The EU Social Market Economy and the Law

Illustrating how the goal of a 'highly competitive social market economy' mentioned in of Art. 3(3) of the Treaty on the European Union fits in the overall EU constitutional framework, this book tests whether it has been pursued actively and to what extent it has been achieved. Part I of the book locates the concept of the 'social market economy' within the broader idea of a multi-layered 'Social Europe' and brings together reflections on the EU constitutional history, without neglecting the harsh reality of current EU politics. In Part II of the volume, various strands of EU legislation are analysed and assessed in light of the 'highly competitive social market economy' objective. The chapters look at legislation based on Article 114 TFEU, and at legislation that implements the Treaty freedoms, pursues primarily economic objectives, or regulates particular market sectors.

In the aftermath of Brexit, and in the 60th anniversary of the Treaty of Rome, the book is particularly timely and topical, offering new and deeper insights on the complex and constantly evolving social dimension of the EU, ultimately reflecting on whether and how the objective of (re)constituting the EU as a 'social market economy' might be achieved.

Dr. Delia Ferri is a Lecturer in Law at Maynooth University Department of Law

Prof. Dr. Fulvio Cortese is Full Professor of Administrative Law at the Faculty of Law of the University of Trento

Routledge Research in EU Law

Available titles in this series include:

The Evolving EU Counter-terrorism Legal Framework
Maria O'Neill

The Early Warning System for the Principle of Subsidiarity
Constitutional theory and empirical reality
Philipp Kiiver

The European Constitution, Welfare States and Democracy
The four freedoms vs. national administrative discretion
Christoffer C. Eriksen

New Governance and the European Strategy for Employment
Samantha Velluti

Human Rights and Minority Rights in the European Union
Kirsten Shoraka

Centralized Enforcement, Legitimacy and Good Governance in the EU
Melanie Smith

EU External Relations and Systems of Governance
The CFSP, Euro-Mediterranean Partnership and migration
Paul James Cardwell

Gender and the Court of Justice of the EU
Jessica Guth and Sanna Elfving

The EU Social Market Economy and the Law
Theoretical Perspectives and Practical Challenges for the EU
Edited by Delia Ferri and Fulvio Cortese

For more information about this series, please visit: https://www.routledge.com/Routledge-Research-in-EU-Law/book-series/ROUTEULAW

The EU Social Market Economy and the Law

Theoretical Perspectives and Practical Challenges for the EU

Edited by Delia Ferri and Fulvio Cortese

Routledge
Taylor & Francis Group
LONDON AND NEW YORK

First published 2019
by Routledge
2 Park Square, Milton Park, Abingdon, Oxon OX14 4RN

and by Routledge
52 Vanderbilt Avenue, New York, NY 10017

First issued in paperback 2020

Routledge is an imprint of the Taylor & Francis Group, an informa business

British Library Cataloguing-in-Publication Data
A catalogue record for this book is available from the British Library

Library of Congress Cataloging-in-Publication Data
A catalog record for this book has been requested

ISBN 13: 978-0-367-58809-0 (pbk)
ISBN 13: 978-1-138-47848-0 (hbk)

Typeset in Galliard
by Apex CoVantage, LLC

Contents

Contributors

Christopher Bovis is Professor of Business Law at the University of Hull. He is an internationally renowned specialist in Public Sector Management, Public Procurement and Public Private Partnerships.

Lucia Busatta is a Postdoctoral Research Fellow at the Department of Public, International and EU Law of the University of Padua. She collaborates with the BioLaw Research Team at the University of Trento and is an associate editor for the *BioLaw Journal*.

Stefano Civitarese Matteucci is Professor of Administrative Law at the University 'Gabriele d'Annunzio' of Chieti-Pescara and Honorary Visiting Professor at York University. His research focuses on methodological and theoretical aspects of public law.

Fulvio Cortese is Professor of Administrative Law at the Faculty of Law at the University of Trento, where he teaches Institutions of Public Law and Judicial Review of Administrative Action. He is a member of the European Group of Public Law.

Marco Dani is Associate Professor of Comparative Public Law at the University of Trento. He is member of the International Society of Public Law and the *Associazione Diritto Pubblico Comparato ed Europeo*.

Giacomo Delledonne is a Postdoctoral Researcher in Comparative Public Law at the Institute of Law, Politics and Development (Dirpolis) of *Scuola Superiore Sant'Anna* of Pisa, where he is one of the editors of the STALS project.

Michael Doherty is Professor of Law and Head of the Law Department at Maynooth University. He lectures and researches in the areas of Employment Law, Industrial Relations Law and Policy and EU law. He is a frequent media contributor on labour market issues.

Sondra Faccio is Adjunct Lecturer of International Law at the University of Verona and associate attorney at Santosuosso Avvocati. Her areas of expertise are Public International Law, Trade Law, Investment Law and International Commercial and Investment Arbitration.

Delia Ferri is a Lecturer in Law at Maynooth University and member of the Maynooth Centre for European and Eurasian Studies. She is an affiliated researcher at the Dirpolis Institute of *Scuola Superiore Sant'Anna* of Pisa and at the Blatt Institute of Syracuse University.

Raphael Heffron is Professor in Global Energy Law and Sustainability at the Centre for Energy, Petroleum, Mineral Law and Policy at the University of Dundee. His work is international and combines a mix of Law, Policy and Economics.

Andreas Heinemann is Professor of Commercial, Economic and European Law at the University of Zurich, permanent visiting Professor at the University of Lausanne and President of the Swiss Competition Commission.

Tamara Hervey is Jean Monnet Professor of EU Law at the University of Sheffield. Her research interests include EU Health Law. She is currently Special Advisor to the House of Commons Health Committee on health implications of Brexit.

Vivian Kube is a Ph.D. researcher at the European University Institute. She studied Law in Hamburg and Leiden, and holds a LL.M. in Comparative, European and International Laws from the European University Institute.

Vanessa Mak is Professor of Private Law and Vice Dean for Research at Tilburg Law School. Her research focuses on private law in the economic regulation of the European consumer market, with particular focus on consumer contract law.

Gokce Mete has seven-year-long practical and academic experience in the field of energy and natural resources law. She is currently a Research Fellow at the Extractives Resource Hub at the Centre for Energy, Petroleum, Mineral Law and Policy at the University of Dundee.

Charles O'Sullivan is an Irish Research Council funded Doctoral Student and Associated Lecturer at the Law Department at Maynooth University. His research focuses on Social Welfare and Immigration Law.

Luigi Pedreschi is a Ph.D. researcher at the European University Institute. He has previously worked as a Solicitor in Commercial Litigation for an International Law Firm and as a tutor of EU Law at the University of Edinburgh.

Silvia Pellizzari is a Senior Lecturer in Administrative Law and Social Services at the University of Trento, and an affiliated researcher at the European Research Institute on Cooperative and Social Enterprises (EURICSE).

Juan Jorge Piernas López is an Assistant Professor of EU and International Law at the University of Murcia and consultant to the World Bank in State Aid Law and Policy. He holds a Doctorate in Law from the European University Institute in Florence.

Caterina Sganga is an Associate Professor at the Department of Legal Studies and the Department of Economic and Business of the Central European University of Budapest. Her research focuses on Comparative Intellectual Property Law and IP strategic management.

Foreword

The Lisbon Treaty inserted into primary EU law new language expressing the ambition of the authors of the Treaty to give the European Union a more social face. The formulation of the basic values and objectives of the European Union was expanded. The relevant Treaty articles (Articles 2 and 3 TEU) now include wording that rebalances the weight of market and non-market values in the foundational provisions of the European Union. Article 3, which lists the Union's main objectives, starts with the ringing sentence that 'The Union's aim is to promote peace, its values and the well-being of its people', and then mentions, among the other main objectives, 'a highly competitive social market economy' and 'social progress'. The Union is, furthermore, directed to 'combat social exclusion' and 'promote social justice and protection'. At first sight, these amendments to the EU Treaty may seem largely rhetorical or 'decorative' because they are not fleshed out, elsewhere in the Treaties, by new lawmaking competences and decision-making procedures in the field of social policy. Article 153 TFEU, in the chapter on Social Policy, maintains a strict distinction between the available means of EU action: whereas the social protection of workers may form the object of minimum harmonization by the EU, the 'combating of social exclusion' and the 'modernization of social protection' may form the object only of measures 'designed to encourage cooperation between Member States'. This disjunction between Treaty proclamations and lack of lawmaking instruments was not an oversight of the drafters of the Lisbon Treaty, but rather the result of a power struggle. A consensus was eventually reached on including the lofty but rather innocuous statements of principles, while excluding – due to the opposition of a number of country delegations – any extension of the Union's lawmaking competences.

This does not render the new language contained in Articles 2 and 3 TEU entirely useless or misleading. That language may come to play another, more indirect, role by prompting the EU institutions, including the Court of Justice, to give more consideration to social welfare implications when applying and interpreting *other rules* of EU law. Article 9 TFEU contains a new mainstreaming clause that aims precisely at achieving this. It states that, in defining and implementing all its policies and activities, 'the Union shall take into account requirements linked to the promotion of a high level of employment, the guarantee of adequate social protection, the fight against social exclusion, and a high level of education, training and protection of human health'. This horizontal clause, again, does not transfer any new competences to the EU. It cannot be used as a legal base for the establishment of a proactive and comprehensive EU social policy, covering the domains mentioned in the text of the article. But, by mainstreaming social policy into all EU policy fields, Article 9 TFEU affirms that social objectives are equivalent to economic objectives within EU primary law. Thereby it requires all EU actors to find a proper balance between economic, social and other aims in all fields of public policy making and implementation in which the EU is engaged. The fields that are particularly relevant in this context are internal market law, competition and state aid law, European citizenship law and external trade law. 'To find a proper balance' concretely means – one might argue – that social considerations should play a greater role than they have done so far in EU policies outside the strict domain of social policy. Only such an understanding of the clause could make a difference compared to the pre-Lisbon situation and could thereby adequately mirror the increased recognition given to the idea of a social Europe by the text of the Treaties in their post-Lisbon version.

The new synthesis between market values and social objectives is synthetically represented by the intriguing notion of the 'highly competitive social market economy' that was inserted in the text of Article 3 TEU. This is the core notion of this book, in which the contributors seek to flesh out the meaning of that notion when applied to different areas of EU law, both in its internal and its external dimensions. None of the contributors would claim that the Treaty reference to the social market economy has concrete legal implications by itself. But it offers a useful vantage point from which to examine the extent to which social considerations do, in fact, infuse the content and scope of the whole range of EU policies. Such a systematic examination has not been undertaken before, and this book thereby offers a rich and intriguing contribution to the literature on EU law.

Bruno De Witte
Florence-Maastricht, 28 February 2018

Acknowledgements

We first thought about writing a volume that dealt in an original way with the theme of balancing social rights with economic freedoms in the European Union (EU) almost twelve years ago, long before the Lisbon Treaty. The entry into force of the revised Treaty on the European Union, with its new provision on the 'a highly competitive social market economy', provided us with a new impetus to collect our thoughts and reflections around this theme within a book. Our travels, as well as our respective academic and personal benchmarks, kept us from realizing this until now. However, we feel this is the ideal moment to take stock of the extent to which the EU pursues social goals alongside economic objectives, without the first being subject to the latter and to market imperatives. This book is therefore an attempt to approach the well-known theme of the 'social dimension' of the EU from a new perspective, and in the context of a dynamic legal analysis of a number of different fields of regulation. It is also an attempt to gather together scholars from different backgrounds, coming from various academic communities around Europe and at different stage of their careers.

As editors, we would like to thank all the authors that helped us to shape this innovative contribution, which aims to advance the current state of the art. Compiling this volume was indeed a demanding endeavour, but we would not have been able to do so without the commitment and patience of all our co-authors, who revised their pieces and responded to all our requests in a timely manner, and with equal enthusiasm for the project as a whole. Special thanks go to Prof. Bruno De Witte for writing the foreword to this book. Some of the contributions to this volume were discussed in two conferences convened by Dr. Delia Ferri at Maynooth University (MU) in September 2016 and in March 2017, in order to test the approach to the volume and engage in a dynamic legal analysis. Thus, we want to thank the MU Department of Law for its generous support, and, in particular, the Head of the Department, Prof. Michael Doherty, who supported this project from the beginning. We would also like to thank those participants in these conferences who made a valuable contribution to the debate, despite not contributing to the final volume.

This book would not have been possible without the constant support of Mr. Charles Edward O'Sullivan, who, besides being a committed author, has acted as assistant editor for the volume. He carried out a linguistic revision of every chapter within the final book, and achieved wonders whilst often working to impossible deadlines. Special thanks go also to Ms. Claire McGovern, Ph.D. candidate at MU Department of Law, who provided editorial support in the latter phase of the project.

Our thanks go also to Siobhan Poole, Nicola Sharpe and the publishing team at Routledge for their advice, patience as well as their efficient management support, to the anonymous reviewers that helped to streamline the research objectives and to our colleagues for the many kind words of friendship and wisdom.

Delia Ferri and Fulvio Cortese

Introduction

The social market economy in the European Union. Theoretical perspectives and practical challenges

Delia Ferri and Fulvio Cortese

1 The starting point: a European Union melancholia

In 2017, the European Union (EU) celebrated the 60th anniversary of the Treaty of Rome. However, in the aftermath of a harsh economic crisis that hit several Member States and of the austerity measures adopted in the context of the European Financial Stability Mechanism (EFSM) and the European Financial Stability Facility (EFSF), the atmosphere has been far from jubilant. As De Burca noted, '[t]he economic maelstrom convulsing the EU . . . has unquestionably been the most severe and profound crisis which the European integration project has confronted in its 60 years of existence', and has raised existential questions 'of whether not only Europe's currency, the Euro, but even the EU itself could survive the wrenching economic circumstances'.[1] The Brexit referendum and its outcome, as well as the election of Trump in the United States, have helped overshadow the celebration of this anniversary.

Across Europe, a disparate *ensemble* of anti-EU parties champions the idea of an EU far-removed from its citizens, which takes unpopular political decisions with little regard for (or even actively against) the will of the EU citizenry and pursues austerity as well as purely market-based values over social interests. By positioning the EU as a soulless technocratic organization built by *élites*, these parties reach out to the 'losers of market opening projects',[2] namely those that feel European integration poses a threat to their way of life. The outcome of the Brexit referendum was, in this vein, rhetorically portrayed by some as the 'weakening of a non-accountable, technocratic superstate, and a strengthening of liberal democracy'.[3] Many Europeans perceive the EU 'as one of the agents of socio-economic distress, and a significant causal factor in the nature and degree of economic and social pain'.[4]

The political situation in Poland and Hungary is another set of events which frame this melancholic anniversary. Indeed, the 'dictatorship-like' laws passed by the governments in power in these countries are eroding the very foundation of the EU – the rule of law. As Steinbeis put it,[5] 'if the legal system in a Member State is broken, the legal system in the whole of the EU is broken'. Following successive failed attempts at political dialogue, soft mediation and various recommendations, in December 2017, the European Commission proposed that the

Council adopt a decision under Article 7(1) of the Treaty of the European Union (TEU). This triggered an action for infringement under Article 258 of the Treaty on the Functioning of the European Union (TFEU) by referring the Polish Law on the Ordinary Courts Organization to the Court of Justice of the EU (CJEU). At this moment in time, it remains to be seen whether Polish authorities will step back, and what consequences the Commission's action will have on the entire EU framework.

Consequently, echoing the title of a post-Brexit paper authored by Joerges, the EU is quite unwell, yet alive.[6] However, the current political malaise represents more than just a momentary unexpected difficulty. As Corkin affirms, 'the political class had already prepared the ground work' for a populist backlash, by treating the EU 'as some sort of alien other, rather than as a means for governments (nothing happens in the EU without them) to cooperate and co-ordinate'.[7] This appears to hold true across each of the EU Member States. Academics, journalists and politicians have, on the one hand, long claimed that the EU suffers from a democratic deficit.[8] Many remember that, not long ago, in an influential editorial,[9] Weiler argued that one of the major shortcomings of the EU is the lack of a strong democracy at the Union level. On the other hand, these same persons have blamed what they view as the ingrained neoliberal values of the EU. These claims have in turn resulted in a choral call to wholly re-think the European project, to avoid 'a requiem for a European dream'.[10] Such desires will inevitably require that the EU, its Member States and its citizenry reflect on the existential question of '*Quo vadis Europa*?'. This is by no means a novel question. Three years ago, the *German Law Journal* published an interdisciplinary special issue titled 'Regeneration Europe'. Its editorial initiative called for 'a new normative paradigm for the EU', and solicited a reflection on European identity, interrogating from different points of view the substance of European integration.[11] This is just one of the large number of initiatives and discussion fora created in recent years. It underlines an enduring debate taking place on the EU's political and legal trajectory, on its constitutional nature, on the values and principles which it posits, and ultimately on its very identity.

This academic discourse on the constitutional nature of the EU and its procedures as well as the prevalent rhetoric on the unbridgeable 'democratic deficit' go hand in hand with a broader debate on the substance of European economic integration, and with a critical analysis of what Ashiagbor calls the 'embedded liberal bargain'.[12] In a recent volume, edited by Joerges, Chalmers and Jachtenfuchs evocatively titled 'The End of the Eurocrats' Dream',[13] the crisis facing the EU is analysed from a series of differing perspectives by multiple authors. The common thread that emerges however is the interrelationship between the (unsuccessful, according to the authors) economic integration and technocratic modes of governance, developed especially after the Maastricht Treaty. Similarly, Floris De Witte noted that '[t]he fact that most textbooks on the EU's internal market devote only one chapter to social policy is indicative of the nature of the Union's market'.[14] In his analysis, he also highlighted, from an historical perspective, that the EU 'integration process was meant to expand the size of the (economic) cake, and the Member States were meant to redistribute that cake internally'. He concludes, harshly, by stating that:

> the current legal architecture of the internal market, and the increased political focus on social policies as a complement to the EMU, make it impossible for the EU to create a social market economy. In the simplest terms, the EU lacks the institutional sophistication required in order to do so.[15]

De Witte's conclusions are in line with what was noted by Scharpf. This author observed that, within the history of the EU, the reach of the four freedoms has been progressively extended and, in a similar vein, competition law has been extended to promote access for private undertakings to a range of public services. Consequently, there is no area of law that has remained unaffected by internal market legislation, the European economic freedoms and the rules aimed at guaranteeing undistorted competition.[16] The appeal of a 'Social Europe', somewhat evoked by Jacque Delors, has been replaced by the free market orientation that has characterized the EU since the early 1990s. A natural consequence of this is that the neoliberal inclination of the EU, whose 'ethos has become gradually harder to distinguish from that of the faceless, naturalised wisdom of global markets',[17] has prevailed since then. In 2012, the governor of the European Central Bank, Mario Draghi, underlined this point by stating that '[t]he European social model has already gone'.

However, looking closer, the idea of a 'Social Europe' remains present and represents a potential future for the Union. Contouris and Freedland predicted this in 2012, albeit with some significant reservations made on their part. O'Cinneide argues that the idea of a 'Social Europe' is infused in and permeates the many layers of European constitutional governance, and has subsequently acquired both a political and legal dimension.[18] Even those who affirm that the EU should not become a 'welfare state', highlight that the EU has a social dimension (for instance, the still incomplete and piecemeal coordination of social security rights of mobile workers) and that it should not confine its role to economic and monetary policies.[19]

Despite the criticism that surrounds the case law of the Court of Justice of the EU (CJEU) and its neoliberal attitude, which had a recent peak in the widely discussed *Viking* and *Laval* decisions,[20] the Luxembourg judges have consistently acknowledged the social objectives of the Union over time. In 1976, Advocate General (AG) Trabucchi in *Mr. and Mrs. F v. Belgium*,[21] a preliminary ruling made by a Belgian Labour Court on the interpretation of EU social security legislation concerning the grant of allowances to people with disabilities within the context of free movement, evoked the goal of EU law 'to be more than a mere mechanical system of economics and to constitute instead a system commensurate with the society which it has to govern', and 'to be a legal system corresponding to the concept of social justice and to the requirements of European integration, not only of the economy but of the people'. In the same year, in *Defrenne v Sabena*, the CJEU interpreted the equal pay provisions of the Treaty (currently Article

157 TFEU) in light of the 'social objectives' of the former Community, 'which is not merely an economic union, but is at the same time intended, by common action, to ensure social progress and seek the constant improvement of the living and working conditions of their peoples'.[22] The aim of ensuring social progress and citations of *Defrenne* can be found in several other decisions and AG's opinions.[23] In a long line of cases on the freedom of establishment, the Court has also mentioned the 'economic and social interpenetration within the European Union'.[24] Further, the CJEU has quite widely accepted the use of Article 114 TFEU and the competence to pursue non-economic policies as long as there is a contribution to the functioning of the internal market.[25]

With the entry into force of the Lisbon Treaty, the EU constitutionalized a new conception of itself as a 'highly competitive social market economy' in Article 3(3) TEU. The cross-cutting social clause provided by Article 9 TFEU further embeds market-related values within social values by stating that

> [i]n defining and implementing its policies and activities, the Union shall take into account requirements linked to the promotion of a high level of employment, the guarantee of adequate social protection, the fight against social exclusion, and a high level of education, training and protection of human health.

This kind of socially driven interpretative clause has a long history within the Treaties. The Treaty Establishing the European Economic Community (EEC Treaty), for example, included several express mentions of socially driven elements, such as: 'to promote throughout the Community a harmonious development of economic activities, a continuous and balanced expansion, an increase in stability, an accelerated raising of the standard of living and closer relations between the States belonging to it', and 'to promote improved working conditions and an improved standard of living for workers, so as to make possible their harmonization while the improvement is being maintained' provide merely two examples of these social elements. Both the Treaty of Maastricht and Treaty of Amsterdam extended these social ideals even further. The constitutional provisions that predate Article 3(3) TEU, however, emphasized the economic ahead of the social.[26] Contrastingly, the imperative to reconstitute the EU as a 'social market economy' seems to pay homage to the need for economic activity to serve the common social good. The Lisbon Treaty also conferred on the EU Charter of Fundamental Rights (EU CFR), which includes a list of (broad) social rights such as the right to education (Art. 14), the right to choose an occupation and engage in work (Art. 15), the right to social security and social assistance (Article 34), the right to healthcare (Art. 35) and a series of employment rights set out in Articles 27–32, an equal legal status with the Treaties.

With regard to the political dimension, the Europe 2020 Strategy, whilst being primarily focused on growth and competitiveness, has embraced the goal by explicitly 'setting out a vision of Europe's social market economy for the 21st century'.[27] However, this strategy is based on the presumption that these achievements will improve social cohesion. More recently, despite the challenges brought on by Brexit, the rise of populism, the imposition of severe and wide-ranging austerity measures, a social dimension remains present in the dialogues of the EU institutions. In September 2015 Jean Claude Juncker affirmed his commitment to developing a 'European Pillar of Social Rights' (EPSR). Later, in March 2016, the Commission launched a public consultation assessing this same Pillar, and to reflect on the 'EU social *acquis*'. The EPSR, after having received the support of the Parliament in January 2017, was solemnly proclaimed in November 2017. It revolves around three main themes: equal opportunities and access to the labour market; fair working conditions; adequate and sustainable social protection. The Pillar should address common principles, and bring greater convergence of social standards within the EU. While being narrowly, in geographic terms (being restricted to the Euro area), and conceptually (as a reference framework to screen the employment and social performance of Member States) conceived, as well as being a soft law document, the Pillar indicates a commitment to making this European social dimension more tangible and complementary (and intertwined) within the ongoing process of economic integration.

Liebert affirmed that the process of European integration has been shaped by the competitive fight for survival between the two paradigms of an economic project of liberalization and that of social solidarity. However, she argued that European constitutionalism 'has paved some ways for making economic and social rationalities mutually constitutive'.[28] In a similar vein, this book aims to interrogate the constant tension between economic integration and social concerns, and to understand whether and to what extent this tension can be reconciled. By investigating the potential of the objective of a 'highly competitive social market economy', laid down in Article 3(3) TEU, and its realization, this book investigates whether a renewed EU commitment to social goals can go hand in hand with economic objectives, without being subject to market imperatives, as evoked (but partially neglected) by the CJEU in *AGET Iraklis*.[29]

Echoing the title of the volume published by Enzo Traverso,[30] the melancholy surrounding the uncertain future of the EU cannot and should not coincide with the abandonment of the European project launched by Schumann of a 'Social Europe'. Rather, it is the melancholy of an EU critically re-evaluating and reflecting upon itself.

2 The scope of the book: the 'social' in the EU social market economy

2.1 *The origin of the social market economy*

The term 'social market economy' (*soziale Marktwirtschaft*) was originally coined in Germany, after World War II, to show that capitalism could be combined with a strong government presence and an extended social safety net. Put simply, Röpke, Rüstow, Eucken, Böhm, Oppenheimer and, overall, Müller-Armack, the fathers of the 'social market economy', advocated in favour of a form of market freedoms that can achieve social objectives.[31] However, Müller-Armack, who actually coined the term *soziale Marktwirtschaft*, posited the balance between a capitalist economy and regulations aiming at the achievement of social justice,[32] and advancing the ordoliberalism of the Freiburg School of Eucken and Böhm. The latter scholars theorized a self-regulating market, while arguing only for an indirect State governance.[33] In Eucken's discourse, social policy was merely aimed at maintaining competition and at the preservation of the market process as the necessary precondition for solving existing social problems.[34]

In contrast with this latter point of view, which advocated for a form of 'procedural' liberalism in which the State sets the institutional framework and abstains from interference in the market, Müller-Armack emphasized the State's role in actively improving the market and in simultaneously pursuing a social balance. Interestingly, in Müller-Armack's discourse, the 'social market economy' is 'the only possible way of achieving social progress while maintaining the functions of the market'.[35] The 'social market economy' therefore 'presupposes a free market economy, but is not identical with it' and represents 'an attempt to harmonize our desire for freedom and social justice with insights into the working of the market machinery'.[36]

Müller-Armack postulated the existence of an efficient State (arguably not influenced by organized private interests) that enables the markets to work well and ensures a high level of provision in terms of goods and services, in addition to actively protecting social rights. The role of the State in this theorization is not merely to secure an efficient market, but to support market competition and prompting a range of social interventions (such as housing, unemployment benefits, healthcare etc.). In Muller-Armack's words:

> [t]he concept of a social market economy comprises a wider complex of measures of social policy and a narrower complex of measures of economic policy, delicately synchronized with each other.[37]

The term 'social market economy' is now characterized by ambiguities and nuances.[38] However, several authors, such as Šmejkal and Šaroch,[39] building on Müller-Armack's economic theory (as well as more broadly on the Freiburg School), tend to identify the requirements of a 'social market economy' in regulatory policy aimed at addressing market failures and in corrective (social) policies which limit the inequalities that arise from the market system itself.

2.2 *The social market economy in the Treaty*

The very idea of the 'social market economy' began to emerge in the EU legal framework long before the entry into force of the Lisbon Treaty, if not from the inception of the EU. As noted by Dale and El-Enany, in 1948, Müller-Armack's 'social market economy' was adopted as a Christian Democratic Union electoral slogan, and Müller-Armack himself contributed to German policy papers that fed into the drafting of the Treaty of Rome.[40] However, the term 'social market economy' was rarely used in EU soft or hard law. During the 2000s, scant documents made reference to it. One relatively isolated instance in this respect is the Decision of the Council and the European Parliament on Intercultural dialogue of 2006.[41] The decision identifies intercultural dialogue as a tool necessary in achieving a number of the EU's strategic priorities, including 'supporting the EU's commitment to solidarity, social justice, the ***development of a social market economy*** (emphasis added), cooperation and greater cohesion in the respect of its common values'.

It is only with the Lisbon Treaty that the EU has identified it as an essential objective of the EU. As noted by Lianos,[42] while undoubtedly borrowing the expression 'highly competitive social market economy' from the German scholarship,[43] Article 3 TEU leaves the expression formally undefined. It is however somewhat safe to assume that this encompasses the creation of an internal market (i.e. 'an area without internal frontiers in which the free movement of goods, persons, services and capital is ensured in accordance with the provisions of the Treaties'). It also involves the elimination of customs and duties and charges as well as quantitative restrictions and all measures having equivalent effects, harmonized standards to secure the free movement of goods and services and removal of barriers, the prohibition of discriminatory internal taxation, the prohibition of State aid and subsidies unless authorized by the Commission or allowed by EU rules, and open competition among economic players. The post-Lisbon EU continues to be based on the principle of an open market economy with free competition, as provided for in Article 119 TFEU. However, Article 3(3) TEU creates an indissoluble relationship between market goals, on the one hand, and social policy areas on the other,[44] and expresses the willingness to reach a balance between them.[45]

This new constitutional paradigm seems to reject a more radical form of liberal capitalism, as the former Commissioner Andor posited, the term 'social market economy' denotes a third way, 'a halfway house . . . between a *laissez-faire* market-based economy and was centrally planned and State-directed'.[46] Dale and El-Enany[47] recall that, since the 'social market economy' represented a sort of 'third way' between liberal capitalism and more dirigiste economic thoughts, it was embraced by Social Democrats (such as Andor), but also by supporters of Christian Social parties, such as Viviane Reding, former Vice-President of the European Commission. The 'social market economy' was also somewhat embraced by those who were nearer to the neoliberal parties, although, arguably, with a slightly different understanding as to its meaning.

According to Damianovic even though 'the EU is restricted in developing its own redistributive welfare systems', this does not mean that 'the EU cannot be based on a social market economy'.[48] This author argues that 'the task at the EU level is thereby to interpret the EU market rules as social market rules'. De Witte and Dawson[49] stated that the objectives of social inclusion and social protection are a 'set of values that must be mainstreamed and reflected in other fields of EU action', and demanded a reinterpretation of the EU's competition law, State aid law and internal market law in compliance of Articles 3 TEU and 9 TFEU, 'improving the functioning of the "social market economy"'. Schiek argued that the 'EU's unique socio-economic constitution demands equilibrium of socio-economic integration instead of widening the gap between economic integration at the EU levels and social integration at the national level'.[50] This equilibrium seems to be somewhat evoked by the *AGET Iraklis* decision on collective redundancies (and even if the outcome is, at the end, disappointing),[51] where the CJEU referred directly to Article 3(3) TEU. In its reasoning it recalled that

> the European Union is not only to establish an internal market but is also to work for the sustainable development of Europe, which is based, in particular, on a highly competitive social market economy aiming at full employment and social progress, and it is to promote, *inter alia*, social protection.

The Court interestingly stressed that 'the European Union thus has not only an economic but also a social purpose', placing them on an equal footing, and requiring (and this is indeed far from being a novelty) a balancing test among the rights under the provisions of the Treaty on the free movement of goods, persons, services and capital and the objectives pursued by social policy.

2.3 Discussing 'social' dimension in the EU 'social market economy'

The EU still retains a very limited set of competences within social fields, centred on the Union's ability to merely coordinate (but not to harmonize) national social policies and the law of the Member States. EU employment law, social security and social assistance law are primarily focused on facilitating individual free movement as well as preventing discrimination on the ground of nationality. For this reason, the academic debate on how 'social' the EU is has often focused on the interplay between negative and positive integration.[52] It has centred on the role of the CJEU in balancing market freedoms and social rights (or more broadly fundamental rights),[53] and in identifying an EU 'social' strain as a necessary counterweight in the quest to establish the internal market.[54] Most often it has been argued that the social dimension of EU law has remained chronically underdeveloped and that national social provisions are endangered by EU rules on market integration. However, this debate is not entirely representative of the whole picture. This book, further having placed the 'social market economy' clause in the EU constitutional context, attempts to fill this gap and to identify social patterns in market legislation, as well as the resulting implications for the future. It aims to investigate to what extent economic regulations are capable of pursuing social goals and of remedying market failures by setting legal standards for health, security and labour protection, by stimulating the development of industry standards for the accessibility and usability of product, by explicitly protecting social rights, and by protecting vulnerable groups. The book attempts to assess EU law in light of this new objective laid down in the Treaty. This collection of contributions discusses what the addition of this new 'social' element contained in Article 3(3) TEU means within the ongoing evolution of the European project. It analyses, through various lenses and in different domains of EU legislation, the juxtaposition of economic liberalism and social protection which characterizes the legacy of the Müller-Armack 'social market economy'.

The starting point of this book is that economic and social objectives are, at least to some extent, reconcilable, rather than mutually exclusive. From this assumption, the book moves onto reflect the extent to which this 'reconciliation' has occurred in the EU domain. Rather than focusing on fundamental rights as such, this book adopts a conception of the 'social market' that encompasses the protection and promotion of the right to work and other social rights, such as those to housing, health, education and income. The book adopts a broad meaning of the 'social', encompassing environmental protection as part of a balanced and sustainable development of society.

This book, deliberately, does not discuss the relationship between the 'social market economy' concept and the economic governance in the Eurozone, as it has been dealt with extensively (especially in relation to the harsh economic crisis). De Witte and Kilpatrick, in 2014, already analysed how social rights have been diminished or endangered as a consequence of the crisis in the Eurozone,[55] and other authors already addressed the Eurozone governance in time of economic crisis.[56] For this reason, while references to the EFSM are included in several of the chapters,[57] the Eurozone crisis will not be explicitly addressed in the book. The editors have also consciously avoided including a chapter which specifically addresses Brexit. The debate among scholars has been quite intense: several contributions have been published so far to explain the reasons behind the leave vote,[58] to predict future outcomes and to sketch out the numerous problems that Brexit brings about, because 'one does not simply withdraw the EU'.[59] This book does not want to replicate or reproduce these pre-existing arguments.[60] In addition, the UK leaving the EU is a reality, but one defined by less than concrete legal outcomes at present. To a certain extent, despite the ongoing debate, Brexit is more a political slogan than a legal conundrum, and it will be so until the withdrawal treaty has been drafted and agreed upon. In January 2018, when completing this volume, there have been renewed calls for a second referendum and the Irish border issue remains unresolved. Despite the EU's commitment towards the Irish cause, there is a risk that the negotiations on the Brexit withdrawal agreement could stall until a feasible proposal on how to manage the Irish border is found. Thus, Brexit is not our focus, and emerges as an underlying theme in some of the contributions.

All in all, the book sets out to illustrate how the goal of a 'highly competitive social market economy' fits in the EU constitutional framework, and to test whether it has been pursued actively and to what extent it has been achieved.

3 The structure of the book

As highlighted above, the objective of the book is to discuss the very meaning of the 'social market economy', as well as to examine how it has been implemented and might be pragmatically realized in the future. In order to achieve this objective, the volume adopts a bipartite structure. Part I is focused on interrogating the values presented by a 'social market economy' within the EU context, placing them within the theoretical and historical debate on the European integration process as a whole. It provides a theoretical backdrop and lays the groundwork for the investigation conducted in Part II, which is focused on different areas of EU law.

The first chapter of Part I, authored by O'Sullivan, places the concept of the 'social market economy' within the EU's constitutional history and explores how this concept balances two seemingly anachronistic values: the 'social' and the 'market'. In the second chapter, Dani claims that the EU is transforming the 'Social State' by re-orienting its original normative aspirations, associated with emancipation from the markets, to weaker forms of social policies aimed at enabling market participation. Dani explores three different engagements between the 'Social State' and the EU in different phases of the EU history. In the third chapter, Civitarese Matteucci addresses the question of what concept of social rights, if any, fits within the ideal of the 'social market economy'. Delledonne closes Part I by providing an overview of how and to what extent EU citizenship can be viewed as existing at the forefront of the 'highly competitive social market economy'. He looks at whether, after Lisbon, EU citizenship has been constructed 'socially'. The choice to include this chapter in the first part of the volume is premised on the idea that the constitutional development of Union citizenship as a principle of EU law expresses, as discussed in a recent book edited by Kochenov,[61] the constant tension between the EU's origins as an economic organization and its 'federal aspirations', situating itself within the realm of the EU existential features.

Part II of the volume examines various strands of EU legislation in light of the 'highly competitive social market economy' objective. The chapters look at legislation based on Article 114 TFEU (i.e. explicitly aimed at the construction of the internal market), on legislation that implements the Treaty freedoms and pursues primarily economic objectives, or regulates particular market sectors. Each contribution looks at measures considered to fall within the category of 'positive integration', and analyses related case law, addressing the role of the CJEU in interpreting EU legislation. Where relevant, the authors include an analysis of most recent soft law measures. All of the chapters pay particular attention to the post-Lisbon Treaty context, so that they may more fully grasp the impact of Article 3(3) TEU. The choice of case studies of market regulation, while necessarily selective, tries to encompass the most significant fields of EU action. At various junctures, the book will highlight connections, overlaps and inconsistencies among different strands of EU law.

Doherty opens Part II by analysing the interplay between social rights and market goals in EU labour law. This is a traditional field in which the social dimension of Europe has been debated, and still remains the primary (although, as this book demonstrates, certainly not the only) field where 'the market and the social meet'. This chapter examines some key themes such as the autonomous nature of labour law, its scope and function, and labour rights as fundamental human rights. Bovis explores the intrinsic links between EU public procurement regulation and the implementation of social policy objectives in the Member States, and offers insights into how public procurement acts as an indissoluble component of the 'social market economy' within the EU. Heinemann discusses how social considerations are provided for under EU antitrust law, looking at the interpretation of Articles 101 and 102 TFEU by the CJEU, and at their implementation by the Commission. He argues that social policy works as an external limitation to the scope of competition law, and that social considerations may affect the application of competition law by having an impact on the interpretation of prohibitions and justifications. Ferri and Piernas Lopez analyse the extent to which social rights are protected and promoted under EU State aid law. They discuss whether social protection is considered within the analysis of the definition of State aid under Article 107(1) TFEU. Then, they will discuss the 'social' elements in Articles 107(2) and 107(3) TFEU and their assessment in the Commission practice. Piernas Lopez then discusses Article 106 TFEU and how social considerations shape the Services of General Economic Interests (SGEI), focusing on Social Services of General Economic Interest (SSGEI). In a similar and complementary vein, Pellizzari discusses how the freedom to provide services can facilitate the provision of social (non-health related) services, and discusses the boundaries between economic and non-economic activities. Busatta and Hervey examine cross-border healthcare as a paradigmatic example of the intersection between economic and social concerns. Mak's contribution focuses on EU consumer law, and examines to what extent social rights or, more broadly, social interests are becoming more prominent in EU regulation and the case law of the CJEU to protect consumer rights. Sganga investigates the recent and ongoing developments in EU Intellectual Property (IP) law, and evaluates to what extent this has pursued social objectives. Mete and Heffron discuss the extent to which EU energy law achieves social objectives and investigates how continuing imbalances and injustices can be addressed in future energy policy and legislation in the realm of the 'EU social market economy'.

The final chapters of Part II, authored respectively by Kube and Pedreschi and by Faccio, outline and explore whether and to what extent different fields of EU external relations law incorporate social elements. Both of these contributions test the extent to which the EU projects externally the combination of economic and social objectives envisaged internally by Article 3(3) TEU. Kube and Pedreschi focus on the Common Commercial Policy (CCP), while Faccio examines EU investment law and unpacks many of the inconsistencies and shortcomings that exist within a relatively recent field of action.

Cortese and Ferri close this edited collection with a brief reflection on the actual and potential role of Article 3(3) TEU to recalibrate the way in which the EU constructs its internal market.

Notes

1 Grainne De Burca, 'Europe's *Raison d'être*' (2013) 2 *EUI-AEL Working Papers* at <http://cadmus.eui.eu/handle/1814/28098>.

2 Neil Fligstein, *Euroclash: The EU, European Identity, and the Future of Europe* (OUP, 2009).
3 Jeffrey Ketland, 'Remain v Leave: Technocracy vs Liberal Democracy' (2016) at <http://quillette.com/2016/07/08/remain-vs-leave-elite-technocracy-vs-liberal-democracy/>.
4 De Burca, 'Europe's *Raison d'être*' (n 1).
5 Maximilian Steinbeis, 'Polish Courts Are Our Courts' (2017) at <https://verfassungsblog.de/polish-courts-are-our-courts/>.
6 Christian Joerges, 'Europe Unwell, Yet Alive: An Introductory Editorial' in Christian Joerges, 'Brexit and Academic Citizenship' (2016) 20 *EUI Working Paper* at <http://cadmus.eui.eu//handle/1814/44024>.
7 Joseph Corkin, 'Fog in the Channel: Europe Isolated' in Joerges 'Brexit and Academic Citizenship' (n 6).
8 Laurent Pech, *The European Union and Its Constitution: From Rome to Lisbon* (Clarus Press, 2008) 93.
9 Joseph Weiler, '60 Years since the First European Community: Reflections on Messianism' (2011) *European Journal of International Law* 303.
10 Andras Baneth, 'Requiem for a European Dream' (2016) at <https://euobserver.com/opinion/136009>.
11 Moritz Hartmann and Floris de Witte (eds.)'Special Issue: Regeneration Europe' 14 (2013) 5 *German Law Journal.*
12 Diamond Ashiagbor, 'Unravelling the Embedded Liberal Bargain: Labour and Social Welfare Law in the Context of EU Market Integration' (2013) *European Law Journal* 303.
13 Joerges Chalmers and Markus Jachtenfuchs, *The End of the Eurocrats' Dream* (CUP, 2013).
14 Floris de Witte, 'The Architecture of a Social Market Economy' (2015) 13 *LSE Law, Society and Economy Working Papers.*
15 Ibid.
16 Fritz Scharpf, 'The Asymmetry of European Integration, or Why the EU Cannot Be a "Social Market Economy"' (2010) *Socio-Economic Review* 211.
17 Claire Methven O'Brien, 'Reflections of an Outlier' in Joerges 'Brexit and Academic Citizenship' (n 6).
18 Colm O'Cinneide, 'Austerity and the Faded Dream of a Social Europe' in Aoife Nolan (ed.), *Economic and Social Rights after the Global Financial Crisis* (CUP, 2014) 169.
19 Frank Vandenbrouke, 'The Idea of a European Social Union: A Normative Introduction' in Frank Vandenbrouke, Catharine Barnard and Geert de Baere (eds.), *A European Social Union after the Crisis* (CUP, 2017).
20 Case C-438/05, *Viking Line*, EU:C:2007:292; Case C-341/05, *Laval*, EU:C:2007:291. On these two decisions and their consequences, Mark Freedland and Jeremias Prassl (eds.), *EU Law in the Member States: Viking, Laval and Beyond* (Hart, 2015).
21 Opinion of AG Trabucchi, Case 7/75, *Mr. and Mrs. F.*, EU:C:1975:75.
22 Case 43/75, *Defrenne v Sabena*, EU:C:1976:56, para 10.
23 Joined opinion of AG Cosmas, Case C-50/96, *Deutsche Telekom AG v Lilli Schröder*, EU:C:2000:72; Joined Cases C-234/96, *Agnes Vick*; Case C-235/96, *Ute Conze*, EU:C:2000:73, para 79.
24 Among others, Case C-97/09 *Ingrid Schmelz*, EU:C:2010:632.
25 Bruno de Witte, 'A Competence to Protect: The Pursuit of the Nonmarket Aims through Internal Market Legislation' in Philip Syrpis (ed.), *The Judiciary, the Legislature and the EU Internal Market* (CUP, 2012) 25.
26 Their potency was further diminished by the fact that, in *Zaera*, the CJEU ensured that these clauses would remain largely non-judicable and were therefore merely

aspirational in their tone from a judicial perspective. They could be used as an additional basis for judicial decisions to be rendered in a more socially conscious manner, but this did not occur so often (Case 126/86, *Zaera*, EU:C:1987:278, paras 10–11).

27 Communication from the European Commission, 'Europe 2020: A Strategy for Smart, Sustainable and Inclusive Growth', COM(2010)2020.

28 Ulrike Liebert, 'Reconciling Market with Social Europe' in Dagmar Schiek, Ulrike Liebert and Hildegard Schneider (eds.), *European Economic and Social Constitutionalism after the Treaty of Lisbon* (CUP, 2011) 48.

29 Case C-201/15, *AGET Iraklis*, EU:C:2016:972.

30 Enzo Traverso, *Malinconia di Sinistra* (Felitrinelli, 2016).

31 Alfred Müller-Armack, 'The Meaning of the Social Market Economy' in Alan T. Pecock and Hans Wilgerodt (eds.), *Germany's Social Market Economy: Origins and Evolution* (Macmillan, 1989) 83. On the history of the concept see Christian Joerges, 'What Is Left of the European Economic Constitution' (2004) *EUI Working Paper* at <http://cadmus.eui.eu/bitstream/handle/1814/2828/law04-13.pdf?sequence=1>; Alessandro Somma, 'Economia sociale di mercato e scontro tra capitalismi' 24 (2015) 4 *DPCE Online*. See also Stefano Civitarese Matteucci, 'Social Rights, Social Market Economy, and the European Social Model: Tracing Conceptual Boundaries', in this volume.

32 Alfred Müller-Armack, 'The Social Market Economy as an Economic and Social Order' (1978) *Review of Social Economy* 325.

33 Christian Gossner, 'The Making of the German Post-War Economy' (2010) at <www.kas.de/upload/dokumente/2010/06/60_Years_SME/glossner.pdf>.

34 Alexander Ebner, 'The Intellectual Foundations of the Social Market Economy: Theory, Policy, and Implications for European Integration' (2006) 3 *Journal of Economic Studies* 206, at 213.

35 Müller-Armack, 'The Social Market Economy as an Economic and Social Order' (n 32), at 330.

36 Ibid.

37 Ibid., at 328.

38 Nils Goldschmidt and Michael Wohlgemuth, 'Social Market Economy: Origins, Meanings and Interpretations' (2008) 3 *Constitutional Political Economy* 261. See also Peter Koslowski, *The Social Market Economy: Theory and Ethics of the Economic Order* (Springer, 2012); Stefan Muresan, *Social Market Economy: The Case of Germany* (Springer, 2014).

39 Václav Šmejkal and Stanislav Šaroch, 'EU as a Highly Competitive Social Market Economy: Goal, Options, and Reality' (2014) *Review of Economic Perspectives* 393.

40 Gareth Dale and Nadine El-Enany, 'The Limits of Social Europe: EU Law and the Ordoliberal Agenda' (2013) *German Law Journal* 616. These authors critically emphasize that the Treaty of Rome was 'a triumph for German ordoliberalism'.

41 Decision No 1983/2006/EC of the European Parliament and of the Council of 18 December 2006 concerning the European Year of Intercultural Dialogue, [2006] OJ L 412/44.

42 Ioannis Lianos, 'Competition Law in the European Union after the Treaty of Lisbon' in Diamond Ashiagbor, Nicola Countouris and Ioannis Lianos (eds.), *The European Union after the Treaty of Lisbon* (CUP, 2012) 252.

43 László Andor, 'Building a Social Market Economy in the European Union' (2011) *Speech at Manchester Business School* at <http://europa.eu/rapid/press-release_SPEECH-11-695_en.htm>.

44 Luigi Fumagalli, 'Art. 3' in Antonio Tizzano (ed.), *Trattati dell'Unione europea* (Giuffrè, 2014) 18.

45 Christian Joerges and Florian Rödl, '"Social Market Economy" as Europe's Social Model?' (2004) *EUI Working Paper* at <http://cadmus.eui.eu/bitstream/handle/1814/2823/law04-8.pdf?sequence=1>.

46 Andor, 'Building a Social Market Economy in the European Union' (n 43).
47 Dale and El-Enany, 'The Limits of Social Europe: EU Law and the Ordoliberal Agenda' (n 40).
48 Dragana Damjanovic, 'The EU Market Rules as Social Market Rules: Why the EU Can Be a Social Market Economy' (2013) *Common Market Law Review* 1685.
49 Mark Dawson and Bruno De Witte, 'The EU Legal Framework of Social Inclusion and Social Protection: Between the Lisbon Strategy and the Lisbon Treaty' in Bea Cantillon, Herwig Verschueren and Paula Ploscar (eds.), *Social Inclusion and Social Protection in the EU: Interactions between Law and Policy* (Intersentia, 2012).
50 Dagmar Schiek, 'A Constitution of Social Governance for the European Union' in Dora Kostakopoulou and Nuno Ferreira (eds.), *The Human Face of the EU* (CUP, 2016).
51 *AGET Iraklis* (n 29).
52 Among many others, Pedro Caro De Souse, 'Negative and Positive Integration in EU Economic Law: Between Strategic Denial and Cognitive Dissonance?' (2012) *German Law Journal* 979 and the literature cited in it.
53 Vasiliki Kosta, *Fundamental Rights in EU Internal Market Legislation* (Hart, 2015); Among others see also, Mad Adenas, Tarijei Bekkedal and Luca Pantaleo, *The Reach of Free Movement* (Springer, 2017).
54 Among others, Loïc Azoulai, 'The Court of Justice and the Social Market Economy: The Emergence of an Ideal and the Conditions for Its Realization' (2008) *Common Market* 493; Dagmar Schieck, Ulrike Liebert and Hildegard Schneider (eds.), *European Economic and Social Constitutionalism after the Treaty of Lisbon* (CUP, 2011); Dagmar Schieck, *The EU Economic and Social Model in the Global Crisis* (Ashgate, 2013); Niklas Brunn, Klaus Lorcher and Isabelle Schomann (eds.), *The Lisbon Treaty and Social Europe* (Hart, 2012).
55 Claire Kilpatrick and Bruno De Witte (eds.), 'Social Rights in Times of Crisis in the Eurozone: The Role of Fundamental Rights' Challenges' (2014) *EUI Working Paper* at <http://cadmus.eui.eu/handle/1814/31247>.
56 Federico Fabbrini, *Economic Governance in Europe: Comparative Paradoxes and Constitutional Challenges* (OUP, 2016).
57 Among others, Lucia Busatta and Tamara Hervey, 'Cross-Border Healthcare and the "Social Market Economy"', in this volume.
58 Catharine Barnard, '(B)Remains of the Day: Brexit and EU Social Policy' in Vandenbrouke, Barnard and De Baere (eds.), *A European Social Union after the Crisis* (n 26).
59 Steve Peers, 'Article 50 TEU: The Uses and Abuses of the Process of Withdrawing from the EU' (2014) at <http://eulawanalysis.blogspot.ie/2014/12/article-50-teu-uses-and-abuses-of.html>.
60 Among others, Kenneth Armstrong, *Brexit Time: Leaving the EU: Why, How and When?* (CUP, 2017).
61 Dimitry Kochenov (ed.), *EU Citizenship and Federalism: The Role of Rights* (CUP, 2017).

Part I

The EU social market economy

Theoretical perspectives

1 The EU between market state ideals and social market economy objectives

Placing the social market economy within the Union's constitutional history

Charles Edward O'Sullivan

1 Introduction

Following the end of World War II, European States engaged in a period of unprecedented economic redistribution and intervention within their national economies. Market failures of almost any kind were viewed as sufficient grounds for greater State control of the economy.[1] This fit within a wider conceptual framework, according to which 'the political machinery of the nation could be used to improve the lot of mankind and helped give post-war national politicians the justificatory ideology they needed'.[2] The State's responsibility towards its citizens morphed into one based on 'the comprehensive responsibility for the subsistence and development of society in cultural, economic and social terms'.[3] Social market economies were therefore those that blended capitalism with social objectives,[4] and acted as a compromise between classical socialist and liberal economic models. These varied nation by nation, with each utilising a differing form of interventionist capitalism.[5] However, the overarching intent was that 'never again will doles and subsistence levels be tolerated' among the poor and working poor'.[6]

With the entry into force of the Lisbon Treaty, the European Union (EU) has now similarly committed itself to transforming the internal market into a fully formed 'social market economy' by way of Article 3(3) TEU. However, the normative potential of this provision remains to be seen, and this book attempts, as detailed in the introduction,[7] to shed a light on its ability to reshape the foundations on which the EU is built.

The EU and its institutions have never explicitly endorsed a particular economic model for the internal market.[8] Rather, the Union has instead engaged primarily in 'market building' activities,[9] through which it has sought to eliminate barriers to trade and open up its Member States' economies so that the internal market may one day be completed. With this in mind, this contribution will explore whether and to what extent the reformulated Article 3 TEU is capable of reshaping the internal market into a 'social market economy' similar to those operated by its Member States. In order to do so, it will adopt a theoretical framework, which measures the extent to which the EU's structures elevate the market over social objectives, and whether or not the Union should therefore be considered a 'Market' rather than a 'Social' State, the latter of which would be reflective of a 'social market economy'.

The EU cannot be considered a State in the strictest sense. In reality, it exists as an entity with its own entirely 'unique legal order', and can be conceived of as '*sui generis* organisation'.[10] It is however capable of satisfying Almond's definition of a political community[11] as it: regulates behaviour; extracts capital; possesses a (limited) redistributive element; recalibrates its own structures to new challenges through Treaty amendments and ordinary laws; as well as enshrining values. Consequently the Union can be classed as 'State-like', allowing for its constitutional competences, as well as legal and institutional structures to be assessed in this light. This contribution embraces the latter view and argues that Article 3(3) TEU on the EU acting as a 'highly competitive social market economy' is a further example of 'State-like' behaviour.

The contribution will adopt the following structure. Section 2 will explore the concept of the 'social market economy' from a historical perspective and discuss how this concept balances two seemingly anachronistic values: the social and the market. The third section will be divided into two separate subsections. The first will examine how this concept of the 'social market economy' and 'Social State' are context dependent, and that based on a historical view of the Union's constitutional development, it has remained a primarily economic entity with additional competences being subsumed into this to reinforce and support the completion of the internal market. The latter will then look at the specific constitutional provisions which reinforce this trend, and the ways in which EU constitutional law has continually impacted on the social policies of its Member States despite having very few express competences in the social fields. A fourth section will argue that because of this trend towards economic integration and the impact of EU law in social fields the Union is more closely aligned with that of a 'Market State', wherein economic rights and deregulation are of primary importance, and that the potential of Article 3(3) TEU cannot be fully realised without the EU's constitutional legal order being consciously reframed to negate this overall trend. The contribution will finally provide some concluding remarks, underlining these points.

2 The social market economy: a historical perspective

As highlighted in the introduction to this volume,[12] the term 'social market economy' was coined by Röpke, Rüstow, Böhm, Oppenheimer and, overall, Müller-Armack as 'market freedoms that are capable of achieving social objectives'. The most common social objectives are to limit social inequality and to correct or address market failures. These concepts are subsequently often embedded within national constitutions as prescriptive principles of social policy. These prescriptive principles are often referred to as 'Social States', after the German *Sozialstaat*, outlined within Article 20 of the Basic Law as a guarantee that '[t]he Federal

Republic of Germany is a democratic and social federal [S]tate'.[13] Establishing a concise definition for what the 'Social State' means in reality has long proved difficult, however Brezovar has argued that the concept came about when 'The State began to provide its people with certain public services – the State's part is not only to command but also to perform certain duties, to provide assistance'.[14] As a result, this provision creates a quasi-constitutional imperative to provide for the well-being of the German people, and seeks to ameliorate if not solve the 'basic conflict between social rights and market values',[15] and therefore acts as the constitutional basis for the German 'social market economy'. The judiciary has predominantly sought to temper this obligation by underlining that whilst there is an emphasis on the executive and legislative branches 'to ensure the balancing of social differences . . . it leaves the legislature broad latitude for doing so', it is also the case that the State 'must merely create the minimum conditions for its citizens to live in human dignity', with the underlying principle of the 'Social State' in Article 20 establishing nothing in terms of how 'the task is to be accomplished in individual cases'.[16] As Dani notes elsewhere in this volume,[17] the German Constitutional Court wanted to ensure that 'the constitution establishes an open institutional framework amenable to competing political aspirations and, notably, also to alternative renderings of the 'Social State'.

Other constitutional traditions and political regimes have, over time, attempted to enshrine their own 'Social State' provisions within both law and practice, echoing this ideal. As outlined in the introduction to this chapter, there was arguably a common European commitment in the post-WWII era aimed at greater levels of State intervention in the economy, and a more pragmatic concern was that by limiting some of the most notable excesses of market forces, the State could ensure that socialism would not replace the existing capitalistic *status quo*.[18] This political drive for greater State intervention was often spearheaded by some of socialism's most ardent critics.[19]

O'Gorman[20] views the 'German experience', that of the *Sozialstaat* in Article 20 of the Basic Law, as instructive in interpreting and applying Article 3(3) TEU, as it arguably represents the constitutional basis for its national 'social market economy' in the same way that Article 3(3) now does. In his estimation, this does not mean that the EU will adopt the *Sozialstaat* model in a wholesale manner. Rather, the German experience could provide a clear example of how the Court of Justice (CJEU) might reconcile this clause within its own legal framework.[21] However, this to some extent assumes that the way in which economies are regulated or controlled by the State is apolitical, as well as the 'Social State' clause being sufficiently clear and precise that it may be followed by the State in taking action to negate the potential for further interpretation.[22] As alluded to previously, the German Constitutional Court has been quite clear that Article 20 is essentially apolitical, and does not require any specific measures to be carried out or tools to be used. On this basis, it is not possible to assume that the German experience can or should be taken as instructive as it is constantly subject to the political realities of those that interpret it, like any broad prescriptive principle.[23] It acts a site of constant political contestation, continually subject to the particular political, economic and social factors at play within the German State at any given time. Socialist scholars in particular have emphasised that this temporal effect may over time add additional layers of complexity in terms of the application of new measures and removal of others, masking the original intention if one can be said to exist, at least insofar as the first government(s) following its adoption viewed it.

3 A specifically European context

Having briefly outlined the link between the concept of the 'social market economy' and the 'Social State', as well as the potential difficulties in abiding by a prescriptive social policy clause, the following subsections will explore the ways in which the EU will, based on its own constitutional development, find it difficult to comply with Article 3(3) TEU. This is not only because of the economic foundations upon which the Union is based, but due to the previous attempts it has made in adopting more socially orientated provisions in previous Treaties and their muted impact.

3.1 The development of an economic constitution for the EU

If, as the argument surrounding the development of the German 'Social State' and its underlying social market economy attempts to posit, the translation of this proscriptive principle into practice is highly dependent on the specific context in which it is interpreted and applied, it is necessary to look at the way in which the EU has developed and how the recent inclusion of Article 3(3) TEU is likely to sit within this overall process.

Although the EU has consistently deepened the extent to which it can exercise its original constitutional competences as well as widening to incorporate additional political and other competences, it has remained a primarily economic union which increasingly serves additional functions. The European Coal and Steel Community (ECSC) for example, the first iteration of the EU established under the Treaty of Paris, reflected this journey towards a meta-normative system in a very simple way, as it sought to ensure peace between European nations in the post-WWII era.[24] It did so by integrating the coal and steel production of the original signatory States at a supranational level. This effectively depoliticised this particular economic function utilising the theory of comparative advantage (each country would specialise in the fields it was best in, with every country benefitting from this shift in production planning) to assuage the fear of German rearmament in particular. Schuman opined that such a momentous step was not only necessary, but an imperative as 'world peace cannot be safeguarded without the making of creative efforts proportionate to the dangers which threaten it'.[25] He inevitably had loftier ambitions, believing that the further social and political integration of European States would be the next logical step. On a theoretical level, Anderson is extremely supportive of this notion, believing nationalistic divides to be both arbitrary and tribal.[26] This leads 'so many millions of people, not so much to kill . . . to die for such limited imaginings'.[27] However even an eventual 'nation of nations' or supranational European State could equally be considered an arbitrary way of organising society and social boundaries, even if it is one based on the continual reevaluation of itself and its values as it develops over time.

In ensuring its original remit, the ECSC was hugely successful. It would lead to the longest period of peace and integration between European nations in history, as well as shaping a new kind of international organisation. It would in time grow into the organisation it is now, a European Union of twenty-eight Member States, and founded on a new legal order.[28] Circumventing Martinez's four stages of normative development (positivisation, generalisation, internationalisation, specification)[29] almost entirely, the EU demonstrates a reciprocal form of evolutionary legal and constitutional development far beyond the judicially driven form heralded by scholars such as Strauss.[30] It is in fact wholly likely that the Union inverted this process if it engaged with it at all, as it began with a specific function at a regional level and then gradually adopted additional functions where they would help ensure the effective performance of its existing competences. The larger conceptual framework evident in the development of the EU goes further than the earlier enunciated forms of evolutionary constitutionalism as well in that it includes the Treaties, general principles of EU law, the constitutional values common to the Member States, the Charter of Fundamental Rights (EU CFR) and the 'Four Freedoms', as well as ordinary legislative acts and the jurisprudence of the CJEU. It is a form of 'constitutional synthesis' in so far as it does not engage with only one discreet form of adaptation.[31] However, this process will continually be driven by the existing constitutional foundations on which the Union is built, and this cannot be forgotten.

3.2 *The EU's burgeoning 'Social State'*

In the more specific, social context, this drive towards consolidating the existing economic competences of the Union by expanding outwards into other fields is evident in how the EU has adopted socially driven Treaty provisions, which could arguably be seen as the primogenitors of Article 3(3) TEU. The EEC Treaty for example, included clauses such as: 'to promote throughout the Community a harmonious development of economic activities, a continuous and balanced expansion, an increase in stability, an accelerated raising of the standard of living and closer relations between the States belonging to it';[32] and 'to promote improved working conditions and an improved standard of living for workers, so as to make possible their harmonization while the improvement is being maintained'.[33] Provisions of this nature were subsequently incorporated even more frequently from the Maastricht Treaty[34] and Treaty of Amsterdam[35] onwards.

Standing in stark contrast to these Articles is Article 3(c) EC Treaty, which held the EU's objectives to be 'characterized by the abolition, as between Member States, of obstacles to the free movement of goods, persons, services and capital', and thus created a constitutional economic imperative emphasising the limitation of government intervention within the market and enshrining economic values as fundamental to the functioning of the Union. Despite its eventual removal and replacement with Article 3 TEU, Oliver argues that its legacy remains within the four freedoms and the constitutional DNA of the Union.[36] For example, Article 60 TFEU retains the objective of liberalising services within the internal market beyond what is already provided for under existing Union legislation, engraining the view that Markets should not be sheltered from competition and that the Market should have a wider application based on the interests of society.

Consequently, despite the existence of earlier provisions which integrate social objectives into the workings of the internal market, the weight ascribed to these constitutional economic provisions demonstrates that the EU is a result of an overall process of shaped integration, accidental or otherwise.[37] The shaping of this process is firstly evident in the constitutional provisions outlined above that predate Article 3(3) TEU, which emphasise the economic ahead of the social. These are economic objectives that will have social consequences rather than social objectives which will be achieved through the selective use and tight regulation of the market. Their potency was further diminished by the fact that in *Zaera*,[38] the CJEU ensured that these clauses would remain largely non-judicable and were therefore primarily aspirational in their tone. There remains the potential that they could be used as an additional basis for judicial decisions to be rendered in a more socially conscious manner, but this has generally not occurred. This is due to the fact that economic policies and competences had historically been ceded to the Union, while social policies and systems remained the primary jurisdiction of the Member States. The division of these competences was solidified at an early date, with Member States arguing in 1956 through the Spaak Report that the protection of socialised systems such as welfare must be protected and promoted,[39] and the Treaties of Paris and Rome were to some extent viewed as 'buttresses to the welfare [S]tate'.[40] The Ohlin Report,[41] which was delivered two years later in 1958, echoed this sentiment, and established that social policy, particularly in the field of labour standards, should be a soft competence granted to the Commission, while the ability to substantively implement these objectives was a competence retained by the Member States themselves.[42] This was borne out in the division of competences at the Union level, which are considered to be the material fields within which the EU has the power to take legislative action. The Union's competences in fields of social policy (as distinct from where it can engage in 'market building' social policies through the use of economic competences)[43] is far more nebulous than its economic competences.

A significant number of scholars have supported this division between social and economic competences, believing that the existence of nationalised solidarity-based programmes involves defending these against interference from EU law.[44] This view is justified based on the greater levels of social rights enjoyed by EU citizens in comparison to those in other jurisdictions[45] by virtue of their social market economies and the corresponding rights granted to citizens in order to give these effect. Their existence, as well as the ability of the State to positively intervene in the national economy to achieve social objectives, is therefore viewed as important social and political achievements worthy of protection.[46] This attachment leads to a natural instinct to defend these from encroachment on the part of EU Member States.[47] This resistance to opening up the 'Social State' at the national level and developing a corresponding infrastructure at the EU level has even grown in recent years in response to both EU enlargement[48] and the perceived dangers of free movement within the Union.[49]

The belief that the intention of the Treaties has always been to limit the spheres within which Member State can intervene within their national economies has also been widely supported by scholars.[50] Such arguments are somewhat justifiable, given that both the Spaak and Ohlin Reports emphasised the creation of an internal market as a tool for 'levelling' social protections amongst its members,[51] despite also suggesting that they would not be eroded by Union membership.

Dashwood has conversely suggested that the Treaties 'contain a variety of formal indications' regarding the inability of the Union to undermine sovereignty in respect of social policy and how they execute them. In his estimation, membership of the Union is instead governed by the sharing of competences between the EU at the supranational level, and the Member States at the national level. This filters down into how competences are now catalogued within the TFEU, and demonstrates that both normatively and functionally the EU can only assume the power to legislate in a given material field where it has been included within the Treaty by the Member States. The Member States are therefore the drafters of the Treaties, and should be considered their 'masters'.[52] Often this school of thought relies on the presumption the EU can only be considered a State-like entity which performs certain regulatory tasks[53] based on a stricter understanding of the principle of conferral.

However, despite an overall lack of uniformity in its approach over time and never explicitly endorsing a particular economic model,[54] the CJEU has played a significant role in expanding the material scope of the fundamental freedoms, particularly during periods where the Union's legislative competence was underutilised.[55] The result of this 'market building' on the part of the CJEU is that 'there simply is no nucleus of sovereignty that the Member States can invoke, as such, against the community'.[56] EU law has developed to such a significant degree that it touches areas previously considered to be exclusively national competences[57] due to the ever broadening material scope of the economic freedoms, and this will in Schiek's estimation, inevitably have consequences for the ways in which Member States instigate social policies and programmes.[58] This is in spite of the prevalent view within the EU from its inception that the creation of an internal market would act 'as an instrument to enhance social welfare through a variety of objectives (that have expanded over time) and not as an end in itself'.[59]

Even free market, non-interventionist philosophers and economists have argued that

> in a federation, certain economic powers, which are now generally wielded by the national [S]tate, could be exercised neither by the federation nor by the individual [S]tates, implies that there would have to be less government all round if federation is to be practical.[60]

The Union may lack a strictly federal structure, but the extent to which Member States have integrated EU law into their national legal systems, and the development of the Union's competences in even the economic field will inevitably have social and political consequences.

What becomes clear from the process of constitutional development discussed above is that not only is context of primary importance in establishing the potential meaning of Article 3(3) TEU, but also that it can never be said to be neutral. This stands in stark contrast to Fossum and Menendez who continually argue that the evolutionary form of constitutionalism adopted by the EU ensures not only that the Member States retain their distinct identities, but that it at the same consolidates them.[61] It is difficult to reconcile how twenty-eight distinct States could integrate without at least some reorientation of the means through which they achieve their social objectives and their normative values, but using the example of the Canadian constitution, the authors believe this to be the case. Webber by contrast, believes that the Canadian provinces gradually converged on social policy grounds by crafting federalised systems for public goods,[62] which would in this instance suggest that it is an unsuitable comparator for the European Union, which originally integrated specific economic functions with the expectation that this might lead to social convergence.

4 The EU as a 'Market State'?

When one examines the Treaties chronologically and the powers they impart, the trend leans predominantly towards the EU as an economic union with additional political and social functions. It has historically viewed these political and social functions as an extension of its economic basis, rather than as an integrated whole, and this is the greatest failing of the EU due to the fact that it has yet to significantly challenge or alter this balance to demonstrate a more nuanced understanding of how society should ideally be directed.

The expansion of the Union's competences have however been made with the tacit, or at least passive, support of the Member States themselves. As Hooghe and Marks argue, there existed a 'permissive consensus' about further constitutional integration at the Union level on the part of Member States, and it was only later that this consensus was challenged by internal disputes.[63] States felt that despite the legal ceding of power towards the EU, they largely retained decisional autonomy.[64] The very process of integration, whilst it may have been driven at least at first almost unilaterally by the CJEU, retained national support. It is also impossible to hold the European Union solely responsible for the gradual decline of what had been termed the 'century of redistribution'.[65] As alluded to in the introduction to this contribution, this period saw the democratic States of Western and Northern Europe in particular dedicate themselves, using a vary forms of the 'social market economy', to forging a compromise between the liberal capitalistic models that were predominant in the 19th century. The factors that led to its decline are difficult to pinpoint, with the likelihood being that the process of decolonisation, the inability of the welfare systems to respond to rapid social change,[66] the shift from an industrial to service based economy, the slow erosion of the 'Social State' internally by capitalistic actors[67] and the breakdown of standard class distinctions[68] all acted as contributing factors.[69] The European Union instead likely provided an answer to the crises of the 1960s and 1970s, which saw these social democratic States question what they should become next or if they should change at all.[70] Yet this does not negate the role played by the EU in restructuring the societies of its Member States towards a far more capitalistic conception of society, and largely in line with what this contribution would consider to be a 'Market State' model, as distinct from a 'Social State'.

The 'Market State' is a model wherein the economy becomes the primary driver of social and political action, and 'the market has been adopted as a purely technical means of allocating goods and services without consideration of its deeper social and economic implications'.[71] State systems will inevitably be built around the self-interest of the individual,[72] and a largely self-regulating economy becomes the natural facilitator of this. Placing an emphasis on economic rights over social rights, reframing welfare systems as being contingent on the economic value of the individual, the degree to which vulnerable persons accessing welfare are highlighted as financial burdens or of poor character are all potentially indicative of this model.[73]

This is evident within the EU's constitutional structures for a variety of reasons. First and foremost, the expansion of the Union's competences has, in almost all circumstances, emphasised the completion of the internal market, and this has, as outlined earlier, often had negative social consequences for its Member States where it has been achieved through negative integration. It is possible that the EU could adopt positive measures to alleviate these issues, but this is limited by the degree to which the Union can take active steps in social fields due to its limited powers in these areas, and the failure to extend powers directly to the EU in this respect. Secondly, even if the EU was granted explicit competences to take more direct action in social fields, the development of its constitutional legal order has continually emphasised the eradication of barriers to the exercise of the free movements, and this limits the potential application of Article 3(3) TEU unless there is a conscious decision to reorientate EU law in light of this new provision. Consequently, the Union cannot take the necessary steps to apply a more dynamic and socially conscious interpretation of the 'social market economy' clause without an active restructuring of the EU's competences, the jurisprudence of the CJEU and the ordinary legislation underpinning EU constitutional law. Such a task cannot be achieved through one proscriptive 'Social State' principle alone.

5 Concluding remarks

Ferri and Cortese in the introduction to this volume mention that the inclusion of Article 3(3) TEU signals the potential for the EU to significantly recalibrate the way in which the EU constructs its internal market away from one which is characterised by an imperative to liberalize in the name of market building. This could potentially nudge the EU towards that of a social market economy which emulates the 'European social model' that exemplified the golden age of European economic development. However, this contribution, looking at Article 3(3) TEU through a historical lens, shows that without a more significant restructuring of the Union's constitutional legal order, the EU remains more closely aligned with that of a 'Market State' in spite of this 'Social State' objective discussed by O'Gorman being incorporated within EU law post-Lisbon. The analysis shows the weaknesses of including this kind of rhetorical emphasis without a series of structural, legal changes capable of giving effect to this concept of a 'social market economy' in even the broadest sense.

The definition of what constitutes a 'social market economy' is never static, and is as such dependent on the particular social, political, economic and even temporal context in which it is said to exist. Consequently, the current EU legal order leans heavily towards that of a 'Market State', which seeks to continually expand its existing competences, the consequences of which are that the powers of Member States to define and implement their own social policy is eroded without being reinforced at the Union level. Without replacing these policies at the supranational level, the EU will simply continue to be a market economy typified by the removal of barriers to trade. This may be why the primary champions of integration have always been centrist and right-wing parties,[74] as it is easily reconciled with their ideological point of view. With the continual movement of socialist and social democratic national parties towards the centre and centre-right, support has inevitably grown for the EU and further integration, but this does not alter that even the most expansive vision put forward by integrationists, such as Jacques Delors, is unlikely to emulate the robust social institutions of the most interventionist Member States within the Union.[75] For states with a low level of social provision, if the EU were to engage in greater regulation and improve the social character of its economy, this might lead to a rise in national standards.[76] However, this would require that the Union alters its historical interpretation of its fundamental economic freedoms and method of integration, as well as assuming the necessary competences to apply and execute the implied intentions of Article 3(3) TEU.

Gillingham argues that 'the adoption of the Single European Act was a choice for the Market. [. . .] It represented an acknowledgement that the model of the national mixed-economy had had its day'.[77] It would appear that this state of play remains in place even after Lisbon, and that the constitutional framework of the EU operates more like a 'Market State' than that of a true 'Social State'.

Notes

1 Giandomenico Majone, *Regulating Europe* (Routledge, 1996); Alan Milward and Vibeke Sorensen, 'Interdependence or Integration? A National Choice' in Alan Milward *et al.* (eds.), *The Frontier of National Sovereignty: History and Theory 1945–1992* (Routledge, 2015).

2 Alan Milward, *The European Rescue of the Nation-State* (Routledge, 2000) 41–42.

3 Dieter Grimm, 'Il Futuro della Costituzione' in Gustavo Zagrebelsky, Pier Paolo Portinaro and Joerg Luther (eds.), *Il Futuro Della Costituzione* (Einaudi, 1996) 143.

4 Tony Judt, *Postwar: A History of Europe since 1945* (Penguin, 2005) 777.

5 Mark Kleinman, *A European Welfare State? European Union Social Policy in Context* (Palgrave Macmillan, 2002).
6 William Beveridge, *Full Employment in a Free Society* (Allen and Unwin, 1967) 249; Nicholas Barr, *The Economics of the Welfare State* (OUP, 1998); Mica Panic, *Globalisation and National Economic Welfare* (Palgrave Macmillan, 2003).
7 Delia Ferri and Fulvio Cortese, 'Introduction', in this volume.
8 Clemens Kaupa, 'May Be Not Activist Enough? On the Court's Alleged Neoliberal Bias in its Recent Labor Cases' in Mark Dawson, Bruno De Witte and Elise Muir (eds.), *Judicial Activism at the European Court of Justice* (Edward Elgar, 2013) 56, at 59–61.
9 Wolfgang Streeck, 'From Market Making to State Building? Reflections on the Political Economy of European Social Policy' in Stephen Leibfried and Paul Pierson (eds.), *European Social Policy: Between Fragmentation and Integration* (Brookings, 1995) 389, at 399; Fritz Scharpf, 'The European Social Model: Coping with the Challenges of Diversity' (2002) *Journal of Common Market Studies* 645.
10 Case 26/62, *Van Gend en Loos*, EU:C:1963:1.
11 Gabriel Almond, *A Discipline Divided* (Sage, 1990).
12 Ferri and Cortese, 'Introduction' (n 7).
13 Article 20.1 of the Basic Law for the Federal Republic of Germany.
14 Nejc Brezovar, 'Judicial Activism Contributing to the Understanding of Social State Principle(S) – Constitutional Court of Slovenia at the Crossroads' (2017) *Danube: Law and Economics Review* 19, at 20. Elsewhere referred to as 'a normative, prescriptive principle, which defines a specific polity, where the State has the constitutional obligation to assume interventionist functions in the economic and social spheres' (George Katrougalos, 'European "Social States" and the USA: An Ocean Apart?' (2008) *European Constitutional Law Review* 225, at 238).
15 Thomas Marshall, *Social Policy* (Routledge, 1975) 42.
16 Federal Constitutional Court of Germany judgement, *BvE* 2/08, 2 *BvE* 5/08, 2 *BvR* 1010/08, 2 *BvR* 1022/08, 2 *BvR* 1259/08, 2 *BvR* 182/09 (30.6.2009).
17 Marco Dani, 'The EU Transformation of the Social State', in this volume.
18 Gosta Esping-Anderson and Walter Korpi, 'Social Policy as Class Politics in Postwar Capitalism' in John Goldthorpe (ed.), *Order and Conflict in Contemporary Capitalism* (OUP, 1984).
19 Adolph Wagner, 'Three Extracts on Public Finance' in Richard Musgrave and Alan Peacock (eds.), *Classics in the Theory of Public Finance* (Palgrave Macmillan, 1967) 1; Peter Flora and Arnold Heidenheimer, *The Development of Welfare States in Europe and America* (Transaction, 1981); Sidney Whitman, *Personal Reminiscences of Prince Bismarck* (John Murray, 1902); Erich Eyck, *Bismarck and the German Empire* (Allen and Unwin, 1958).
20 Roderic O'Gorman, 'The Irish "Bail-Out" and Cuts to Social Protection Spending: The Case for a Right to a Subsistence Minimum in EU Law' (2014) 4 *German Law Journal* 569, at 589.
21 Ibid., at 580–590.
22 David Gerber, *Law and Competition in Twentieth Century Europe: Protecting Prometheus* (Clarendon, 1998) 246.
23 Nils Goldschmidt and Michael Wohlgemuth, 'Social Market Economy: Origins, Meanings and Interpretations' (2008) *Constitutional Political Economy* 261, at 262.
24 Andrew Moravcsik, *The Choice for Europe* (CUP, 1998); Wayne Sandholz and Alec Stone Sweet, *European Integration and Supranational Governance* (OUP, 1998).
25 The Schuman Declaration (9 May 1950).
26 Benedict Anderson, *Imagined Communities* (Verso, 2006).
27 Ibid., at 7.

28 *Van Gend en Loos* (n 10).
29 Gregorio Peces Barba Martinez, *Teoria dei diritti fondamentali* (Giuffré, 1993); Pasquale Policastro, 'A New Garment for an Old Question: A Clash between Man's Rights and Citizen's Rights in the Enlarged Europe?' in Joakim Nergelius (ed.), *Nordic and Other European Constitutional Traditions* (Martinus Nijhoff, 2006) 61, at 63.
30 David Strauss, *The Living Constitution* (OUP, 2010).
31 John Fossum and Augustín Menendez, *The Constitution's Gift: A Constitutional Theory for a Democratic European Union* (Rowman and Littlefield, 2011) 163–177.
32 Article 2 EEC Treaty.
33 Article 117 EEC Treaty. Article 118 EEC Treaty provided specifically for the Commission's role in driving Member States towards closer cooperation in the sphere of social security, and Recitals 2, 3 and 5 of the Treaty laid out further aspirational provisions.
34 Article 2 EC Treaty stated that the Union would ensure 'a high level of employment and of social protection, the raising of the standard of living and quality of life, and economic and social cohesion and solidarity among Member States' (Maastricht Treaty [1992] OJ (C 191) 1).
35 Treaty of Amsterdam [1997] OJ C 340, Article 2(1) and (2) included the coordination of employment and access to education.
36 Peter Oliver, *Oliver on Free Movement of Goods in the European Union* (Bloomsbury, 2010).
37 Helen Wallace, 'Europeanisation and Globalisation: Complimentary or Contradictory Trends?' (2000) *New Political Economy* 369, at 370.
38 Case 126/86, *Zaera*, EU:C:1987:395, paras 10–11.
39 Milward, *The European Rescue of the Nation-State* (n 2), at 216.
40 Ibid., at 211.
41 International Labour Office, 'Social Aspects of European Economic Co-Operation' (1956) 74 *International Labour Review* 99.
42 Michael Doherty, 'W(h)ither Social Europe? Labour Rights in a Social Market Economy', in this volume.
43 Alina Tryfonidou, *The Impact of Union Citizenship on the EU's Market Freedoms* (Hart, 2016) 168; Charlotte O'Brien, 'Social Blind Spots and Monocular Policy Making: The ECJ Migrant Worker Model' (2009) *Common Market Law Review* 1107, at 1112.
44 Diamond Ashiagbor, 'Unravelling the Embedded Liberal Bargain: Labour and Social Welfare Law in the Context of EU Market Integration' (2013) 3 *European Law Journal* 303.
45 Colm O'Cinneide, 'Austerity and the Faded Dream of a "Social Europe"' in Aoife Nolan (ed.), *Economic and Social Rights after the Global Financial Crisis* (CUP, 2014) 169.
46 Jeremy Rifkin, *The European Dream: How Europe's Vision of the Future Is Quietly Eclipsing the American Dream* (Tarcher, 2005).
47 George Katrougalos, 'The (Dim) Perspectives of the European Social Citizenship' (2007) 5 *Jean Monnet Working Paper* at <https://jeanmonnetprogram.org/paper/the-dim-perspectives-of-the-european-social-citizenship/> at 2.
48 Willfried Spohn and Anna Triandafyllidou (eds.), *Europeanisation, National Identities and Migration: Changes in Boundary Constructions between Western and Eastern Europe* (Routledge, 2003).
49 Financial Times, 'Poll Backlash Expected Amid Hostility to Migrants in EU' (2013) at <www.ft.com/intl/cms/s/0/945b9c46-3810-11e3-8668-00144feab7de.html#axzz2kbZVJyKA>; European Social Survey, 'Attitudes towards

Immigration and Their Antecedents: Topline Results from Round 7 of the European Social Survey' (2016) at <www.europeansocialsurvey.org/docs/findings/ESS7_toplines_issue_7_immigration.pdf>; European Commission, 'Euro Baromater' (2017) at <http://ec.europa.eu/commfrontoffice/publicopinion/index.cfm/Survey/getSurveyDetail/instruments/STANDARD/surveyKy/2142>.

50 John Pinder, 'Positive Integration and Negative Integration: Some Problems of Economic Union in the EEC' (1968) *The World Today* 88; Fritz Scharpf, 'Negative and Positive Integration in the Political Economy of European Welfare States' in Gary Marks *et al.* (eds.), *Governance in the European Union* (Sage, 1996) 15.

51 Simon Deakin, 'Labour Law as Market Regulation: The Economic Foundations of European Social Policy' in Paul Davies *et al.* (eds.), *European Community Labour Law: Principles and Perspectives* (Clarendon Press, 1997) 63, at 67.

52 Alan Dashwood, 'States in the European Union' (1998) *European Law Review* 201, at 202.

53 Phillipe Schmitter, 'Imagining the Future of the Euro-Polity with the Help of New Concepts' in Marks *et al.* (eds.), *Governance in the European Union* (n 50), at 133.

54 Stephan Wernicke, 'Au nom de qui? The European Court of Justice between Member States, Civil Society and Union Citizens' (2007) *European Law Journal* 380, at 381; Michael Malecki, 'Do ECJ Judges all Speak with the Same Voice? Evidence of Divergent Preferences form the Judgments of Chambers' (2012) *Journal of European Public Policy* 59.

55 Jospeh Weiler, *The Constitution of Europe* (CUP, 2005) 30–31.

56 Koen Lenaerts, 'Constitutionalism and the Many Faces of Federalism' (1990) *American Journal of Comparative Law* 205, at 220.

57 Eleanor Spaventa, 'Seeing the Wood Despite the Trees? On the Scope of Union Citizenship and its Constitutional Effects' (2008) *Common Market Law Review* 13, at 28; Gareth Davies, *Nationality Discrimination in the European Internal Market* (Kluwer, 2003) 196–197.

58 Dagamar Schiek, 'Re-Embedding Economic and Social Constitutionalism: Normative Perspectives for the EU' in Dagmar Schiek, Ulrike Liebert and Hildegard Schneider (eds.), *European Economic and Social Constitutionalism after the Treaty of Lisbon* (CUP, 2011) 17; Diamond Ashiagbor, 'Unravelling the Embedded Liberal Bargain: Labour and Social Welfare Law in the Context of EU Market Integration' (2013) *European Law Journal* 303.

59 Erica Szyszczk, 'Building a Socio-Economic Constitution: A Fantastic Object?' (2011) *Fordham International Law Review* 1364, at 1370.

60 Friedrich Hayek, 'The Economic Conditions of Interstate Federalism' in Friedrich Hayek (ed.), *Individualism and Economic Order* (CUP, 1939) 255.

61 Fossum and Menendez, *The Constitution's Gift* (n 31), at 45–76.

62 Jeremy Webber, *Reimagining Canada* (McGill-Queen's UP, 1994) details this process in full from the perspective of a constitutional historian.

63 Liesbet Hooghe and Gary Marks, 'A Postfunctionalist Theory of European Integration: From Permissive Consensus to Constraining Dissensus' (2009) *British Journal of Political Science* 1, at 5–6.

64 Christian Joerges, 'Taking the Law Seriously: On Political Science and the Role of Law in the Process of European Integration' (1996) *European Law Journal* 105, at 121.

65 Pierre Ronsanvallon, *The Society of Equals* (HUP, 2013) 165.

66 Walter Benn Michaels, *The Trouble with Diversity: How We Learned to Love Identity and Ignore Inequality* (Holt and Company, 2006); Ruth Rosen, *The World Split Open: How the Modern Women's Movement Changed America* (Penguin,

2006); Corey Robin, *The Reactionary Mind: Conservatism from Edmund Burke to Sarah Palin* (OUP, 2013).

67 Pierre Bourdieu, *The Social Structures of the Economy* (Polity Press, 2005).

68 Peter Mair calls this 'the tendency towards the decline of collective identities within western electorates, resulting from more or less common socio-economic or socio-cultural processes' (Peter Mair, *Ruling the Void: The Hollowing of Western Democracy* (Verso, 2013) 57).

69 Johanna Bockman, *Markets in the Name of Socialism: The Left-Wing Origins of Neoliberalism* (SUP, 2011).

70 Ronsanvallon, *The Society of Equals* (n 65), at 210.

71 David McNally, *Against the Market: Political Economy, Market Socialism, and the Marxist Critique* (Verso, 1993) 172. Although McNally in this instance refers to the unquestioning adoption of the Market by Social Democrats over time, it still demonstrates the view of the Market by its advocates. Advocates of the Market either knowingly or unknowingly would for the existence of the 'Market State' in that it is the natural consequence of Market principles.

72 Kenneth Arrow, 'Gifts and Exchanges' (1972) *Philosophy and Public Affairs* 343, at 349–350.

73 Michelle Everson, 'The Legacy of the Market Citizen' in Jo Shaw and Gillian More (eds.), *New Legal Dynamics of European Union* (Clarendon, 1995) 73; Niamh Nic Shuibhne, 'The Resilience of EU Market Citizenship' (2010) *Common Market Law Review* 1597; Kanishka Jayasuriya, 'Constituting Market Citizenship: Regulatory State, Market Making and Higher Education' (2015) *Higher Education* 973.

74 Kevin Featherstone, *Socialist Parties and European Integration: A Comparative History* (MUP, 1988) 2.

75 Liesbet Hooghe and Gary Marks, 'The Making of a Polity: The Struggle over European Integration' in Herbert Kitschelt *et al.* (eds.), *Continuity and Change in Contemporary Capitalism* (CUP, 1999) 70; Martin Rhodes and Bastiaanvan Apeldoorn, 'Capitalism versus Capitalism in Western Europe' in Martin Rhodes, Paul Heywood and Vincent Wright (eds.), *Developments in West European Politics* (St. Martin Press, 1997) 171.

76 Liesbet Hooghe, *The European Commission and the Integration of Europe: Images of Governance* (CUP, 2001) 129.

77 John Gillingham, *European Integration 1950–2003: Superstate or New Market Economy* (CUP, 2003) 294.

2 The EU transformation of the social state

Marco Dani

1 Introduction

The expression 'Social State' commonly refers to a legal and political order making capitalism socially acceptable by means of redistributive policies and a democratic public sphere.[1] An elusive notion due to the variety of models it encompasses,[2] it is frequently viewed as a defining element of European constitutional democracies.[3] References to it (or to its main components) feature prominently in eternity clauses,[4] preambles[5] or key principles of national constitutions.[6] Even if not explicitly mentioned in constitutional texts, its structures operate as a key driver of citizens' allegiance to national communities.[7]

The EU Treaties approach the 'Social State' in two different ways. Firstly, they acknowledge at the level of preambles[8] and binding principles[9] the social character of the Member States. Secondly, they deploy social language to qualify the normative profile of the EU institutional framework and policies.[10] Yet, at almost ten years from the ratification of the Lisbon Treaty, the evaluation of the relationship between the Union and the 'Social State' remains problematic. On the one hand, EU projects such as the single market and the Economic and Monetary Union (EMU) seem to have increasingly contributed to a transformation or, in certain circumstances, the impoverishment of national social states. On the other hand, the EU has developed its own set of social policies, which, however, do not amount to a pan-European social State.[11] Thus, what should we make of the EU social dimension? Should we conclude that the EU appropriation of social language is just a cosmetic expedient adding constitutional warmth to an otherwise socially hostile legal and political order?

This chapter resists this hasty and, at any rate, simplistic conclusion. It claims that, in order to understand the EU engagement with the 'Social State', one has to forego gradualist[12] approaches aimed at assessing to what extent the EU can reproduce at a supranational level nation state models. A more productive way to look at the issue is adopting a transformationalist approach and, namely, exploring how concepts and institutions originally developed at national level have both influenced and adapted to the evolving institutional framework of the Union. In this perspective, an examination of the EU social dimension revolves around three different set of questions: 1) how does the incorporation of 'Social

State' language affect the EU institutional architecture and culture? 2) how is the concept of 'Social State' transformed by being appropriated by the Union, i.e. a polity lacking the preconditions for generating a fully fledged social state? 3) considering the interactive linkages existing between the Union and nation state constitutions, what is the impact of the EU transformed notion of 'Social State'? How does it affect the original concept at a national level and, critically, its policy manifestations?

To answer these questions, this chapter explores three different engagements between the 'Social State' and the EU. It starts with the 'Social State' under Embedded Liberalism, the regime articulated by the European Economic Communities between the end of World War II and late 1970s aimed at accommodating state economic and social interventionism and multilateral economic integration (section 2). In this period, it is argued, a dual governmental structure is established: at a national level, the 'Social State' develops with a view to promote the emancipation of citizens from the vagaries of unregulated markets by means of active industrial and redistributive policies; at a supranational level, economic growth is fostered by applying a notion of economic freedoms centred on non-discrimination on the basis of nationality.

The analysis proceeds by looking at the 'Social State' under Advanced Liberalism, the regime developed by the Union to cope with the crisis of national social government since the end of 1970s up to the adoption of the Lisbon Treaty (section 3). In this phase, the EU expands gradually its remit towards economic and social policies and incorporates a number of social motifs in its institutional framework. Yet, these developments do not bring about a pan-European 'Social State'. On the contrary, social motifs are employed to recalibrate the common market and elaborate policies re-orienting national social government from the original goal of emancipation to competitiveness and participation in the markets. This triggers important processes of transformation of 'Social State' structures such as the re-organisation of the systems of direct taxation to attract mobile factors of production, the marketisation of social services and the reconsideration of labour law and employment policies to enable workers' participation in the market.

Finally, the chapter examines the relationship between the social state and Authoritarian Liberalism, the regime introduced by the Union to cope with the economic and financial crisis (section 4). In this context, the 'Social State' is firstly targeted as undermining the stability of the Eurozone and, subsequently, revived in the formally and substantively impoverished form of the European Pillar of Social Rights to improve the sustainability of economic governance.

Overall, the chapter claims that the EU is transforming the 'Social State' by re-orienting its original normative aspirations associated with emancipation from the markets to weaker forms of social policies aimed at enabling market participation or providing a basic safety net for the most vulnerable. This process is not concluded and is in part resisted by rear-guard forces mobilised by the controversial EU management of the economic and financial crisis. Hitherto the EU institutional architecture appears resilient and capable to cope with mounting criticism, owing also to a manipulative and placatory use of 'Social State' language.

2 The social state under Embedded Liberalism

Although the idea of a 'Social State' dates back to the origins of the social question in the 19th century, its post-World War II constitutional manifestations are largely a reaction to the destructive consequences of unconstrained capitalism experienced in the interwar period. This constitutional response manifests itself firstly in negative form by ruling out both socialism and *laissez-faire*, equally regarded as economic models conducive to intractable social and political conflicts. It then finds a positive expression by referring to a social justice as a shared and, yet, undefined horizon[13] in which the distributive conflicts between conservative and left-leaning parties can be mediated through democratic institutions and procedures.[14]

Within a similar institutional framework, the 'Social State' lends itself to a variety of more specific manifestations. Its first important rendering is the social market economy, the economic model influencing economic and social policy in West Germany in the aftermath of World War II.[15] Inspired by the ordoliberal school, the 'social market economy' develops from a position of scepticism towards *laissez-faire* and, notably, its core idea of a spontaneous self-regulating capacity of markets.[16] Markets, by contrast, are viewed as institutions to be established and regulated by the state with a view to promote economic efficiency.[17] Indeed, only the pursuit of economic efficiency can prevent the disruptive tendencies of capitalism and promote social progress. Thus, the State is expected to secure the market against public and private monopolies, a task fulfilled by enforcing the economic constitution.[18] State intervention, therefore, is admitted, but only if compatible with the functioning of the market.[19] As mentioned, this model became predominant in West Germany,[20] but only as a matter of policy. Indeed, against the background of an animated debate on the meaning of Article 20(2) of the German Basic Law between the heirs of Schmitt and Heller,[21] the German constitutional court rejects the idea of reading the constitution as entrenching a specific economic model.[22] The constitution establishes an open institutional framework amenable to competing political aspirations and, notably, also to alternative renderings of the 'Social State'.

Outside Germany, ordoliberalism is far less influential. In countries like France or Italy, free markets are largely discredited as forces operating without regard to reason or justice,[23] and only a minority of scholars or politicians are ready to regard social progress as a side-effect of well-regulated markets.[24] The predominant political culture interprets the 'Social State' in different and more interventionist terms. Key to this rendering is the influence of personalism and its pursuit of human dignity as emancipation.[25] Following this line of thought, democratic constitutions consider liberty as a necessary but insufficient condition for emancipation since in a liberal society freedom is exercised essentially in alienated form by adapting to shifting economic conditions.[26] The 'Social State' instead promises a more ambitious form of emancipation. The individual is no longer conceived in a state of fictitious independence, but is situated in a set of interdependent relationships created by the industrial society.[27] Within a similar context, the 'Social State' enhances individuals and protects their human dignity. Consequently, individuals are shielded from the vagaries of unregulated markets;[28] and at the same time, they are protected also against collectivist drifts and the absorption by the State.[29] In sum, the 'Social State' is expected to engage with the cause of social justice, to tackle the root causes of totalitarianism and, therefore, to protect individuals against economic insecurity and dependence.[30] This results in the establishment of a welfare edifice including programmes of welfare and poverty relief for non-workers; instruments promoting access to the labour market and health and safety at work; social security of workers and their families outside work; instruments defending workers' income and a framework of economic and monetary policies aiming at full employment.[31]

The implementation of the 'Social State' in Europe should not be regarded only as the sum of disconnected national attempts to cope with the social question. Its achievement is situated in a broader context of multilateral cooperation rejecting both disembedded *laissez-faire* and uncoordinated economic nationalism. Embedded liberalism is the term referring to this new international regime grounded on free movement of goods and services, capital controls and respect to national interventionist economic and monetary policies aimed at economic growth, full employment and social justice.[32] To a considerable extent, this is the model inspiring also the process of European integration in its formative period. As widely known, in this period market building is the pre-eminent goal pursued by supranational institutions,[33] whereas the harmonisation of social policies is rejected.[34] This leads to a comprehensive institutional framework grounded on a rather artificial demarcation between the economic and social domains: while redistributive social policies are carried out in national constitutional democracies, at a supranational level institutions operate in the light of economic rationality to promote a system of open markets and undistorted competition.[35]

The market designed in the Treaty of Rome is a project strongly influenced by ordoliberalism.[36] This emerges, first of all, at a conceptual level since the market is not regarded as a given requiring protection against state interferences, but as a goal to be actively achieved by public institutions by means of strategies of negative and positive harmonisation. Secondly, ordoliberal influence is visible also in the idea of considering economic freedoms and competition law as the key instruments for integration.[37] Thirdly, economic integration is regarded as self-sufficient. According to the treaties, the pursuit of social progress does not require direct state intervention in that it is just the side-effect of economic integration.[38]

In the formative period, however, an embedded rather than a disempowering understanding of economic freedoms prevails.[39] Due to the difficulties in pursuing active market integration by means of positive harmonisation under the Luxembourg Compromise, the Court of Justice (CJEU) favours a construction of the economic freedoms as the concretisation of the principle of non-discrimination on the basis of nationality.[40] A decentralised model of market integration[41] prevails in which economic multilateralism is not inimical to interventionist industrial[42] and social policies.[43] The common market allows the development of social government, its only concern being contrasting excesses such as protectionism and discrimination.

However, this embedded notion of market integration as well as the complementary relationship established with the social state is built on shaky ground. Firstly, the boundary between non-discrimination and obstacle-based interpretations of economic freedoms is by no means clear-cut.[44] This emerges in *Cassis de Dijon*,[45] where the CJEU promotes a key shift towards an obstacle-based interpretation of the free movement of goods, ushering in a competitive model of market regulation.[46] Moreover, the distinction between economic and social spheres is also quite ephemeral. Already in this formative period, for instance, the Community introduces pieces of social legislation under the guise of market making policies.[47] This arises as an ambivalent achievement: on the one hand, the efficiency of the market is improved by removing distortions on competition and, arguably, social dumping; on the other, the Community nourishes the idea that intervention on social issues is possible not for its contribution in terms of individuals' emancipation, but based on economic rationality.[48] Both of these dynamics erode Embedded Liberalism and expose it to influences leading to a more problematic institutional regime in which multilateral economic cooperation, rather than strengthening or complementing national Social States, operates to transform them.

3 The social state under Advanced Liberalism

The demise of Embedded Liberalism, which began at the end of the 1970s, is a process exceeding European boundaries.[49] Globalisation and, notably, increased capital mobility undermine the ability of national governments to perform their ordinary tasks in industrial, economic and fiscal policy. Destabilised in one of its key elements, Embedded Liberalism leaves room for a renewed international regime developing an entirely different relationship with national social states.

The unravelling of Embedded Liberalism coincides with a phase of profound transformations in the Community and, later, EU institutional framework. Change takes place firstly within the original project of economic integration. The shift in understanding of economic freedoms from a non-discrimination to an obstacle-based construction experimented in *Cassis de Dijon* is consolidated[50] and extended outward to the other factors of production.[51] Home control arises as the main criterion governing free movement[52] and inspires the competitive model of market regulation introduced by the White Paper on the completion of the single market[53] and the Single European Act (SEA). Once extended to free movement of capital,[54] this rendering of economic freedoms ends up overturning the relationship between markets and social government. No longer capable to govern markets with a view to emancipation, the social state is pressured to adapt to market forces, for the latter are now in the position to decide which arrangements are affordable and which ones are a liability.[55]

Admittedly, the regulatory strategy pursued ever since the SEA also includes important progresses in the field of positive harmonisation. Supranational political institutions gain increased political capacity under qualified-majority voting[56] and their legislative competences are expanded to include social regulation in the fields of environmental, consumer and health protection. Moreover, the completion of the single market sets the ground for the introduction of a single currency and, as a direct consequence, to the coordination of national economic and social policies. All these developments take place in an institutional framework that gradually incorporates the iconography and the institutions of national constitutionalism.[57] It is in this context that the Lisbon Treaty, alongside consolidating the single market project and the economic and monetary Union, commits *inter alia* to solidarity[58] and a 'highly competitive social market economy' aimed at full employment and social progress.

The demise of Embedded Liberalism, therefore, also brings to an end the dual polity grounded on the division of labour between supranational and national law. Whereas it is difficult to disagree on this point, opinions greatly diverge on the characterisation of the next evolutionary phase and, in particular, on the assessment of the actual impact of the incorporation of the social state within the EU institutional framework.

According to a first view, the move away of the Union from its ordoliberal matrix and its constitutionalisation ushers in a supranational legal and political order grounded on solidarity.[59] This view makes the most of the constitutional innovations adopted in this period, namely the commitment to social market economy and the composite set of social values and rights inserted in the EU Charter and Treaties. It is a narrative buttressed on the procedural dimension by the increasing influence of the European Parliament in legislative decision-making and the Union's embrace of representative democracy as mode of operation.[60] However it is also a narrative which overlooks a number of structural aspects which not only call into question the existence of a pan-European 'Social State' but also its viability.[61] Indeed, the EU lacks the political capacity and the budgetary resources to sustain the establishment of a European Social State or the regulation of salient aspects of national welfares such as direct taxation and workers' rights,[62] industrial relations[63] and social security.[64] In addition, divergences persist in the organisation and normative orientation of national welfare state traditions, a fact reflected in the reluctance of national electorates and governments to harmonise social protection. Most of all, this view neglects the particular goals and architecture of the economic and monetary Union, notably the priority assigned to price stability over full employment[65] which, arguably, forecloses the edification of a 'Social State' along Keynesian lines.

Thus, the impact of the 'Social State' on the EU institutional framework does not bring about a conversion to activist economic and redistributive social policies. Upon closer examination, the incorporation of social motifs by the Union triggers two less spectacular developments: the social revaluation of the internal market and the neoliberal reconceptualisation of national economic and social policies.

The social revaluation[66] of the internal market is a process involving both negative and positive harmonisation. In negative harmonisation, the obstacle-based reading of economic freedoms and the expansion of their scope is, at least in part, balanced by a more open construction of their derogations.[67] This emerges in judgements mainstreaming constitutional rights in market adjudication[68] or admitting as legitimate justifications the pursuit of goals ranging from the cohesion of the tax system[69] to the financial balance of the social security system.[70] A socially enriched conception of the internal market is even more evident in positive harmonisation. Here, EU institutions are expected to take into account the non-economic principles included in horizontal clauses. The fundamental rights listed in the EU Charter are factored into the impact assessment procedures conducted by the Commission, the European Parliament and the Council throughout the legislative process.[71] These attempts at re-embedding the market at a supranational level contribute to a renewed conception of the market. Market regulation is no longer conceived in liberal terms as a task merely directed at increasing the volume of trade.[72] Market regulation is increasingly re-interpreted in holistic terms as an opportunity to attain virtually any public policy goal.[73] The consequences of a similar regulatory strategy are ambivalent: one the one hand, market regulation, especially if conducted by means of minimum harmonisation, may protect from regulatory competition the capacity of Member States to pursue their favourite non-economic policies;[74] on the other, the use of market legal bases to attain non-economic goals comes at the price of exposing to market influence a broad range of public policies. As a result, the internal market does not end up being subsumed by the flanking policies added with each Treaty amendment;[75] quite the contrary, it establishes its normative grip on social regulation and also reframes non-economic values in accordance with economic rationality.[76]

The predominance of economic rationality also emerges quite starkly if the EU coordination of national social policies is considered.[77] Again, the appropriation of social language by the Union is a source of ambiguities. On the one hand, the idea of coordinating national social states by means of procedures encouraging policy learning rather than further centralisation may sound appealing: some degree of collective action is promoted while preventing the disembedding of core issues associated with national Social States.[78] On the other hand, the type of coordination actually promoted by the Union does not aim at genuinely confronting different ways to cope with the challenges of social government. Analyses conducted on the outcomes of coordination on industrial,[79] employment[80] or education[81] policies reveal how these procedures have been largely instrumental in steering social policies towards predetermined goals such as employability, entrepreneurship and adaptability and, more broadly, to the supply-driven strategies inspiring the EMU.[82]

The enduring prevalence of economic rationality is key to understanding how the EU transforms the idea of a Social State. In the period reviewed it is misleading to portray the Union as an agent merely promoting *laissez-faire* economic policies and the dismantlement of national social government. The Union's engagement with the 'Social State' is more complex: on the one hand, it employs social principles and regulation to complete economic integration; on the other, it re-orients national social government from emancipation to competitiveness. Arguably, Advanced Liberalism is the most accurate term to define this policy agenda:[83] the Union does not seem interested in coordinating social policy with a view to shielding individuals from the vagaries of markets.[84] The EU is genetically entwined with market building; thus, it is more interested in employing social policy to enable individuals' participation in highly competitive markets.[85] This has a remarkable influence on the direction of supranational coordination: the Union promotes weak forms of social policies[86] enabling individuals to operate as well-functioning market participants or compensating them for losses of market income.[87] In essence, the expansion of European integration towards social policy and its appropriation of social motifs appear an entirely different endeavour from establishing a pan-European Social State. The Union does not commit itself to securing the democratic governance of global capital; rather, it facilitates globalisation by securing market freedoms and offering national governments a viable vehicle to promote otherwise unworkable structural reforms.[88] Notably, the economic and monetary Union functions as a strategic lever to counter vested interests or circumvent national legal or political hurdles.[89] In this phase, therefore, the Union strengthens its role of *vehiculo externo* for structural change.[90] In the newly acquired policy fields, it operates as a major driver of transformation: by dictating the direction of national policy making and pushing forward the reforms experimented in *avant-garde* countries,[91] it challenges the original normative claims and institutional structures of national social states. Constitutionalisation and socially minded discourses facilitate this process by rendering legally viable and politically palatable a policy agenda that, ultimately, enables capitalist dynamics.[92]

By adopting the Advanced Liberalism agenda, the Union triggers a series of transformations targeting specific elements of the welfare state edifice. Direct taxation is the first field in which the impact of the EU's transformative capacity can be appreciated. Absent political consensus on measures of positive harmonisation,[93] the European Court of Justice undertakes a rather aggressive application of market principles.[94] On the whole, these rulings intensify tax competition between the Member States,[95] but mainly the more mobile factors of production profit from this development repositioning in countries with more favourable tax regimes.[96] Following a trend common to all advanced economies, the Union's tax burdens gradually shift towards less mobile sources of income (*in primis*, workers' wages), giving rise to a rather disturbing asymmetry.[97]

A second important development concerns social services. Here, transformative pressures concentrate on public monopolies in the provision of healthcare, education, social security and assistance. A considerable push towards privatisation is exerted by means of the application of market principles to welfare provision.[98] Whereas under Embedded Liberalism the CJEU tended to exempt social policies from the application of economic freedoms, in this phase the Court appears more open to their review in the light of market principles.[99] Exposure to economic rationality triggers processes potentially disruptive of the original configuration of the Social State. Individuals are encouraged to spend in other Member States or in private markets the invisible voucher corresponding to their individualised quota of welfare expenditure.[100] This sets the ground for a market of welfare in which individuals are no longer regarded as citizens entitled to public goods but as consumers operating in a market of services.[101]

Lastly, labour law and industrial relations are also subject to neoliberal transformation. The shift from emancipation to empowerment has the effect of redefining the identity of these key elements of the welfare edifice. Thus, whereas under Embedded Liberalism their main task was redistributing income and power between employers and employees, in the new landscape they are expected to contribute to competitiveness and productivity.[102] Similarly, education, employment and training policies are also re-oriented with a view to improving the quality of the workforce and adapting it to the contingent demands of the 'knowledge society'.[103]

4 The social state under Authoritarian Liberalism

The transition from the emancipatory to the enabling Social State promoted by Advanced Liberalism is a gradual and uneven process. This may explain why resistance against it erupts only sporadically.[104] It takes a profound economic and financial crisis to accelerate and radicalise this development[105] and, correspondingly, to make the Union politically more salient and divisive.[106] Indeed, to cope with the crisis, the Union reiterates in more assertive forms the policy goals and institutional framework introduced under Advanced Liberalism. This ushers in a highly contentious type of economic governance evoking Authoritarian Liberalism,[107] the political regime experienced in Germany in the late 1920s and early 1930s.[108] Reasons of space preclude detailed examination of these reforms. To expose their dubious democratic credentials and justify this label, it is sufficient to highlight their main characteristics:

(a) the new instruments of economic governance radicalise the EU's commitment to transforming national economic and social policies. This course of action is coherent with a diagnosis whereby the crisis exposed the structural weaknesses of the economies of the Member States more reluctant to embracing Advanced Liberalism.[109] Against this background, the Union engages with recalcitrant Member States by granting financial assistance[110] subject to reforms of national social government being implemented;[111]

(b) coordination is maintained as the mode of governance to promote and oversee the transformation of national Social States, but its scope is expanded to virtually all policy fields affected by the economic and monetary Union.[112] In this way, economic governance absorbs issues situated at the core of national Social States such as wages, industrial relations, productivity, social security and assistance, private and public indebtedness.[113] Accordingly, economic rationality is exported well beyond the competence limits defined in the Lisbon Treaty[114] accentuating the subservient role of social policies;

(c) the coordination of economic and social policies becomes more stringent. Budget constraints are strengthened at a supranational level by intensifying the set of macroeconomic indicators steering economic policy and introducing semi-automatic sanctions in case of violation.[115] At a national level, balanced budget rules are incorporated within national constitutional law, alongside mechanisms of automatic correction in case of deviations from the medium term budget objective.[116] Being calibrated on the soundness of the financial situation and fiscal discipline, the intensity of budgetary and policy constraints varies considerably between member states. Thus, in situations close to insolvency the Union requires the adoption of specific measures preempting almost entirely the room for manoeuvre of national parliaments; in situations apparently normal, the existence of economic coordination and the steering capacity of the Union are hardly perceived;
(d) reforms of economic governance consolidate the closed character of the EU institutional framework: price stability, competitiveness, adaptability remain the predefined uncontested goals of, respectively, EU monetary, economic and social policy. Indeed, neither the criticalities in the institutional framework of the EMU exposed by the crisis nor the eruption of a debate between Keynesian and neoclassical approaches to its handling[117] motivate the Union to reconsider the entrenchment of the latter economic and social paradigm.[118] The Union maintains its previous economic and social agenda requiring the reduction of public expenses and the promotion of an export led economic growth by means of supply side measures;[119]
(e) from a substantive standpoint, the new economic governance prioritises macroeconomic indicators as the main coordinates steering national economic and social policies.[120] By conditioning the protection of constitutional rights to the respect of predefined macroeconomic quantities, a similar institutional framework downsizes their role and disables their emancipatory potential;
(f) from a procedural perspective, the new economic governance constrains considerably national democratic and representative policy making on behalf of supranational decision-making.[121] National parliaments are subjected to intensive oversight by intergovernmental and technocratic institutions[122] operating according to the style and rationale of the regulatory state.[123]

Leaving aside its dubious capacity to stabilise the Eurozone, this newly established institutional setting also reveals its own questionable social credentials. Firstly, its main strategy is not inspired by solidarity ideals such as redistributing the dividends of the single currency or assisting the states negatively affected by the imbalances created by the EMU. A more controversial course of action is followed in which the stick of stringent rules plus sanctions and the carrot of financial support are engineered to reform national social government. Secondly, by maintaining an institutional framework primarily committed to price stability and competitiveness, the new economic governance forecloses the possibility to cope with the crises by means of robust countercyclical policies strengthening demand, economic growth and full employment. Thirdly, absent the possibility of achieving full employment and promoting economic growth, national Social States are pressured to downsize their structures and reduce the level of social provision to make up for declining tax revenues.

While EU institutions contribute to the implementation of this policy agenda, the EU legal framework offers neither sufficient guarantees to prevent the corrosion of the social state nor equivalent supranational substitutes. In the initial and more dramatic part of the financial crisis, the Memoranda of Understanding and adjustment plans seem to have been elaborated in complete disregard of the social horizontal clauses set out in the treaties. Nor has the EU Charter of Fundamental Rights been able to constrain this process of desocialisation.[124] Indeed, the CJEU has ruled that its fundamental rights jurisdiction does not extend to the activity of EU institutions conducted in the context of the European Stability Mechanism.[125] National measures implementing conditionality obligations have also been regarded as falling outside the remit of the EU Charter.[126] Tellingly, even the Commission, in reporting on the implementation of the EU Charter, has omitted entirely any assessment of the impact of the EU Charter on adjustment measures and EU coordination of economic and social policy.[127] Lacking the intervention of the Court of Justice, national constitutional courts have been called into question in cases concerning adjustment measures encroaching on national constitutional rights. This has generated an interesting series of judgements in which national constitutional courts attempt to cope with the difficult task of accommodating the national measures with an EU imprimatur and the integrity of national Social States.[128]

More recent judgements reveal a slightly different approach. The CJEU has accepted to review in the light of EU fundamental rights the conduct of EU institutions in the fulfilment of their tasks under the European Stability Mechanism and other instruments of financial support.[129] It is a significant move in that it (re)situates the activity of EU institutions within a shared framework of constitutional guarantees. Yet, the deferential standards of review adopted in these judgements do not seem to offer yet any tangible contribution to the actual protection of the affected economic and social rights.

This trend of paying only lip-service to the protection of fundamental rights pervades the much advertised 'European Pillar of Social Rights' (EPSR).[130] An initiative promoted by the Commission to revive the EU social dimension, this document aims at increasing the visibility of social rights and, possibly, strengthening their actual impact in the EU economic governance.[131] It acknowledges and reaffirms most of the rights listed in title IV of the EU Charter (Solidarity),[132] although the focal point is centred on the rights related to employment and the working environment. Three categories of rights are highlighted: equal opportunities and access to labour markets; fair working conditions; social protection and inclusion. Following a trend experimented at an informal level,[133] the principles contained in the Pillar are to be mainstreamed in the new instruments of economic governance with a view to embolden their social profile.

However, for all of its emphasis on social rights, the EPSR invites a number of critical observations. Firstly, in no parts of the document does the Commission seem to reconsider the EU management of the crisis and, in particular, the draconian measures imposed upon the Member States receiving financial assistance. On the contrary, the upshot of the document is updating and completing EU economic governance[134] by replicating the revaluation strategy inaugurated with the single market. In other words, according to the Commission, the EU social deficit exposed by the crisis does not require an institutional reconsideration of the EU institutional framework and policies. What is needed is not a structural reform of EU economic governance, but a modicum of social warmth to make it more palatable. Secondly, even if we are to accept this as a valid strategy, social rights remain subordinate to economic rationality. This emerges first of all at a formal level: the *soft law* nature of the document reveals that the crisis has not only hardened economic governance but it has also softened social rights.[135] Rather than requiring the mainstreaming of the EU Charter of Fundamental Rights or Treaty-based social clauses (hard law in hardened governance), the Commission opts for a legally innocuous instrument such as the recommendation which neither can interfere with the policy directions and redistributive strategies inspiring the EMU, nor can establish tangible side-constraints on the resulting policy measures (soft law in hard governance).[136] Subordination to economic rationality is also evident from a substantive standpoint: the European Pillar reiterates the type of weak social policies inspiring Advanced Liberalism.[137] It does not promise (and cannot deliver) emancipation, the reduction of social inequalities or fairer tax systems. The Pillar insists either on measures enabling market participation[138] or on a basic safety net to render economic governance socially sustainable.[139] Thirdly, the appropriation of social rights language in the context of the economic governance transforms their nature. Originally, social rights were goals inspiring political struggle and social mobilisation; in the current context, they are deprived of their subversive potential and operate at best as negative limits to structural reform.[140] Moreover, they are treated just as an additional element to be taken into account in complex and opaque procedures conducted under the ethos of managerialism.[141] Thus, it is not surprising that in a similar context social rights are normalised as another variable amenable to quantification and measurement in a scoreboard.[142] Lastly, despite paying lip-service to subsidiarity and diversity, the European Pillar is presented also as a cooperative effort involving EU and national institutions, social partners and stakeholders. As already experimented in the holistic single market, social rights are employed to make legally and politically more attractive the EMU, an undertaking in which all players are expected (and, sometimes, coerced) to row in the same direction.[143]

In sum, under Authoritarian Liberalism the EU accelerates the transformation of the 'Social State' envisioned under Advanced Liberalism. In a first and dramatic phase, different national social states are viewed as problematic for the stability of the EMU.[144] Next, the social state is revived both as a discourse and a source of policies contributing to the sustainability of regulatory and distributive strategies with questionable constitutional pedigree. On the whole, the 'Social State' emerges from this phase either confirmed in its renewed vocation to enable market participation or in an impoverished form securing protection only to the most vulnerable members of national communities. In both of these manifestations, its original promise of emancipation is obscured.

5 Conclusion

This chapter has examined three different engagements between the 'Social State' and the EU corresponding to as many evolutionary stages of the process of European integration. The focal point of the process of European integration in its formative period has been the instauration of an embedded form of economic integration complementing national social states. In a similar context, the 'Social State' has largely fulfilled the promise of emancipating individuals from the risks associated with unregulated markets. It has also been shown that the demise of this institutional arrangement coincides with the expansion of the scope of operation of supranational policy making and the appropriation by the Union of several motifs associated with the social state. The incorporation of 'Social State' language, however, does not reflect a genuine attempt at establishing a pan-European Social State. In this phase, social discourse is more modestly employed to reframe in holistic terms the common market project and promote social policies fostering competitiveness and enabling participation in markets. This process of reorientation of the social state in the light of economic rationality culminates in the institutional arrangements adopted to cope with the economic and financial crisis. Here, the diversity of national social states has initially been viewed as undermining the stability of the EMU. More recently, social language has been rehabilitated with a view to make more sustainable the new economic governance and secure a basic safety net for the most vulnerable individuals.

If this account is accurate, the resulting trajectory reveals a rather disturbing process in which European integration transforms the 'Social State' from a system delivering emancipation from the markets to a set of policies either enabling market participation or offering an impoverished form of social protection. It is unclear to what extent this dynamic is reversible. What is granted is that if a possibility exists to overturn it, it largely rests more with politics and social mobilisation than with law. During the economic and financial crisis the EU, by radicalising its transformative commitment, has grown increasingly controversial and awakened a considerable amount of resistance and resentment. At the time of writing, however, its institutional architecture appears resilient and capable to cope with mounting criticism. In this regard, a key role is certainly played by EU social discourses. Rather than inspiring mobilisation, the latter distract from the real challenges to the social state posed by European integration. While leaving intact institutional structures with questionable social pedigree, social discourses try to restore the aura of the 'Social State' by offering an emotional cushion and, ultimately, a form of camouflage to the Union policy strategies.[145] Social language, it has been shown, adapts quite easily to a variety of institutional arrangements, even to those transforming or contradicting its original normative claims. Denouncing this as a dangerous manipulation should probably come high in the list of the priorities of those interested in reviving emancipation as the original promise of the European Social State.

Notes

1 Fritz Scharpf, *Governing Europe: Effective and Democratic?* (OUP, 1999) 33.
2 Fritz Scharpf, 'The European Social Model: Coping with the Challenges of Diversity' (2002) *Journal of Common Market Studies* 650. Differences regard a range of variable such as the amount of available resources, the institutional framework and the normative aspirations.
3 Jurgen Habermas and Jacques Derrida, 'February 15, or What Binds Europeans Together: A Plea for a Common Foreign Policy, Beginning in the Core of Europe' (2003) *Constellations* 291; Claus Offe, 'The European Model of "Social" Capitalism: Can It Survive European Integration?' (2003) *The Journal of Political Philosophy* 437. On the historical evolution of national welfare states, Michael Stolleis, 'The European Welfare State: A Model under Threat' (2017) *Quaderni Fiorentini* 25.
4 E.g. Articles 20(1) and 79(3) of the German Basic Law and Article 288 of the Portuguese Constitution.
5 E.g. The Preamble to the 1946 Constitution of France, recalled by the Preamble to the 1958 Constitution.
6 E.g. Articles 1(1) and 9(2) of the Spanish Constitution, Article 2 of the Polish Constitution and Article 3(2) of the Italian Constitution.
7 Thomas Marshall, *Citizenship and Social Class* (CUP, 1950) 47.
8 See the attachment to the fundamental rights defined in the European Social Charter (1961) and the Community Charter of the Fundamental Social Rights of Workers (1989).
9 Article 2 TEU, where justice and solidarity feature among the values common to the Member States. This provision (alongside Article 49 TEU) could also be read as prescribing a social component in the legal and political orders of the Member States.
10 Article 3 TEU. See also Title IV of the EU CFR (Solidarity), the horizontal clauses fostering the promotion of equality (Article 8 TFEU), high levels of employment, social protection, health and education (Article 9 TFEU), and the policies included in titles IX-XV and XVIII of the TFEU.
11 Christian Joerges, '*Sozialstaatlichkeit* in Europe? A Conflict-of-Laws Approach to the Law of the EU and the Proceduralisation of Constitutionalisation' (2009) *German Law Journal* 343; Scharpf, *Governing Europe: Effective and Democratic?* (n 1), at 8–9; Offe, 'The European Model of "Social" Capitalism: Can It Survive European Integration?' (n 3), at 457–460.
12 The distinction between gradualist and transformationalist approaches to the study of the EU is traced in Francis Cheneval and Frank Schimmelfennig, 'The Case for Democracy in the European Union' (2012) *Journal of Common Market Studies* 336.
13 Dieter Grimm, 'The Democratic Costs of Constitutionalization: The European Case' (2015) *European Law Journal* 464, observes that 'the function of constitutions is to legitimise and to limit political power, but not to replace it. Constitutions are a framework for politics, not the blueprint for all political decisions'.
14 Marco Dani, 'Rehabilitating Social Conflicts in European Public Law' (2012) *European Law Journal* 621.
15 Charles Edward O'Sullivan, 'The EU between "Market State" Ideals and "Social Market Economy" Objectives: Placing the "Social Market Economy" within the

Union's Constitutional History', in this volume; Delia Ferri and Fulvio Cortese, 'Introduction', in this volume.

16 Flavio Felice, *L'economia sociale di mercato* (Rubettino, 2008) 21.
17 Ibid.
18 Ibid., at 22–23 and 29.
19 Ibid., at 39–40.
20 David Gerber, 'Constitutionalizing the Economy: German Neo-Liberalism, Competition Law and the "New" Europe' (1994) *The American Journal of Comparative Law* 60.
21 On the debate between Forsthoff (claiming that the reference to the social state had only programmatic value) and Abendroth (arguing that the promise of social justice is inherent in the idea of democratic rule), Joerges, '*Sozialstaatlichkeit* in Europe? A Conflict-of-Laws Approach to the Law of the EU and the Proceduralisation of Constitutionalisation' (n 11), at 336–337.
22 BVerfGE 4, 7 (*Investitionshilfe*); Alexander Somek, *The Cosmopolitan Constitution* (OUP, 2014) 82 and 84, claiming that democratic constitutions are only formally programmatic as they do not contain a detailed blueprint of social life.
23 Ibid., at 158.
24 Giuliano Amato, 'Il mercato nella Costituzione' (1992) *Quaderni Costituzionali* 8; Felice, *L'economia sociale di mercato* (n 16), at 75–79.
25 Somek, *The Cosmopolitan Constitution* (n 22), at 123–124.
26 Ibid., at 164.
27 Georges Burdeau, *La democrazia* [1956] (Edizioni di Comunità, 1964) 25–41.
28 Somek, *The Cosmopolitan Constitution* (n 22), at 127.
29 Ibid., at 142.
30 Ibid., at 153–156.
31 Offe, 'The European Model of "Social" Capitalism: Can It Survive European Integration?' (n 3), at 450–453.
32 John Ruggie, 'International Regimes, Transactions, and Change: Embedded Liberalism in the Postwar Economic Order' (1982) *International Organisation* 393.
33 Damian Chalmers, 'The Single Market: From Prima Donna to Journeyman' in Jo Shaw and Gillian Moore (eds.), *New Legal Dynamics of European Union* (Clarendon Press, 1995) 61–62.
34 Scharpf, 'The European Social Model: Coping with the Challenges of Diversity' (n 2), at 646.
35 Joerges, '*Sozialstaatlichkeit* in Europe? A Conflict-of-Laws Approach to the Law of the EU and the Proceduralisation of Constitutionalisation' (n 11), at 341.
36 Gerber, 'Constitutionalizing the Economy: German Neo-Liberalism, Competition Law and the "New" Europe' (n 20), at 59–75; Chalmers, 'The Single Market: From Prima Donna to Journeyman' (n 33), at 56–66.
37 Augustin Menéndez, 'The Existential Crisis of the European Union' (2013) *German Law Journal* 472.
38 Barnard Catharine, 'EU "Social" Policy: From Employment Law to Labour Market Reform' in Paul Craig and Grainne de Búrca (eds.), *The Evolution of EU Law* (OUP, 2011) 642.
39 Menéndez, 'The Existential Crisis of the European Union' (n 37), at 473.
40 Ibid.
41 Miguel Maduro, *We, the Court: The European Court of Justice & the European Economic Constitution* (Hart, 1999) 143–149.
42 Gian Tosato, 'La disciplina comunitaria degli aiuti tra economia di mercato ed interessi generali' in Cesare Pinelli and Tiziano Treu (eds.), *La costituzione economica: Italia, Europa* (il Mulino, 2010) 253.
43 Case C-263/86, *Humbel*, EU:C:1988:451.

44 Grainne De Búrca, 'Unpacking the Concept of Discrimination in EC and International Trade Law' in Catharine Barnard and Joanne Scott (eds.), *The Law of the Single European Market. Unpacking the Premises* (Hart, 2002) 188.
45 Case 120/78, *Cassis de Dijon*, EU:C:1979:42. In this case, the Court departs from a non-discrimination construction of Article 34 TFEU in order to review indistinctly applicable regulatory measures hindering free movement. The same outcome could have been achieved by arguing that the measure at hand was discriminatory in that it imposed a dual burden on imported goods; Stephen Weatherill and Paul Beaumont, *EU Law* (Penguin, 1999) 608–699.
46 Maduro, *We, the Court: The European Court of Justice & the European Economic Constitution* (n 41), at 126–143.
47 Barnard, 'EU "Social" Policy: From Employment Law to Labour Market Reform' (n 38), at 647, referring to health and safety and collective redundancies directives.
48 Ibid., at 645; Floris de Witte, 'The Architecture of a Social Market Economy' (2015) 13 *LSE Law, Society and Economy Working Papers*.
49 John Ruggie, 'Globalization and the Embedded Liberalism Compromise: The End of an Era?' (1997) *Max-Planck Institut fur Gesellschaftsforschung Working Paper*.
50 Its more extreme applications, however, have been partially curbed in Case C-267/91, *Keck and Mithouard*, EU:C:1993:905.
51 Case C-76/90, *Manfred Säger*, EU:C:1991:331 (services); Case C-415/93, *Bosman*, EU:C:1995:463 (workers); Case C-212/97, *Centros*, EU:C:1999:126 (establishment); Case C-112/05, *Commission v Germany*, EU:C:2007:623 (capital).
52 Paul Craig, 'The Evolution of the Single Market' in Barnard and Scott (eds.), *The Law of the Single European Market: Unpacking the Premises* (n 44), at 35–36.
53 European Commission White Paper, 'Completing the Internal Market', COM(1983)310.
54 Directive 88/361/EEC for the implementation of Article 67 EEC, [1988] OJ L178/5.
55 Offe, 'The European Model of "Social" Capitalism: Can It Survive European Integration?' (n 3), at 463.
56 Article 100A EEC Treaty.
57 Reference can be made to fundamental rights (Article 6 TEU), European citizenship (Articles 9 TEU and 20 TFEU), horizontal clauses (Articles 8–17 TFEU) and parliamentarisation (Articles 10 and 14 TEU).
58 EU CFR, Title IV.
59 Armin von Bogdandy, 'Constitutional Principles' in Armin von Bogdandy and Jurgen Bast (eds.), *Principles of European Constitutional Law* (Hart, 2007) 32.
60 Article 10 TEU.
61 Joerges, '*Sozialstaatlichkeit* in Europe? A Conflict-of-Laws Approach to the Law of the EU and the Proceduralisation of Constitutionalisation' (n 11), at 344–345.
62 Articles 114(2) and 115 TEFU.
63 Article 153(5) TFEU.
64 Articles 48 and 156 TFEU.
65 Article 127 TFEU; Matthias Herdegen, 'Price Stability and Budgetary Restraints in the Economic and Monetary Union: The Law as Guardian of Economic Wisdom' (1998) *Common Market Law Review* 9.
66 Loic Azoulai, 'The European Court of Justice and the Duty to Respect Sensitive National Interests' in Mark Dawson, Bruno De Witte and Elise Muir (eds.), *Judicial Activism at the European Court of Justice* (Edward Elgar, 2013) 180.
67 This opening was already visible in *Cassis de Dijon* with the mandatory requirements doctrine.
68 Case C-112/00, *Schmidberger*, EU:C:2003:333, and, more controversially, Case C-438/05, *Viking*, EU:C:2007:772.

69 Case C-204/90, *Hanns-Martin Bachmann*, EU:C:1992:35.
70 Case C-385/99, *V.G. Müller-Fauré*, EU:C:2003:270.
71 Communication from the European Commission, 'Strategy for the Effective Implementation of the Charter of Fundamental Rights by the European Union', COM(2010)573.
72 Alexander Somek, *Individualism: An Essay on the Authority of the European Union* (OUP, 2008) 90.
73 Ibid., at 115 and 137.
74 De Witte, 'The Architecture of a Social Market Economy' (n 48), at 10–12.
75 Chalmers, 'The Single Market: From Prima Donna to Journeyman' (n 33), at 67–69.
76 Somek, *Individualism: An Essay on the Authority of the European Union* (n 72), at 94.
77 Article 5 TFEU.
78 Giandomenico Majone, *Dilemmas of European Integration* (OUP, 2005) 162–180. On the dangers lurking behind cognition and policy learning: Offe, 'The European Model of "Social" Capitalism: Can It Survive European Integration?' (n 3), at 462–468.
79 Marco Dani, 'Lo sviluppo dell'imprenditorialità nello spazio costituzionale europeo: le politiche pubbliche tra sostegno ed emancipazione' (2005) *Diritto Pubblico Comparato ed Europeo* 396.
80 Barnard, 'EU "Social" Policy: From Employment Law to Labour Market Reform' (n 38), at 678–685.
81 Sacha Garben, 'The Future of Higher Education in Europe: The Case for a Stronger Base in EU Law' (2012) *LEQS Paper* at <www.lse.ac.uk/europeanInstitute/LEQS%20Discussion%20Paper%20Series/LEQSPaper50.pd>.
82 Articles 146(1) and 148(2) TFEU. On the subordination of coordination to economic rationality, William Scheuermann, 'Democratic Experimentalism or Capitalist Synchronisation? Critical Reflections on Directly-Deliberative Polyarchy' (2004) *Canadian Journal of Law and Jurisprudence* 101.
83 Nikolas Rose, *Powers of Freedom: Reframing Political Thought* (CUP, 1999) 139–142.
84 Alexander Somek, 'The Individualisation of Liberty: Europe's Move from Emancipation to Empowerment' (2013) 4 *Transnational Legal Theory* 261.
85 Ibid., at 274–275.
86 Alexander Somek, 'De-Commodification Revisited: On the Absence of Emancipation in Europe' (2004) 6 *University of Iowa Legal Studies Research Paper* at <https://papers.ssrn.com/sol3/papers.cfm?abstract_id=927967> at 14–16.
87 Somek, 'The Individualisation of Liberty: Europe's Move from Emancipation to Empowerment' (n 84), at 227, observing that, in this perspective, what remains of justice is an equal entitlement to market activation.
88 Chris Bickerton, *European Integration: From Nation-States to Member States* (OUP, 2012) 127–128.
89 Kevin Featherstone, 'The Political Dynamics of the *Vincolo Esterno*: The Emergence of EMU and the Challenge to the European Social Model' (2001) *Queen's Papers on Europeanisation* 9.
90 Bickerton, *European Integration: From Nation-States to Member States* (n 88), at 131–136.
91 Featherstone, 'The Political Dynamics of the *Vincolo Esterno*: The Emergence of EMU and the Challenge to the European Social Model' (n 89), at 6–13.
92 In retrospect, it can be argued that constitutionalisation has largely succeeded not only in defusing the legal resistances of national constitutional courts towards increased integration but also in co-opting the political Left in the transformative agenda of the Union; Wolfgang Streeck, 'Heller, Schmitt and the Euro' (2015) *European Law Journal* 365.

93 According to Articles 114(2) and 115 TFEU, harmonisation of fiscal provision is subject to unanimity voting.
94 Case C-118/96, *Jessica Safir*, EU:C:1998:170.
95 Wolfgang Schön, 'Tax Competition in Europe: General Report' in Wolfgang Schön (ed.), *Tax Competition in Europe* (International Bureau of Fiscal Documentation, 2003) 17–18.
96 Only in rather extreme cases of opportunistic exercise of free movement the Court of Justice reinforces national measures aimed at defending the tax base, Case C-196/04, *Cadbury Schweppes*, EU:C:2006:544.
97 Mario Monti, *A New Strategy for the Single Market: At the Service of Europe's Economy and Society* at <http://ec.europa.eu/internal_market/strategy/docs/monti_report_final_10_05_2010_en.pdf> at 80.
98 Gareth Davies, 'The Process and Side-Effects of Harmonisation of European Welfare States' Jean Monnet WP 2/06 at <https://jeanmonnetprogram.org/paper/the-process-and-side-effects-of-harmonisation-of-european-welfare-states/>.
99 This line of judgements is inaugurated by Case C-120/95, *Decker*, EU:C:1998:167, and Case C-158/96, *Kohll*, EU:C:1998:171.
100 Case C-368/98, *Abdon Van Braeckel and others ANMC*, EU:C:2001:400.
101 John Baldock, 'On Being a Welfare Consumer in a Consumer Society' (2003) *Social Policy and Society* 65.
102 Hugh Collins, 'Is There a Third Way in Labour Law?' in Joanne Conaghan, Richaed Fischl and Karl Klare (eds.), *Labour Law in an Era of Globalization: Transformative Practices and Possibilities* (OUP, 2004) 451.
103 Barnard, 'EU "Social" Policy: From Employment Law to Labour Market Reform' (n 38), at 678–685.
104 For an account on EU social conflicts before the economic and financial crisis, Neil Fligstein, *Euroclash. The EU, European Identity, and the Future of Europe* (OUP, 2008).
105 Agustin Menéndez, 'The Crisis of Law and the European Crises: From the Social and Democratic *Rechtsstaat* to the Consolidating State of (Pseudo-)technocratic Governance' (2017) *Journal of Law and Society* 64.
106 Damian Chalmers, Markus Jachtenfuchs and Christian Joerges, 'The Retransformation of Europe' in Damian Chalmers, Markus Jachtenfuchs and Christian Joerges (eds.), *The End of the Eurocrats' Dream: Adjusting to European Diversity* (CUP, 2016) 6.
107 William Scheuermann, 'Hermann Heller and the European Crisis: Authoritarian Liberalism Reedux?' (2015) 21 *European Law Journal* 302, Michael Wilkinson, 'Authoritarian Liberalism in the European Constitutional Imagination: Second Time as farce?' (2015) *European Law Journal* 313.
108 Hermann Heller, 'Authoritarian Liberalism?' (2015) *European Law Journal* 295.
109 Communication from the European Commission, 'Europe 2020: A Strategy for Smart, Sustainable and Inclusive Growth', COM(2010)2020, at 7–9.
110 Financial assistance has been provided via intergovernmental financial vehicles such as the *European Financial Stability Facility*, the *European Financial Stabilisation Mechanism* and *European Stability Mechanism* and ECB programmes such as the *Security Markets Programme, Outright Monetary Transaction* and *Asset Purchase Programme.*
111 Edmondo Mostacci, 'La sindrome di Francoforte: crisi del debito, *costituzione finanziaria europea* e torsioni del costituzionalismo democratico' (2013) *Politica del diritto* 506.
112 Article 9 of the Treaty on Treaty on Stability, Coordination and Governance in the Economic and Monetary Union (TSCG).

113 Chalmers, Jachtenfuchs and Joerges, 'The Retransformation of Europe' (n 106), at 19.
114 Mark Dawson and Floris de Witte, 'Constitutional Balance in the EU After the Euro-Crisis' (2013) *Modern Law Review* 824.
115 The application of these indicators has been uneven and discretionary. As a consequence, Menéndez, 'The Crisis of Law and the European Crises: From the Social and Democratic *Rechtsstaat* to the Consolidating State of (Pseudo-) technocratic Governance' (n 105), at 76–78, observes that they have only the semblance of rules.
116 Article 3(2) TSCG.
117 Clemens Kaupa, 'Has (Downturn-)Austerity Really Been 'Constitutionalized' in Europe? On the Ideological Dimension of Such a Claim' (2017) *Journal of Law and Society* 36.
118 Mostacci, 'La sindrome di Francoforte: crisi del debito, *costituzione finanziaria europea* e torsioni del costituzionalismo democratico' (n 111), at 492–495.
119 Fritz Scharpf, 'After the Crash: A Perspective on Multilevel European Democracy' (2015) *European Law Journal* 391.
120 Marco Dani, 'Numeri e principio democratico: due concezioni a confronto nel diritto pubblico europeo' in Chiara Bernardi, Silvia Borelli and Andrea Guazzarotti (eds.), *La legge dei numeri. Governance economica europea e marginalizzazione dei diritti* (Jovene, 2016) 101.
121 Article 2a of Regulation No 1466/97 as amended by regulation n. 1175/2011 (European Semester) and Article 4 of Regulation No 473/2013 (Common Budgetary Timeline).
122 De Witte, 'The Architecture of a Social Market Economy' (n 48), at 17.
123 Damian Chalmers, 'The European Redistributive State and a European Law of Struggle' (2012) *European Law Journal* 685.
124 Francesco Saitto, '"Risocializzare l'Europa". La dimensione sociale europea tra economia di mercato e integrazione sovranazionale' (2017) *Rivista di diritti comparati* 86.
125 Case C-370/12, *Pringle*, EU:C:2012:756, paras 179–180.
126 Case C-128/12, *Sindacato dos Bancários do Norte, do Centro, do Sul e Ilhas*, EU:2013:149.
127 Only the 2016 Report contains a brief reference in this regard. European Commission, *2016 Report on the Application of the EU Charter of Fundamental Rights* (2016) at <http://ec.europa.eu/newsroom/just/item-detail.cfm?item_id=59189> at 13–14.
128 Massimo Luciani, 'Diritti sociali e livelli essenziali delle prestazioni pubbliche nei sessant'anni della corte costituzionale' (2016) *Rivista AIC* 4. On the role of national constitutional courts in the context of the new economic governance, Marco Dani, 'National Constitutional Courts in Supranational Litigation: A Contextual Analysis' (2017) *European Law Journal* 207.
129 Joined Cases C-8/15 P and C-10/15 P, *Ledra and Others*, EU:C:2016:701, and Case C-258/14, *Eugenia Florescu and Others*, EU:C:2017:448.
130 Communication from the European Commission, 'Establishing a European Pillar of Social Rights', COM(2017)250, and European Commission, 'Recommendation of 26 April 2017 on the European Pillar of Social Rights', C(2017)2600.
131 European Commission, 'Commission Recommendation of 26 April 2017 on the European Pillar of Social Rights' (n 130), Recital 14.
132 Ibid., Recitals 3–5.
133 Johnaton Zeitlin and Bart Vanhercke, 'Socializing the European Semester: EU Social and Economic Policy Co-Ordination in Crisis and Beyond' (2018) *Journal of European Public Policy* 157.

134 Saitto, '"Risocializzare l'Europa"' (n 124), at 114–119.

135 Stefano Giubboni, 'Appunti e disappunti sul pilastro europeo dei diritti sociali' (2017) *Quaderni costituzionali* 960.

136 Soft law allows generous promises. For instance, the recommendation enshrines for young people 'the right to continued education, apprenticeship, traineeship or a job offer of good standing within 4 months of becoming unemployed or leaving education' (4b), for workers a 'right to fair wages that provide for a decent standard of living' (6a) and for everyone lacking sufficient resources a 'right to adequate minimum income benefits ensuring a life in dignity at all stages of life, and effective access to enabling goods and services' (14).

137 Giubboni, 'Appunti e disappunti sul pilastro europeo dei diritti sociali' (n 135), at 956.

138 Particular emphasis is put on active labour market policies (4–5), expanding childcare provision (11), lifelong learning (1).

139 The right to unemployment benefits (13), minimum income (14), housing and assistance for the homeless (19) and access to essential services (20).

140 Saitto, '"Risocializzare l'Europa"' (n 124), at 89.

141 It is noteworthy that the relationship between social rights and other economic indicators as well as their role in the procedure remains in the document undefined.

142 The EPSR includes a scoreboard to 'track trends and performances across countries and to inform policy guidance in the context of the European Semester of economic policy coordination'. Tellingly, 'For the EU as a Whole, the Scoreboard Will Also Serve to Assess Progress towards Its "Social Triple A"' (n 130), at 3.

143 'Delivering on These Principles and Rights Is a Joint Responsibility' (Ibid), at 2.

144 De Witte, 'The Architecture of a Social Market Economy' (n 48), at 13–17.

145 Ulrich Haltern, 'On Finality' in von Bogdandy and Bast, *Principles of European Constitutional Law* (n 59), at 741.

3 Social rights, social market economy and the European social model

Tracing conceptual boundaries

Stefano Civitarese Matteucci

1 Introductory remarks

The aim of this chapter is to address the question of what concept of social rights, if any, suits the idea of 'social market economy' best and particularly whether the (alleged) 'constitutional' entrenchment of such rights is consequent on (or even compatible with) the tenets of this idea. To do this, one should understand first what is meant by 'social market economy', given that it is an expression mainly employed to describe a set of economic theories and ideas which allegedly shaped post-WWII Germany politics, and was then made into a legal concept once it was inserted into the TEU after the Lisbon Treaties. In Article 3(3) TEU, the term 'social market economy' has replaced that of a mere 'market economy' as an objective to pursue. However, besides being 'social', the market economy must also be 'highly competitive'. Hence, there seems to be a specific conception of 'social market economy' that is being embraced by the European Union (EU) and which shapes its economic and social constitution on the face of which one should set out any feasible concept of social rights.

At first glance, the novelty of the qualification of the market as 'social' may lead one to think of a counterbalance to the neoliberal emphasis on the free market and unfettered competition, in order to underpin principles of social justice and foster redistributive policies. Yet, if we consider the actual impact of other policies on the 'social question' and the type of response the EU institutions have issued to the financial crisis – namely austerity measures and labour market reforms across the Member States as a condition for financial assistance[1] – we are tempted to wonder whether the internal market project, with its strong reliance on a complex system of competition law, does not stand in sharp contrast to such an interpretation and instead suggests an understanding of 'social market economy' in line with its historical roots. In fact, the ideal of 'social market economy' is intertwined with ordoliberalism, although it is not entirely coincident with it. Therefore, there is scope to speculate that a highly competitive 'social market economy' is at odds with redistributive justice as well as a conception of the welfare state which hinges upon the commitment to social rights and social services.

The welfare state is in turn a highly disputed notion. The conception we have referred to is widely acknowledged by social policy research. Although it is neither exclusive nor exhaustive,[2] it encapsulates a normative stance inherent to the pioneering advocates of social citizenship in post-WWII Great Britain.[3] A definition which conveys this stance has been given by Girvetz:

> The welfare state is the institutional outcome of the assumption by a society of legal and therefore formal and explicit responsibility for the basic well-being of all of its members. Such a state emerges when a society or its decision-making groups become convinced that the welfare of the individual [. . .] is too important to be left to custom or to informal arrangements and private understandings and is therefore a concern of government.[4]

The assumption then is that, by taking the reference to 'social market economy' seriously, we mean something different from this 'archetypical' welfare state and even more so if we try to figure out the contours of a 'highly competitive' one. Therefore, whilst there are approaches which set the interpretation of Article 3(3) in a wider context of social engagement by EU legal sources and institutional practice,[5] we will try, in the interest of the central research question, to treat, as much as is practicable, the wording of Article 3(3) as a genuine reference to the original notion.

The European social model, which is sometimes considered to be tantamount to a 'social market economy', is itself quite a fluid notion, characteristically forged as a thick or umbrella concept, whereby one can adapt a variety of policies.[6] As has been ironically observed, 'the European social model is not wholly European, not wholly social and not a model'.[7] It is apparent, then, that we must extricate ourselves from three vague overlapping notions such as the European social model, the 'social market economy', and the welfare state.

In light of the foregoing,[8] the next section examines the historical development of 'social market economy' as a highly disputed concept, to determine how it can be legally understood and articulated in the context of EU law and practice. The ensuing discussion in section 3 will argue that the concept of the 'social market economy' can be more easily reconciled with so-called activation policies and social investment than with universalistic rights-based approaches. In this vein, it will become clear that it remains wise to continue to draw a distinction between a welfare state regime and a 'social market economy'. This raises the question of whether a welfare state regime can be reconciled with the idea of a 'highly competitive social market economy'. In section 4, the notion of 'social market economy' will be assessed against the EU social acquis to show that it is somewhat inappropriate to rely on the former to expand upon the latter. In the final section, firstly we restate the main findings of the contribution, which boil down to the suggestion that interpreting Article 3(3) TEU as a commitment to rebalance the EU's current trajectory towards a more 'social Europe' is ineffective. Secondly, a hint to the debate on how to account for a normative stance towards a European Social Union is made.

2 The social market economy between German scholarship and the Constitutional Treaty for Europe draft

It is hardly disputed that, despite the foresaid presence of numerous provisions on social policy in the EU Treaties and elsewhere, the actual trajectory of the EU is one which can be regarded as welfare rights-driven.[9] We can flesh out this assumption by looking at the constitutional locus of the 'market' and the 'social' within the EU. Even though, as Garben has held, there are arguments that EU social law may enjoy a good deal of input, output and 'throughput' legitimacy,[10] this is based on the acknowledgement that 'the objectives for which the Social Title permits the adoption of EU legislation are generally not of a redistributive nature and thereby deny the EU the power to take the most consequential decisions on "the social" and "the market" from the outset'.[11]

Joerges and Rödl have contextualised this separation in a deeper, more constitutional sense, by holding that the original choice made in the Treaty of Rome to sever the economic from the political sphere, as well as pushing the 'social' into the latter, was a conscious decision made in order to shape the 'economic constitution' according to ordoliberal ideals. For such ideals 'discretionary' politics must be kept at safe distance from the functioning of the market as well as the enjoyment of economic freedoms.[12] The provocative reading which Joerges and Rödl offer of the *Maatricht Urteil* of the German Federal Constitutional Court of 1993 reveals how the acceptance of the Treaty on the European Union by the strongest competitor of the CJEU ends up sealing the 'political decoupling of economic integration and social-protection issues'.[13] In fact, the German Constitutional Court's strenuous defence of national sovereignty by wielding the counter-limit bar over the democratic argument leads paradoxically to the full legitimation of the ordoliberal constitutional order of the European Monetary Union. Price stability and economic integration are treated as politically detached matters thereby legitimately left to the supranational level of competence.[14]

This constitutional arrangement is key to understanding the particular shift which led to the introduction of the concept of the 'social market economy' within the Treaties as part of the deliberative process for the now abandoned, Constitutional Treaty. An important point that must be made at this juncture is that despite ordoliberalism being German in origin, this division between the realm of law and economics and the realm of politics was never within the German constitutional and political mode. On the contrary, the incursion of politics in the supposedly non-political domain of economic regulation was pragmatically professed and practised.[15]

It is often said in the literature that 'social market economy' is a very ephemeral notion.[16] Sometimes the expression is even used to refer to the experience of Germany as a whole, irrespective of the values that the concept of the 'social market economy' is supposedly imbued with.[17]

This open-textured nature was possibly the key of the broad favour it encountered at the time of its introduction in the social and political arenas of post-war

Germany. As observed by Watrin, the scholars whose theories are at the root of 'social market economy' all belonged to the German (neo)liberal movement during the 1940s and 1950s and, while they agreed that personal liberty is a value in itself, they argued that a free society cannot be justified solely on the basis of economic efficiency arguments.[18] Ordoliberals, such as Eucken and Bohm, thought that competition must be actively defended in a modern liberal state through appropriate legislation, because it was not sufficient for maintaining a free market to guarantee property rights and enforce private contracts. Müller-Armack, who, as mentioned by others in this volume,[19] coined the term 'social market economy', held that although social policy may be necessary to make the market economy work, it can never be such as that competition is threatened.[20]

While the 'social market economy' may more closely resemble a blend of socio-political ideas rather than a fully developed theory in its own right, it nonetheless exerted a powerful influence on both political and public discourse. By adopting the "social market economy" as a form of catchphrase, the Christian Democrats won the first elections in 1949. Ludwig Erhard, minister for economic affairs from 1949 to 1963 and the 'father of the economic miracle' in post-war Germany, viewed the 'social market economy' as a sort of 'capitalism of the people', which would use increases in wages, consumption and property for all social classes rather than welfare benefits provided by the state as its main ingredients.[21] The means through which this would be achieved was to be anti-inflation, monetary and pro-competition policies. As Leisering has stressed 'it was not a variety of, but an antidote to the welfare state. In reality, Erhard viewed the 'welfare state' negatively, and considered it to be a 'modern paranoia'.[22]

If the vagueness of the notion was key to its success, it also appears to be – once taken out of the historical and economic context of post-war Germany – its primary shortcoming. The 'social market economy' has been often used as a proxy for the quest for an alternative socio-economic order between the extremes of *laissez-faire* liberalism and centrally planned economic model. The broad nature of this reconceptualisation of the term makes one doubt that it is even capable of being translated into a workable legal principle. The same can arguably be said of the debate surrounding the inclusion of the term 'social market economy' in the Lisbon Treaty. This story is worthy of a discussion, being mindful, though, of the many pitfalls that an originalist interpretation of constitutional texts entails[23] as well as the actual attitude of the CJEU as regards legal reasoning and interpretation.[24]

A proposal was made by Working Group XI-'Social Europe', an offshoot of the Economic Governance Working Group within the European Convention for the Future of Europe, to insert the 'social market economy' as an EU objective. Section II of the Final Report issued on 4 February 2003 addresses the question of what objectives should be included in Article 3 of the preliminary draft Constitutional Treaty in order to define the Union's general objectives.[25] Para 14, after recalling that the Lisbon Strategy is based on the balance between economic, employment and social policies, as well as environmental policy, puts forward that, according to several Member States, this balance should be enshrined in the future Constitutional Treaty by providing that alongside economic growth and prosperity, sustainable development, the promotion of full employment and a high degree of social protection should be listed and taken into account in Union decision-making. While there was 'very broad support' for the introduction of full employment as a goal, it was disputed how the social protection clause should be phrased. The proposal to include the 'European Social Model' among the objectives was apparently rejected because it would have yielded uncertainty. In para 17 this objection is apparently overcome by noting that the European social model 'allows for a diversity of approaches in order to promote shared European values and that this diversity should be treated as an asset and a source of strength'. However, it is stated two lines below this that 'several members considered that the objectives should refer to the Union as a "social market economy", to underline the link between economic and social development and the efforts made to ensure greater coherence between economic and social policies'. Thus, even in attempting to apply a charitable interpretation in this instance – which adds to the bold interpretive decision to treat this document as a source for a subjective originalist interpretation of the 'will be' Article 3(3) of the TEU – it is difficult to discern what the intention of working group was in using a term like 'social market economy' rather than the aforementioned European social model.[26] One wonders, for example, whether in this phrasing it is used as a refinement of the European social model to better express the connection between the 'economic' and the 'social', or as a completely different concept which allegedly avoids the porous nature of the first expression. In either case, one is left clueless about how the balance between economic and social policies should be struck, not least because social market economy is arguably even vaguer than the concept of the European social model. If, however, we rely on the largely accepted tenets of social market economy, it is difficult to suggest that market freedoms will not be granted priority.[27] The many inconsistencies and drawbacks that the idea of incorporating this 'economic style' into the Treaty as an objective to pursue have been thoroughly analysed by Joerges and Rödl, who present three sets of arguments.

Firstly, that 'social market economy' – which was probably auspiciously associated by the EU Treaty constitution drafters with the German economic revival of the 1950s and 1960s – was unlikely to be the sole driving 'force' of the 'German miracle'. Much of it depended on the corporatist structures that played a prominent role in shaping German post-war development[28] and, in fact, social policy research was undertaken to retroactively forge a specific corporatist welfare regime. From a legal viewpoint, the enshrinement in the German Constitution of the 'principle of the social state', despite the initial self-restraint of the Constitutional Federal Court to interpret it as a social right-generating clause,[29] represented another important counterbalance to ordoliberal ideals. Secondly, the 'social market economy' was never established as a specific 'objective', even by its advocates in Germany. It was a means unto an end, rather than an end in and of itself. Thirdly, that, even conceiving the 'social market economy' as a social protection objective – in conflict with its aspiration to restrict social objectives – it would be unattainable within the actual constitutional structure of the EU.[30]

Even an interpretation that could potentially unite the disparate references to the European Social Model and 'social market economy' in the XI Working Group's final report could lead to an outcome which undermines the commitment to social welfare and rights. Indeed, the Green Paper and the White Paper on social policy of 1993 and 1994[31] were said to 'represent a significant new stage in EU social policy making',[32] as it is there that 'Social Europe' became a more flexible 'European social model' rooted in shared liberal-democratic values. The new principles which were set up were 'convergence which respects diversity' – that suits well a market (negative) integration through law – and 'the establishment of a framework of basic minimum standards'.[33] This sounds as quite another music vis-à-vis the project of building a 'social Europe' through harmonisation policy put forward during the 1980s particularly by Jaques Delors and culminated in the adoption of the Social Charter in 1989.[34] The tone of the White Paper 'is almost a plea for recognition of the role of social policy in economic integration. This reflects an anxiety that social policy is in fact playing "second string" to the development of the internal market and EMU'.[35]

On the face of it, one can observe that since the introduction of the 'social market economy' as a Union objective, the attitude towards social policy has potentially worsened. This may have nothing to do with the introduction of the expression at stake, for in any legal order we find a number of unimplemented constitutional mandates, and one may want to embrace the thesis that the financial crisis was a sort of 'state of exception'. Nonetheless, it underscores the limited potential of the 'social market economy' clause in restraining unfettered market competition. In other words, the question is whether the adding of 'social' to the objective of working for a competitive market economy changes the course of the EU trajectory, or simply makes explicit something which was already in place.

3 Social market economy, activation policies and rights-based approaches

Even if it is possible to suggest that the proposal to introduce the Union level objective of creating a 'social market economy' was inspired by the desire to rebalance the almost exclusive orientation of the EU away from the free market and towards core principles of the welfare state core,[36] its eventual introduction was not in and of itself sufficient to give it legal substance. In our opinion, either the reference to 'social market economy' is largely symbolic[37] or, if we take heed of the intimation to a 'highly competitive' social market economy, it represents a constitutional shift away from a social Europe to the sort of European social model envisaged in the previously mentioned commission white paper of 1993 'European Social Policy: A Way Forward for the Union'. Giorgio Monti, a former commissioner for competition, argued that the term 'social market economy' 'calls for a maximum of free market, for reliance on competition wherever possible'.[38]

Arguably, the concept which best encapsulates the kinds of socio-economic measures congenial to a 'social market economy' is post-welfare 'social investment', with its emphasis on activation vis-à-vis the delivery of passive universal benefits. Key to this approach are policies that foster the development of human capital and its 'efficient use', such as early childhood education, lifelong training, active labour market services, etc.[39] Notably, the social investment approach has buttressed the Lisbon Agenda, which the EU adopted in 2000 with the aim of making Europe 'the most dynamic and competitive knowledge-based economy in the world'.[40] Strictly linked to this, in the EU Commission's view, is the modernisation of social policies to give activation measures a more prominent role. To do this 'support schemes should provide an exit-strategy, so they should in principle be temporary. Conditionality to achieving an appropriate and specific goal (e.g. participation in training) is part of this'.[41] Conditionality, in fact, is what primarily underpins social investment and activation policies and refers to arrangements that require people to behave in particular ways in order to access and maintain cash benefits or other welfare supports and services.

To what extent conditionality is reconcilable with a rights-based perspective is a contentious point. Making the enjoyment of welfare services conditional seems to imply that the access to such goods is used as a tool to pursue various political goals, rather than being conferred as a right. In other words, the question is whether such an instrumental view is compatible with a concept of rights *qua* entitlement. Leaving aside the moral aspect of this question,[42] we can observe that some kind of conditionality is pragmatically inherent to any right and, especially, social right. The individual right to social benefits has always been in some way conditional, and conditionality can therefore be viewed as cornerstone and basis for risk management in welfare states.[43] Norms that confer rights describe facts which entitle someone to claim something from someone else. In this sense, for example, even universal healthcare is only available on condition of being sick. The point, then, is not conditionality *per se* but what kinds of conditions are attached to the enjoyment of a given benefit. Clasen and Clegg have classified such conditions in three groups: conditions of category, conditions of circumstance, and conditions of conduct. Despite the fact that also category (e.g. old age for pension) and circumstance (e.g. disability) are subject to legal qualification to discriminate between who is 'in' and who is 'out', they are more easily associated with universal welfare rights. This is so also when the 'in-out' condition is not straightforward (as it is in case of bright line rules) but is dependent on means-tested discretionary decision-making.[44] Indeed, even if we consider constitutional (programmatic) rights – which by nature are vague – we can still conceive them as justiciable 'legal rights' as long as we adopt a rights interest-based theory in which the bearer of the correspondent duty is the state.[45]

The conditionality of conduct is the lever that is meant to change the traditional features of welfare state by providing for active behaviour to be or remaining an eligible welfare recipient. It is when the balance between category, circumstance and conduct – which may be seen as forming a spectrum – considerably swerves towards 'conduct' that a concept of social rights as entitlement-claim is put under much stress. We cannot know, in abstract terms, what is the level of 'conduct conditionality' that would be compatible with such a serious constitutional-like entrenchment of social rights as to encompass a social welfare regime.[46] Empirically one can assess what is, say, a situation in which social minimum[47] is not guaranteed under a certain constitutional arrangement. This chapter argues, though, that making social rights conditional to the functioning of a highly competitive market is what suits a 'social market economy' best. This is in fact the actual model of EU socio-economic constitutional arrangement, which does not amount to a welfare state regime objective.[48] As we will see in the next section, the institutional practice reflects such an arrangement.

4 Unravelling the EU social acquis

One might contend – relying on abundant literature – that the social objectives of the EU are placed at the forefront in the Treaties.[49] The preamble of the TEU refers to the reverence of the signing parties to 'fundamental social rights as defined in the European Social Charter signed at Turin on 18 October 1961 and in the 1989 Community Charter of the Fundamental Social Rights of Workers'. Article 3 TEU, after having depicted the EU as a 'social market economy' aiming at full employment and social progress, expresses its commitment to fight 'social exclusion and discrimination' and to promote 'justice and social protection'. The TFEU preamble, in turn, promises to guarantee 'the social progress of their States through a common action to eliminate the barriers dividing Europe'. Especially the 'social' horizontal clause of Article 9 TFEU can be linked to such objectives, as it commits the EU to promote a high level of employment, the guarantee of adequate social protection, and the fight against social exclusion in all its policies. Nonetheless, when dealing with the EMU and macroeconomic and budgetary surveillance, this mainstreaming obligation has never been considered.

The EU Charter of Fundamental Rights (EU CFER) in turn recognises an array of social rights, particularly in Chapter IV which is entitled 'Solidarity'. Most of these rights require positive action to fulfil their attainment and therefore they should be seen as mandates for the European legislator to act accordingly. Title X of the TFEU, entitled 'Social Policy' (particularly Articles 153 and 156), which could have contained this kind of mandate as well as a series of directly enforceable rights, has not been amended by the Treaty of Lisbon, and therefore the EU can do no more than 'supporting and integrating' the Member States' lawmaking in such areas as labour law and social security.

These provisions of EU primary law set up important goals for the Union to pursue. However, they do not establish directly enforceable social rights or any obligation for the Member States to implement a harmonised European welfare regime. The same can be said with regard to the recently adopted European Pillar of Social Rights (EPSR), an instrument which identifies important goals in an attempt to fill the EU gap on social rights protection, but whose legal status is all the more dubious. As already critically noted by Dani, it belongs to the domain of soft law[50] and consequently, as well as being a mere instrument of moral persuasion towards the Member States, it could at best be used by the CJEU as an additional tool to interpret those provisions of the Charter which are echoed by the Pillar. Moreover, even though it is taken for granted that social rights figure among the (unwritten) fundamental rights recognised by the CJEU as part of the general principles of EU law, their use has been nearly negligible.[51]

There are two different points of view – respectively, one descriptive and the other normative – for dealing with the social acquis in relation to the 'social market economy' objective.

Firstly, the social acquis objection can be judged as not pertinent to the case. Indeed, all of the so-called social acquis could be meant as a means of expressing the tension between the tentative social orientation scattered within primary EU law and the highly competitive social market economy objective. Tensions and compromises are typical of any constitutional-like document. In fact, all of the sources which amount to the social acquis can be interpreted in the light of SME as driven by market dependent non-redistributive principles.

Secondly, from a normative point of view, it could be claimed that the 'social market economy' objective must be interpreted in the light of the social acquis. As mentioned in section 1, this is the approach which is sometimes implicit within one strand of the literature. Yet, this boils down to a paradox, because from this approach the 'social market economy' objective ends up being unfeasible and largely irrelevant. This relates somewhat to the work conducted by Scharpf on the asymmetry of European integration,[52] which posits that the process of European integration, driven by judge-made law, has notably curtailed the political leeway of the Member States in favour of European competences. This vertical 'integration through law' negatively impacts on the socio-economic regimes of EU Member States. In particular, Continental and Nordic 'social market economies' would be affected by the constraints of market imperatives, epitomised by the '*Dasonville*'[53] doctrine and its successive refinements. This partly involves a set of citizenship's rights, built around freedom of movement and non-discrimination on grounds of nationality which may involve access to welfare benefits. However, in the CJEU's view:

> European citizenship . . . is not about collective self-determination. It is about individual rights of exit from, and entry into, democratically shaped and collectively financed systems of national solidarity. For the new social liberties as for economic liberties, therefore, integration through law maximizes negative integration at the expense of democratic self-determination in the national polity.[54]

This structural asymmetry cannot be rebalanced by political action at the European level and this is why the EU cannot be, according to Scharpf, a 'social market economy'. Here 'social market economy' stands for Continental and Nordic welfare regimes as opposed to liberal regimes.[55] This claim, then, could be reversed by arguing that, given the asymmetry of European integration, a highly competitive social market economy as opposed to a welfare state regime is the maximum one can aspire to within the actual EU economic constitution.

This issue risks becoming purely nominalistic, but the meaning of 'social market economy', in light of what we have discussed in the previous section, and entailed by the foregoing first descriptive approach, suits the EU constitutional orientation better. More importantly, what we have just observed as regards integration through law put forward by the CJEU invites us to be wary of those positions that rely on the Court to swim against the tide of the highly competitive economy. It is indeed both simplistic and inappropriate to call upon the CJEU for a reinterpretation of 'social market economy' as a catalyst for social citizenship. Recent analyses confirm that not even the conferment to the Charter of the status of primary law has significantly enhanced the rank of social rights within the CJEU jurisprudence.[56]

Case law of the CJEU in litigation not directly relating to welfare entitlements upholds this conclusion. A good viewpoint is constituted by cases concerning the relationship between freedom to provide services and non-economic services of general interest as well as agreements concluded between social partners in the context of their collective bargaining, which will be discussed later in this volume.[57] A scrupulous study of the relevant case law has convincingly demonstrated, on the one hand, that the Court's consolidated approach on issues of protection of competition in those fields – for example as regards the progressive erosion of the exemption provided by Protocol 26 of the Treaty for non-economic services of general interest[58] – has not changed after the inception of 'social market economy' objective into the Treaty, which is by the way never used in its reasoning. And on the other hand, that this is the case because those rulings are somewhat consistent with this new EU goal.[59]

Finally, the only two cases in which we find the Court using the phrase at stake are worthy of a mention. One is *AGET Iraklis* already mentioned at the outset of this volume,[60] where the Grand Chamber in listing possible overriding reasons in the public interest transcribes the whole content of Article 3(3) TEU (para 76). In this instance, the decision is in favour of the freedom to conduct a business vis-à-vis workers' right to protection against unjustified dismissal pursuant to Article 30 of the Charter. To be fair, the latter is treated not as rights-claim, but just as hypothetical limitations for the proportionality test against the right enshrined in Article 16 of the Charter (para 89–91). In fact, the Court limits itself to disregarding a national authorisation regime based on the assessment of the 'interests of the national economy' as a valid limitation to the freedom of business rather than balancing the two rights – defined alternatively interests by the Court – against each other.

Corsica Ferries France SAS v Commission[61] is the only one in which 'social market economy' is taken on to directly uphold the Court's reasoning aimed at pinning down the notion of a 'reasonable private investor' to assess whether a private investor could have been prompted to make a certain capital contribution to a company undertaking public transport service. This was a way of determining whether a contribution made by the State should be deemed to be an unlawful State aid. Even though, in 'a social market economy', a reasonable private investor would not disregard either its responsibility towards all stakeholders in the company or the social, economic and environmental context in which it continues to develop, it is the Court's view that the assumption of the burden of additional costs because of such 'legitimate concerns cannot follow an exclusively social, even political, objective, as it would otherwise go beyond the framework of the private investor test'.[62]

To summarise, it cannot be entirely accidental that the decision by the CJEU to refer to the 'social market economy' objective in these rare cases has occurred in a context where business freedom and entrepreneurial behavioural precepts were at stakes, in order to strike a balance between the functioning of the market and general social policy concerns, which in both cases were ruled following an economic rationale.

5 Concluding remarks: beyond the social market economy

The discussion thus far leads us to the conclusion that interpreting Article 3(3) TEU as creating a kind of imperative which necessitates that the Union rebalance itself in favour of a more 'social Europe' may be misleading.[63] However, this can still be done out of a deliberate normative choice to charitably interpret the reference to a 'social market economy' as generically encompassing all the provisions in the Treaties which mention social issues. As it stands, neither the CJEU nor the other EU institutions have been ready to use it as a 'social state' clause or to articulate through it a commitment to meaningful social rights.

Given that the concept of the 'social market economy' is centred on the correction of pure market competition, it is not a principle on which one can coherently build a 'European Social Union'. The extent and scope of what can be 'extracted' from it is confined to coordination of social security rights for mobile workers and standards for health and safety in the workplace, which are rooted in the principle of non-discrimination. As discussed in section 3, the dimension of 'conditionality of conduct' regarding social rights best suits its tenets. If one wants to advocate for a shift towards a European social union, in which social policy has equal pedigree as competitive economy, other principles should be taken on board. The actual living notion of a 'social market economy' in the EU is disengaged with any specific concept of social rights according to European constitutional traditions, and its overarching ideology is instead closer to other notions underpinning recent social policy projects such as social investment and activation.

In order to go beyond the present crisis of the social Europe – exacerbated by the financial crisis and the ensuing austerity era, which laid bare the interdependency between creditor and debtor states as well as deep social inequalities between them – both a theory of justice for the EU[64] and a multi-layered approach to welfare policies[65] are necessary.

Since any concept of social (constitutional) rights entails the recognition of entitlements that a person can claim against the State, the bone of contention is against whom precisely a person can claim such entitlements within the complex arrangement of the European integrated polity/order. In other words, who is the bearer of the corresponding duty to a social minimum? The decoupling of economic integration and social protection leaves such rights in between, for the constraints on fiscal policy which come from the technical needs of the internal market functioning make the political leeway supposedly reserved to the Member States empty. At the same time, the very idea of social rights is intertwined with the notion of the welfare state: the bearer of the obligation, however the latter is variously qualified, has to be the political entity in charge of deciding and delivering any in-kind or in-cash benefit. Hence, any transnational social duties are to be understood as complementary to the national arrangements in place, which retain much of their autonomy and diversity. As Crum affirms:

> [t]he EU level thus emerges as an additional layer that, on the one hand, helps to protect and stabilize the national welfare states and, on the other hand, redresses for arbitrary inequalities as they operate in transnational interactions and provides some inroads into the transnational sharing of the common wealth in Europe. The transnational duties that European integration generates can be understood to operate on two levels. In the first instance they speak to states, the relations they maintain with each other in the framework of the EU, and the duties they owe to each other's citizens. But more than merely governing interstate relations through the states, these duties also have direct implications for the individual citizens of these states.[66]

Thus, the normative stance on which to build a European social union is one of coordination, as opposed to a harmonisation of the diverse European welfare state regimes under the Union's guidance. An advancement towards an articulation and guarantee of constitutional social rights at the EU level neither can leave the common market objective untouched, nor can it be achieved under the ideal of a 'social market economy'. Such an arrangement, which would entail a boost in the CJEU's powers relating to social rights issues, leaves the decision-making on social policy with the Member States but within a European constitutional social clause.

Notes

1 Stefano Civitarese Matteucci and Simon Halliday (eds.), *Social Rights in Europe in an Age of Austerity* (Routledge, 2017).
2 David Garland, *The Welfare State: A Very Short Introduction* (OUP, 2016) 31–43, who identifies two other approaches, welfare as assistance to the poor and welfare as the government of the economy towards social goals.
3 Thomas Marshall, *Citizenship and Social Class* (CUP, 1950).
4 Harry Girvetz, 'Welfare State' in David Sills (ed.), *International Encyclopedia of the Social Sciences* (Palgrave Macmillan, 1968) 512.
5 Fritz Scharpf, 'The Asymmetry of European Integration, or Why the EU Cannot Be a "Social Market Economy"' (2010) *Socio-Economic Review* 211; Simon Deakin, 'The Lisbon Treaty, the Viking and Laval Judgments and the Financial Crisis: In Search of New Foundations for Europe's "Social Market Economy"' in Niklas Bruun, Klaus Lorcher, and Isabelle Schomann (eds.), *The Lisbon Treaty and Social Europe* (Hart, 2012) 20; Loïc Azoulai, 'The Court of Justice and the

Social Market Economy: The Emergence of an Ideal and the Conditions for its Realization' (2008) *Common Market Law Review* 1335.

6 Maria Jepsen and Amparo Serrano Pascual, *Unwrapping the European Social Model* (Policy Press, 2006).

7 Anthony Giddens, *Turbulent and Mighty Continent: What Future for Europe?* (Polity Press, 2014) 88.

8 Delia Ferri and Fulvio Cortese, 'Introduction', in this volume.

9 Alexander Kornezov, 'Social Rights, the Charter, and the ECHR: Caveats, Austerity, and Other Disasters' in Frank Vandenbroucke, Catherine Barnard and Geert De Baere (eds.), *A European Social Union after the Crisis* (CUP, 2017) 407.

10 Sacha Garben, 'The Constitutional (im)Balance between "the Market" and "the Social" in the European Union' (2017) *European Constitutional Law Review* 23, who uses the legitimacy vocabulary developed by Vivien Schmidt, 'Democracy and Legitimacy in the European Union Revisited: Input, Output and "Throughput"' (2013) *Political Studies* 2.

11 Ibid., at 25.

12 Christian Joerges and Florian Rödl, 'Social Market Economy as Europe's Social Model?' in Lars Magnusson and Bo Stråth (eds.), *A European Social Citizenship? Preconditions for Future Policies from a Historical Perspective* (Peter Lang, 2004) 130.

13 Fritz Scharpf, 'The European Social Model: Coping with the Challenges of Diversity' (2002) *Journal of Common Market Studies* 646.

14 Joerges and Rödl, 'Social Market Economy as Europe's Social Model?' (n 12), at 133.

15 Ibid.

16 Alexander Lorch, 'Advancing the Notion of a Social Market Economy' in Christian Glossner and David Gregosz (eds.), *Sixty Years of Social Market Economy: Formation, Development and Perspectives of a Peacemaking Formula* (Konrad-Adenauer-Stiftung, 2010) 69.

17 Sorin Mureşan, *Social Market Economy: The Case of Germany* (Springer, 2014), where the roots of RSU are found in the larger philosophical and historical tradition than German neo-liberalism.

18 Christian Watrin, 'The Social Market Economy: The Main Ideas and Their Influence on Economic Policy' in Peter Koslowski (ed.), *The Social Market Economy: Theory and Ethics of the Economic Order* (Springer, 1998) 17.

19 Ferri and Cortese, 'Introduction' (n 8).

20 Joerges and Rödl, 'Social Market Economy as Europe's Social Model?' (n 12), at 145.

21 Lutz Leisering, 'Germany: A Centrist Welfare State at the Crossroads' in Pete Alcock and Gary Craig (eds.), *International Social Policy: Welfare Regimes in the Developed World* (Palgrave Macmillan, 2009) 154.

22 Ibid.

23 Andrei Marmor, *Interpretation and Legal Theory* (Hart, 2005) 141–170. Without committing ourselves to any theory regarding the constitutional substance of the European Treaties, it seems nonetheless plausible to analogise them to a constitutional document as they possess the following features pinned down by Marmor: supremacy, longevity, rigidity, moral content (human rights), and generality and abstraction.

24 Gerard Conway, *The Limits of Legal Reasoning and the European Court of Justice* (CUP, 2012) 52.

25 The European Convention, The Secretariat, *Final Report of Working Group XI on Social Europe* (2003) CONV 516/1/03.

26 The initiative of proposing this formula is attributed to the Foreign Ministers of Germany and France Joschka Fischer and Dominique Villepin (Christian Joerges, 'Sozialstaatlichkeit in Europe? A Conflict-of-Laws Approach to the Law of the

EU and the Proceduralisation of Constitutionalisation' (2009) *German Law Journal* 344).

27 It is fitting to note that at the time of the Convention, except for Germany, all the largest countries of the continental bloc were run by centre-right or liberalistic cabinets (France, Italy, Spain, the Netherlands, Belgium, Denmark, Austria). In the UK the 'New Labour' was in office, whose orientation towards marketization is well-known.

28 Alexander Ebner, 'The Intellectual Foundations of the Social Market Economy: Theory, Policy, and Implications for European Integration' (2006) *Journal of Economic Studies* 218.

29 Ulrike Lembke, 'Germany' in Civitarese Matteucci and Halliday, *Social Rights in Europe in an Age of Austerity* (n 1), at 54.

30 Joerges and Rödl, 'Social Market Economy as Europe's Social Model?' (n 12), at 150.

31 European Commission, *European Social Policy: Options for the Future, Green Paper* (1993); European Commission, 'European Social Policy: A Way Forward for the Union, White Paper', COM(1994)333.

32 Michael Newman, *Democracy, Sovereignty and the European Union* (Hurst & Co., 1996) 85.

33 European Commission, 'European Social Policy' (n 33).

34 Newman, *Democracy, Sovereignty and the European Union* (n 33), at 97.

35 Norman Ginsburg, 'Postmodernity and Social Europe' in John Carter (ed.), *Postmodernity and the Fragmentation of Welfare* (Routledge, 1998) 282.

36 As mentioned in section 1, some commentators use the expression as a synonym for welfare state.

37 Jean-Claude Piris, *The Constitution for Europe: A Legal Analysis* (CUP, 2006) 188, for the thesis that in the economic and social fields the Constitutional Treaty was neutral, it did not change the 'existing balance between "market-friendly" and "worker-friendly" provisions.'

38 Mario Monti, 'Competition in a Social Market Economy' (2001) 1 *Competition Policy Newsletter* 2.

39 Nathalie Morel, Bruno Palier and Joakim Palme, 'Beyond the Welfare State as We Knew It?' in Nathalie Morel, Bruno Palier and Joakim Palme (eds.), *Towards a Social Investment Welfare State? Ideas, Policies and Challenges* (Policy Press, 2012) 1–30.

40 Lisbon European Council 23 and 24 March 2000. Presidency Conclusions, para I, 5 <www.europarl.europa.eu/summits/lis1_en.htm>.

41 Communication from the European Commission, 'Towards Social Investment for Growth and Cohesion-Including Implementing the European Social Fund 2014–2020', COM(2013)83.

42 Stuart White, 'Should a Minimum Income Be Unconditional?' in Civitarese and Halliday (n 1), at 179.

43 Jochen Clasen and Daniel Clegg, 'Levels and Levers of Conditionality: Measuring Change within Welfare States' in Jochen Clasen and Nico Siegel (eds.), *Investigating Welfare State Change: The 'Dependent Variable Problem' in Comparative Analysis* (Edward Elgar, 2007) 171.

44 Which in a valuable strand of literature is held as either inescapable or even desirable to achieve social justice Richard Titmuss, 'Welfare "Rights", Law and Discretion' (1971) *The Political Quarterly* 113; Robert Goodin, 'Structures of Mutual Obligation' (2002) *Journal of Social Policy* 579.

45 Cécile Fabre, *Social Rights under the Constitution: Government and the Decent Life* (OUP, 2000) 152–182.

46 It is possible to describe social rights as relating to specific legal traditions which, in turn, are loosely linked to certain welfare regimes. Three models of

constitutional incorporation of social rights within Europe have been outlined. In the first there is little scope for judicial interference with the setting of priorities; the second is characterised by a sizeable recourse to provisions conferring social rights on individuals which are enforceable; the third blends liberal stances with a variable degree of commitment to the protection of social rights, whether as individual rights, as general goals of the State (e.g. the social state clause in Germany), or as policies. These three types of welfare labelled respectively as liberal, Southern and corporatist roughly correspond. See Stefano Civitarese Matteucci and Simon Halliday, 'Constitutional Law and Social Welfare after the Economic Crisis' in Francesco Merloni and Alessandra Pioggia (eds.), *European Democratic Institutions and Administrations. Cohesion and Innovation in Times of Economic Crisis* (Springer, 2018).

47 Jeff King, *Judging Social Rights* (CUP, 2012) 33–37.

48 The constitutionalisation of social rights does not guarantee generous welfare state, and a fully developed and universally inspired welfare state can thrive with no constitutional social rights. This is the case of the UK.

49 Bruun, Lorcher, Schomann, *The Lisbon Treaty and Social Europe* (n 5).

50 It has taken the form of a recommendation by the Commission pursuant to Article 292 TFEU, and afterwards of a 'inter-institutional proclamation' by the European Parliament, the Council and the European Commission issued on 17 November 2017, which as such lacks formal basis in primary law. The Commission points out that delivering on the rights and principles mentioned in the Pillar is joint responsibility where 'most of the tools required to . . . are in the hands of local, regional and national authorities, as well as the social partners, and civil society at large (Communication from the European Commission, 'Establishing a European Pillar of Social Rights', COM(2017)250).

51 Bruno De Witte, 'The Trajectory of Fundamental Social Rights in the European Union' in Gráinne De Búrca and Bruno De Witte (eds.), *Social Rights in Europe* (OUP, 2005) 162.

52 Scharpf, 'The Asymmetry of European Integration, or Why the EU Cannot Be a "Social Market Economy"' (n 5).

53 Case 8/74, *Dassonville*, EU:C:1974:82.

54 Scharpf, 'The Asymmetry of European Integration, or Why the EU Cannot Be a "Social Market Economy"' (n 5), at 223.

55 Gosta Esping-Andersen, *The Three Worlds of Welfare Capitalism* (PUP, 1990).

56 Kornezov, 'Social Rights, the Charter, and the ECHR: Caveats, Austerity, and Other Disasters' (n 8).

57 Juan Jorge Piernas Lopez, 'Services of General Economic Interest and Social Considerations', and Silvia Pellizzari, 'Social Services, Services Providers and Non-Economic Activities in the Realm of the EU Social Market Economy', in this volume.

58 Stefano Civitarese Matteucci, 'Servizi Sanitari, Mercato e "Modello Sociale Europeo"' (2009) *Mercato Concorrenza Regole* 192.

59 Václav Šmejkal, 'Competition Law and the Social Market Economy Goal of the EU', (2015) *International Comparative Jurisprudence* 33, at 35.

60 Case C-201/15, *AGET Iraklis*, EU:C:2016:972.

61 Case T-565/08, *Corsica Ferries France SAS v Commission*, ECLI:EU:T:2012:415.

62 Ibid. para 82. There is in another case revolving around State aid and environmental protection in which the 'social market economy' of Article 3(3) TEU is mentioned: Case T-57/11, *Castelnou Energía*, ECLI:EU:T:2014:1021.

63 Christian Joerges, 'Social Europe in an Ever More Diverse Union' in Frank Vandenbroucke, Catherine Barnard and Geert De Baere (eds.), *A European Social Union after the Crisis* (CUP, 2017) 103 admonishes that 'the "highly competitive social market economy" is an oxymoronic notion. . . . To be sure we are free – and

need to be free – to redefine and reconceptualise the social market economy. But we should then be aware of the continuities and discontinuities in our operations. We should also remain sensitive for the bases of popular appeal of this legacy'.

64 Frank Vandenbroucke, 'The Idea of a European Social Union: A Normative Introduction' in Vandenbroucke, Barnard and De Baere (eds.), *A European Social Union after the Crisis* (n 63), at 6.

65 Ben Crum, 'A Multi-Layered Social Europe? Three Emerging Transnational Social Duties in the EU' in Amandine Crespy and Georg Menz (eds.), *Social Policy and the Euro Crisis: Quo Vadis Social Europe?* (Palgrave Macmillan, 2015) 161–210.

66 Ibid., at 163.

4 EU citizenship and the social market economy

Shifting balances

Giacomo Delledonne

1 Introduction

The purpose of this chapter is to discuss whether and to what extent citizenship of the European Union (EU) has been affected by the commitment to a 'highly competitive social market economy', by now enshrined in Article 3 TEU. Is EU citizenship being constructed in a way which satisfactorily takes into account social concerns?

In many respects, EU citizenship – as well as its interplay with the 'social market economy' in the broadest sense – has been at the forefront of some of the crises which have plagued the EU in the last decade.[1] The debate triggered by the *Dano* and *Alimanovic* judgements of the Court of Justice of the European Union (CJEU) and the discussion about 'social tourism' in the EU – with the latter playing a relevant role in the run-up to the Brexit referendum[2] – are closely related to different understandings of what EU citizenship entails and, more particularly, of the combination of the right to move and reside freely and access to social assistance systems.

Developments in the case law of the CJEU over the last decade have pointed out to some inherent difficulties of the very concept of EU citizenship as it has been devised in EU primary and secondary law. Essentially, the somehow oscillating case law of the CJEU has shown the growing contradiction 'between market logic and the "social and democratic *Rechtsstaat*"'.[3] This chapter will discuss the relations between the social dimension of EU citizenship and supranational integration: in so doing, it will make some points on the relevance of social concerns to any notion of citizenship. Moreover, this analysis will inevitably lead to a consideration of the way in which EU law has shaped the balance between national concerns and supranational integration in this area of the composite legal system of the EU. After the decline of so-called embedded liberalism, attempts have been made to strengthen the social component of EU citizenship and enrich it with a genuinely social dimension. Has such a shift been accomplished now? Is a reconciliation between citizenship and the 'social market economy' taking place at the supranational level?

The chapter is structured as follows: section 2 will look back to the decline of 'embedded liberalism' and its controversial relationship with supranational integration. Section 3 will consider whether and to what extent primary law provisions regarding EU citizenship reflect social concerns. After that, the implementation of the primary law provisions and the relevant case law of the CJEU prior to the economic and financial crisis will be considered. Section 4 will focus on more recent judgements of the CJEU and political attempts at redefining the balance between transnational solidarity and national concerns in a period of ongoing crisis. Finally, section 5 will summarize the results of the analysis and make explicit the answers to the research question.

The methodological perspective of this chapter is one of EU constitutional law, with a focus on the composite European constitution, and meaning that supranational and national constitutional materials will be considered jointly.[4] As will be discussed later, concepts whose meaning has been defined in the national legal and political environment are now playing a crucial role for assessing the ambitions and achievements of an autonomous supranational citizenship. Furthermore, the chapter combines a theoretical approach – revolving around the meaning of social citizenship – with a critical discussion of the relevant legislation and case law of the CJEU. Indeed, the interaction between judicial and political actors offers a number of tools which can be used in deciphering the tortious evolution of this area of EU constitutional law.

2 Early assumptions: social citizenship and the decline of embedded liberalism

The first part of the story is quite well-known: there is consensus on its factual background, although interpretations of cause-effect links may diverge. Since the early 1980s, the progress of supranational integration has contributed to the weakening of the normative and factual premises of social citizenship(s) in the Member States.[5] More precisely, it marked the decline of the paradigm of embedded liberalism (or 'Smith abroad, Keynes at home'), a *de facto* division of labour between the supranational and national institutional layers which relativized the alleged social frigidity of the Treaties.[6] This embedded liberalism made it possible for economic integration to avoid undermining 'the preconditions of social cohesion and stability at the national level',[7] thereby meaning, among other things, long-standing assumptions concerning social security and healthcare systems. This is of the greatest relevance for the topic of this chapter. In the first post-war years, T. H. Marshall coined the label 'social citizenship' in order to define the most recent stage in the evolution of this notion.[8] As Brubaker observed in his seminal study, there is a very tight link between the *institution of citizenship* and contemporary welfare states, of which the post-war European systems were prime examples:

> The modern territorial welfare state, to be sure, has a vital interest in the legal, political and administrative capacity to control access to its territory, labour market, and welfare system, and the control of access pivots on the institution of citizenship.[9]

On the other hand, the social dimension which was injected into the concept of citizenship played a pivotal role in redefining the conditions of legitimacy of nation states in the post-war order.[10] In the very peculiar legal landscape of the European Communities, this made (and possibly still makes) it plausible to locate the legitimating basis of the integration process in the constitutional charters of the Member States, which generally correspond, more or less closely, to the normative ideal of the social and democratic *Rechtsstaat*.[11] On a different note, nation States' control over access to social security systems perfectly illustrates the inherent paradox of citizenship: for all its universalist character, the organizational form in which equal citizenship could historically develop has been a more limited one, i.e. the nation state.[12]

As Scharpf put it, the peculiar division of labour which characterized embedded liberalism did not apply to all the Member States of the former Communities, but only to those of them which can – or could – be described as social market economies, i.e. a 'continental core' of Member States in Western Europe, combining 'a coordinated market economy with either a Continental or Scandinavian type of welfare state'.[13] On the other hand, the United Kingdom, Ireland and possibly the Netherlands can more properly be described as *liberal market economies*.

Such a state of affairs has been questioned more and more overtly because of concurring pressures related to the case law of the CJEU, with the rise of positive integration, and the liberalization of capital markets – as well as, more recently, enlargement to the East; other factors, e.g. a generalized push towards deregulation, are not specifically European but have also played a role. The result has been a decisive weakening of Member States' control over their own social security systems. Meanwhile, the extension of personal mobility rights has also created institutional conditions favouring a convergence of national welfare models 'towards the liberal minimum of social protection'.[14] However, different interpretive paradigms have objected that a decisive crisis of European national welfare systems had already started in the 1970s, independently of supranational integration.[15] All in all, it seems difficult to establish a clear link between cause and effect: still, some peculiar characters of the European integration process did affect the legal, political and social environment in which national welfare systems had developed and which had contributed to shaping social citizenship. Furthermore, current crises in a vast majority of the national political systems in Europe are directly related to this major challenge for nation states.[16]

3 The entrenchment of citizenship in EU primary law: is there room for social concerns?

The introduction of a citizenship of the EU has been routinely labelled – alongside the establishment of the Monetary Union and the launch of the Second and Third Pillars of the Union – as one of those Maastricht innovations which created a clear challenge for national constitutional orders.[17] In light of what has been discussed in section 2, the main research questions that this chapter attempts to answer can be rephrased as: how much does EU citizenship correspond with the normative ideal of social citizenship, which has played a major role in post-war European constitutionalism? Does EU citizenship, as it has been defined and regulated by EU law, contribute to enhancing the constitutional ambitions of the Union? Is the current legal framework of EU citizenship able to provide solutions for the crisis of social citizenship(s) at the national level?

In order to answer these questions, EU primary and secondary law and the case law of the CJEU should be considered simultaneously. In fact, as it has frequently happened throughout the constitutionalization of the Union, these legal formants have all contributed to enhancing the potential of EU citizenship. In this regard, formal constitutionalization – thereby meaning entrenchment in the form of primary law – has often acted as the final step, rather than the starting point, in an evolutionary process of change and adaptation. Constitutional theorists have made resort to the label 'achievement constitution' precisely in order to summarize those characters in the supranational process of constitutionalization.[18] These features are even more striking when it comes to EU citizenship, which has been said to 'bind together' a number of historically distinct regulatory layers, 'without reversing distinctive rules and rationales, which characterize different circumstances'.[19]

At first sight, the content of primary law provisions does not seem to be very promising when it comes to the social dimension of EU citizenship. By contrast, one might feel that the wording of the relevant provisions sounds somehow tautological ('the rights and . . . the duties provided for in the Treaties', as Art. 20(2) TFEU goes).[20] The drafters of the Lisbon Treaty tried to address some of the concerns related to the possible vagueness of those primary law provisions. For this reason, and as part of an effort to emphasize the social inspiration of the Treaties, the former Art. 18 TEC was amended by the Lisbon Treaty in order to overcome doubts about a lack of competence of the supranational institutions in this area and to bring 'social security and social protection matters within the scope of EU citizenship'.[21] In its current form, Art. 21(3) TFEU states:

> For the same purposes as those referred to in paragraph 1 and if the Treaties have not provided the necessary powers, the Council, acting in accordance with a special legislative procedure, may adopt measures concerning social security or social protection. The Council shall act unanimously after consulting the European Parliament.

On the other hand, it should be noted that the procedural requirement of unanimity reduces the innovative potential of that same provision, which, by the way, should be read together with the merely supporting competence of the Union in the domains of social security and social protection of workers (Art. 153 TFEU).

Of course, the social inspiration of EU primary law has been considerably strengthened by the recognition of the binding value of the Charter of Fundamental Rights, which includes a number of provisions protecting social rights. Still, the provisions of the Charter – most notably those in its Chapter IV – are of limited interest for this analysis, as they do not focus specifically on the rights related to EU citizenship. The broad formulation of Art. 34(2) testifies to this feeling, as it focuses primarily on those 'residing and moving legally within the European Union'. Furthermore, reference is made to 'Union law and national laws and practices', which are primarily responsible for defining the practical implications of the right to social security and social assistance under the Charter. In itself, '[a]s a free-standing provision, Article 34 offers little'.[22]

Consequently, much of the discussion about the social component of EU citizenship has revolved around the interpretation of the right to move and reside freely within the territory of the Union entrenched in Art. 21 TFEU or, put more clearly, its capacity to go beyond a far from innovative 'market citizenship'. Consequently, secondary law must not only specify the scope and substance of this right, but also, possibly, to limit them.[23] On the other hand, those limitations have to be interpreted narrowly and have to be applied in accordance with the principle of proportionality.

In spite of early scepticism about the actual normative content of Articles 20 and 21 TFEU, the case law of the CJEU greatly contributed to enriching EU citizenship and the right to move and reside freely within the territory of the Union from a social perspective. In a way, the Luxembourg judges have tried to take seriously a famous claim made by Advocate General Jacobs in *Konstantinidis*, prior to the entry into force of the Maastricht Treaty: he argued that a European worker or self-employed should

> be treated in accordance with a common code of fundamental values, in particular those laid down in the European Convention on Human Rights. In other words, he is entitled to say '*civis europeus sum*' and to invoke that status in order to oppose any violation of his fundamental rights.[24]

The implications of this claim are further-reaching than the Treaty provisions alone might suggest.

The CJEU clarified that rights arising from Art. 21 TFEU, with particular regard to their enjoyment by economically inactive citizens, should mean something more than the mere right to free movement.[25] As a consequence, access to social security and social assistance were 'decoupled from the status as a worker or other economically active person' and went on to become 'issues which fall under the general principle of free movement or, indeed, fundamental rights'.[26] In doing so, the Court relied on a systemic reading of Articles 18 and 21 TFEU: the prohibition of all discrimination on grounds of nationality 'must be read in conjunction with [Article 21(1) TFEU], which proclaims the right to move and reside freely within the territory of the Member States'.[27] The seminal judgements in that line of case law of the CJEU, which mostly date back to the late 1990s or the early 2000s, also deserve special attention due to the way in which they highlight the tension between the normative programme of supranational citizenship and traditional national prerogatives in the domain of social citizenship. In this regard, they show an ongoing transition from the previous state of affairs and a new 'settlement', in which the balance between the competing claims of the supranational and national institutional layers would be redefined. The underlying assumption in the reasoning of the CJEU was that supranational citizenship should turn into the 'fundamental status of nationals of the Member States'.[28] In defining the balance between supranational and national claims, the Court made it clear that the right under Art. 21 TFEU

> is conferred directly on every citizen of the Union by a clear and precise provision of the . . . Treaty . . . the application of the limitations and conditions acknowledged in Article [21(1)] TFEU in respect of the exercise of that right of residence is subject to judicial review. Consequently, any limitations and conditions imposed on that right do not prevent the provisions of Article [21(1)] TFEU from conferring on individuals rights which are enforceable by them and which the national courts must protect.[29]

In the *Grzelczyk* case, the issues at stake were access to a non-contributory social benefit and the (ir)relevance of whether or not a national of a Member State other than the host State fell within the scope of Regulation 1612/68 on the freedom of movement for workers.[30] In a nutshell, the CJEU held that its joint reading of Articles 18 and 21 TFEU also applied to access to social benefits like the Belgian minimex. In the same judgement, the Court also considered a possible justification for limiting the right to equal treatment: the main pieces of secondary law in force at the time[31] 'accept[ed] a certain degree of financial solidarity between nationals of a host Member State and nationals of other Member States, particularly if the difficulties which a beneficiary of the right of residence encounters are temporary' and so long as 'beneficiaries of the right of residence [do] not become an unreasonable burden on the public finances of the host Member State'.[32] For the purposes of this chapter, this meant that 'Member States therefore retain a certain discretion in determining what those circumstances are'.[33] This claim stressed the possible contradiction between the implications of transnational movement in terms of enjoyment of the rights of a *civis Europaeus*, on the one hand, and the regulatory prerogatives of Member States, on the other hand. The same line of reasoning was confirmed in subsequent cases like *Dany Bidar*, in which the CJEU also made reference to the relevance, for students claiming access to maintenance grants, of 'demonstrat[ing] a certain degree of integration into the society' of the host State.[34] In that case, a French citizen who had finished secondary education in the United Kingdom had been refused a university student loan by the British authorities. A similar integration – or 'real link' – requirement would apply to jobseekers applying for financial benefits.[35]

In spite of the abovementioned nuances, the Court proved to be fully aware of the far-reaching implications of the radically innovative wording of Art. 21 TFEU. The extent to which economically inactive citizens were included among those entitled to move freely, as well as the question of their access to the social security system of their host Member State, was however soon put under the spotlight.

The possible clash between the normative programme related to the implementation of primary law provisions regarding EU citizenship and traditional assumptions about national social citizenship(s) was acutely detected by some scholars:

> The 'inclusion' of EU citizens who are nationals of other Member States into the distinct national legal systems, which has been triggered by this case law, goes so far as to threaten the very foundations of national constitutional law and nation states themselves. What is left of the nation and the state people (*Staatsvolk*) if the state, which is supposed to constitute them, does not have at its disposal exclusion mechanisms any longer?[36]

As can be inferred from this passage, the establishment and implementation of EU citizenship were a crucial element in the discussion about the possibility (or desirability) of a fully-fledged Constitution for the Union.

Secondary legislation should now be considered more carefully. The main reference is provided by Directive 2004/38/EC, which replaced three pre-existing sectorial disciplines and, quite importantly, came into force after a EU citizenship had been created.[37] This piece of secondary law tries to strike a balance between the exercise of the right of residence by economically inactive citizens on the one hand, and the financial concerns of the Member States on the other. The enactment of Directive 2004/38 was preceded by the publication of a Communication in which the Commission highlighted that '[t]rue free movement . . . is not possible without protecting the social security rights of migrant workers and their families'.[38] In order to define an appropriate balance between the competing expectations of the involved actors, Articles 6 and 7 of the Directive provide for different legal regimes for, respectively, residence for up to three months and residence for more than three months. Economically inactive persons are entitled to reside within the territory of another Member State for more than three months if they

> have sufficient resources for themselves and their family members not to become a burden on the social assistance system of the host Member State during their period of residence and have comprehensive sickness insurance cover in the host Member State.
>
> (Art. 7(1)(b))[39]

Moreover, those requirements have to be fulfilled at any time in order for the right of residence to be retained (Art. 14(2)). Meanwhile, and in accordance with Art. 18 TFEU, EU citizens exercising their right of residence are entitled to equal treatment with the nationals of the host Member State (Art. 24(1), with lawful exceptions laid down at paragraph 2). Another interesting element in Directive 2004/38 is the attempt to establish a link between the novel right of permanent residence and the promotion of 'social cohesion, which is one of the fundamental objectives of the Union'.[40] According to the intention of the drafters of the Directive, there is a tight link between the rights arising from Art. 21 TFEU and social cohesion within the Union. As will be examined later in greater detail, this connection has somehow been loosened in more recent judgements of the Court. Thus, lawful residence has been identified by Directive 2004/38 as meaningful enough for establishing a 'link of belonging' with the host Member State.[41] On the other hand, the enduring relevance of the distinction between economically active and inactive citizens reflects the persistent influence of market citizenship: 'if migrant Union citizens do not belong to the category of economically active or post-active persons, their right to reside and their recourse to social assistance in the host Member State is much more controversial, both legally and politically'.[42] This point is clearly crucial when it comes to the full enjoyment of the right to reside – and, consequently, to equal treatment for social benefits. Still, 'the legal borderline between economically active and economically inactive persons remains blurred'.[43] As mentioned previously, this is a consequence of the peculiar genesis of the provisions regulating rights under Art. 21 TFEU, in which different 'layers' of legal materials coexist. Legal and political uncertainty concerning the actual meaning of this 'borderline' has come to the forefront more clearly in the latest line of case law of the CJEU.

Finally, with regard to the notion of social assistance under Article 7 of Directive 2004/38, the Court has stuck to a comprehensive definition, given that

> the aim of Directive 2004/38 is to facilitate and strengthen the exercise of the primary and individual right – conferred directly on all Union citizens by the Treaty – to move and reside freely within the territory of the Member States . . . for the purposes of Article 7(1)(b) of Directive 2004/38, the concept of 'social assistance system' must be defined by reference to the objective pursued by that provision . . . and not by reference to formal criteria.[44]

4 A shift back? Assessing the impact of the crisis on the case law of the CJEU

Since the onset of the economic and financial crisis throughout the Union, the intertwined issues of exercise of the right to move by economically inactive EU citizens and their access to social benefits in the host Member State have become increasingly topical. This is shown, first and foremost, by statements and initiatives of political leaders, both at the domestic and EU level. Of course, the core of this discussion had to be found in the British public debate before and after the Brexit referendum, with enlargement to Bulgaria and Romania. The right to free movement of their nationals has been 'the ostensible catalyst for this debate'.[45] However, fears related to 'benefit tourism' have also shaped the public debate in other Member States. It should be noted, by the way, that arguments against 'benefit tourism' concern not only economically inactive persons but also some categories of workers, e.g. frontier workers.[46] From the viewpoint of the regulation of supranational citizenship, those discussions all reflect a growing uneasiness on the part of nation states and their desire to take back control over what they perceive as their own welfare systems. On a slightly different note, these national reactions might also be interpreted as being part of a revival of government intervention aiming at coping with the effects of the crisis.[47] The European Commission was also involved in the debate about 'social tourism' and collected evidence in order to study the actual dimension of this supposed trend – and sometimes ended up debunking some recurring fears.[48]

However, the legal materials which have been scrutinized most carefully are some judgements of the Court of Justice. Some scholars have questioned the actual innovative potential of some of the claims made by the Court in decisions like *Dano*. The most important point there is that by itself EU citizenship is not sufficient to ensure equal treatment under Art. 18 TFEU: 'it is legally relevant only in conjunction with other, more specific rules'.[49] Indeed, 'the Court had insisted since *Martínez Sala* that equal treatment should be limited to those who are "lawfully resident in the territory of the host Member State"'.[50] The Court considered this issue more closely in *Commission v United Kingdom*. In the latter case, although the requirement of lawful residence for granting social benefits is indirectly discriminatory, the CJEU held that

> it is clear from the Court's case-law that the need to protect the finances of the host Member State justifies in principle the possibility of checking whether residence is lawful when a social benefit is granted in particular to persons from other Member States who are not economically active, as such grant could have consequences for the overall level of assistance which may be accorded by that State.[51]

Furthermore, in *Dano* the preconditions for the recognition of the right of residence laid down in Directive 2004/38 are interpreted as 'seek[ing] to prevent economically inactive Union citizens from using the host Member State's welfare system to fund their means of subsistence'.[52] By then, the focus was placed on those 'economically inactive Union citizens who exercise their right to freedom of movement solely in order to obtain another Member State's social assistance although they do not have sufficient resources to claim a right of residence'.[53] In the *Dano* case, the Court of Justice developed an interpretation of the relevant legal provisions in the field of EU citizenship which was probably at odds with the original intent of the drafters of Directive 2004/38.

From the specific viewpoint of the social dimension of EU citizenship, the *Alimanovic* case is no less interesting than *Dano*. In this judgement, the Court admits that a EU citizen may well retain a right of residence and, at the same time, be deprived of his/her right to access the social assistance system of the host Member State. It also held that a worker who has become unemployed in accordance with Article 7(3)(c) of Directive 2004/38 and has registered as jobseeker 'retains his right of residence in the host Member State under Article 7 of Directive 2004/38 and may, consequently, rely on the principle of equal treatment, laid down in Article 24(1) of that directive'.[54] On the other hand,

> in such a case, the host Member State may rely on the derogation in Article 24(2) of that Directive in order not to grant that citizen the social

> assistance sought. It follows from the express reference in Article 24(2) of Directive 2004/38 to Article 14(4)(b) thereof that the host Member State may refuse to grant any social assistance to a Union citizen whose right of residence is based solely on that latter provision.[55]

The analysis of the above-mentioned judgements seems to show that the case law of the CJEU regarding EU citizenship has experienced a significant shift since the beginning of the 2010s. However, overemphasizing changes in the case law of courts is an inherent risk in studies which, almost inevitably, focus on the most relevant pieces of case law and risk neglecting the wider body of 'ordinary' judicial decisions. In this respect, two scholars have tried to analyse the impact of the crisis on the citizenship-related case law of the CJEU in quantitative terms. The overall picture which they have sketched does not hint at radical change in the attitude and orientations of the Court. Although the CJEU seems to show greater deference towards the national courts and their autonomy in decision-making, the most relevant changes in its general approach do not concern EU citizens, but third country nationals: the latter are most likely not to succeed in their claims in the areas of free movement, immigration and national security. On the other hand, '[t]he fraction of pro citizenship outcomes in the category of social advantages granted to EU citizens, irrespective of subcategory, and residence disputes that involve EU citizens have been high and relatively stable'.[56]

A distinct question, which inevitably affects the institutional balance between the Union and the Member States, is how the reference, included in Art. 7(1)(b) of Directive 2004/38, to a 'burden on the social assistance system of the host Member State' should be interpreted. The CJEU seems to have 'fluctuated between a primary focus on the individual and systemic implications'.[57] Whereas a systemic evaluation focuses on the impact of the access of EU citizens to social benefits on the overall sustainability of the social assistance system of a given host Member State, in other cases, like *Dano*, an individualized, applicant-centred approach has prevailed. In *Brey*, in which the CJEU expounded a double proportionality test, the aim of the systemic assessment was defined as 'ascertain[ing] more precisely the extent of the burden which that grant would place on the national social assistance system'.[58] These statements of the Court of Justice confirm the permanent significance of national welfare systems in the composite architecture of the EU. On the one side, an individualized approach focuses on the personal situation of each citizen applying for access to social benefits, with the possibility of denying it in cases in which a given Member State does not face 'the risk of systemic breakdown of social services as a result of free movement'.[59] On the other side, interestingly, the specific features of national welfare systems are seen as the primary reference for assessing the sustainability of transnational movement of EU citizens: this confirms, at least for the time being, their crucial role in the current legal architecture of EU citizenship and the rights related thereto. Individual claims based on citizens' rights under EU law have to be measured against the capacity of national welfare systems to address them.

5 Concluding remarks

The evolving legal scenario which has been presented in the preceding sections hardly lends itself to an unambiguous concluding assessment. Undoubtedly, the uncertainties and contradictions which characterize the social dimension of EU citizenship reflect the flaws of the two-decade long semi-permanent Treaty revision process,[60] not to mention the plans to build a Social Union within, or next to, a reformed Economic and Monetary Union.[61] In this regard, it is often difficult to decouple specific, citizenship-related issues from the wider context in which they are located. The growing exasperation with which the social implications of EU citizenship have been received in some Member States results from, among other possible explanations, the unresolved asymmetry between negative integration and positive integration in the architecture of the Union.[62] Furthermore, the breakdown of the multiple crises of the Union has significantly affected the ongoing legal and political context, with growing doubts about the stability of the relevant regulatory framework. Some of the basic implications of the new economic governance obviously affect social citizenship:

> the entrenchment of internal deflation as the policy of choice for Member States of the Eurozone suffering structural crises implies turning the Social state upside down. Internal deflation requires public intervention that not only reduces the tax burden on some of the members of society with the highest levels of economic wealth and income . . . but also a structural reduction of welfare benefits.[63]

Still, it is possible to sketch a tentative assessment of this ongoing evolutionary process. Thus far, the new primary law provisions introduced by the Lisbon Treaty, which were supposed to strengthen the social character of the Treaties, have not played a crucial role in this field of EU law.[64] In this respect, the coexistence of evolutionary constitutionalism and 'achievement constitutions' does not seem to have been significantly altered. On the other hand, one might get a feeling of an interrupted path: the rise of a

> new constitutional dimension [of] European citizenship, finally destined to transcend the nation-States' particularistic allegiances in order to revive and expand the universal . . . promise of a society of free and equal individuals built on the jus-naturalistic foundations of modern citizenship,[65]

is clearly far from settled. In strategic terms, injecting social components into EU citizenship is a crucial step in the process of establishing an autonomous supranational citizenship.[66] The CJEU took an audacious stance in the 1990s, when it developed its systemic reading of Articles 18 and 21 TFEU. This made it possible for the Luxembourg judges to enrich the content of EU citizenship from the outset. Meanwhile, it allowed EU citizenship to get closer to the normative ideal of social citizenship, which had been formally entrenched in a number of Member States. It is also worth mentioning that the Court could take the lead in the construction of citizenship law even because a comprehensive, consistent legal framework for the exercise of rights under Art. 21 TFEU was enacted only in 2004. Its early case law on citizenship has been defined as one of '*disembedded* freedoms, the substantive content of which is autonomously established at the supranational level'[67] and, consequently, somehow undermines the regulatory claims arising at the national level. However, recent developments in the case law of the CJEU have led many scholars to conclude that 'the notion of the freedom of movement and access to social benefits appears to end at the borders of the individual Member States':[68] such has been the case with *Dano*, *Alimanovic* and *Commission v United Kingdom*. Conversely, it has been mentioned earlier that those judgements may not be representative of a generalized trend in the case law of the Court. Moreover, further evidence shows that EU citizens who could be seen as 'problematic'[69] in light of Directive 2004/38 are just a minority among the overall number of EU citizens who exercise their right to move, so much so that '[t]his restricting of access to benefits therefore appears to be more of a populist strategy of the governing parties, which finds support in the decisions of the Court of Justice and which turns social myths into legal reality'.[70]

Some of the potential transformations which have been envisaged in the public debate in the last few years are even difficult to reconcile with the primary law framework. One example will suffice: the difficulties and tensions which are reflected in the latest wave of judgements of the CJEU peaked in winter 2016, during the negotiations which preceded the Brexit referendum. The conclusions of the European Council meeting held on 18–19 February 2016 are particularly worth quoting:

> Member States have the possibility of refusing to grant social benefits to persons who exercise their right to freedom of movement solely in order to obtain Member States' social assistance although they do not have sufficient resources to claim a right of residence.
>
> Member States may reject claims for social assistance by EU citizens from other Member States who do not enjoy a right of residence or are entitled to reside on their territory solely because of their job-search. This includes claims by EU citizens from other Member States for benefits whose predominant function is to cover the minimum subsistence costs, even if such benefits are also intended to facilitate access to the labour market of the host Member States.[71]

As was written immediately afterwards, some of the contents of the (ultimately unsuccessful) settlement between the EU and the UK would significantly undermine the effectiveness of fundamental freedoms under EU law. Among other things:

> First, workers' access to the benefit system would be restricted by the need to show a 'real and effective degree of connection' between the person concerned and the labour market of the host Member State. Secondly, the modifications proposed by the Decision would restrict the right of job seekers to access social benefits in a host State.[72]

In general terms, one might get the feeling that Member States have developed quite slowly, and only to the price of growing political resistance, a consciousness of the fundamental transformation which a nation state undergoes after joining the EU as a member. This point has been studied and commented above all with regard to the interpretation of the constitutional identity clause of Art. 4(2) TEU.[73] Still, this point is relevant also for interpreting the balance between supranational and national powers and competences in this area.

Distinct concerns are related not so much to the balance between the EU and the Member States as to the respective weight of legislation and judicial decision-making. It has been mentioned previously that a gap has emerged between some aspects of the case law of the CJEU and the political will of the Member States, partly channelled through the political branches. More broadly, the CJEU tried to strengthen the substantial connection between the regulation of EU citizenship in primary and secondary law and the normative ideal of citizenship, including its social dimension.[74] But those attempts by the CJEU were not without risk, as demonstrated by the reactions to some of its judgements. This has to do, at least in part, with the inherent limitations of courts in adjudicating social rights disputes. As Lon Fuller once argued, 'there are polycentric elements in almost all problems submitted to adjudication', and 'generally speaking, it may be said that problems in the allocation of economic resources present too strong a polycentric aspect to be suitable for adjudication'.[75] Polycentrism, need for technical expertise and democratic concerns seem to suggest that in this area 'judges depart from the *status quo* only to a certain extent and, when they have to deal with macro-policies, they should preserve margins of flexibility for the legislative and administration'.[76] But this risk is deeply rooted in the 'juridification and judicialization of citizenship'[77] which took place from the 1990s onwards.

In conclusion, it seems clear that EU citizenship is an area of the EU legal order in which the relevance of the 'social market economy' is most crucial. As has been said before, the main issue is how to reconcile positive law provisions with the normative ideal of citizenship, which was conceived and developed at the national level, inevitably provides a reference and a benchmark, and has already been implemented, at least to a certain extent, at the supranational level. As developments in legislation and case law illustrate, it would be incorrect to claim that EU citizenship has not significantly departed from its basis of market citizenship. The idea of market citizenship has kept some of its early strength, and is illustrated within judgements like *Dano*. Yet the underlying (and unresolved) issue is the balance of powers which has taken shape since the decline of embedded liberalism and which, in many respects, has proved unsatisfactory. Taking for granted that 'all systems of solidarity and redistribution need borders',[78] transnational solidarity must be considerably strengthened if an actual shift in the law of EU citizenship is to take place.

Notes

1 Menéndez affirms that:'[t]he European Union is not undergoing one crisis, but is instead suffering several simultaneous, interrelated, and intertwined crises – crisis, which are global, not exclusively European'; still, the EU 'is not only experiencing those crisis, but is significantly responsible for the crises in the first place' (Agustín Menéndez, 'The Existential Crises of the European Union' (2013) *German Law Journal* 453, at 453–454)

2 Alessandra Silveira, 'On the CJEU's Post-Brexit Case-Law on European Citizenship: The Recovery of the Identity Ariadne's Thread?' (2017) *Union – EU Law Journal* 48.

3 Urška Šadl and Mikael Rask Madsen, 'Did the Financial Crisis Change European Citizenship Law? An Analysis of Citizenship Rights Adjudication before and after the Financial Crisis' (2016) *European Law Journal* 40, at 43.

4 As defined by Leonard Besselink, *A Composite European Constitution* (Europa Law Publishing, 2007).

5 Fritz Scharpf, 'The Asymmetry of European Integration, or Why the EU Cannot Be a "Social Market Economy"' (2010) *Socio-Economic Review* 211.

6 John Ruggie, 'International Regimes, Transactions, and Change: Embedded Liberalism in the Postwar Economic Order' (1982) *International Organisation* 379; Robert Gilpin, *The Political Economy of International Relations* (PUP, 1987) 355; GiuseppeFederico Mancini, 'Principi fondamentali di diritto del lavoro nell'ordinamento delle Comunità europee' in *Il lavoro nel diritto comunitario e l'ordinamento italiano* (Cedam, 1988) 23, at 26.

7 Scharpf, 'The Asymmetry of European Integration, or Why the EU Cannot Be a "Social Market Economy"' (n 5), at 215.

8 Thomas Marshall, *Citizenship and Social Class and Other Essays* (CUP, 1950).

9 Rogers Brubaker, *Citizenship and Nationhood in France and Germany* (HUP, 1992) 181.

10 Dagmar Schiek, 'Perspectives on Social Citizenship in the EU: From *Status Positivus* to *Status Socialis Activus* via Two Forms of Transnational Solidarity' in Dimitry Kochenov (ed.), *EU Citizenship and Federalism: The Role of Rights* (CUP, 2017) 341, at 342; Charles Edward O'Sullivan, 'The EU between "Market State" Ideals and "Social Market Economy" Objectives: Placing the "Social Market Economy" within the Union's Constitutional History', in this volume.

11 Agustín Menéndez, 'Which Citizenship? Whose Europe? The Many Paradoxes of European Citizenship' (2014) *German Law Journal* 907, at 912.

12 Michel Rosenfeld, *The Identity of the Constitutional Subject: Selfhood, Citizenship, Culture, and Community* (Routledge, 2010) 216.

13 Scharpf, 'The Asymmetry of European Integration, or Why the EU Cannot Be a "Social Market Economy"' (n 5), at 234. As regards classification of welfare models, Gøsta Esping-Andersen, *The Three Worlds of Welfare Capitalism* (PUP, 1990); Maurizio Ferrera, 'The Four "Social Europes": Between Universalism and Selectivity' in Martin Rhodes and Yves Mény (eds.), *The Future of European Welfare: A New Social Contract?* (Palgrave Macmillan, 1998) 81, at 85–86.

14 Scharpf, 'The Asymmetry of European Integration, or Why the EU Cannot Be a "Social Market Economy"' (n 5), at 238.
15 Francesco Saitto, '"Risocializzare l'Europa". La dimensione sociale europea tra economia di mercato e integrazione sovranazionale' (2017) *Rivista di Diritti comparati* 86, at 94–95.
16 Delia Ferri and Fulvio Cortese, 'Introduction', in this volume.
17 Bruno De Witte, 'The Lisbon Treaty and National Constitutions: More or Less Europeanisation?' in Carlos Closa (ed.), *The Lisbon Treaty and National Constitutions: Europeanisation and Democratic Implications* (2009) 3 *ARENA Report 25*, at 33.
18 Neil Walker, 'Post-Constituent Constitutionalism? The Case of the European Union' in Martin Loughlin and Neil Walker (eds.), *The Paradox of Constitutionalism: Constituent Power and Constitutional Form* (OUP, 2007) 247, at 260–261.
19 Daniel Thym, 'The Elusive Limits of Solidarity: Residence Rights of and Social Benefits for Economically Inactive Union Citizens' (2015) *Common Market Law Review* 17, at 18.
20 Antoine Bailleux and Denis Duez, 'La libre circulation dans l'ornière? Penser ensemble, libre circulation, (dé)régulation et légitimité dans l'Union européenne' in Heidi Mercenier *et al.* (eds.), *La libre circulation sous pression. Régulation et dérégulation des mobilités en Europe* (Bruylant, 2018) 11, at 21.
21 Alina Kaczorowska, *European Union Law* (Routledge, 2013) 641; Paula García Andrade, 'Privileged Third-Country Nationals and Their Right of Free Movement and Residence to and in the EU: Questions of Status and Competence' in Elspeth Guild, Cristina Gortázar Rotaeche and Dora Kostakopoulou (eds.), *The Reconceptualization of European Union Citizenship* (Brill, 2014) 111, at 126.
22 Robin White, 'Article 34: Social Security and Social Assistance' in Steve Peers *et al.* (eds.), *The EU Charter of Fundamental Rights: A Commentary* (Hart, 2014) 927, at 936.
23 Niamh Nic Shuibhne, 'Limits Rising, Duties Ascending: The Changing Legal Shape of Union Citizenship' (2015) *Common Market Law Review* 889, at 889.
24 Opinion of AG Jacobs, Case C-168/91, *Konstantinidis*, EU:C:1992:504, para 46.
25 Costanza Margiotta, 'I nuovi limiti alla cittadinanza europea alla luce delle sue originarie contraddizioni' (2017) *Sant'Anna Legal Studies Research Paper* 3, at 9.
26 Allan Rosas and Lorna Armati, *EU Constitutional Law: An Introduction* (Hart, 2010) 138.
27 Case C-184/99, *Grzelczyk*, EU:C:2001:458, para 37.
28 Opinion of AG Alber, Case C-184/99, *Grzelczyk*, EU:C:2000:518, para 31. Opinion of AG Maduro, Case C-135/08, *Rottmann*, EU:C:2009:588, para 23 ('a new form of civic and political allegiance on a European scale. It does not require the existence of a people, but it is founded on the existence of a European political area from which rights and duties emerge'); Opinion of AG Szpunar, *Alfredo Rendón Marín*, EU:C:2016:75, para 117.
29 Case C-413/99, *Baumbast*, EU:C:2002:493, paras 84 and 86.
30 Council Regulation (EC) No 1612/68 of 15 October 1968 on freedom of movement for workers within the Community [1968] OJ L257.
31 Council Directive (EC) No 93/96 of 29 October 1993 on the right of residence for students [1993] OJ L317; Council Directive (EC) No 90/364 of 28 June 1990 on the right of residence [1990] OJ L180; Council Directive (EC) No 90/365 on the right of residence for employees and self-employed persons who have ceased their occupational activity [1990] OJ L180.
32 *Grzelczyk* (n 27), para 44.
33 Opinion of AG Alber, *Grzelczyk* (n 28), para 123.
34 Case C-209/03, *Bidar*, EU:C:2005:169, para 57.
35 Case C-138/02, *Collins*, EU:C:2004:172.

36 Peter Huber, 'Unionsbürgerschaft' (2013) *Europarecht* 637, at 638 (the translation is my own).
37 European Parliament and Council Directive 2004/38/EC of 29 April 2004 on the right of citizens of the Union and their family members to move and reside freely within the territory of the Member States amending Regulation (EEC) No 1612/68 and repealing Directives 64/221/EEC, 68/360/EEC, 72/194/EEC, 73/148/EEC, 75/34/EEC, 75/35/EEC, 90/364/EEC, 90/365/EEC and 93/96/EEC [2004] OJ L158/77. See also Regulation (EC) No 883/2004 of the European Parliament and of the Council of 29 April 2004 on the coordination of social security systems [2004] OJ L166/1.
38 Communication from the European Commission, 'Free Movement of Workers: Achieving the Full Benefits and Potential', COM(2002)694.
39 It should be noted, however, that recital 10 of the preamble of Directive 2004/38 makes reference to 'an unreasonable burden' (Opinion of AG Wahl, Case C-140/12, *Peter Brey*, EU:C:2013:337, para 76).
40 European Parliament and Council Directive 2004/38/EC, Recital 17 of the preamble.
41 Maria Antonia Panascì, 'Legal Values and Hermeneutic Virtues: The *Status Quo* of European Social Citizenship' (2017) *Politiche Sociali* 429, at 430–431.
42 Herwig Verschueren, 'The Right to Reside and to Social Benefits for Economically Inactive EU Migrants: How to Balance Freedom of Movement and Solidarity?' in Mercenier *et al.* (eds.), *La libre circulation sous pression* (n 20), 33, at 37.
43 Ibid., at 36.
44 *Peter Brey* (n 39), paras 53 and 60.
45 'Editorial Comments: The Free Movement of Persons in the European Union: Salvaging the Dream While Explaining the Nightmare' (2014) *Common Market Law Review* 729, at 730.
46 Case C-20/12, *Elodie Giersch*, EU:C:2013:411, para 80.
47 Giulio Napolitano, 'Looking for a Smarter Government (and Administrative Law) in the Age of Uncertainty' in Susan Rose-Ackerman, Peter Lindseth and Blake Emerson (eds.), *Comparative Administrative Law* (Edward Elgar, 2017) 352.
48 Communication from the European Commission, 'Free Movement of EU Citizens and Their Families: Five Actions to Make a Difference', COM(2013)837; Herwig Verschueren, 'Preventing "Benefit Tourism" in the EU: A Narrow or Broad Interpretation of the Possibilities Offered by the ECJ in *Dano*?' (2015) *Common Market Law Review* 363, at 364.
49 Thym, 'The Elusive Limits of Solidarity: Residence Rights of and Social Benefits for Economically Inactive Union Citizens' (n 19), at 24.
50 Ibid.
51 Case C-308/14, *Commission v United Kingdom*, EU:C:2016:436, para 80; Verschueren, 'The Right to Reside and to Social Benefits for Economically Inactive EU Migrants: How to Balance Freedom of Movement and Solidarity?' (n 42), at 46.
52 Case C-333/13, *Dano*, EU:C:2014:2358, para 76; Francesco De Cecco, 'False Friends and True Cognates: On Fundamental Freedoms, Fundamental Rights and Union Citizenship' in Mads Andenas, Tarjei Bekkedal and Luca Pantaleo (eds.), *The Reach of Free Movement* (Asser Press, 2017) 253, at 269–270.
53 *Dano* (n 52), para 78.
54 Case C-67/14, *Alimanovic*, EU:C:2015:597, para 53.
55 Ibid., paras 57–58.
56 Šadl and Madsen, 'Did the Financial Crisis Change European Citizenship Law? An Analysis of Citizenship Rights Adjudication before and after the Financial Crisis' (n 3), at 43.
57 Thym, 'The Elusive Limits of Solidarity: Residence Rights of and Social Benefits for Economically Inactive Union Citizens' (n 19), at 28.

58 *Peter Brey* (n 39), para 78.
59 Thym, 'The Elusive Limits of Solidarity: Residence Rights of and Social Benefits for Economically Inactive Union Citizens' (n 19), at 30.
60 Bruno de Witte, 'The Closest Thing to a Constitutional Conversation in Europe: The Semi-Permanent Treaty Revision Process' in Paul Beaumont, Carole Lyons and Neil Walker (eds.), *Convergence and Divergence in European Public Law* (Hart, 2002) 39.
61 Frank Vandenbroucke, Catherine Barnard and Geert De Baere (eds.), *A European Social Union after the Crisis* (CUP, 2017).
62 Thorsten Kingreen, 'Fundamental Freedoms' in Armin von Bogdandy and Jürgen Bast (eds.), *Principles of European Constitutional Law* (Hart, 2009) 515, at 527–528.
63 Menéndez, 'Which Citizenship? Whose Europe? The Many Paradoxes of European Citizenship' (n 11), at 929–930.
64 Václav Šmejkal and Stanislav Šaroch, 'EU as a Highly Competitive Social Market Economy: Goal, Options, and Reality' (2014) *Review of Economic Perspectives* 393, at 407.
65 Stefano Giubboni, 'Free Movement of Persons and European Solidarity Revisited' (2015) *Perspectives on Federalism* 1, at 3.
66 Dimitry Kochenov, 'EU Citizenship without Duties' (2014) 20 *European Law Journal* 482, at 496.
67 Menéndez, 'Which Citizenship? Whose Europe? The Many Paradoxes of European Citizenship' (n 11), at 922.
68 Nadine Absenger and Florian Blank, 'From Social Myths to Legal Reality: Limiting the Freedom of Movement of EU Citizens' (2017) *Politiche sociali* 469, at 471.
69 Ibid., at 472.
70 Ibid.
71 European Council, 'A New Settlement for the United Kingdom within the European Union', 2016/C 69 I/01.
72 Rossella Pulvirenti, 'A New Settlement for the United Kingdom in the European Union: A New Challenge to EU Citizens' Social Benefits and Freedom of Movement?' (2016) *European Papers* 727, at 739.
73 Armin von Bogdandy and Stephan Schill, 'Overcoming Absolute Primacy: Respect for National Identity under the Lisbon Treaty' (2011) *Common Market Law Review* 1417, at 1425.
74 Menéndez, 'Which Citizenship? Whose Europe? The Many Paradoxes of European Citizenship' (n 11).
75 Lon Fuller, 'The Forms and Limits of Adjudication' (1978) *Harvard Law Review* 353, at 397 and 400.
76 Christian Joerges and Florian Rödl, '"Social Market Economy" as Europe's Social Model?' (2004) 8 *EUI Working Papers* 22; Bruno Brancati, 'Decidere sulla crisi: le Corti e l'allocazione delle risorse in tempi di "austerità"' (2015) *Federalismi.it* 1, at 6.
77 Menéndez, 'The Existential Crisis of the European Union' (n 1), at 483.
78 Stefano Giubboni, *Diritti e solidarietà in Europa. I modelli sociali nazionali nello spazio giuridico europeo* (il Mulino, 2012) 12 (the translation is my own).

Part II

The EU social market economy

Practical challenges

5 W(h)ither social Europe?

Labour rights in a social market economy

Michael Doherty

1 Introduction

Labour law is where the market and the social meet.[1] From the outset, the EU Treaties, secondary legislation, and case law of the Court of Justice of the European Union (CJEU) have explicitly recognised the unique role of labour in the creation of the internal market. In part, of course, this is because labour is not the same as physical goods, traded services or capital. Work is central to the human experience, and labour law, be it at EU or national level

> is much more directly central to the peoples of Europe than the regulation of capital movements, financial services, take-overs and mergers, international trade or customs duties or other barriers to free movement of goods and services, which absorbs most of the attention of (EU) lawyers.[2]

However, perhaps precisely because of the centrality of work to peoples' lives, the tensions between regulation at national, or local level, and regulation at the level of the EU are intensely felt and contested; particularly where economic and social rationales intersect.

In this chapter, it is not proposed, nor is it feasible, to attempt to cover the entire terrain of EU regulation pertaining to labour relations, in order to investigate the intersection between the economic and the social. Rather the chapter sets out to examine some key themes in relation to labour regulation- the autonomous nature of labour law, the scope and function of labour law, and labour rights as fundamental human rights – in order to examine the interplay between economic internal market rules, and the role of the EU in protecting, defending and reinforcing labour standards. The chapter will also focus predominantly on collective labour rights, where the Court, and the legislature, has in recent years had to reconcile the interaction of the economic and the social in an explicit manner.

The chapter is set out as follows. In the next section, a brief historical overview of the development of 'EU Labour Law' is outlined, and relevant Treaty provisions, secondary legislation, and CJEU decisions are presented. In section 2, the chapter considers the 'autonomous' nature of labour law, and how this fits with the role of the EU in labour relations. Here, the chapter considers 'direct attacks' on this autonomy in terms of the interpretation of treaty articles, and secondary legislation, as well as 'indirect attacks', most notably those institutionalised as a response to the socio-economic crisis that erupted in 2008, and manifested in the new economic governance arrangements. In section 3, the shift in the objectives of labour law is examined; from the 'protective' to the 'flexibility' function. Here, the chapter analyses developments in the labour relations field post-Lisbon, where economic interests and labour rights intersect, and note that decisions of the CJEU tend to move, albeit not definitively, in the direction of (indirectly) undercutting labour rights at national level. Section 4 considers the question of fundamental rights, and explores how effective the appeal to labour rights as human rights has been in terms of protecting labour standards in the EU, particularly where a fundamental labour right comes into conflict with a fundamental economic freedom. In the concluding section, the chapter appeals for a closer examination of, and greater respect for, not norms or ideals, but the crucial roles of actors and institutions. It is by looking at agency and process, rather than only focusing on the reforms of norms and laws, that effective reconciliation of the social and the market in the sphere of labour rights will be achieved.

2 Labour rights and market-making in the EU

This chapter started, above, by proclaiming that the unique role of labour was recognised from the outset in the EU Treaties. However, there was almost a complete absence of explicit social policy, and labour law, provisions in the Treaty of Rome in 1957. Article 118 of the Treaty of Rome provided that the Commission 'shall have the task of promoting close cooperation between Member States in the social field', particularly in matters relating to, *inter alia*, employment; labour law and working conditions; the right of association; and collective bargaining between employers and workers. This, however, was clearly a role that would not involve 'hard' lawmaking, as it was to be achieved by 'making studies, delivering opinions and arranging consultations'. Article 117 provided that (emphasis added) 'Member States agree upon the need to promote improved working conditions and an improved standard of living for workers. . . . They believe that such a development will ensue *not only from the functioning of the common market*' but would also need regulatory action. Clearly, then, any objectives the then-EEC, via the Commission, might have in the social field were to be achieved only in an intergovernmental fashion, with Member States in the driving seat, and were to be achieved primarily via market mechanisms, and not legislative action.[3] The key 'social provisions', therefore, in respect of which legislative action was permitted were those closely tied to the needs of a single market: Article 48 on free movement of workers, and Article 119 on equal pay as between men and women.[4]

The story of the development of EU social policy, as it relates to labour rights, between the entry into force of the Treaty of Rome in 1958, and that of the Treaty of Lisbon in 2009, has been discussed extensively elsewhere,[5] and will not be repeated here. Instead, some key points of relevance to succeeding sections will be highlighted. First, the role of the CJEU should be noted. Decisions of the Court, and opinions of the Advocates General (AG), acknowledged at a relatively early stage the interpenetration of the economic and the social in EU law, in decisions involving the 'hard law' Treaty provisions. AG Trabucchi in *Mr. and Mrs. F v. Belgium*, in the context of free movement of workers, noted that 'the migrant worker is not regarded by Community law . . . as a mere source of labour but is viewed as a human being'.[6] As noted in the introduction to this volume,[7] the famous decision of *Defrenne v Sabena* involving the equal pay provisions in Article 119 saw the Court explicitly acknowledge the social objectives of the EEC,[8] and, by 2000, the Court had acknowledged in *Deutsche Telekom*, that the

> economic aim pursued by Article 119 of the Treaty, namely the elimination of distortions of competition between undertakings established in different Member States, *is secondary to the social aim* pursued by the same provision, which constitutes the expression of a fundamental human right.[9]

Secondly, we should note the manner in which the Union's competence in matters related to labour rights has evolved. Whilst social competences initially were very limited, the idea that social progress would be achieved through market integration alone has long come to be questioned. So, for example, by the 1970s, following the widespread social unrest of the late-1960s, and economic devastation wreaked by the oil crises, a Social Action Programme was adopted (1974–76), with the aim of providing the EEC with a more 'human face'.[10] This resulted in the adoption of a number of legislative measures concerned with worker protection in the face of mass redundancies and corporate restructuring in an attempt to harmonise labour legislation across the Member States.[11] However, given that the Treaty of Rome provided no real competence in the field of social and labour policy, the directives were adopted on the basis of Article 100 (now Article 115 TFEU), which allowed for legislation 'for the approximation of such laws, regulations or administrative provisions of the Member States as directly affect the establishment or functioning of the common market'. As Bercusson notes, the formal, legal, justification for such measures 'was, and had to be, not social policy, but as contributing to the common market'.[12]

The period of Conservative party rule in the UK, from the election of Thatcher's Conservative government in 1979, until New Labour's victory in 1997, meant that the unanimity required to pass measures under Article 100 was not an option. Two developments are of particular interest to this chapter. First, there was a progressive expansion, beginning with the Single European Act (SEA) of 1986 and continuing in the Treaties of Maastricht, Amsterdam and Nice, of the use of 'Qualified Majority Voting' (QMV), which circumvents Member States' veto rights in enacting legislative measures. Secondly, beginning with Article 118A (now Article 153 TFEU) inserted by the SEA, which allowed for Community action (by QMV) in the area of protecting workers' health and safety, there was an accompanying extension of the areas in which legislation affecting labour rights could be enacted, including 'working conditions' and the 'information and consultation of workers'.[13] As will be discussed later, the fact that the Union, post-Lisbon, still has no competence to legislate in 'core' labour law areas such as pay, and the right to strike, has not prevented EU law from having a significant impact on national law in these spheres.

The final area in which significant, pre-Lisbon developments, should be noted is that of social dialogue. From the mid-1980s, the social partners at EU level – the workers' representative organisation, the European Trade Union Confederation (ETUC), and the employer groups BusinessEurope (private sector), and *Centre Européen des Entreprises à Participation Publique et des enterprises d'intérêt économique general* (CEEP – public sector) – have been given a unique role in relation to policy- and law- making in the EU.[14] The European Social Partners were intimately involved in the process which led to the declaration (with the dissent of the UK), of a Charter of the Fundamental Social Rights of Workers in 1989, in the inclusion, in the Maastricht Treaty, of a Protocol to the Treaty on European Union (TEU) on Social Policy and an Agreement on Social Policy, and in the approval, in 2000, of an EU Charter of Fundamental Rights (EU CFR), including many social and labour rights, as well as in the aforementioned expansion of legal competence in the field of labour rights.[15] Thus, the EU has long-recognised the key role that autonomous social partners play in labour regulation, at both the EU and national level.

The following sections, in discussing developments of relevance to the social market economy post-Lisbon, will refer back to these key themes of the role of the CJEU, of the nature of the Union's competence in terms of labour rights, and of the role of autonomous social partners in the regulation of labour relations. In the next section, it is to this concept of the 'autonomy of labour law' the chapter turns.

3 Labour law's autonomy and EU law

Labour lawyers and labour relations practitioners (such as trade unionists and human resource management professionals) often feel quite protective of the 'autonomous' nature of labour law. This section will consider two elements of 'autonomy' of particular significance to this volume. First, and most significantly, the very varied nature of industrial relations and collective bargaining practices, and their interaction with the law, across the Union, has meant that Member States have resisted ceding lawmaking powers in the labour relations field to the EU in 'core' areas such as wage-setting, freedom of association and the right to strike. There is no legislative competence in these areas, even post-Lisbon. Secondly, in some Member States, labour rights are largely regulated by social partner agreements, whilst in others, legislative intervention is more significant. In some Member States collective bargaining at sectoral, or national, level is hugely important in setting labour standards; in others, collective bargaining is left to enterprise level. Thus, the role of the social partners, at the national and (as briefly introduced above) EU level will be considered. Title X of the TFEU, the title on 'Social Policy', begins with Article 151 TFEU, which sets out various objectives for the Union and the Member States, including the promotion of dialogue between management and labour. Article 153 TFEU sets out the specific fields in which the Union is to support and complement the activities of the Member States, which include, *inter alia*, working conditions; social security and social protection of workers; the information and consultation of workers; and equality between men and women with regard to labour market opportunities and treatment at work. The Parliament and the Council may adopt 'measures' designed to encourage cooperation between Member States (but excluding any harmonisation of the laws and regulations of the Member States), and, in the fields outlined in Article 153 (a) to (i), may adopt directives that set out minimum requirements for gradual implementation.[16] Article 151(5) TFEU provides that pay, the right of association, the right to strike or the right to impose lock-outs, are excluded from the scope of the Article.

Whilst a number of important directives have been adopted pursuant to these provisions (as they existed under previous treaties), the last of any significance was Directive 2008/104 on Temporary Agency Work, which was adopted prior to the entry into force of the Lisbon Treaty,[17] almost a decade ago. The competence afforded the Union in this sphere, therefore, has lain dormant. The competence not afforded the EU in Article 151(5), however has been the subject of much debate in the years following Lisbon. As noted by Syrpis and Novitz, for many years the Court of Justice managed to avoid conflicts between internal market norms and national labour laws, by maintaining a certain autonomy for labour law.[18] So, in *Rush Portuguesa*, the Court held that:

> Community law does not preclude Member States from extending their legislation, or collective labour agreements entered into by both sides of industry, to any person who is employed, even temporarily, within their territory, no matter in which country the employer is established.[19]

Similarly, in *Albany*,[20] the Court refused to apply competition law rules to collective agreements aimed at improving working conditions. However, as is now well documented, the *Viking* and *Laval* cases,[21] decided just before the entry into force of the Lisbon Treaty, 'destroyed any cosy assumptions to the effect that labour law may in some way be insulated from the internal market case law of the Court'.[22] In these widely known cases, the CJEU was called upon to deliver its judgement with regard to disputes that arose from the collision of an economic freedom (the right of establishment in *Viking*; the freedom to provide services in *Laval*) with a trade union right (to engage in collective action, which the Court acknowledged as a fundamental right, which forms an integral part of the general principles of EU law). Instead of framing the issue as involving the confrontation of two opposed rights of equal value,[23] the Court organised its reasoning on the basis that the economic freedom was considered to be 'the rule', and the collective labour right was identified as 'the exception'.[24] Whilst the Court in *Laval* recognised that the restriction on market freedoms inherent in the taking of collective action could be justifiable, in principle, if such action were aimed at preventing 'social dumping', it considered the action in the case connected with negotiations on rates of pay for such workers could not be justified on public interest grounds.[25] Therefore, in the balancing of the social and the economic, in these cases, the weighting was overwhelmingly in favour of the latter.

More alarmingly, in many ways, is that, as Novitz argues, the Court, in an attempt to promote employer exercise of market freedoms, engaged in 'backdoor regulation of the right to strike'; the exercise of the right to strike has been regulated by the CJEU, even though the legislature was barred from intervention under Article 153(5) TFEU.[26] So much for the 'autonomous nature' of labour law.

Turning from the jurisprudence of the Court, a second area where measures have been taken that impact significantly on national collective bargaining, and wage-setting, relates to the establishment of a strict economic governance package for all Eurozone countries.[27] Notwithstanding again the lack of competence in the sphere of labour law afforded to the EU legislator in the Treaties, the Euro Plus Pact is quite clear about what Member States must do in order to 'foster competitiveness':[28]

> Review the wage setting arrangements, and, where necessary, the degree of centralisation in the bargaining process, and the indexation mechanisms.

The 'Country-Specific Recommendations' (CSRs) now issued to Member States have become ever more intrusive in the area of labour law, focussing increasingly on wage-setting mechanisms.[29] Thus, we have increasingly seen EU employment policy being directed by the Ecofin Council, made up of the economics and finance ministers of the Member States.[30] As Novitz argues, the EU's attempts to regulate Member States' macroeconomic policies regarding public spending and wage-setting, have resulted in a limitation on access to the right to strike, 'not only when industrial action has cross-border effects, but also when action would achieve collectively bargained wage (and other) gains internal to Member States'.[31]

In the context of these direct and indirect attacks on core areas of labour rights, social dialogue seems to have been in abeyance. Articles 154 and 155 TFEU grant a unique, and privileged, role to the EU social partners, which mandates consultations with them on any proposals for Union action in the social field, and allows them to make agreements on specified matters in this field, which may subsequently be passed into law by the EU legislature. At the national level, social partners may be entrusted with the implementation of EU legislative measures in accordance with Article 153(3). By contrast, then, with matters relating to pay, and collective bargaining/action, the Treaty *guarantees* to respect the autonomous role of the social partners at the EU and Member State levels. However, a role for social dialogue has not been a feature of developments at EU level since the entry into force of the Lisbon Treaty. No legislative measures resulting from social partner agreement have been passed. At the national level, social partners in the countries most affected by the crisis have largely been ignored, and, as noted, the new economic governance regime explicitly allows for EU interference in national collective bargaining, and wage-setting, particularly in relation to sectoral agreements.[32] The role for the social partners, then, in the 'social market economy' is somewhat opaque.

4 From protection to regulation: labour rights in the EU post-Lisbon

The previous section has outlined the attacks, directly from the Court's jurisprudence, and indirectly via the Commission's economic surveillance function, on the autonomous nature of labour law in the Union. This section moves on to examine how judicial developments, post-Lisbon, have continued to impact on the protection of labour standards.

For much of the twentieth century, the perspective that labour law should be defined by reference to its 'protective' function was the dominant one amongst labour law scholars.[33] Therefore, laws regulating employment relations should focus on protecting workers from unjust, unfair or exploitative treatment by employers, by means of creating individual labour rights for workers, or permitting and/or encouraging collective representation of workers' interests, generally via trade unions. By the late twentieth, and early twenty-first, century, however, the dominance of the protective perspective came to be questioned. In terms of labour law, scholars have argued that the changed political landscape, and:

> in particular, the acceptance across party political divides of a market logic forcefully resistant to regulatory 'interference' appeared to render futile any attempt to remain tied to old notions of labour law as state intervention to guarantee fair terms and conditions of employment.[34]

Attention has, therefore, focused increasingly on the interaction between *labour law* and *labour markets*, and the impact of legal regulation on competitiveness, flexibility and labour market access.[35]

These arguments hold particular sway in the context of the EU, given its economic foundations, and (relatively) limited competence in the sphere of worker protection. In this section, the interaction between the drive for business flexibility and competitiveness in the internal market, and measures protecting labour rights in the interests of social sustainability, will be addressed by looking at three areas of EU law: the law on transfer of undertakings, competition law and the law on collective redundancies. The areas chosen are useful illustrations as all have been the subject of important post-Lisbon decisions of the CJEU, in which economic freedoms needed to be balanced with the collective representation of workers, and in each of which the Court invoked the Charter of Fundamental Rights in its reasoning.[36] In *Alemo-Herron*, the Court had to confront the issue of whether, in the context of a transfer of undertaking, 'dynamic clauses' by virtue of which the transferee could be bound not only by collective agreements in force at the time of the transfer at issue, but also subsequent to that transfer, could be enforced.[37] The Court noted that the provisions of the measure in question,

Directive 2001/23,[38] had to be interpreted in a manner consistent with the fundamental rights as set out by the EU CFR. However, it was not the articles of the Charter dealing with collective bargaining (Article 28), or freedom of association (Article 12) to which the Court referred. The Court instead focused on Article 16 of the Charter on the freedom to conduct a business. Enforcing a 'dynamic clause' in a collective agreement, the Court concluded, would mean that the transferee's 'contractual freedom is seriously reduced to the point that such a limitation is liable to adversely affect the very essence of its freedom to conduct a business'.[39]

Turning to the intersection between collective bargaining and competition rules,[40] we note a similar, if more nuanced, trajectory in the Court's thinking. The competition rules in the Treaties include the principled prohibition of cartels (Article 101 TFEU). Collective agreements, which explicitly aim to 'directly or indirectly fix purchase or selling prices or any other trading conditions' in relation to the price of labour (Article 101 (a)) are often referred to as 'wage cartels'. However, 'this is a cartel which is perfectly legitimate, if one accepts the necessity for employees to combine in order to overcome structural market imbalance'; indeed 'the whole process of collective bargaining is based on combining employees in order to alleviate the pressure to undercut the price of each other's labour'.[41] Advocate General Wahl in *FNV Kunsten* made it clear that there are 'good socio-economic reasons to restrict, or even to eliminate, wage competition among workers through collective bargaining', and that collective bargaining can help workers and employers in reaching a balanced and mutually acceptable outcome.[42]

As will be further discussed in Chapter 9, in *Albany*, the Court held that collective agreements do not fall within the scope of Article 101 TFEU when two cumulative conditions are met: 1) they are entered into in the framework of collective bargaining between employers and employees, and 2) they contribute directly to improving the employment and working conditions of workers.[43] As the Court's case law refers explicitly to 'employees', collective agreements involving the self-employed fall outside of the '*Albany* exception'. This issue came before the Court in *FNV Kunsten*,[44] where the question was whether EU competition rules applied to a Dutch collective labour agreement which contained provisions on the minimum fees to be paid not only to *employees* of an orchestra, but also to *self-employed musicians* who work for orchestras on an occasional basis as substitutes for employed musicians. The Court proceeded along predictable lines, holdings that a self-employed musician should 'in principle' be treated as an 'undertaking', and that an organisation negotiating on behalf of self-employed service providers should not be treated as a social partner but should be characterised as an 'association of undertakings'.[45] Therefore, the agreement in question could not fall under the '*Albany* exception'. However, the Court went on to note that the boundaries between the self-employed (as undertakings) and employees are not so easy to determine in a fluid employment market, and it identified a category of workers which it called the 'false self-employed'; namely 'service providers [who are] in a situation comparable to that of employees' who, subject to certain conditions, *can* benefit from an *Albany*-type exemption.[46] The Court might be commended here for not applying an overly formalistic interpretation of 'self-employment'; it could, and might have been expected to, have held simply that competition rules apply to all those who are not 'employees'. However, the Court did not engage with AG Wahl's much more nuanced balancing of the interests of collective bargaining and antitrust rules. The AG also concluded that the '*Albany* exception' could not cover contractual provisions concluded on behalf of self-employed persons. He did accept, however, the argument that the provisions of the collective agreement *did* improve the working conditions of the employees concerned (the musicians employed directly by the Orchestra), by aiming to prevent social dumping.[47] Applying the terms of the agreement to the self-employed musicians would help ensure these employees could not be replaced by lower-cost self-employed workers; not applying it to the self-employed, equally, would weaken the collective bargaining power of employees in negotiations.

The third example of the Court's balancing of collective labour rights and economic freedoms relates to the decision in *AGET Iraklis*.[48] At issue here was a Greek law allowing the Minister of Labour to refuse to authorise, and thus render invalid, collective redundancies sought by an employing organisation. The Minister, in coming to a decision under the law in question, was to consider the 'conditions in the labour market'; 'the situation of the undertaking'; and 'the interests of the national economy'. When the Minister refused to authorise redundancies sought by AGET Iraklis, the company argued the national law was not compatible with Directive 98/59, or Articles 49 TFEU (freedom of establishment) and 63 TFEU (free movement of capital).

What is of most concern to this chapter was the Court's decision in relation to Article 49 TFEU. Predictably, the Court held the national measure was 'liable to constitute a serious obstacle to the exercise of freedom of establishment in Greece'.[49] The Court also noted that the measure amounted to a limitation on exercise of the freedom to conduct a business enshrined in Article 16 of the Charter.[50] The Court ruled that such a restriction might be justified by overriding requirements in the public interest, such as 'the protection of workers' or 'the encouragement of employment and recruitment', but in the instant case, the three criteria which the Minister was to take into account for the purpose of deciding whether to oppose collective redundancies, were formulated in terms that were too 'general and imprecise' to be capable of justifying the restriction on freedom of establishment.[51] Nor, the Court concluded, could the measure be saved by the particular Greek context, i.e. that 'the context in a Member State may be one of acute economic crisis and a particularly high unemployment rate'.[52]

At first blush, then, there appears to be 'nothing to see here'; a measure aimed at protecting the collective interests of workers is deemed to be a disproportionate restriction on an economic freedom. However, the decision of the Court is notable for its more measured, and balanced, approach to the competing economic and social objectives. First, as noted in the Introductory chapter,[53] the Court makes explicit reference to Article 3(3) TEU.[54] There is also an explicit reference to Article 9 TFEU.[55] Secondly, in stark contrast to *Alemo-Herron*, the scope of, and possible limitations to, Article 16 of the Charter are noted.

So, 'a mechanism imposing a framework on collective redundancies [allowing a national authority, in certain circumstances, to oppose projected redundancies on grounds relating to the protection of workers and of employment] does not seem – in principle – to be such as to affect the essence of the freedom to conduct a business'.[56] Moreover, 'the freedom to conduct a business is not absolute, but must be viewed in relation to its social function'.[57] Thirdly, again by contrast with *Alemo-Herron*, other provisions of the Charter are considered by the Court, notably Article 30 (protection against unjustified dismissal). Ultimately, the Court concluded, the Greek measure failed on its particular merits; however, it left open the possibility of a new mechanism being devised which would *not* be formulated in very general and imprecise terms.

The picture that emerges from the Court jurisprudence post-Lisbon examined in this section is, therefore, somewhat mixed. *Alemo-Herron* is squarely in the *Laval* mode, where social considerations are barely acknowledged in the Court's assessment of whether economic freedoms have been infringed. However, that decision is dismissed fairly swiftly in *AGET Iraklis*, where there is much more discussion by the Court of the Union's social aims in the worker protection field. *FNV Kunsten* is also somewhat more moderate in its balancing exercise, in recognising the complexities of contemporary employment relationships,[58] and in not automatically applying competition rules to the collective bargaining situation of workers who may not be employees. However, Schiek et al. have questioned why collective agreements should be subject to competition rules at all; if, as is the case, collective bargaining is a fundamental right and a general principle of EU law, is the essence of the right not compromised when the autonomy of the parties is subject to control by competition authorities?[59]

Arguably, the decision in *AGET Iraklis* sees the Court at its most engaged in assessing the arguments for and against the economic and social rights at issue. However, here we must link back to the argument in the preceding section of this chapter concerning the role of the Commission, the Greek creditors and the new economic governance regime. As Markakis has argued, in 'an attempt to bring a dose of realism to the debate', whilst the Court left open the possibility that the Greek law might be saved, and modified to meet the Court's criteria, 'it should not escape our attention that the new law would be drafted by the Greek authorities in cooperation with [its creditors] the European Commission, the ECB, the IMF, and the ESM'; as such, without an authoritative interpretation by the CJEU on the nature of any new mechanism, 'the Greek authorities are likely to succumb to the pressure exerted by the country's lenders to create a more "flexible" labour market'.[60]

Sober realism indeed.

5 Labour rights as human rights?

The preceding section considered some key decisions of the CJEU, where economic freedoms and labour rights intersected, since the entry into force of the Lisbon Treaty, when the EU CFR became a legally binding instrument. In this section, the extent to which conceptualising labour rights as fundamental human rights adds value in terms of achieving adequate protection for workers in EU law is considered.[61]

Mantouvalou outlines three different approaches to examining labour rights as human rights.[62] The positivistic approach sees a fundamental right as being recognised as such when it has been adopted in international treaties or other sources of international law. The instrumental approach looks at the consequences of using strategies, primarily litigation, which promote labour rights as human rights. The third approach is a normative one; the rights in question are seen to have a compelling moral weight and are universal and imperative (implying that such rights are not subordinate to other interests).

In terms of the positivistic view, there are long-standing declarations on the fundamental status of labour rights from the International Labour Organization (ILO) and in the European Convention on Human Rights and Fundamental Freedoms (ECHR). Now, of course, the EU CFR has the same legal status as the Treaties. The Charter explicitly protects the rights of freedom of association (Article 12), the freedom to choose an occupation and the right to engage in work (Article 15) and, in Title IV (Solidarity), the rights to collective bargaining and action (Article 28) and the right to fair and just working conditions (Article 31). There has been an ongoing debate about the extent to which the Charter's new status following Lisbon will impact on the Court's jurisprudence, in particular in the area of labour rights.[63] Chalmers and Trotter note that between 1 December 2009 and 31 December 2014, the Charter has been cited no less than 353 times by the Court of Justice; however, 'scratch beyond these headlines and its transformative effects seem limited'.[64] The picture in the cases discussed previously, and in others such as *Commission v Germany*,[65] and *Palhota*[66]give little indication of a fundamental rethinking of its approach by the Court, notwithstanding some of the comments of the Advocates General in the cases.[67] Indeed, the decision in *Alemo-Herron* forcefully reminds us that some fundamental economic rights, like the freedom to conduct a business in Article 16, also gained an 'upgrade' post-Lisbon.

In terms of EU law, then, and the approach of the Court, it seems that the instrumental appeal to fundamental rights as a defence to attacks on labour standards has failed spectacularly in recent years. The ease with which 'fundamental' rights have been dispensed in order to implement austerity policies has been instructive. However, we may well see an increasing appeal to fundamental human rights arguments in the context of labour law, which might involve, in Langille's formulation, envisaging labour law as a tool to be used to help achieve, ultimately, the 'maximising of human freedom'.[68] This appeal to human rights, though, has been questioned as, first being framed too abstractly ('maximisation of human freedom') to be of practical significant to workers, and, secondly, as a symptom of the labour movement's weakness, rather than a positive programme for the future.[69]

Nonetheless, Jaspers and Roozendaal, whilst concluding that fundamental social rights add value, at best, in a very modest way to worker protection in the EU, note that 'their moral weight should not be underestimated'.[70] This is undoubtedly true, but we cannot leave matters there. The idea of fundamental human rights protection is often discussed at too abstract a level, or in merely symbolic terms. Labour law and policy could (should) be a means of concretising human rights; 'labour law has the potential to bring human rights (declared in a very abstract and general manner and acknowledged by constitutions and many international treaties) into people's everyday lives'.[71] As Doherty notes,

> achieving this would make it much more difficult for such rights to be set aside . . . whenever it is deemed they cannot be afforded. It is here that those seeking to reinforce and defend labour standards, notably, but by no means exclusively, trade union movements, have failed. Labour rights in general, and collective labour rights in particular, simply do not register (certainly in the 'Anglo' world) as 'fundamental'.[72]

However, even if one does not wish to invoke fundamental rights arguments, the 'public relations' battle must be fought and fought harder. A good crisis should never be wasted; the value of labour standards, and how these should be promoted and defended, should be at the centre of debates about the future of the EU project and of the type of social and economic model desired by European workers and citizens.

6 Concluding remarks: norms and rights to agency and institutions

> Failure to protect the pay and conditions of vulnerable workers . . . is unlikely to contribute to social cohesion and popular support for national or international governing institutions in an era of crisis.[73]

Recent political events across the EU, most significantly, of course, the decision of the UK to leave the Union, have done little to suggest the sentiments expressed above are no longer valid. It was in this context that the European Commission published a communication outlining the core principles of a new 'European Pillar of Social Rights' (EPSR),[74] which was 'proclaimed' in November 2017. The EPSR 'lays out a number of principles relevant to the issues discussed in this chapter, for example, 'adequate minimum wages shall be ensured. . . . All wages shall be set in a transparent and predictable way according to national practices and respecting the autonomy of the social partners'.[75] The Pillar also focuses on social dialogue and the need to both encourage the autonomy of the social partners in terms of negotiating and concluding agreements, and encourage their capacity to promote social dialogue.

The precise terms of the ESPR need not detain us long. The Pillar has already come in for significant criticism for being 'embedded in a deep and overarching economic rhetoric in which economic growth appears to be the main goal'.[76] Moreover, as with the Charter, it is unclear what legal effects the ESPR will have;

it would be seem the answer would be virtually none, given that the Union does not have the powers necessary either to give effect to all of its rights and principles, or to adopt measures requiring the Member States to ensure that all the rights and principles are enforceable by those to whom they are directed. The ESPR, then, is really a political, rather than a legal instrument.

The argument in this closing section is that this might not necessarily be a terrible thing. In conclusion, this chapter looks to the roles of actors and institutions, not norms and laws, as providing hope for the greater future reconciliation of the social and the market. Fudge has argued that the lawyer's (natural) preoccupation with norms and values may not be the optimum way to ensure a more effective balancing of economic freedoms and labour rights in the EU. First, she suggests 'there is a tendency to treat the rights contained in (various International instruments) as Platonic Forms, only the expert legal study of which can provide the rest of us, including politicians, with genuine knowledge', an approach which 'ignores the extent to which the meaning of the values embodied in the international and European rights instruments is contested, contingent and provisional'.[77] Secondly, Fudge notes, a key problem with 'a values-based approach to resocializing Europe is that it runs the risk of ignoring the instrumentalities needed to put values to work'.[78]

In this respect, when norms and values are so contested between the EU institutions, between Member States, and between actors in the labour relations spheres, perhaps it is best to focus less on the 'Platonic Forms' and grand ideological debates, and further on the (more mundane) matters of what can be achieved on the ground, within the context of the EU social market economy. So, for example, a robust approach by national and local authorities to the possibilities opened up by the Public Procurement Directives of 2014, which focuses on using taxpayers' money, not in a protectionist manner, but in a manner which enshrines decent labour standards in public contracts.[79]

It surely cannot be inconceivable that competition authorities (national and at EU level) can take greater account of the implications of an overly economistic reading of antitrust rules. As the AG in *FNV Kunsten* demonstrated clearly, competition rules may have to be balanced with legitimate concerns around social dumping, most notably where clear empirical evidence of social dumping can be adduced. As noted earlier, the questions in *FNV Kunsten* will inevitably fall to be decided again in the context of 'gig economy' work. We cannot simply accept that work in the 'gig economy' is outside the scope of labour law regulation; in this respect, we can welcome the recent engagement of the Commission with this issue.[80]

The role of enforcement authorities, at all levels, must also be emphasised. Ford, writing in the context of the UK, has noted 'the current fashion for collateral attacks on substantive worker rights',[81] whereby substantive rights are set down in law, but procedural constraints (costs, delays, etc) render their exercise by workers increasingly difficult. He recounts that there have been developed a range of principles controlling the means by which Member States give proper effect to EU law; this includes the case law of the Court (*Von Colson*), and Articles of the Treaties (Article 19 TEU) and the Charter (Article 47). There is a role here for the EU to re-double efforts to ensure there are no 'rights without remedies', when it comes to labour relations. In this regard, it should be noted that, in September 2017, President Juncker announced, in his State of the Union address, plans to create a common Labour Authority (a new European inspection and enforcement body) noting it is 'absurd to have a Banking Authority to police banking standards, but no common Labour Authority for ensuring fairness in our single market'.[82] Although clearly not a judicial body, this new EU Authority may well provide greater expert guidance on cross-border, and internal, disputes involving labour rights guaranteed under EU Law.

Of course, for a labour lawyer, the key actors (alongside State agencies) are the social partners. Here it is important to flag values and principles. The EU cannot continue to reference 'social dialogue' in key policy documents, where 'it has become unclear what this can mean in the context of the intentional reduction of trade union bargaining power through various means, including prevention of collective action'.[83] This is particularly, as noted previously, where legal restrictions on trade union action come via 'the back door' of the Court's jurisprudence. Therefore, the 'contours and parameters' of what we genuinely mean by collective bargaining and collective action should be the subject of a transparent debate, in the political sphere.[84]

The question framed by Bercusson more than a decade ago remains pertinent:

> Is EU labour law to be constitutionally embedded as the social partners become institutional actors in the EU' s lawmaking and law enforcement processes? Is the social model a central and integral element of European integration? Or is EU labour law a mere adjunct to legal regulation of an internal market in which the social partners are subordinate players in an industrial relations sub-system?[85]

This, of course, is the question with which this volume grapples, in various spheres of EU law. For labour rights, however, it will be actors, agency, and political debate and renewal, rather than legal change, that are likely to determine the answer.

Notes

1 Judy Fudge, 'The Way Forward for Social Europe: How Do We Get There from Here?' (2014) *MLR* 808.
2 Brian Bercusson, *European Labour Law* (CUP, 2009) 5.
3 Paul Davies, 'The Emergence of European Labour Law' in William McCarthy (ed.), *Legal Intervention in Industrial Relations: Gains and Losses* (Blackwell, 1992) 324–325.
4 The chapter will not address Chapter 2 of the Social Policy Title III of the Treaty of Rome on the European Social Fund, the main function of which was 'to improve employment opportunities for workers in the common market'.
5 Catherine Barnard, *The Substantive Law of the EU* (OUP, 2016).
6 Opinion of AG Trabucchi, Case 7/75 *Mr. and Mrs. F.*, ECLI:EU:C:1975:75, para 5.
7 Delia Ferri and Fulvio Cortese, 'Introduction', in this volume.

8 Case 43/75, *Defrenne v. Sabena*, EU:C:1976:56, para 10.
9 Case C-50/96, *Deutsche Telekom AG v. Schroder*, EU:C:2000:72, para. 57 (emphasis added).
10 The need for the Union to achieve in the social, as well as the economic realm, is invoked regularly over the period of its existence; famously, for example, in Jacques Delors's comment that 'you don't fall in love with a Common Market, you need something else', and in Mario Monti, *A New Strategy for the Single Market: At the Service of Europe's Economy and Society* (2010) at <http://ec.europa.eu/internal_market/strategy/docs/monti_report_final_10_05_2010_en.pdf>.
11 For example, Council Directive 75/129/EEC of 17 February 1975 on the approximation of the laws of the Member States relating to collective redundancies [1975] OJ L48/29; and Council Directive 77/187/EEC of 14 February 1977 on the approximation of the laws of the Member States relating to the safeguarding of employees' rights in the event of transfers of undertakings, businesses or parts of undertakings or businesses [1977] OJ L61/26.
12 Bercusson, *European Labour Law* (n 2), at 110.
13 Brian Bercusson, 'Regulatory Competition in the EU System: Labour' in Daniel Esty and Damien Geradin (eds.), *Regulatory Competition and Economic Integration: Comparative Perspectives* (OUP, 2000).
14 For an outline of the development of the social dialogue in the Community, see European Commission, *The Social Dimension of the Internal Market, Interim Report of the Interdepartmental Working Party of the Commission* (1988).
15 Tiziano Treu, 'European Collective Bargaining Levels and Competences of the Social Partners' in Paul Davies *et al.* (eds.), *European Community Labour Law: Principles and Perspectives: Liber Amicorum Lord Wedderburn* (OUP, 1996).
16 Unanimity is required if the directives relate to social security/social protection, dismissal, collective representation/defence of the interests of workers and employers, or the conditions of employment for third country nationals legally residing in Union territory.
17 Directive 2008/104/EC of the European Parliament and of the Council of 18 November 2008 on temporary agency work [2008] OJ L 327/9.
18 Phil Syrpis and Tonia Novitz, 'The EU Internal Market and Domestic Labour Law: Looking Beyond Autonomy' in Alan Bogg *et al.* (eds.), *The Autonomy of Labour Law* (Hart, 2015) 294.
19 Case C-113/89, *Rush Portuguesa*, EU:C:1990:142, para 8.
20 Case C-67/96, *Albany International*, EU:C:1999:430.
21 Case C-438/05, *Viking Line*, ECLI:EU:C:2007:772; Case C-341/05, *Laval*, EU:C:2007:809.
22 Sypris and Novitz, 'The EU Internal Market and Domestic Labour Law' (n 18), at 295.
23 Among many others, Edoardo Ales and Tonia Novitz (eds.), *Collective Action and Fundamental Freedoms in Europe: Striking the Balance* (Intersentia, 2010).
24 Eftychia Achtsioglou and Michael Doherty, 'There Must Be Some Way Out of Here: The Crisis, Labour Rights and Member. States in the Eye of the Storm' (2014) *European Law Journal* 219.
25 *Laval* (n 21), para 107.
26 Tonia Novitz, 'The EU and the Right to Strike: Regulation through the Back Door and Its Impact on Social Dialogue' (2016) *KLJ* 46, at 57.
27 Eleni Balamoti, 'Evaluating the New Rules of EU Economic Governance in Times of Crisis' (2014) *ELLJ* 97.
28 Euro Plus Pact at <www.consilium.europa.eu/uedocs/cms_data/docs/pressdata/en/ec/120296.pdf>.
29 Sonia Bekker and Sonja Klosse, 'Changing Legal Context of Employment Policy Coordination: How do Social Policy Issues Fare after the Crisis?' (2014) *ELLJ* 6.

30 Michael Doherty, 'New Morning? Irish Labour Law Post-Austerity' (2016) *DULJ* 62.
31 Novitz, 'The EU and the Right to Strike: Regulation through the Back Door and Its Impact on Social Dialogue' (n 26), at 47.
32 Michael Doherty, 'When You Ain't Got Nothin', You Got Nothin' to Lose: Union Recognition Laws, Voluntarism and the Anglo Model' (2015) *ILJ* 469.
33 Bill Wedderburn, *The Worker and the Law* (Penguin, 1965).
34 Ruth Dukes, *The Labour Constitution* (OUP, 2014), 2.
35 Simon Deakin and Frank Wilkinson, *The Law of the Labour Market* (OUP, 2005).
36 There are, of course, many other areas that could be considered here: public procurement law and company law spring immediately to mind; Michael Doherty, 'Back to the Future of EU Labour Law' (2014) *KLJ* 467.
37 Case C-426/11, *Alemo-Herron v Parkwood Leisure Ltd*, EU:C:2013:521.
38 Council Directive 2001/23/EC of 12 March 2001 on the approximation of the laws of the Member States relating to the safeguarding of employees' rights in the event of transfers of undertakings, businesses or parts of undertakings or businesses [2001] OJ L82/16.
39 *Alemo-Herron* (n 38), para 35.
40 See *infra* Andreas Heinemann, 'Social Considerations in EU Competition Law', in this volume, section 4.2.
41 On the 'fallacy of labour markets' see Dagmar Schiek *et al.*, *EU Social and Labour Rights and EU Internal Market Law: Study for the EMPL Committee* at <www.europarl.europa.eu/RegData/etudes/STUD/2015/563457/IPOL_STU(2015)563457_EN.pdf> at 40.
42 Case C-413/13, *FNV Kunsten Informatie en Media*, ECLI:EU:C:2014:2215, para 33.
43 *Albany* (n 20).
44 *FNV Kunsten* (n 42).
45 Ibid., paras 27–28.
46 Ibid., paras 31–32. The factors to be considered in establishing 'false' self-employment would include the extent to which the worker acts under the direction of another; whether the worker shares in the employer's commercial risks, and whether, for the duration of the relationship, the worker forms an integral part of the employer's undertaking (para 36).
47 Ibid., paras 74–79.
48 Case C-201/15, *AGET Iraklis*, EU:C:2016:972.
49 Ibid., para 57.
50 Ibid., para 66.
51 Ibid., paras 96–97.
52 Ibid., para 108.
53 Ferri and Cortese 'Introduction' (n 7), in this volume.
54 *AGET Iraklis* (n 48), para 76.
55 Ibid., para 78.
56 Ibid., para 84.
57 Ibid., para 85.
58 The case involved quite traditional employment (musicians); the application of the reasoning in the context of 'gig economy' work cannot be far away. See Jermias Prassl, *Humans as a Service* (OUP, 2018).
59 Schiek *et al. EU Social and Labour Rights and EU Internal Market Law: Study for the EMPL Committee* (n 47), 41.
60 Menelaos Markakis, 'Can Governments Control Mass Layoffs by Employers? Economic Freedoms vs Labour Rights' at <http://eulawanalysis.blogspot.ie/2017/01/case-c-20115-aget-iraklis-can.html>.

61 Teun Jaspers and Willemijn Roozendaal, 'Fundamental Social Rights: An Added Value to the Protection of Workers' in Marc Rigaux, Jan Buelens and Amanda Latinne (eds.), *From Labour Law to Social Competition Law?* (Intersentia, 2014).
62 Virginia Mantouvalou, 'Are Labour Rights Human Rights?' (2012) *European Law Journal* 151.
63 See, for example, Sybe de Vries, 'Balancing Fundamental Rights with Economic Freedoms According to the European Court of Justice' (2013) *Utrecht Law Review* 169.
64 Damian Chalmers and Sarah Trotter, 'Fundamental Rights and Legal Wrongs: The Two Sides of the Same EU Coin' (2016) *European Law Journal* 9, at 9.
65 Case C-271/08, *Commission v Germany*, EU:C:2010:183.
66 Case C-515/08, *dos Santos Palhota and Others*, EU:C:2010:589.
67 Phil Syrpis, 'Reconciling Economic Freedoms and Social Rights: The Potential of Commission v Germany (Case C-271/08, Judgment of 15 July 2010)' (2011) *ILJ* 222.
68 Brian Langille, 'Labour Law's Theory of Justice' in Guy Davidov and Brian Langille (eds.), *The Idea of Labour Law* (OUP, 2011) 114.
69 Doherty, 'Back to the Future of EU Labour Law' (n 36).
70 Teun Jaspers and Willemijn Roozendaal, 'Fundamental Social Rights: An Added Value to the Protection of Workers' in Marc Rigaux, Jan Buelens and Amanda Latinne (eds.), *From Labour Law to Social Competition Law?* (Intersentia, 2014) 107, at 122.
71 Barbara Kresal, 'Mutating or Dissolving Labour Law?' in Marc Rigaux, Jan Buelens and Amanda Latinne (eds.), *From Labour Law to Social Competition Law?* (Intersentia, 2014) 149–160, at 151.
72 Doherty, 'Back to the Future of EU Labour Law' (n 36), at 472.
73 Michael Doherty, 'Battered and Fried? Regulation of Working Conditions and Wage-Setting after the John Grace Decision' (2012) *DULJ* 97, at 120.
74 Communication from the European Commission, 'Establishing a European Pillar of Social Rights', COM(2017)250. The text of the Pillar prclaimed in November 2017 is available at <https://ec.europa.eu/commission/priorities/deeper-and-fairer-economic-and-monetary-union/european-pillar-social-rights_en>.
75 Section 6.
76 Klaus Lörcher and Isabelle Schömann, *The European Pillar of Social Rights: Critical Legal Analysis and Proposals* (ETUI, 2017) 18.
77 Fudge, 'The Way Forward for Social Europe: How Do We Get There from Here?' (n 1), at 815.
78 Ibid., at 817.
79 Doherty, 'New Morning? Irish Labour Law Post-Austerity' (n 30). On the social elements of public procurement see Christopher Bovis, 'The Social Dimension of EU Public Procurement and the "Social Market Economy"', in this volume.
80 Proposal for a Directive of the European Parliament and of the Council on transparent and predictable working conditions in the European Union COM/2017/0797.
81 Michael Ford, 'The Effect of Brexit on Workers' Rights' (2016) *KLJ* 398, at 409.
82 President Juncker's State of the Union Address 2017 at <http://europa.eu/rapid/press-release_SPEECH-17-3165_en.htm>.
83 Novitz, 'The EU and the Right to Strike: Regulation through the Back Door and Its Impact on Social Dialogue' (n 26), at 47.
84 Ibid.
85 Bercusson, *European Labour Law* (n 2), at 25.

6 The social dimension of EU public procurement and the 'social market economy'

Christopher Bovis

1 Introduction

The strategic importance of public procurement for the European integration process has been recognised by the 2011 Single Market Act[1] which has prompted a series of reforms to the European Union (EU) Public Procurement acquis.[2] These reforms aim at linking directly public procurement with the European 2020 Strategy, which focuses on growth and competitiveness. Hence, after 2011, the importance of a liberalised and integrated public procurement as an essential component of the single market has been clearly established.[3]

The conceptual origins of public procurement regulation in the EU can be traced in policy instruments which identified purchasing practices of Member States as considerable non-tariff barriers and as hindering factors for the functioning of a genuinely competitive internal market.[4] Economic justifications for regulating public procurement have pointed towards introducing competitiveness into the relevant markets in order to increase cross-border trade of products and services destined for the public sector and to achieve price transparency and price convergence across the EU, thus achieving significant savings.[5] The need for competitiveness and transparency in public procurement markets is also considered as a safeguard to fundamental Treaty principles,[6] such as the free movement of goods and services, the right of establishment and the prohibition of discrimination on grounds of nationality.[7]

Against this background this chapter aims to explore the intrinsic links of public procurement regulation with the implementation of social policy objectives in the Member States and offer insights to the dimension of public procurement as an indissoluble component of the 'social market economy' in the EU. The chapter is structured as follows. Section 2 offers a critical exposition to the structure and characteristics of the regulation of public procurement. Section 3 advances the discourse to the option for externalisation of public services and the ensuing outcomes for the public sector of EU Member States. Section 4 leads to the exposition of the connection of public services and their delivery with the regulation of public procurement. Section 5 offers a critical disposition of the underpinning ordoliberal approach to public procurement regulation as the conduit of its connection with the 'social market economy' in the EU. Section 6 concludes the analysis and synthesises the arguments made to provide evidence of the social dimension of public procurement regulation in the EU and its links with 'social market economy'.

2 The structure and nature of public procurement regulation

The current public procurement acquis[8] has prescribed a different regulatory treatment to public sector procurement and utilities procurement, for two reasons. Firstly, a more relaxed regime for utilities procurement, irrespective of their public or privatised ownership, has been justified and accepted as a result of the positive effects of liberalisation of network industries which has stimulated sectoral competitiveness.[9] Secondly, a codified set of rules, covering supplies, works and services procurement in a single legal instrument for the public sector aims at producing legal efficiency, simplification and compliance in order to achieve the opening up of the relatively closed and segmented public sector procurement markets. A decentralised dimension of the public procurement rules has been introduced by the procurement Remedies Directives.[10]

Public procurement regulation has an introvert focus on the internal market. It envisages bringing the respective behaviour of the public sector in parallel to the operation of private markets. Public procurement regulation reveals distinctive *sui generis* markets which function within the EU internal market and have as main feature the pursuit of public interest.[11] They are referred to as 'public markets' where the pursuit of public interest is the main behavioural driver. Further variances distinguish public markets from private markets apart from the substitution of profit maximisation.[12] These focus on structural elements, competitiveness, demand and supply conditions, pricing and risk.

Public procurement regulation relies on harmonisation, through Directives, as legal instruments, which have been utilised to provide the framework of the *acquis communautaire*, but at the same time afford the necessary discretion to the Member States as to the forms and methods of their implementation. By allowing for discretion to Member States, an element of public policy is inserted in public procurement regulation, which reveals ordoliberal policy inferences and decentralised features. Competition regulation, on the other hand, is enacted through the principle of uniformity, utilising directly applicable regulations, and possesses a corrective character,[13] whereas public procurement regulation has a convergence character. The corrective character of competition policy aid aims at restoring competitive market equilibria, while the convergence character of public procurement regulation aims at adjustment towards behavioural norms. To that extent, the Single Market Act[14] identified public procurement as an essential component of competitiveness and growth and as an indispensable instrument in delivering public services[15] in the EU.

The public procurement acquis has prescribed a different regulatory treatment to public sector procurement and utilities procurement, for two reasons. Firstly, a more relaxed regime for utilities procurement, irrespective of their public or privatised ownership has been justified and accepted as a result of the positive effects of liberalisation of network industries which has stimulated sectoral competitiveness.[16] Secondly, a codified set of rules, covering supplies, works and services procurement in a single legal instrument for the public sector aims at producing legal efficiency, simplification and compliance in order to achieve the opening up of the relatively closed and segmented public sector procurement markets. A decentralised enforcement of the public procurement rules has been introduced by the procurement Remedies Directive,[17] introducing a clear divide between pre-contractual and post-contractual stages, a balance between effective review of public contracts and need of efficient public procurement, a strict standstill requirement for contract conclusion, including direct awards by contracting authorities and extensive communication and monitoring requirements.

The axiomatic assumption is that public procurement serves as negation agent to State aid and competition regulation. The presence of public procurement is a safeguard of the internal market in as much as the transfer of public financial resources to private or public undertakings in a contractual format or in any other format is not deemed as state aid when and where public procurement rules are followed. Public procurement is deemed as a market calibration exercise in the relations between public and private sectors for two reasons: the competitive process in the engagement of the private sector and the justification of such engagement through contract award criteria.

The Court's jurisprudence has influenced the interpretation of public procurement legal concepts such as contracting authorities,[18] the remit of selection and qualification criteria,[19] and the parameters for contracting authorities to use environmental and social considerations[20] as award criteria.[21]

3 The externalisation dilemma of public services

Traditionally the role of the State has been as the conduit for providing public services.[22] The term 'public services', which often refers to services that are offered to the general public, highlights that a service has been assigned a specific role in the public interest, or refers to the ownership or status of the entity providing the service. In the latter situation, public service fuses with the concept of 'public sector', which covers the State and its organs, bodies governed by public law and undertakings controlled by public authorities.

Two models for the treatment and regulation of public services have been developed based on different theoretical and conceptual values. One model theorises that public services capture the general needs of the public and are delivered through market-based mechanisms, whereby the public sector interfaces or competes with private sector undertakings; by contrast, other models describe public services as being essential facilities (for example defence, policing) which should be sheltered from competition in order to ensure the integrity of their delivery.[23]

The public interest task conferred on a contracting authority might ultimately be carried out by resources external to the contracting authority. This can be the case where the competence for the given public task is transferred, as such, to another public authority. The performance of a given task may also be entrusted to another entity altogether. This may be done 1) without establishing contractual links, 2) by calling on another contracting authority, which enjoys an exclusive right or 3) through joint procurement with other contracting authorities or through central purchasing bodies. Legal competence for a public task could be understood as the exclusive obligation and right to fulfil the task by an entity's own administrative, technical or other means, or even by calling upon external entities. The term 'competence' for a given public task includes the official authority necessary to establish the regulatory framework for fulfilling the task at the level of the authority concerned.

4 The notion of public services and its link to procurement regulation

The term public service often refers to a service that is offered to the general public, or highlights that a service has been assigned a specific role in the public interest, or refers to the ownership or status of the entity providing the service. In the latter situation, public service fuses with the concept of public sector which covers the state and its organs, bodies governed by public law and undertakings controlled by public authorities. Two models for the treatment of public services have been developed, based on different theoretical and conceptual values. On the one hand, public services which capture general needs of the public are delivered through market-based mechanisms where the public sector interfaces or competes with private sector undertakings. This model is based on Art 106 TFEU, sectoral primary and secondary legislation, as well as State aid rules. On the other hand, public services which are described as essential facilities (for example defence, policing) should be sheltered from competition in order to ensure the integrity of their delivery.[24] The provision of these types of public services is the prerogative of the State and not affected by the thrust of EU law.[25]

Although the term public services does not feature in the *acquis communautaire* relevant to Article 106 TFEU, surrogate concepts have attributed in constructing a notion where the State is expected or even obliged[26] to enter the marketplace in order to deliver directly or organise the delivery of public services. These surrogate concepts are reflected in the terms of 'public service obligations' and 'universal service obligations', which have supported the liberalisation process of sectoral policies of the EU.[27] The term public service obligations refers to specific quality and price requirements that are imposed by public authorities on the provider of the service in order to ensure that certain public interest objectives applicable at Community, national or regional level are met.[28] The term 'universal service obligations' denotes contractual or regulatory requirements imposed by public authorities upon undertakings with a view to maintaining regularity and affordability[29] in the provision of the relevant services.[30] Alongside public service obligations and universal service obligations, Art 106(2) TFEU has introduced the term of Services of General Economic Interest (SGEI), a term which its significance has been augmented by virtue of Article 16 TFEU. As highlighted by Piernas Lopez in this volume,[31] the term services of general economic interest is not defined further in the Treaty or in secondary legislation. The term refers to services of an economic nature which the Member States or the EU subject to specific public service obligations or universal service obligations by virtue of a general interest criterion. Thus, SGEI cover services provided by utilities or network industries such as transport, water, postal services, energy and communications but also extend to any other economic activities which may be subject to public service obligations.

It is the absolute discretion of public authorities to decide whether to provide a service themselves or to entrust it to a third party by means of contractual externalisation. The public procurement rules only apply if the public authority decides to externalise the service provision by entrusting it to a third party against remuneration.

One of the fundamental characteristics of public services is their economic nature. The funding of public services, which may emerge through different formats such as payment or remuneration under a contract, payment of annual subsidies, preferential fiscal treatment or lower social security contributions to an entrusted undertaking, reveals such a characteristic. This means that public services have a cost and a value attached to them. Cost reflects upon capital considerations, whereas value reflects upon revenue considerations. Even the provision of SGEI[32] which include health services, long-term care, social security, employment services and social housing is compatible with their economic character assessment.[33]

However, public services lack industrial or commercial character. The non-commercial or industrial character of a service[34] is a necessary criterion intended to clarify needs in the general interest. However, there might be needs of general interest, which have an industrial and commercial character and that it is also possible private undertakings can meet needs of general interest, which do not have industrial and commercial character. Nevertheless, the test for needs in the general interest which do not possess industrial or commercial character is that the state or other public authorities choose themselves to meet these needs or to have a decisive influence over their provision. In parallel, it is assumed that if an activity which meets general needs is pursued in a competitive environment, there is a strong indication that it possesses commercial characteristics.[35] The absence of commerciality from a public service or the absence of competitive forces within the markets it is delivered represents a strong indication of the *sui generis* marketplace public services are delivered or organised. The first implication of such nature is the non-applicability of general competition law. In addition to the provisions of Art 106 TFEU, sector specific regulation has removed the treatment of financing public services from the general provisions of competition law and placed it within the state aid regime.[36] Furthermore, the *sui generis* nature of public service markets provide the conceptual bridge to engage the public procurement regime as a guardian of the principles of accountability and transparency in the delivery of services of 'general interest having non industrial or commercial character'.[37]

5 The ordoliberal approach to public procurement regulation

5.1 Harmonisation of laws and regulatory flexibility

As mentioned earlier, harmonisation has been entrusted to carry the progress of public procurement regulation. Directives, as legal instruments, have been utilised to provide the framework of the *acquis communautaire*, but at the same time afford the necessary discretion to the Member States as to the forms and methods of their implementation. This is where the first deviation from the traditional economic approach of public procurement occurs. Antitrust law and policy is enacted through the principle of uniformity across the internal market, utilising directly applicable regulations. By allowing for discretion to the Member States, an element of public policy is inserted in the equation, which often has decentralised features. Traditionally, discretion afforded by Directives takes into account national particularities and sensitivities as well as the readiness of domestic administrations to implement the acquis within a certain deadline. In addition, individuals, who are also subjects of the rights and duties envisaged by the Directives, do not have access to justices, unless provisions of Directives produce direct effect.

However, the public policy dimension of public procurement regulation is not exhausted in the nature of the legal instruments of the regime. The genuine connection of an ordoliberal perspective[38] with public procurement regulation is reflected in the award criterion relating to the most economically advantageous offer. The public sector can award contracts by reference to 'qualitative' criteria, in conjunction with price, and thus can legitimately deviate from the strict price competition environment set by the lowest offer criterion.[39] There are three themes emanating from such approach: one reflects on public procurement as a complementary tool of the European integration process; the second regards public procurement as an instrument of contract compliance; last, the ordoliberal perspective can reveal a rule of reason in public procurement, where the integration of public markets in the EU serves as a conveyer belt of common policies, such as environmental policy, consumer policy, social policy, industrial policy and takes into account a flexible and wider view of national and community priorities, and a type of 'European public policy'.

5.2 The award criteria as a vehicle to promote social considerations

Historically, two criteria laid down in the public procurement Directives provide the conditions under which contracting authorities award public contracts: the lowest price or the most economically advantageous offer.

The first criterion indicates that, subject to the qualitative criteria and financial and economic standing, contracting authorities do not rely on any other factor than the price quoted to complete the contract. The tenderer who submits the cheapest offer must be awarded the contract. It should be mentioned that the Directives provide for an automatic disqualification of an 'obviously abnormally low offer', subject to the requirement imposed upon contracting authorities to examine the details of the tender before deciding the award of the contract. The contracting authorities are under duty to seek from the tenderer an explanation for the price submitted or to inform him that his tender appears to be abnormally low and to allow a reasonable time within which to submit further details, before making any decision as to the award of the contract.

The meaning of the most economically advantageous offer includes a series of factors chosen by the contracting authority, including price, delivery or completion date, running costs, cost-effectiveness, profitability, technical merit, product or work quality, aesthetic and functional characteristics, after-sales service and technical assistance, commitments with regard to spare parts and components and maintenance costs, security of supplies. This list is not exhaustive and the factors listed therein serve as a guideline for contracting authorities in the weighted evaluation process of the contract award. The Court reiterated the flexible and wide interpretation of the relevant award criterion[40] and had no difficulty in declaring that contracting authorities may use the most economically advantageous offer as award criterion by choosing the factors which they want to apply in evaluating tenders,[41] provided these factors are mentioned, in hierarchical order or descending sequence in the invitation to tender or the contract documents,[42] so tenderers and interested parties can clearly ascertain the relative weight of factors other than price for the evaluation process. However, factors, which have no strict relevance in determining the most economically advantageous offer by reference to objective criteria do involve an element of arbitrary choice and therefore should be considered as incompatible with the Directives.[43]

The most economically advantageous offer as an award criterion has provided the CJEU for the opportunity to balance the economic considerations of public procurement with policy choices. Although in numerous instances the Court has maintained the importance of the economic approach[44] to the regulation of public sector contracts, it has also recognised the relative discretion of contracting authorities to utilise non-economic considerations as award criteria. In *Beentjes*,[45] the Court ruled that social policy considerations, and in particular measures aiming at the combating of long-term unemployment, could only be part of the award criteria of public contracts, especially in cases where the most economically advantageous offer is selected. The CJEU accepted that the latter award criterion contains features that are not exhaustively defined in the Directives, therefore there is discretion conferred on contracting authorities to specify what would the most economically advantageous offer for them. However, contracting authorities cannot refer to such measures as a selection criterion and disqualify candidates, which could not meet the relevant requirements. The selection of tenderers is a process, which is based on an exhaustive list of technical and financial requirements expressly stipulated in the relevant Directives and the insertion of contract compliance as a selection and qualification requirement would be considered *ultra vires*. The Court held that a contractual condition relating to the employment of long-term unemployed persons is compatible with the public procurement Directives, if it has no direct or indirect discriminatory effect on tenders from other Member States. Furthermore, such a contractual condition must be mentioned in the tender notice.[46] Rejection of a contract on the grounds of a contractor's inability to employ long-term unemployed persons has no relation to the checking of the contractors' suitability on the basis of their economic and financial standing and their technical knowledge and ability. The Court maintained that measures relating to employment could be utilised as a feature of the award criteria, only when they are part of a contractual obligation of the public contract in question and on condition that they do not run contrary to the fundamental principles of the Treaty. The significance of that qualification has revealed the Court's potential stance over the issue of contract compliance in public procurement.

In *Nord-pas-de-Calais*, the Court considered whether a condition linked to a local project to combat unemployment could be considered as an award criterion of the relevant contract. The Commission alleged that the French Republic had infringed the procurement rules by referring to the criterion linked to the campaign against unemployment as an award criterion in some of the disputed contract notices. The Court held that the most economically advantageous offer does not preclude all possibility for the contracting authorities to use as a criterion a condition linked to the campaign against unemployment provided that that condition is consistent with all the fundamental principles of EU law, in particular the principle of non-discrimination deriving from the provisions of the Treaty on the right of establishment and the freedom to provide services.[47] Furthermore, even if such a criterion is not in itself incompatible with public procurement rules, it must be applied in conformity with all the procedural rules laid down in that directive, in particular the rules on advertising.[48] The Court therefore accepted the employment considerations as an award criterion, part of the most economically advantageous offer, provided it is consistent with the fundamental principles of EU law, in particular the principle of non-discrimination and it is advertised in the contract notice.

5.3 *Public procurement as part of the horizontal policies of EU integration*

Procurement rules and the public markets do not operate in a vacuum. Irrespective of the often publicised nature of public procurement as the most significant non-tariff barrier for the functioning of the internal market and the clinical presentation of the arguments in favour of an integrated public market across the EU, public purchasing is indissolubly linked with national policies and priorities.[49] In the history of European economic integration, public procurement has been an important part of the Member States' industrial policies. It has been utilised as a policy tool[50] in order to support indigenous suppliers and contractors and preserve national industries and the related workforce.

There has been a great deal of controversy over the issue of the compatibility of preferential procurement with EU law. Preference schemes have been linked with regional development policies, a fact that indicates the close interplay between public procurement and State aids.[51] Protectionist public procurement practices, when strategically exercised, has resulted in the evolution of vital industries for the state in question.[52] The sustainability of 'national champions' has brought about benefits for a sector or an industry, which, when protected from competition in the short-run, managed to achieve specialisation and internationalisation.

Preferential public procurement reveals a double dimension. Firstly, it appears in the form of an exercise which aims at preserving some domestic sectors or industries at the expense of the principles of the European integration process. In such format, there is obviously no exit plan. Impact assessment studies undertaken by the European Commission showed that the operation of preference schemes had a minimal effect on the economies of the regions where they had been applied, both in terms of the volume of procurement contracts, as well as in terms of real economic growth attributed to the operation of such schemes. Thus, in such format, preferential public procurement perpetuates the sub-optimal allocation of resources and represents a welfare loss for the economy of the relevant State. On the other hand, preferential purchasing in the format of strategic investment to the sustainability of selected industries might represent a viable instrument of industrial policy, to the extent that the infant industry, when specialised and internationalised, would be in a position to counterbalance any welfare losses during its protected period. In the above form, preferential public procurement, as an integral part of industrial policy could possibly result in welfare gains.

Although the utilisation of public procurement as a tool of regional development policy in the form of State aids may breach directly or indirectly primary Treaty provisions on free movement of goods, the right of establishment and the freedom to provide services, it is far from clear whether the European Commission or the Court could accept the legitimate use of public procurement as a means of State aid. Prior notification to the European Commission of the measures or policies intended to be used as State aid does not, apparently, legitimise such measures and absolve them from the well-established framework of the four freedoms. The parallel applicability of rules relating to State aid and the free movement of goods, in the sense that national measures conceived as State aid must not violate the principle of free movement of goods, renders the thrust of regional policies through State aid practically ineffective. It appears that the Court of Justice has experimented with the question of the compatibility between State aids and free movement of goods in a number of cases where, initially, it was held that the two regimes are mutually exclusive, to the extent that the principle of free movement of goods could not apply to measures relating to State aid.[53] The acid test for such mutual exclusivity was the prior notification of such measures to the European Commission. However, the Court departed from such a position, when it applied free movement of goods provisions to a number of cases concerning State aid, which had not been notified to the Commission.[54] Surprisingly, the Court also brought notified State aid measures under the remit of the provision of free movement of goods and reconsidered the whole framework of their mutual exclusivity.[55]

Preferential procurement does contradict directly the fundamental principles of free movement of goods and services. However, the notification of Member States' intention to utilise it as a form of State aid aims to move the focus of potential disputes towards the antitrust remit of the acquis. Two reasons seem to support the above assumption. Firstly, the public procurement legal framework is positively in favour of strategic subcontracting.[56] The nomination of regional or national firms in the award process of public contracts under such premises could, legitimately, elevate preferential procurement as an instrument of industrial policy. This might shift the debate from the potential violation of internal market provisions towards the overall compatibility of the regime with national or EU-wide industrial policies, thus positioning preferential public procurement in the remit of antitrust. Secondly, there is a fundamental change in perceptions about the role and responsibilities expected from governments in delivering public services. The public sector not only initiates and facilitates the delivery of public services, but also can actively be involved in the actual delivery process. Such changes, in practical terms viewed through the evolution of public-private partnerships,[57] are translated into a new contractual interface between public and private sectors,[58] which in turn encapsulates an era of contractualised governance.

5.4 Contract compliance and public procurement

The most economically advantageous offer as an award criterion has provided the Court with the opportunity to balance the economic considerations of public procurement with policy choices. Although in numerous instances the Court has maintained the importance of the economic approach[59] to the regulation of public sector contracts, it has also recognised the relative discretion of contracting authorities to utilise non-economic considerations as award criteria.

The term contract compliance[60] could be best defined as the range of secondary policies relevant to public procurement, which aim at combating discrimination on grounds of sex, race, religion or disability.[61] When utilised in public contracts, contract compliance is a system whereby, unless the supply side (the industry) complies with certain conditions relating to social policy measures, contracting authorities can lawfully exclude tenderers from selection, qualification and award procedures. The concept is well-known and practised in North American jurisdictions and, in particular, in the United States,[62] as it has been in operation for some time in an attempt to reduce racial and ethnic minority inequalities in the market and to achieve equilibrium in the workforce market.

The potential of public purchasing as a tool capable of promoting social policies has been met with considerable scepticism.[63] Policies relevant to affirmative action or positive discrimination have caused a great deal of controversy, as they practically accomplish very little in rectifying labour market equilibria. In addition to the practicality and effectiveness of such policies, serious reservations have been expressed with regard to their constitutionality,[64] since they could limit, actually and potentially, the principles of economic freedom and freedom of transactions.

Contract compliance legislation and policy is familiar to most European member states, although the enactment of public procurement Directives has changed the situation dramatically.[65] The position of EU institutions on contract compliance has been addressed in three instances before the CJEU.[66] The Court maintained that contract compliance with reference to domestic or local employment cannot be used as a selection criterion in tendering procedures for the award of public contracts. The selection of tenderers is a process which is based on an exhaustive list of technical and financial requirements expressly stipulated in the relevant Directives and the insertion of contract compliance as a selection and qualification requirement would be considered *ultra vires*. The Court ruled that social policy considerations can only be part of award criteria in public procurement, and especially in cases where the most economically advantageous offer is selected, provided that they do not run contrary to the basic principles of the Treaty and that have been mentioned in the tender notice.

The Court's approach has also opened an interesting debate on the integral dimensions of contract compliance and the differentiation between the 'positive' and 'negative' approaches. The concept of positive approach within contract compliance encompasses all measures and policies imposed by contracting authorities on tenderers as suitability criteria for their selection in public procurement contracts. Such positive action measures and policies intend to complement the actual objectives of public procurement which are confined in economic and financial parameters and are based on a transparent and predictable legal background.[67] Although the complementarity of contract compliance with the actual aims and objectives of the public procurement regime was acknowledged, the Court (and the European Commission) were reluctant in accepting such an overflexible interpretation of the Directives and based on the literal interpretation of the relevant provisions disallowed positive actions of a social policy dimension as part of the selection criteria for tendering procedures in public procurement.

However, contract compliance can not only incorporate unemployment considerations, but also promote equality of opportunities and eliminate sex or race discrimination in the relevant market.[68] Indeed, the Directives on public procurement stipulate that the contracting authority may require tenderers to observe national provisions of employment legislation when they submit their offers. The ability to observe and conform to national employment laws in a Member state may constitute a ground of disqualification and exclusion of the defaulting firm from public procurement contracts.[69] In fact, under such interpretation, contract compliance may be a factor of selection criteria specified in the directives, as it contains a 'negative approach' to legislation and measures relating to social policy.

There are arguments in favour and against incorporating social policy considerations in public procurement.[70] The most important argument in favour focuses on the ability of public procurement to promote parts of the Member States' social policy, with particular reference to long-term unemployment, equal distribution of income, social exclusion and the protection of minorities. Under such a positively oriented approach, public purchasing could be regarded as an instrument of policy in the hands of national administrations with a view to rectifying social equilibria. Contract compliance in public procurement could also cancel the stipulated aims and objectives of the liberalisation of the public sector. The regulation of public markets focuses on economic considerations and competition. Adherence to social policy factors could derail the whole process, as the public sector will pay more for its procurement by extra or hidden cost for the implementation of contract compliance in purchasing policies.[71]

Member States can require tenderers and their subcontractors to undertake the obligation to pay staff the minimum wage laid down in the relevant domestic legislation, and in the event that these tenderers or their subcontractors refuse to undertake such obligation,[72] their exclusion from participation in the procedure for the award of a public contract can be justified.[73] However, tenderers cannot be put under a requirement to pay their subcontractors the minimum wage which is stipulated by domestic legislation if those subcontractors are established in a different Member State.[74]

5.5 *A rule of reason in the social dimension of public procurement*

In EU law, the rule of reason serves as an expansion of the determined exemptions from a prohibition principle.[75] The rule of reason is a juridical development where the Court interprets the margins of discretion allotted to an executive authority (Member States and/or the Commission), as well as the grounds, the limits and the levels of deviation from a prohibition's exemptions. For public procurement, a rule of reason has emerged through the application of the most economically advantageous offer criterion. The Court, through a steady accumulation of case law adopted a bi-focal stance: positive yet restrictive. Where the rules allow for discretion, the Court did not claw back any margin of appreciation from Member States and their contracting authorities; in fact, in many instances, it gradually expanded the grounds of flexibility in the award procedures.

The meaning of the most economically advantageous offer includes a series of factors chosen by the contracting authority, including price, delivery or completion date, running costs, cost-effectiveness, profitability, technical merit, product or work quality, aesthetic and functional characteristics, after-sales service and technical assistance, commitment with regard to spare parts and components and maintenance costs, and security of supplies. This list is not exhaustive and the factors listed therein serve as a guideline for contracting authorities in the weighted evaluation process of the contract award.

The Court reiterated the flexible and wide interpretation of the relevant award criterion[76] and had no difficulty in declaring that contracting authorities may use the most economically advantageous offer as award criterion by choosing the factors which they want to apply in evaluating tenders,[77] provided these factors are mentioned, in hierarchical order or descending sequence in the invitation to tender or the contract documents,[78] so tenderers and interested parties can clearly ascertain the relative weight of factors other than price for the evaluation process. However, factors which have no strict relevance in determining the most economically advantageous offer by reference to objective criteria do involve an element of arbitrary choice and therefore should be considered as incompatible with the public procurement Directives.[79]

A question arises whether, under the most economically advantageous offer, each individual award factor has to provide an economic advantage which directly benefits the contracting authority, or it is sufficient that each individual factor has to be measurable in economic terms, without the requirement that it directly provides an economic advantage for the contracting authority in the given contract. This question intends to assess the integral function of the factors that comprise the most economically advantageous offer for contracting authorities. Although there is wide discretion conferred to them in compiling the relevant factors, subject to the requirements of relevance to the contract in question and their publicity, their relative importance, in economic terms, remains somehow unknown.

If the second interpretation were accepted, the discretion conferred to contracting authorities would permit a wide range of factors to feature as part of award criteria in public contracts, without the need to demonstrate a direct economic advantage to a contracting authority which is attributable to each of these factors. On the contrary, if each individual factor has to establish a measurable (in quantifiable terms) economic advantage to the contracting authority, which is directly attributed to its inclusion as part of the award criterion, the discretion of contracting authorities is curtailed, since they would be required to undertake and publicise in the tender or contract documents a clear cost-benefit analysis of the relevant factors that comprise in their view the most economically advantageous offer.

There are two instances where the rule of reason as applied in public procurement brought the relevant regime in line with European policy. The first is the case of transfer of undertakings, where the Court expanded the remit of the Acquired Rights Directive to the public procurement contractual relations.[80] The second instance is the permissibility of environmental factors[81] as part of the award criteria for public contract and the explicit recognition of the environmental policy of the EU as being complementary to all legal and policy activities of the internal market.

The latter development reveals also the importance of public procurement in relation to harmonisation and even standardisation of national policies. Public procurement in such cases serves as a conveyer belt for transferring homogenous legal or policy standards across the internal market.[82] The protection of the environment as an award criterion in public contracts is a classic example of the potential of public procurement regulation as an instrument of public policy. There will be instances in the future where positive integration will be required by EU institutions and Member States equally in areas such as social security, business ethics and anti-corruption policies. Harmonisation of laws and policies within the common market has traditionally sought a common denominator amongst divergences and differences of national administrations. Under an ordoliberal approach, the rule of reason seems an essential tool to convey effectively rights and obligations of EU law.

6 Conclusions

There is an infant attempt to install a modality of strategy and social consideration across the EU for the delivery of public services. The symbiotic relation of public procurement with the social policy of the internal market reveals the commonality of regulatory features inherent to the notion of the public services. The notion of public service in its incarnations is pivotal for the applicability of public procurement regulation. The symbiosis also reveals the flexibility embedded in the public procurement acquis which is translated as discretion conferred to contracting authorities to introduce social policy considerations in dispersing public services. In parallel to the flexibility of public procurement, State aid regulation projects flexibility either as regional development considerations, or as part of a national of EU-wide industrial policy.

The social dimension of public procurement is in direct contrast with the economic approach of its regulation. Productivity rises, competitiveness, industrial restructuring exercises, privatisation, employment relations, taxation and corporate governance are mere examples of the features which the EU and its Member States will be facing under the auspices of the Europe 2020 Strategy. Public procurement will play a pivotal role in carrying over the European legal and policy standards of growth into national systems and as such, its social could be diluted in favour of a neoliberal approach, which is based on the costs in public sector as well as the latter's relation with private sector actors in delivering public services.

Notes

1 Communication from the European Commission, 'Europe 2020: A Strategy for Smart, Sustainable and Inclusive Growth', COM(2010)2020.
2 European Commission, 'Green Paper on the Modernization of EU Public Procurement Policy: Towards a More Efficient European Procurement Market', COM(2011)15/47.
3 Communication from the European Commission, 'Towards a Single Market Act', COM(2010)608.
4 European Commission, 'White Paper for the Completion of the Internal Market', COM(1985)310; European Commission, 'Green Paper on Public Procurement in the European Union: Exploring the Way Forward', COM(96)583; Communication from the European Commission, 'Public Procurement in the European Union', COM(98)143.
5 Commission of the European Communities, 'The Cost of Non-Europe in Public Sector Procurement' in *The Cost of Non-Europe, Basic Findings, Vol. 5 Part A* (Official Publications of the European Communities, 1988); Paolo Cecchini, *1922, the European Challenge: The Benefits of a Single Market* (Wildwood House, 1988).
6 Cases C-223/99 and C-260/99, *Excelsior*, EU:C:2001:259; Case C-360/96, *Gemeente Arnhem Gemeente Rheden*, EU:C:1998:525; Case C-44/96, *Mannesmann Anlangenbau*, EU:C:1998:4.

7 Berend Jan Drijber and Hélène Stergiou, 'Public Procurement Law and Internal Market Law' (2009) *Common Market Law Review* 805.
8 Directive 2014/24 on the coordination of procedures for the award of public works contracts, public supply contracts and public service contracts and Directive 2014/25 coordinating the procurement procedures of entities operating in the water, energy, transport and postal services sectors.
9 Christopher Bovis, *The Law of EU Public Procurement* (OUP, 2015).
10 Public Sector Remedies Directive 89/665, [1989] OJ L395/33, and the Utilities Remedies Directive 92/13, [1992] OJ L76/14.
11 Christopher Bovis, 'La notion et les attributions d'organisme de droit public comme pouvoirs adjudicateurs dans le régime des marchés publics' (2003) *Contrats Publics*, Moniteur Juris, Septembre 2003, 26–30
12 On the issue of public interest and its relation with profit, see the cases cited at (n 6).
13 Andreas Heinemann, 'Social Considerations in EU Competition Law: The Protection of Competition as a Cornerstone of the Social Market Economy', in this volume.
14 European Commission, 'Towards a Single Market Act' (n 3).
15 European Commission, 'Guide to the Application of the European Union Rules on State Aid, Public Procurement and the Internal Market to Services of General Economic Interest, and in Particular to Social Services of General Interest', SEC(2010)1545 final; European Commission, 'Buying Social: A Guide to Taking Account of Social Considerations in Public Procurement', SEC(2010)1258; European Commission, 'Supporting Social Responsibility in the Economy through Public Procurement' (2016) at <https://ec.europa.eu/growth/content/supporting-social-responsibility-economy-through-public-procurement-0_en>.
16 Christopher Bovis, 'Developing Public Procurement Regulation: Jurisprudence and Its Influence on Law Making' (2006) *Common Market Law Review* 461.
17 Directive 2007/66, [2007] OJ L335/31.
18 Case C-237/99, *Commission* v *France*, EU:C:2000:577; Case C-470/99, *Universale-Bau and Others*, EU:C:2002:746; Case C-373/00, *Adolf Truley*, EU:C:2002:207; Case C-84/03, *Commission v Spain*, EU:C:2005:14; *Strohal* (n 6); Case C-31/87, *Beentjes*, EU:C:1988:422; *BFI Holding* (n 6); Case C-223/99, *Agora*, EU:C:2001:65 and Case C-260/99, *Excelsior*, EU:C:2001:259; Case C-343/95, *Diego Cali et Figli*, EU:C:1997:160; Case C-380/98, *University of Cambridge*, EU:C:2000:229; Case C-26/03, *Stadt Halle*, EU:C:2005:5; Case C-107/98, *Teckal*, EU:C:1999:562; Case C-18/01, *Korhonen and Others*, EU:C:2002:448.
19 Case C-315/01, *GAT*, EU:C:2002:573; Cases C-21/03 and C-34/03, *Fabricom*, EU:C:2004:709; Case C-285/99 and Case C-286/99, *Lombardini and Mantovani*, EU:C:2001:314; Case C-324/98, *Telaustria and Telefonadress*, EU:C:2000:669; Case C-126/03, *Commission v Germany*, EU:C:2004:391; Case C-176/98, *Holst Italia*, EU:C:1999:447, para 29; Case C-399/98, *Ordine degli Architetti and Others*, EU:C:2000:671, para 92; Case C-314/01, *Siemens and ARGE Telekom*, EU:C:2003:628, para 44; Case C-57/01, *Makedoniko Metro and Mikhaniki*, EU:C:2002:450.
20 *Beentjes* (n 18); Case C-225/98, *Nord-Pas-de-Calais*, EU:C:2000:121; Case C-513/99, *Concordia Bus*, EU:C:2001:686.
21 Brian Bercusson and Niklas Bruun, 'Labour Law Aspects of Public Procurement in the EU' in Ruth Nielsen and Steen Treumer (eds.), *New EU Public Procurement Directives* (DJØF, 2005) 97; Catharine Barnard, 'Using Procurement Law to Enforce Labour Standards' in Guy Davidov and Brian Langille (eds.), *The Idea of Labour Law* (OUP, 2011) 256; Catharine Barnard, 'To Boldly Go: Social Clauses in Public Procurement' 46 (2017) 2 *Industrial Law Journal* 208; Karen

Jaehrling, 'The State as a "Socially Responsible Customer"? Public Procurement between Market-Making and Market-Embedding' (2015) 21 *European Journal of Industrial Relations* 149.

22 Christopher Bovis, 'The State, Competition and Public Services' in Patrick Birkinshaw and Michael Varney (eds.), *The European Union Legal Order after Lisbon* (Wolters Kluwer, 2010), 137–152; Andre Moriceau, 'Services d'"intérêt économique general et valeurs communes' (2008) 519 *Revue du Marché Commun et de l'Union Europénne* 358; Malcolm Ross, 'Article 16 EC and Services of General Interest: From Derogation to Obligation?' (2000) *European Law Review* 22.

23 Tony Prosser, *The Limits of Competition Law* (OUP, 2005); Cosmo Graham, 'Essential Facilities and Services of General Interest' (2007) *Diritto e Politiche dell'Unione Europea* 22; Wolf Sauter, 'Services of General Economic Interest and Universal Service in EU Law' (2008) *European Law Review* 172.

24 Graham, 'Essential Facilities and Services of General Interest' (n 23), at 29.

25 Moriceau, 'Services d'intérêt économique general et valeurs communes' (n 22), at 358.

26 Ross, 'Article 16 E.C. and Services of General Interest: From Derogation to Obligation?' (n 22).

27 Christopher Bovis, 'The Application of Competition Rules to the European Union Transport Sectors' (2005) *Columbia Journal of European Law* 1.

28 In the context of air transport, public service obligation is defined in Council Regulation 2408/92 as any obligation imposed upon an air carrier to take, in respect of any route which it is licensed to operate by a Member State, all necessary measures to ensure the provision of a service satisfying fixed standards of continuity, regularity, capacity and pricing, which standards the air carrier would not assume if it were solely considering its economic interest.

29 Sauter, 'Services of General Economic Interest and Universal Service in EU Law' (n 24), at 172.

30 In the context of the Universal Services Directive EC 2002/22, universal service obligations are services made available to the public at the quality specified to all end-users in their territory, independently of geographical location, and, in the light of specific national conditions, at an affordable price.

31 Juan Jorge Piernas Lopez, 'Services of General Economic Interest and Social Considerations', in this volume.

32 European Commission, 'Green Paper on Services of General Interest', COM(2003)270.

33 Communication from the European Commission, 'A Single Market for 21st Century Europe-Services of General Interest, Including Social Services of General Interest: A New European Commitment', COM(2007)725; Christian Joerges and Florian Rödl, '"Social Market Economy" as Europe's Social Model?' (2004) 8 *EUI Working Papers*.

34 *BFI Holding BV* (n 18).

35 Joined Cases C-223/99, *Agora Srl*, EU:C:2001:65.

36 Christopher Bovis, 'Financing Services of General Interest, Public Procurement and State Aid: The Delineation between Market Forces and Protection' (2005) 1 *European Law Journal* 79.

37 The term 'industrial and commercial character' features in the public procurement *acquis* and corresponds to the presence of market competitiveness supported through the factors of profitability and demand substitutability (Christopher Bovis, 'Redefining Contracting Authorities under the EC Public Procurement Directives: An Analysis of the Case C-44/96, *Mannesmann Anlangenbau Austria AG et al. v Strohal Rotationsdurck GesmbH*' (1999) *Common Market Law Review* 41).

38 Alexis Jacquemin and Henry de Jong, *European Industrial Organisation* (Palgrave Macmillan, 1997); Wernhard Möschel, 'Competition Law from and Ordo Point of View' in Alan Peackock and Hans Willgerodt (eds.), *German Neo-Liberals and the Social Market Economy* (Palgrave Macmillan, 1989) 143.
39 Interpretative Communication from the European Commission, 'Community Law Applicable to Public Procurement and the Possibilities for Integrating Social Considerations into Public Procurement', COM(2001)566; Interpretative Communication from the European Commission, 'Community Law Applicable to Public Procurement and the Possibilities for Integrating Environmental Considerations into Public Procurement', COM(2001)274.
40 *Beentjes* (n 18), para 19.
41 Case C-324/93, *R. v The Secretary of State for the Home*, EU:C:1995:84, where the national court asked whether factors concerning continuity and reliability as well as security of supplies fall under the framework of the most economically advantageous offer, when the latter is being evaluated.
42 *Beentjes* (n 18), para 22.
43 Ibid., para 37.
44 *Cambridge University* (n 18), para 17; *Strohal* (n 6), para 33; *BFI Holding BV* (n 18), paras 42 and 43.
45 *Beentjes* (n 18).
46 Case 28/86, *Bellini*, EU:C:1987:276.
47 *Beentjes* (n 18), para 29.
48 Para 31 of the judgement, where the Court stipulated that an award criterion linked to the campaign against unemployment must be expressly mentioned in the contract notice so that contractors may become aware of its existence.
49 Anja Wiesbrock, 'Socially Responsible Public Procurement: European Value or National Choice?' in Beate Sjåfjell and Anja Wiesbrock (eds.), *Sustainable Public Procurement Under EU Law: New Perspectives on the State as Stakeholder* (CUP, 2016) 75; ACL Davies, *The Public Law of Government Contracts* (OUP, 2008) 260–296; Christopher McCrudden, *Buying Social Justice: Equality, Government Procurement & Legal Change* (OUP, 2007); Sue Arrowsmith and Peter Kunzlik (eds.), *Social and Environmental Policies in EC Procurement Law: New Directives and New Directions* (CUP, 2009).
50 The legislation on public procurement in the early days clearly allowed for 'preference schemes' in less favoured regions of the common market which were experiencing industrial decline (Articles 29(4) and 29(a) of the EC Public Works Directive 71/305; Article 26 of EC Public Supplies Directive 77/62). Such schemes required the application of award criteria based on considerations other than the lowest price or the most economically advantageous offer, subject to their compatibility with Community law in as much as they did not run contrary to the principle of free movement of goods and to competition law considerations with respect to State aid. Since the completion of the internal market, they have been abolished, as they have been deemed capable in contravening directly or indirectly the basic principle of non-discrimination on grounds of nationality stipulated in the Treaty of Rome.
51 Jose Fernadez-Martin and Martin Stehmann, 'Product Market Integration versus Regional Cohesion in the Community' (1991) *European Law Review*.
52 Christopher Bovis, *The Liberalisation of Public Procurement in the European Union and Its Effects on the Common Market* (Ashgate, 1998).
53 Case 74/76, *Ianelli and Volpi Spa*, EU:C:1977:23.
54 Case 103/84, *Commission v Italy*, EU:C:1986:229; Case 244/81, *Commission v Ireland*, EU:C:1982:402.
55 Christopher Bovis, 'Public Procurement as an Instrument of Industrial Policy in the European Union' in Thomas Lawton (ed.), *Industrial Policy and Competitiveness in Europe* (Palgrave Macmillan, 1998) Chapter 7.

56 Subcontracting plays a major role in the opening up of public markets as it is the most effective way of small- and medium-sized enterprises' participation in public procurement. All Directives on Public Procurement, influenced by Commission's Communications on subcontracting and small and medium enterprises encourage the use of subcontracting in the award of public contracts. Particularly, in public supplies contracts, the contracting entity in the invitation to tender may ask the tenderers on their intention to sub-contract to third parties part of the contract. In public works contracts, contracting authorities awarding the principal contract to a concessionaire may require the subcontracting to third parties of at least 30% of the total work provided for by the principal contract.
57 An example of such approach is the views of the UK Government in relation to the involvement of the private sector in delivering public services. Christopher Bovis, *Public Private Partnerships in the EU* (Routledge, 2013); Department of Environment, *Working Together: Private Finance and Public Money* (DOE Publications, 1993); Private Finance Panel and HM Treasury, *Private Opportunity, Public Benefit: Progressing the Private Finance Initiative* (HM Treasury, 1995).
58 Of interest is the case *ARGE* (para 26), where even the receipt of aid or subsidies incompatible with the Treaty by an entity may be a reason for disqualification from the selection process, as an obligation to repay an illegal aid would threaten the financial stability of the tenderer in question. Case C-94/99, *ARGE*, EU:C:2000:330 where the Court concluded that if the legislature wanted to preclude subsidized entities from participating in tendering procedures for public contracts, it should have said so explicitly in the relevant Directives.
59 *Strohal* (n 6), para 33; *BFI Holding BV* (n 18), paras 42 and 43.
60 Christopher Bovis, 'The Compatibility of Compulsory Tendering with Transfer of Undertakings: The case of Contract Compliance and the Acquired Rights Directive' in High Collins, Alan Davies and Roger Rideout (eds.), *Legal Regulation of the Employment Relations* (Kluwer, 2000) Chapter 21.
61 ILEA Contract Compliance Equal Opportunities Unit, *Contract Compliance: A Brief History* (London, 1990).
62 Peter Morris, 'Legal Regulation of Contract Compliance: An Anglo-American Comparison' (1990) *Anglo-American Law Review* 87.
63 For an overview of the Social Policy in North American systems, Christine Cnossen and Christopher Bovis, 'The Framework of Social Policy in Federal States: An Analysis of the Law and Policy on Industrial Relations in USA and Canada' (1996) 12 *International Journal of Comparative Labour Law and Industrial Relations.*
64 In the US, Case 93-1841, *Adarand Constructors* v *Pena* [1995] Annual Volume of US Supreme Court. The United States Supreme Court questioned the constitutionality in the application of contract compliance as a potential violation of the equal protection component of the Fifth Amendment's Due Process Clause and ordered the Court of Appeal to reconsider the employment of socio-economic policy objectives in the award of federal public procurement contracts.
65 For example, in the UK, every initiative relating to contract compliance has been outlawed by virtue of the Local Government Act 1988. Contract compliance from a public law perspective has been examined by Terence Daintith, 'Regulation by Contract: The New Prerogative' (1979) *Current Legal Problems* 41. For a comprehensive analysis of the issue of contract compliance in relation to public contracts, see Christopher McCrudden, *Contract Compliance and Equal Opportunities* (OUP, 1997).
66 *Beentjes* (n 18).
67 For a more in-depth discussion, Anna Tryfonidou, 'Reverse Discrimination in Purely Internal Situations: An Incongruity in a Citizens' Europe' (2008) 35 *Legal Issues of Economic Integration* 43; Dominic Hanf, 'Reverse Discrimination in EU Law: Constitutional Aberration, Constitutional Necessity, or Judicial

Choice' (2011) 18 *Maastricht Journal of European and Comparative Law* 29; Peter Van Elsuwege, 'The Phenomenon of Reverse Discrimination: An Anomaly in the European Constitutional Order?' in Lucia Serena Rossi and Federico Casolari (eds.), *The EU after Lisbon: Amending or Coping with the Existing Treaties?* (Springer, 2014) 161.

68 There are a number of legal instruments relevant to social policy at the EU level that may apply to public procurement. They include directives on safety and health at work, working conditions and the application of employment law.

69 It should be mentioned that adherence to health and safety laws have been considered by a British court as part of the technical requirements specified in the Works Directive for the process of selection of tenderers; *General Building and Maintenance v Greenwich Borough Council*, [1993] IRLR 535. Along these lines, the Interpretative Communication from the European Commission, 'Community Law Applicable to Public Procurement and the Possibilities for Integrating Social Considerations into Public Procurement', COM(2001)566.

70 Kai Kruger, Ruth Nielsen and Niklas Brunn, *European Public Contracts in a Labour Law Perspective* (DJOFg, 1997).

71 Christopher Bovis, 'Social Policy Considerations and the European Public Procurement Regime' (1998) 3 *International Journal of Comparative Labour Law and Industrial Relations.*

72 Francesco Costamagna, 'Minimum Wage between Public Procurement and Posted Workers: Anything New after the *RegioPost* Case?' (2017) *European Law Review* 101.

73 Case C-115/14, *RegioPost*, EU:C:2015:760.

74 Case C-549/13, *Bundesdruckerei*, EU:C:2014:2235.

75 See the application of the rule of reason to the principle of free movement of goods and also the competition law principle prohibiting cartels and collusive behaviour.

76 *Beentjes* (n 18), para 19.

77 *R. v The Secretary of State for the Home* (n 41), where the national court asked whether factors concerning continuity and reliability as well as security of supplies fall under the framework of the most economically advantageous offer, when the latter is being evaluated.

78 *Beentjes* (n 18), para 22.

79 Ibid., para 37.

80 Directive 77/62, [1977] OJ C 61/26, as amended by Directive 98/50, [1998] OJ L132 and consolidated by Directive 2001/23, [2001] OJ L82/16. For a comprehensive analysis of the implications of transfer of undertakings in public procurement, Case C 29/91, *Redmond Stichting* v *Bartol*, EU:C:1992:144; Case C-382/92, *Commission* v *United Kingdom*, EU:C:1994:233; Case C-24/85, *Spijkers*, EU:C:1986:24; Case C-209/91, *Rask*, EU:C:1992:436; Case C-392/92, *Schmidt*, EU:C:1994:134; Case C-48/94, *Rygaard*, EU:C:1995:290; Case C-324/86, *Tellerup*, EU:C:1987:537.

81 *Concordia Bus* (n 18).

82 Herwig Verschueren, 'The European Internal Market and the Competition between Workers' (2015) *European Labour Law Journal* 128.

7 Social considerations in EU competition law

The protection of competition as a cornerstone of the social market economy

Andreas Heinemann

1 Introduction

The new self-identification of the European Union (EU) as a 'highly competitive social market economy, aiming at full employment and social progress' is of greatest interest for competition lawyers, given that competition law plays a major role in an economic system conceived as a 'social market economy'. At the same time, questions have emerged regarding the balance between free competition, on the one hand, and social progress, on the other, and on how these two potentially competing interests can be reconciled.

In addressing this question, the remainder of this chapter is divided into five sections. Section 2 starts with the task of competition law in a social market economy. Section 3 offers a general discussion on the hierarchical objectives of the Union in the context of competition, welfare and society. This discussion draws on the realization that the term 'social' and its variants are virtually absent from EU competition law, not only from primary and secondary legislation, but also with regard to the relevant soft law, i.e. the many communications, notices and guidelines issued by the European Commission in the field of competition law. The adoption of the Lisbon Treaty has done little to alter this fact. However, the 'social deficit' within competition law is surprising only at first glance. There is an important consideration underlying this absence of the 'social' within EU competition law which must not be taken for granted: competition law is effective in so far as its application is restricted to economic and, in particular, to competitive arguments. If this was to change, and the assessment of restraints to competition is subject to a comprehensive *bilan économique et social*, the institutions responsible for the control of anti-competitive behaviour would be granted a much wider discretion in this field.[1] Predictability and legal certainty would therefore be jeopardized by the integration of a wide range of social goals within this balancing exercise.[2] A more subjective approach such as this is not up to the task of maintaining a competitive economic system, and falls short of the international standards in the field of competition policy.[3] It is commonly accepted that for competition law systems to be effective, they must not allow competition law to be diluted with other public policy goals. In US antitrust law, for example, it is recognized that the 'rule of reason' analysis does not allow for social objectives to be taken into consideration, and must be confined to 'a consideration of [the] impact on competitive conditions'.[4] It is instead the competence of the legislature to decide if specific industries shall be granted an exemption from these general rules for social purposes. In the EU, the interface between competition law and social policy follows a similar trajectory. According to Art. 9 TFEU, the Union shall take into account the 'requirements linked to the promotion of a high level of employment, the guarantee of adequate social protection [and] the fight against social exclusion'. This obligation applies to all policies and activities including competition policy,[5] and must also be read in line with Article 7 TEU, which requires that EU ensures 'consistency between its policies and activities, taking all of its objectives into account and in accordance with the principle of conferral of powers'. In the Treaty, there are very few express provisions on conflicts between social policy and competition rules, partially because many social services in the Member States fall outside the scope of EU competition law as they do not have an effect on trade between Member States.[6] One of them is however Article 42 TFEU, which restricts the application of competition law to agriculture for different reasons, including the achievement of specific social objectives.[7] In the absence of written rules, the relationship between competition law and social policy must be determined by the relevant competition authorities and the courts. In several lines of causal precedent, the CJEU has limited the application of competition law due to conflicts with social policy. For this purpose, the Court has expressly emphasized that primary law contains at the same time competition rules and social rules (the latter to be found in Part Three – Title X: Social Policy).[8] As there is no hierarchy between the different policy fields, they must be reconciled with each other within a given context.[9] In some circumstances, social considerations may lead to competition law being wholly un-applicable in a certain field or in respect of certain concerns within that same field. Section 4 discusses these cases, and argues that social policy works as an external limitation to the scope of competition law. On the other hand, social considerations may affect the application of competition law from inside by having an impact on the interpretation of prohibitions and justifications. Section 5 discusses these aspects and examines the way in which social considerations work within competition law. The external and the internal functionality of social goals with respect to competition law will form the central parts of this contribution. Section 6 will conclude.

2 The role of competition law in the social market economy

2.1 From ordoliberalism to the social market economy

As discussed in the introduction to this volume and earlier by Civitarese Matteucci,[10] the concept of the 'social market economy' dates back to German economic policy adopted immediately after the World War II. It has been made popular by the then minister for economic affairs Ludwig Erhard who borrowed the term from his staff member Alfred Müller-Armack. The concept of the social market economy was primarily based on the post-1930s Ordoliberalism of the Freiburg School, headed and elaborated by the economist Walter Eucken and the lawyer Franz Böhm in opposition to the Nazi regime.[11] For them, economic policy must strive towards a system which is at the same time effective and humane (*funktionsfähig und menschenwürdig*). Ordoliberals advocated for a strong State which must guarantee that markets are protected against distortions due to cartels and monopoly power.[12] The proposals of the Freiburg School are closely linked to social objectives. However, Eucken wanted to solve the 'social question' by controlling markets, not by intervening within their processes. Thus, social objectives do not directly impact on the application of competition law, but may take precedence in other policy areas.

Müller-Armack took over the central elements of the Freiburg School, but replaced the notion of *Ordo* (stemming from early medieval philosophy) with the more 'catchy' 'Social Market Economy'.[13] His thinking was influenced by other theories, such as Christian social teaching, in particular by the Catholic Social Doctrine ('*Katholische Soziallehre*') as conceived by Oswald von Nell-Breuning with its principles of personality, solidarity and subsidiarity. However, from the very beginning, the term 'Social Market Economy' was not precisely defined, and was instead used as a general framework which places the market economy at the centre of economic policy with the addition of different social elements. Competition law plays an essential role in the concept of the Social Market Economy.[14] Erhard described this relation quite clearly:

> In my conception the social market economy does not recognize the freedom of the entrepreneur to exclude competition through cartel agreements; it imposes far more the obligation to gain the favour of the consumer through one's own efforts in competition against rivals.[15]

For Erhard, competition law has a constitutional dimension.[16] Its goal is to protect consumers.[17] However, the link between competition law and the social function of consumer protection is rather indirect: protecting free and fair competition leads to 'the best possible quality and quantity and at the proper price'.[18] Consumers will benefit the most if the competitive process is protected against distortions. Hence, social goals are promoted in two ways: on the one hand, the decentralized coordination over markets rewards those who create the biggest value for society; on the other hand, social policy intervenes where market results are not satisfactory. These measures must however be compatible with the market mechanism.

2.2 *The reception of the social market economy in the EU and competition law*

Prior to the Lisbon Treaty, the term 'Social Market Economy' did not exist in EU legal texts. It has however been part of the official discourse within the European institutions for a long time.

For example, a speech of the former Competition Commissioner Mario Monti on the topic 'Competition in a Social Market Economy' dates back to 2000.[19] The general context was the preparation of the new enforcement system in European competition law.[20] Monti underlined the importance of the market mechanism and pointed repeatedly to its capacity for creating jobs. Rejecting *'Laissez-faire-*capitalism', he pleaded for a strong framework encompassing on the one hand, social standards, and on the other, a strong body of competition law capable of ensuring 'that the beneficial workings of the market forces are not blocked, restrained or distorted by short-sighted actions of the market actors themselves'.[21]

This interpretation of European economic law is emblematic of the openness on the part of the EU to the concept of the social market economy. From the very beginning, the European Communities had an effective body of competition law as well as strong institutions, and thus started from the idea that the market economy is not conceived purely as a system of *laisser faire* capitalism. Rather, it has to be protected against restrictions by state *and* market actors. Regarding legal texts, the Communities were initially reticent to make programmatic statements. With the Maastricht Treaty, however, primary law adopted 'the principle of an open market economy with free competition' (Art. 3a(1) EC Treaty). As these terms appeared too general in character, the Treaty establishing a Constitution for Europe (TCE) mentioned 'a highly competitive social market economy, aiming at full employment and social progress' (Art. I-3(3) TCE). As fifty years earlier in Germany, the irenic expression combining the 'cold' market mechanism with 'warm' social goals was intended to foster goodwill, in this case in order to ensure the Constitutional Treaty's passing where ballot measures were utilized at the Member State level, particularly the referendum in France. After this plan failed, an identical wording was transposed within the Lisbon Treaty in Article 3(3) TEU.

In this context, it is quite significant that the objective is further qualified: the 'social market economy' has to be 'highly competitive'. In fact, as discussed in Section 2.1, the term 'social market economy', no matter how difficult it may be to precisely capture its meaning, presupposes the existence of an effective body of competition law. The qualification 'highly competitive' makes this link even stronger. On the other hand, the Lisbon Treaty has relegated the aim of undistorted competition to Protocol 27 on the Internal Market and Competition.[22] This relocation was considered by some scholars as a degradation of the principle of competition: competition shall not be regarded as an end in itself, but as a means of achieving other objectives, including social progress.[23] For critics of the principle of competition, these higher objectives may be likewise achieved through the use of other policy instruments, including but not limited to industrial policy.[24]

However, such a devaluation on the competitive principle has not been successful.[25] On the one hand, according to Art. 51 TEU, protocols have the same legal value as the Treaties themselves. Protocol 27 therefore is a sufficient basis on which to consider 'a system ensuring that competition is not distorted' as an essential part of the internal market. On the other hand, the integration function of EU competition law, i.e. the goal of not having state barriers to trade replaced by private restrictions (for example in distribution systems), continues to have great significance. Recently, this has been confirmed by the European Commission's Digital Single Market Strategy which extends the prohibition of excluding passive sales even beyond the scope of competition law.[26] Also the Court of Justice of the European Union (CJEU) has underlined the importance of the principle of competition and of Protocol 27 recalling 'the vital nature of the Treaty rules on competition'.[27]

The crucial significance of competition law in the EU economic system is subsequently supported by the pledge to adopt a 'social market economy' since this concept encompasses – as we have seen – a strong competition law preventing market actors from destroying economic freedom.

3 Competition, efficiency and social progress

Competition law is characterized by a fundamental debate on its goals and the way in which these goals shall be pursued. This section aims to show that the search for the social content of competition law touches upon the very essence of the 'market economy'.

3.1 The impact of the goals of competition law on social considerations

A market economy is the best system in order to maximize wealth and social welfare. The allocation of scarce production factors is optimized and dynamic efficiency is enhanced because markets allow rapid adaptation to changing circumstances, and market processes yield innovation.[28] In competition law, there is a long-standing controversy surrounding the degree of directness with which these goals are to be pursued.[29] According to the concept of 'freedom to compete', competition is an open-ended 'discovery procedure',[30] and its results cannot be predicted. Therefore, the task of competition law is to protect the freedom to compete, rather than targeting welfare or other objectives.[31] By contrast, the Chicago School has put efficiency at the centre of its reasoning and has – on the basis of neoclassical equilibrium theory – criticized traditional competition law analysis.

With regard to social considerations, these two opposing views have the following consequences: for the proponents of the freedom-to-compete-approach, prosperity and, concomitantly, other social goals must not be pursued directly. The welfare of citizens will be a natural outcome if the freedom to compete is being protected.[32] Therefore, social considerations are excluded from competition law from the outset. For the Chicago School, efficiency and thus welfare, is the direct goal of competition law. However, Chicago School scholars do not accept objectives other than efficiency, meaning that there is similarly no room for social considerations.

The picture gets more complex when it comes to the real application of competition law: a pure freedom-to-compete approach does not give the standards to decide between conflicting freedom positions. And, for Chicago School scholarship, the measurement of efficiencies may become an extremely complex procedure.[33] Therefore, middle ground has to be found between the opposing views. This seems to be also the position of the European institutions. The CJEU has repeatedly underlined that Art. 101 TFEU 'aims to protect not only the interests of competitors or of consumers, but also the structure of the market and, in so doing, competition as such'.[34] The European Commission, which – because of its 'more economic approach' – is suspected to lean towards the efficiency paradigm, has often emphasized the importance and the preponderance of the process aspect over efficiencies.[35]

3.2 Total welfare versus consumer welfare in EU competition law

Even though competition law must not be weakened by a general balancing with public policy goals, it is not socially neutral. The most fundamental discussion concerns the question of whether competition law (assuming that its application is open to efficiency considerations, which is affirmed here to a certain extent) should apply a *total welfare* or a *consumer welfare standard*. Whereas the total welfare standard maximizes total surplus, i.e. the sum of producer and consumer surplus, the consumer welfare standard takes into consideration exclusively consumer surplus.[36] Often, an increase in total welfare implies also an increase of consumer surplus. However, this is not necessarily the case. It is very well conceivable that certain measures, including for example price discrimination between customers in different EU Member States on the basis of their willingness to pay, maximizes total surplus but is detrimental at least with respect to certain groups of consumers. The question then is if total or if consumer welfare governs the application of competition law. Whereas many economists exclude distribution issues and plead for a maximization of total welfare,[37] the practice of competition law worldwide pleads for the consumer welfare standard.[38] In the EU, e.g. several communications of the European Commission take this position.[39]

One of the reasons is that Article 101(3) TFEU requires for an exemption to apply that consumers receive a fair share of the resulting benefit. For example, the European Commission states that 'negative effects on consumers in one geographic market or product market cannot normally be balanced against and compensated by positive effects for consumers in another unrelated geographic market or product market'.[40] According to Art. 2(1)(b) of the EU Merger Regulation, the Commission – when appraising concentrations – shall take into account the interests of consumers as well as technical and economic progress 'provided that it is to consumers' advantage and does not form an obstacle to competition'. Moreover, Art. 12 TFEU demands consumer protection requirements be taken into account in defining and implementing other Union policies and activities. The consumer welfare standard is best suited to fulfil this mission in the area of competition law. A deeper reason for preferring the consumer welfare standard is that the ultimate goal of the social market economy is the well-being and the autonomy of consumers. In this perspective, consumer sovereignty is the most fundamental expression of the social content of competition law.[41]

4 Social considerations as a limitation to the scope of competition law

4.1 The concept of undertaking and social considerations

Competition law only applies to the activities of 'undertakings', and not to the behaviour of entities which do not qualify as such. Therefore, purely social activities are not caught by competition law. An undertaking is defined as 'any entity engaged in an economic activity, irrespective of its legal status and the way in which it is financed. [. . .] any activity consisting in offering goods and services on a given market is an economic activity'.[42] An intent to realize a profit is not necessary in this regard.[43] The definition of undertaking and, consequently, of the personal scope of application of competition law is very broad. Not only are commercial and industrial activities in the classical sense covered, but also the liberal professions and the world of commercialized arts and sports. Competition rules apply likewise to private and public undertakings. Public undertakings are – in conformity with the Transparency Directive[44] – any undertakings over which the public authorities may exercise directly or indirectly a dominant influence. A dominant influence is presumed if public authorities hold the major part of the undertaking's subscribed capital.[45] Therefore, for competition law to apply, it is not relevant if a certain economic activity is performed by a private or a public undertaking: both sorts of undertaking shall be treated equally in competition law (Art. 106(1) TFEU). Regarding public undertakings, it is not relevant if the activity is performed by a defined sub-unit of the state or by the state in general.[46] It is only important that there is an economic activity. Legal capacity of the acting entity is not required.[47] Consequently, activities in the social sector can constitute an economic activity as long goods or services are offered on a given market.[48] For example, employment procurement services,[49] patient transport services[50] as well as specialist medical services[51] and hospital services[52] have been qualified an economic activity, thus triggering the application of the EU competition rules. However, an intensely debated exception has been crafted by the CJEU through the distinction between purchasing and selling activities. In the *FENIN* case, the Court has affirmed that the purchasing activities of the Spanish national health system SNS cannot be separated from the subsequent use of the purchased goods. Therefore, if the provision of medical treatment by SNS is of a purely social nature, the purchasing activities of SNS cannot be qualified as an economic activity.[53] This reasoning is in conformity with the usual definition of 'economic activity' according to which the 'offering', hence not the 'purchasing' of goods and services on a given market is relevant. As a result, public procurement, which is discussed earlier in this volume,[54] is outside the realm of competition law if the subsequent use of the purchased goods or services is not offered over markets. In the *FENIN* case, for example, suppliers complained about systematic payment delays by the national health system averaging 300 days to pay the debts. Under competition law, it would have been possible to examine if these delays amount to an abuse of a dominant position (Art. 102 TFEU). As such backlog of payments indicates the exploitation of an uncontrolled scope of action due to the strong position of SNS on health markets, a violation of Art. 102 TFEU appears likely. However, in absence of an economic activity, the way into competition law is barred, and there are no equivalent rules in public procurement law.

The definition of undertaking does not encompass the State when it acts *de iure imperii* (as opposed to *de iure gestionis*). The State, acting in the exercise of official authority and in the core of its public competences, is not an undertaking in the sense of competition law.[55] This is the case if the activities in question are, by their nature, their aim and the rules to which they are subject, connected with the exercise of powers which are typically those of a public authority.[56] Examples are the army and the police, air and maritime navigation control as well as anti-pollution surveillance.[57] The fact that an entity has been given the power to adopt regulations of a public law character is not sufficient to assume the exercise of official authority. The decisive question is if the rule-making power relates to economic activities.[58] Generally, the fact that a certain activity may be exercised by a private undertaking may be used as an argument in order to deny the exercise of official authority and to affirm the applicability of competition law.[59]

An important area where public activity may be exempted from competition law is social security, e.g. statutory accident and health insurance as well as old age pension schemes. The CJEU has always recognized the competence of the Member States to organize their social security systems as they see fit.[60] It is settled case law that social security systems do not perform an 'economic activity' if certain conditions are fulfilled: the insurance scheme must have an exclusively social function, it must apply the principle of solidarity, so that no direct link between the contributions paid and the risk covered or the benefits granted is realized, for example because the contributions also depend on the earnings of the insured person, and it must be subject to the supervision of the State.[61] If this is the case, the insurance scheme is not an undertaking and Articles 101 and 102 TFEU are not applicable. This means that for example, compulsory affiliation to a scheme cannot be qualified as abuse of a dominant position. However, sometimes it is difficult to assess if a certain social security scheme meets the requirements excluding an economic activity. An economic scheme, as opposed to a solidarity-based scheme, may be characterized by optional membership, the principle of capitalization (i.e. a direct link between contributions and later earnings), its profit making nature or by its supplementary character adding to a basic scheme.[62] If the insurance scheme presents elements of both types, an overall assessment has to be made.[63] The freedom to engage in some competition with other social security funds does not exclude the solidarity-based character.[64]

CJEU case law on the application of competition law to social security entities is diverse and does not provide absolute guidance.[65] There is no general exemption from competition law for the social security sector. Rather EU law adopts a 'case-by-case' approach, by examining whether the single social security body under review performs an economic activity. An alternative would be either to withdraw social security systems completely from the application of competition law, or, to the contrary, to subject social security in its entirety to competition law control while assessing the specific aspects of this sector under Art. 106(2) TFEU which provides for exceptions in favour of undertakings entrusted with the operation of services of general economic interest.[66] However, on the one hand, a general social security exemption would put at risk the autonomous term of 'undertaking' in EU competition law. On the other hand, a general application of competition law to social security bodies would interfere with the competence of Member States to organize their social security systems. Therefore, even though it might create legal uncertainty, the individual assessment of the respective social security entities under competition law is best suited to reconcile social and general economic goals.

4.2 *Labour markets, workers' rights and competition law*

4.2.1 *Preliminary remarks*

Workers' rights, including the right to collective bargaining, are recognized as human rights, guaranteed by Art. 23(4) of the Universal Declaration of Human Rights, Art. 8 of the International Covenant on Economic, Social and Cultural Rights, Art. 2(a) of the ILO Declaration on Fundamental Principles and Rights at Work,[67] Art. 5 and 6 of the European Social Charter of the Council of Europe and by Articles 12 and 28 of the EU Charter of Fundamental Rights.[68] However, as already discussed by Doherty in this volume,[69] from a different angle, collective bargaining may – in economic terms – be assessed as a 'wage cartel'. Terms and conditions of labour contracts are not negotiated individually by the contracting parties, but by groups of employers and employees. In spite of the 'cartel' character of collective bargaining, competition law has always shown flexibility when it comes to the exercise of labour rights.[70] In US antitrust law, there are express rules on that aspect. In particular, according to § 6 Clayton Act, 'the labor of a human being is not a commodity or article of commerce' so that antitrust law does not interfere on the way of labour organizations to carry out their legitimate objectives. Such organizations cannot be considered illegal combinations or conspiracies under antitrust law.[71] In a similar vein, the CJEU has always refused to apply EU competition law to the legitimate exercise of labour rights. Unlike US law, the argument is not based on the commodity aspect of labour, but on the assumption that the employee is not an undertaking. Employees form an economic unit with the undertakings they are working for and therefore do not themselves constitute 'undertakings' within the meaning of competition law.[72] Even taken collectively, they are not undertakings,[73] so that competition law does not apply.

4.2.2 *The Albany exception: content and scope*

Art. 155 TFEU expressly encourages 'management and labour' to undertake a dialogue at the Union level which may lead to 'contractual relations, including agreements'. As mentioned previously by Doherty,[74] in the *Albany* case, the Court has drawn a far-reaching conclusion from this institutional setting, which is fundamental for the general relationship between competition law and social policy. The Court held that it is beyond question that certain restrictions of competition are inherent in collective agreements between organizations representing employers and workers. However, it stated that 'the social policy objectives pursued by such agreements would be seriously undermined if management and labour were subject to' Article 101(1) TFEU when 'seeking to adopt measures to improve conditions of work and employment.' It therefore follows from an interpretation of the provisions of the Treaty as a whole, which is both effective and consistent, that agreements concluded in the context of collective negotiations between management and labour in pursuit of such objectives must, by virtue of their nature and purpose, be regarded as falling outside the scope of 'Article Art. 101(1) TFEU'.[75]

This reasoning goes much further than the argument in the *Becu* case, which merely stated that employees and trade unions are not 'undertakings' in the sense of competition law.[76] The *Albany* decision establishes a general 'inherency doctrine' according to which competition law has to step back insofar as its application would undermine the social policy objectives pursued by certain rules and institutions. It has to be underlined, though, that this line of reasoning is reserved to collective bargaining between employers and employees. It cannot be extended, for example, to collective arrangements between members of the liberal professions,[77] to employees' organizations which also represent the interests of self-employed service providers (since these are not employees but undertakings in the sense of competition law)[78] or to inter-trade agreements between two independent links of the production chain.[79] The inherency approach is not unknown to competition law. In the *Wouters* case, the Court had to assess the prohibition of multi-disciplinary partnerships of lawyers and accountants which the Bar of the Netherlands justified with the goal of guaranteeing the complete independence of lawyers and of avoiding all risk of conflict of interest. The Court was confronted with the question of whether 'the consequential effects restrictive of competition are inherent in the pursuit of those objectives'[80] and answered this question in the affirmative since the rules in question were necessary to ensure the proper practice of the legal profession.[81] In later case law, the Court has reiterated the admissibility of such inherency arguments in different contexts.[82] It has emphasized, though, that the inherency argument only works insofar as the restriction of competition in question is necessary to ensure the implementation of legitimate objectives.[83]

There is no uniform interpretation of the relationship between the '*Albany* exception'[84] and the *Wouters* jurisprudence. Some observers are of the opinion that *Albany* has brought a general exemption from competition law in favour of collective labour agreements.[85] For others, there is – deviating from *Wouters* – no general immunity of collective agreements from the application of competition law since only such agreements which pursue recognized social aims will profit from the '*Albany* exception'.[86] In our view, there is no structural difference between *Wouters* and *Albany*. The inherency doctrine of the CJEU is context-sensitive. On the one hand, the CJEU recognizes that social aims are acknowledged by EU law. On the other hand, exceptions must be restricted to what is necessary in order to achieve the respective high-ranking goals. In this sense, inherency is not equivalent to immunity; the CJEU examines each case and applies the proportionality principle.

However, it is contested what these general principles mean *in concreto*. In the *Albany* case, Advocate General (AG) Jacobs had proposed some conditions for an exception from competition law to apply. Apart from requiring a formal framework of collective bargaining between management and labour, he pleaded the application of the principle of good faith. He argued that collective agreements do not benefit from an exception if they merely function 'as a cover' for restrictive agreements of employers on product markets.[87] Moreover, he 'tentatively' suggested to restrict the exception to collective agreements which deal with 'core subjects of collective bargaining such as wages and working conditions and which [do] not directly affect third parties or markets', 'such as clients, suppliers, competing employers, or consumers'.[88] The Court did not take over the latter requirement, but required that the collective agreement must aim at adopting measures to improve conditions of work and employment in order to be exempted from the scope of competition law.[89] In fact, a requirement, such as that envisaged by the AG, excluding effects on third parties or markets seems to go too far. Collectively negotiated employment conditions will very often have an effect beyond the relationship between the parties.[90] It would put the right of collective bargaining at risk if collective agreements were systematically to be subject to an obligation of justification under competition law. Therefore, the general proportionality test as to the necessity of the restriction of competition for recognized social aims should be sufficient in order to renounce on the application of competition law.

The limits of the *Albany* exception have become relevant for the EFTA Court in the *Holship Norge* case. In a collective agreement, a fixed pay scheme for dockworkers in the largest ports of Norway had been adopted. The agreement contained a priority clause: unloading or loading cargo from or to incoming ships was reserved to dockworkers of the Administration Office of the home port. The trade union participated in the management of this entity and therefore had a business objective going beyond its core tasks. As a company used its own employees for unloading and loading instead of the incumbent's one, a boycott was initiated. The EFTA Court decided that the *Albany* exception did not apply, because the trade union was engaged in the management of the home port's firm, therefore did not limit itself to the improvement of working conditions of the workers and thus went beyond the objective of collective bargaining.[91] The case makes clear that social goals justify exceptions from competition law, but that they cannot be used as an excuse to unduly restrict competition in the pursuit of objectives which are different from social ones.

It is important to note that the *Albany* exception is relevant only in the context of competition law. In the *Viking* case, the CJEU has held that inherency arguments cannot be invoked when applying fundamental freedoms.[92] Moreover, in the context of labour markets, the extension of the fundamental freedoms to associations or organizations with legal autonomy is relevant and contributes to limit the scope of the *Albany* exception. While normally the fundamental freedoms are addressed to the Member States and not to private entities, associations or organizations may be included in the group of addressees if otherwise the abolition of State barriers could be neutralized by obstacles erected collectively by these autonomous entities. As a result, the fundamental freedoms may be relied upon also against trade unions.[93]

4.3 *Some concluding remarks on social policy and the scope of application of competition law*

Social security organisms and labour markets are the most prominent examples for exceptions to the application of competition law. However, these fields exhibit specific characteristics and do not allow for a general assumption that competition law will never apply in the field of social policy.[94] In reality, the opposite can be said to be true. As soon as an entity performs an economic activity (as to be distinguished from a social activity), it qualifies as an undertaking and has to respect competition law. EU competition law has been applied frequently within social policy contexts. The most prominent example is the *Höfner* case where the CJEU found the German public employment agency in violation of Arts. 106 and 102 TFEU because it was incapable of satisfying the demand prevailing on the market for executive recruitment activities. As it is further discussed in Chapter 12, the fact that the statutory monopoly of this agency (dating back to the Great Depression of 1929) was based on social policy considerations did not prevent this finding. For the Court, it is crucial that placement services are an economic activity, and that the agency abused its dominant position by not satisfying the demand.[95] From that, the general lesson can be learned that the competition rules apply to the field of social policy except if its conditions of application are not met. The most important arguments for an exception ensue from the concept of undertaking and from the inherency doctrine.

5 Social considerations within EU competition law

EU competition law has its own categories which focus on the competitive assessment of relevant markets, but, at the same time, it is only one of the very many policy fields in the EU domain. As mentioned in the Introduction to this volume and discussed further in other chapters, according to the horizontal social clause in Article 9 TFEU, social values have to be respected in all policy fields of the EU. The CJEU in its own case law has expressly stated that European economic law has to be reconciled with social goals.[96]

Against this background, the following analysis aims to establish the current status of social considerations within the prohibitions and exemptions of EU competition law. As discussed in Section 4, tensions between competition law and social policy have been reconciled by restricting in limited instances the application of competition law. The following section however shows that there are additional 'mechanisms' which provide a degree of flexibility in reconciling social policy and competition law. The analysis focuses on substantive law, in particular Articles 101 and 102, and merger control. Article 106 TFEU is not discussed in this chapter as it is examined at length in Chapter 12. It should not however be overlooked, that social considerations may play a role in procedural law including sanctions. If a fine jeopardizes the economic viability of an undertaking, the European Commission will take account 'of the undertaking's inability to pay in a specific social and economic context'.[97] The basic goal of allowing the Commission with flexibility in such a case is to prevent assets from losing all their value and to weaken competition; however the reference to the social context makes clear that the safeguarding of employment is at least an additional factor to be considered.[98]

5.1 Article 101(1) TFEU: prohibition of cartels

Agreements between undertakings, decisions by associations of undertakings and concerted practices having as their object or effect a restriction of competition and affecting trade between Member States are prohibited. The core phrase in the prohibition laid out in Article 101(1) TFEU is that of a 'restriction of competition'. This is linked to the 'requirement of independence',[99] according to which each undertaking must determine its behaviour autonomously. This does not mean, however, that any restriction of autonomy amounts to a restriction of competition. The entire factual, legal and economic context has to be taken into account.[100] However, outside the inherency doctrine, social considerations have not gained importance in the realm of application of Art. 101(1) TFEU. Cooperation between undertakings in order to promote social goals has to comply with EU competition law. This has been criticized insofar as the cartel prohibition 'also restricts economic entities mainly motivated by aims other than profit maximization in any endeavour to civilise or even socialise markets'.[101] This objection is – subject to the possibility of justifications, for example based on Art. 101(3) TFEU – true since the cartel prohibition applies to all restrictions of competition once the activity is qualified as 'economic'.

However, in applying Article 101(1) TFEU the Commission has a wide leeway. It is recognized that competition law is not violated if undertakings renounce on behaving illegally.[102] Therefore, there is no restrictive agreement if, for example, firms agree with each other not to infringe tax laws, money laundering provisions or social policy rules. As a consequence, it must be possible for undertakings to cooperate in order to advance social goals. The efforts to establish and to strengthen Corporate Social Responsibility (CSR) are an example. There is no restriction of competition if a firm adheres to recognized CSR initiatives (such as the UN Global Compact) insofar as existing obligations are confirmed.[103] For voluntary commitments going beyond statutory requirements, coordination may lead to a restriction of competition which would require a justification.[104] Competition law should be open with respect to CSR, since, by accepting its corporate social responsibility, the firm qualifies for the 'social licence to operate' in addition to the legal license.[105] However, CSR must not be used as a cover for hard-core cartels. An example is the 'washing powder' cartel fined by the European Commission in 2011.[106] The starting point of this cartel was an environment-friendly initiative of the trade association *Association Internationale de la savonnerie, de la détergence et des produits d'entretien* (AISE) representing the manufacturers of laundry detergents. AISE launched a code of conduct in order to reduce the consumption of detergents, their packaging, poorly biodegradable ingredients and washing temperatures thus decreasing CO2 emissions.[107] On this basis, detailed discussions between AISE members on the reduction of detergents' weight and volume took place. Major manufacturers used this framework in order to agree on prices, for example not to decrease prices when the weight or volume of the product was reduced, but also by increasing prices directly. Moreover, they agreed to restrict their promotional activity and they exchanged sensitive information on prices and trading conditions. A justification was not possible since the environmental objectives of the cooperation do not require price fixing. This case shows that, while the coordinated pursuit of social objectives may fall outside the application of competition law, deeds aimed at the pursuit of social goals cannot be used as a smokescreen for anti-competitive behaviour.

5.2 *Article 101(3) TFEU: justification of restrictive agreements*

If a restrictive agreement is caught by Art. 101(1) TFEU, it might still be compatible with EU rules. For example, the restriction may be covered by a block exemption regulation (BER); however, BERs do not concern social rights or environmental reasons. There are no Commission Guidelines in the field of social policy either. The Guidelines on horizontal cooperation agreements[108] address some forms of coordination including production and commercialization agreements, but they do not touch upon the field of codes of conduct and CSR. Therefore, individual exemptions based directly on Art. 101(3) TFEU are of special importance in this context.

The central condition for an exemption under Art. 101(3) TFEU is the improvement of the production or distribution of goods or the promotion of technical or economic progress. Social progress is not mentioned. In some cases, the European institutions have interpreted Art. 101(3) TFEU broadly so that, e.g. concerns for employment were accepted as an efficiency ground.[109] Also the protection of the environment, public health and cultural policy has been taken into account by the European Commission.[110] However, Art. 101(3) is not a gateway to general policy reflections (which should be reserved to the legislator[111]) and is instead a legal norm listing four conditions for an exemption to apply. In this sense, the European Commission has stated in its Guidelines on the interpretation of Art. 101(3) TFEU: 'Goals pursued by other Treaty provisions can be taken into account to the extent that they can be subsumed under the four conditions of [Art. 101(3)]'.[112] Therefore, social considerations are relevant only insofar as they have an impact on (static or dynamic) efficiency or on the other conditions laid down in that provision, such as the fair participation of consumers at the resulting benefits.[113] It is not possible to refer to public policy interests which are in contradiction to the system of undistorted competition.[114]

5.3 Article 102 TFEU

Art. 102 TFEU prohibits the abuse of dominant positions within the internal market or in a substantial part of it insofar as trade between Member States is affected. Normally, competitive markets ensure that the other market side gets the best and most innovative products at an appropriate price. If, however, an undertaking has the power to behave independently of other market actors like competitors, suppliers, customers and consumers,[115] fair and efficient results are not guaranteed any longer. The control by competition then is replaced – at least in part – by a special competition law control aiming at preventing any abuse which is made of the dominant position. Art. 102 TFEU protects consumers already by guaranteeing competition as such: dominant firms are barred from foreclosing competitors in an anti-competitive way; they have to compete on the merits.[116] However, Art. 102 TFEU has also a more direct impact on consumers and therefore a social component which is more visible than the protection of economic freedom under Art. 101 TFEU. Art. 102 TFEU not only prohibits exclusionary conduct but also exploitative abuses, for example the imposition of unfair purchase or selling prices or of other unfair trading conditions.

Traditionally, it is inferred from Art. 102(a) TFEU that exploitative abuse constitutes a category which is distinct from exclusionary behaviour. Under the more economic approach and under the influence of US law, which does not allow direct price control through antitrust law,[117] the category of exploitative abuse has been criticized.[118] It has been proposed to restrict price control to regulated markets insofar as they are not able to self-correct in the short to medium term.[119] This position appears problematic: Art. 102 TFEU does not contain a limitation to regulated markets.[120] Moreover, the self-correcting forces of the market mechanism may be absent for other reasons than regulation, for example because of network effects in the digital world. Many other barriers to entry exist. Price control against dominant firms is expressly provided for in Art. 102(a) TFEU, and insofar as consumers are the victims, it directly prevents welfare transfers from consumers to dominant firms and thus has a social dimension.

5.4 Merger control

The Merger Regulation[121] posits that concentrations which would not significantly impede effective competition in the internal market or in a substantial part of it, in particular as a result of the creation or strengthening of a dominant position, are considered compatible with the internal market. According to Art. 2(2) and (3) of this Regulation, the compatibility of concentrations is linked on whether or not there is a 'Significant Impediment to Effective Competition' (SIEC). The SIEC test requires a competition-related examination.[122] Nevertheless, the Merger Regulation opens some space to extra-competitive aspects. According to Recital 23 of that Regulation, 'the Commission must place its appraisal within the general framework of the achievement of the fundamental objectives referred to' in the articles which correspond today to Art. 3 TEU. As these 'fundamental objectives' include social goals, the third pillar of European competition law seems the most open one to social considerations. In the *Vittel* case, the General Court has held that

> the primacy given to the establishment of a system of free competition may in certain cases be reconciled, in the context of the assessment of whether a concentration is compatible with the [internal] market, with the taking into consideration of the social effects of that operation.[123]

As a result, the Court has confirmed that the Commission has to examine the impact of the concentration on the collective interests of the employees.[124] However, in the European Commission's practice, such reflections have been rare and never decisive.[125] General social considerations cannot be found in the list of aspects regarding the appraisal of concentrations in Art. 2(1) Merger Regulation or in the accompanying merger guidelines. Moreover, it is hard to conceive how such criteria could be operationalized. The commitment to the social market economy within the Lisbon Treaty does not alleviate these concerns. Therefore, only exceptionally, there will be room for general social considerations going beyond consumer interest, which is expressly underlined in Art. 2(1)(b) Merger Regulation.[126]

The question to be asked is whether it would be desirable to introduce a system in which social consideration have greater weight in merger control at the EU level. In some Member States, a two-tiered system is in place where the competition authority makes a strictly competitive analysis of mergers whereas the government has the possibility – after the prohibition of a merger – to grant an exceptional authorization for public interest reasons.[127] Transposing such a system at the EU level would mean that a political body would be granted the competence to overturn merger prohibitions for public policy considerations including social aspects like for example the preservation of jobs. The advantage would be that the first examination of the merger made by the European Commission would be completely relieved from general political pressure and could rely on a mere competitive analysis. Of course, the existing law prevents the European Commission from proceeding to general weighing exercises. But critics argue that the Commission is *de facto* influenced by political constraints. In a two-tiered system, the separation between competition authority and a political body would clearly restrain the Commission to a competitive analysis. Then, at a later stage, it would be the task of a political body to assess the general consequences of the merger. However, this system would trigger a reflection on which institution would be more suitable to carry out these tasks, and whether the competence of applying competition law should be transferred from the European Commission to a newly set up, independent EU competition authority.[128]

6 EU competition law: a cornerstone of the 'social market economy'

Competition law is crucial for economic success: well-functioning markets protected against formation of cartels, the abuse of dominant positions and anti-competitive mergers are the basis of wealth, growth and innovation. In competitive markets consumers are provided with the most advanced products of highest quality and at best prices, and they have the possibility to choose. By protecting consumer sovereignty and by preventing value transfers in form of cartel and monopoly rents, competition law is social in itself.

Nevertheless, the relationship of competition law with other policy fields including social policy is still problematic and requires further reflection.[129] The analysis has shown that public interests of a non-economic or non-competitive nature should be primarily addressed by the respective policy fields. Competition law does not stand in the way of such measures: if the legislature excludes the competition principle with respect to certain subject-matters,[130] there is no economic activity and hence no undertaking to which competition law could be applied. In this sense, there is an 'exception sociale' to competition law, for example regarding collective bargaining by social partners or social security systems subject to the principle of solidarity. If there is an economic activity which has not been dispensed from the market mechanism, competition law applies. This does not mean, however, that social considerations are completely excluded. Due to the symbiotic relationship between competition law and the social market economy, preference should be given to the consumer welfare standard over the total welfare standard when it comes to efficiency analysis. If social considerations overlap with efficiency considerations, they may lead to the justification of restrictive agreements. Cooperation in the field of CSR, for example, benefits to a large extent from the applicable justifications. The prohibition against abuse of dominant positions has a strong relationship to social goals given that it not only promotes effective competition with its welfare-enhancing effects, it also protects customers, particularly against abusive prices and conditions. For EU merger control, a two-tiered system might lead to a sharper distinction between a purely competitive analysis, reserved to the competition authority, and a public policy assessment, attributed to a political instance.

The entry into force of the Lisbon Treaty has not altered the central tenets of EU competition law. Although the principle of undistorted competition has been relegated from the Treaty to a mere Protocol, the autonomy of competition law has not been affected by this change. With regard to the strengthening of social objectives within the Lisbon Treaty, competition law had always to define its relationship to other policy areas. The case law and the discussion post-Lisbon regarding the intersection between competition law and social goals follow the same lines as before. On the other hand, and unintended by those who wanted to weaken the competition principle, the Lisbon Treaty has confirmed a fundamental insight: even though, as this volume demonstrates, the meaning of 'social market economy' is still subject to debate and largely undefined, it is not disputed that competition law is one of its cornerstones since it is essential for the creation of wealth, which the State can avail for the pursuit of social goals.

Notes

1 David Gerber, *Law and Competition in Twentieth Century Europe: Protecting Prometheus* (Clarendon Press, 1998) 328, who describes, taking the example of Germany after WWII, how law was given preponderance over policy and administrative discretion regarding the application of competition law.
2 Ariel Ezrachi, 'Sponge' (2017) *Journal of Antitrust Enforcement* 49, at 59.
3 OECD Global Forum on Competition, 'The Objectives of Competition Law and Policy: Note by the Secretariat' CCNM/GF/COMP(2003)3.
4 US Supreme Court, *National Society of Professional Engineers v US*, [1978] 435 U.S. 679, 690 and its interpretation by Lawrence Sullivan, Warren Grimes and Christopher Sagers, *The Law of Antitrust: An Integrated Handbook* (West Publishing, 2016) 222–223.
5 Dagmar Schiek *et al.*, *EU Social and Labour Rights and EU Internal Market Law* (2015) Study for the EMPL Committee of the European Parliament, para 1.3.1, at < http://www.europarl.europa.eu/RegData/etudes/STUD/2015/563457/IPOL_STU(2015)563457_EN.pdf>.
6 European Commission, 'Guidelines on the Effect on Trade Concept Contained in Articles 81 and 82 of the Treaty', [2004] OJ C101/81. However, the cross-border condition is met relatively easy: A direct or indirect, actual or potential influence on the pattern of trade between Member States (which is not only insignificant) is sufficient, for example Case C-475/99, *Ambulanz Glöckner*, EU:C:2001:577, paras 47–49.
7 Article 39(1)(b) TFEU which reads 'thus to ensure a fair standard of living for the agricultural community, in particular by increasing the individual earnings of persons engaged in agriculture'.
8 Case C-67/96, *Albany*, EU:C:1999:430, para 54.
9 Anne Witt, 'Public Policy Goals under EU Competition Law: Now Is the Time to Set the House in Order' (2012) *European Competition Journal* 443, at 465.
10 Delia Ferri and Fulvio Cortese, 'Introduction', and Stefano Civitarese Matteucci, 'Social Rights, Social Market Economy, and the European Social Model: Tracing Conceptual Boundaries', in this volume.
11 For an overview of ordoliberalism, Gerber, *Law and Competition in Twentieth Century Europe: Protecting Prometheus* (n 1), at 232.
12 Leonhard Miksch, *Wettbewerb als Aufgabe ('Competition as Task')* (Helmut Küpper, 1947).
13 Alfred Müller-Armack, *Wirtschaftslenkung und Marktwirtschaft* (Verlag für Wirtschaft und Sozialpolitik, 1947). However, the term *ordo* has not completely disappeared from the German language, but is used for example in the word *'Ordnungspolitik'* which describes fundamental market economy policy in an ordoliberal sense.
14 The English title of Erhard's most successful book (*Wohlstand für Alle*, Econ, 1957) underlines this context more clearly than the German one: it reads '*Prosperity Through Competition*' (Frederich Praeger, 1958).
15 Erhard, *Prosperity Through Competition* (n 14), at 126.

16 Gerber, *Law and Competition in Twentieth Century Europe: Protecting Prometheus* (n 1), 270, at 277.
17 Erhard, *Prosperity Through Competition* (n 14), at 117.
18 Ibid., at 129.
19 Mario Monti, 'Competition in a Social Market Economy' (2001) 1 *Competition Policy Newsletter* 2. Since then, the 'social market economy' has become a standard reference for EU competition law, Joaquín Almunia, 'How competition policy contributes to competitiveness and social cohesion' (2011) SPEECH/11/17, at 2.
20 Passage from the centralized notification and authorization system to the system of legal exception, implemented by Council Regulation (EC) No 1/2003 of 16 December 2002 on the implementation of the rules on competition laid down in Articles 81 and 82 of the Treaty, [2003] OJ L1/1.
21 Monti (n 19), at 3.
22 Article 3(1)(g) EC Treaty included among the aims of the treaties 'a system ensuring that competition in the internal market is not distorted'.
23 Josef Drexl, 'Competition Law as Part of the European Constitution' in Armin von Bogdandy and Jürgen Bast (eds.), *Principles of European Constitutional Law* (Hart, 2010) 659, at 660–661; Heike Schweitzer and Kiran Klaus Patel, 'EU Competition Law in Historical Context' in Kiran Klaus Patel and Heike Schweitzer (eds.), *The Historical Foundations of EU Competition Law* (OUP, 2013) 207, at 227; Witt, 'Public Policy Goals under EU Competition Law: Now Is the Time to Set the House in Order' (n 9), at 465–466.
24 Schweitzer and Patel (eds.), *The Historical Foundations of EU Competition Law* (n 23).
25 Václav Šmejkal, 'Competition Law and the Social Market Economy Goal of the EU' (2015) *International Comparative Jurisprudence* 33, at 35.
26 Recital 34 and Article 6 of Regulation (EU) 2018/302 of the European Parliament and of the Council of 28 February 2018 on addressing unjustified geo-blocking and other forms of discrimination based on customers' nationality, place of residence or place of establishment within the internal market, [2018] OJ L60 I/1.
27 Case C-496/09, *Commission v Italy*, EU:C:2011:740, para 60; Case C-52/09, *TeliaSonera Sverige*, EU:C:2011:83, paras 20–22; Case C-610/10, *Commission v Spain*, EU:C:2012:781, para 126.
28 Joshua Gans, 'Economics of Innovation' in Roger Blair and Daniel Sokol (eds.), *Antitrust, Intellectual Property, and High Tech* (CUP, 2017) 3.
29 Daniel Zimmer (ed.), *The Goals of Competition Law* (Edward Elgar, 2012).
30 Friedrich August von Hayek, 'Competition as a Discovery Procedure' (2002) *The Quarterly Journal of Austrian Economics* 9.
31 Oles Andriychuk, *The Normative Foundations of European Competition Law: Assessing the Goals of Antitrust through the Lens of Legal Philosophy* (Edward Elgar, 2017).
32 Roger Zäch and Adrian Künzler, 'Freedom to Compete or Consumer Welfare: The Goal of Competition Law according to Constitutional Law' in Roger Zäch, Andreas Heinemann and Andreas Kellerhals (eds.), *The Development of Competition Law: Global Perspectives* (Edward Elgar, 2010) 61.
33 Robert Bork, *The Antitrust Paradox: A Policy at War with Itself* (Free Press, 1993) 117, one of the most prominent proponents of the Chicago School, warns against the direct measurement of efficiencies.
34 Joined Cases C-501/06P, C-513/06P, C-515/06P and C-519/06P, *GlaxoSmithKlines*, EU:C:2009:610, para 63; Case C-286/13P, *Dole Food and Dole Fresh Fruit Europe*, EU:C:2015:184, para 125.
35 European Commission, 'Guidelines on the Application of Article 81(3) of the Treaty', [2004] OJ C101/97, para 105; European Commission, 'Guidance

on the Commission's Enforcement Priorities in Applying Article 82 of the EC Treaty to Abusive Exclusionary Conduct by Dominant Undertakings', [2009] OJ C45/7, para 6.

36 Massimo Motta, *Competition Policy: Theory and Practice* (CUP, 2004) 17.

37 Ibid., at 21–22. Motta adds, though, that policy recommendations based on the two standards rarely differ. There is no consensus among economists. Damien Neven and Lars-Hendrik Röller, 'Consumer Surplus vs. Welfare Standard in a Political Economy Model of Merger Control' (2005) *International Journal of Industrial Organisation* 829, argue in a merger control context that the consumer surplus standard is more appropriate if lobbying from large firms is strong or if an important part of mergers fail to yield significant efficiencies.

38 UNCTAD, 'The Benefit of Competition Policy for Consumers' (2014) TD/B/C.I/CLP/27, para 4; Phil Evans, 'The Consumer and Competition Policy: Welfare, Interest and Engagement' in Ariel Ezrachi (ed.), *Research Handbook on International Competition Law* (Edward Elgar, 2012) 545.

39 European Commission, 'Guidelines on the Application of Article 81(3) of the Treaty' and 'Guidance on the Commission's Enforcement Priorities in Applying Article 82 of the EC Treaty to Abusive Exclusionary Conduct by Dominant Undertakings' (n 35), para 19.

40 European Commission, 'Guidelines on the Application of Article 81(3) of the Treaty' (n 35), para 43.

41 On the position of consumers in competition law, Neil Averitt and Robert Lande, 'Consumer Sovereignty: A Unified Theory of Antitrust and Consumer Protection Law' (1997) *The Antitrust Law Journal* 713.

42 Case C-185/14, *EasyPay and Finance Engineering*, EU:C:2015:716, para 37.

43 Case C-209/78, *Van Landewyck*, EU:C:1980:248, para 88; Case C-244/94, *FFSA and Others*, EU:C:1995:392, para 21.

44 Commission Directive 2006/111/EC of 16 November 2006 on the transparency of financial relations between Member States and public undertakings as well as on financial transparency within certain undertakings, [2006] OJ L318/17.

45 Ibid., Article 2.

46 Case C-118/85, *Commission v Italy*, EU:C:1987:283, para 8; Case C-343/95, *Calì and Figli*, EU:C:1997:160, para 17.

47 *Commission v Italy* (n 46), para 11.

48 Delia Ferri and Juan Piernas Lopez, 'State Aid Law in a Social Market Economy', in this volume.

49 Case C-41/90, *Höfner*, EU:C:1991:161, paras 21–23.

50 Case C-475/99, *Ambulanz Glöckner*, EU:C:2001:577, paras 19–20.

51 Joined Cases C-180/98 to C-184/98, *Pavlov*, EU:C:2000:428, paras 76–77.

52 Commission Decision, Case COMP/M.4010, *Fresenius v Helios*, [2006] OJ C26/9.

53 Case C-205/03P, *FENIN*, EU:C:2006:453, paras 25–27.

54 Christopher Bovis, 'The Social Dimension of EU Public Procurement', in this volume.

55 *Commission v Italy* (n 46), paras 7–8; Case T-462/13, *Comunidad Autónoma del País Vasco and Itelazpi v Commission*, EU:T:2015:902, para 61.

56 Case C-364/92, *SAT Fluggesellschaft v Eurocontrol*, EU:C:1994:7, para 30.

57 Communication from the European Commission, 'The Application of the European Union State Aid Rules to Compensation Granted for the Provision of Services of General Economic Interest', [2012] OJ C8/4, para 16.

58 Case C-41/83, *Italy v Commission*, EU:C:1985:120, paras 18–20; *Pavlow* (n 51), paras 85–88; Case C-1/12, *Ordem dos Técnicos Oficiais de Contas*, EU:C:2013:127, paras 39–56.

59 Case C-82/01 P, *Aéroports de Paris v Commission*, EU:C:2002:617, para 82.

60 Case C-238/82, *Duphar*, EU:C:1983:226, para 16; Case C-158/96, *Kohll v Union des caisses de maladie*, EU:C:1998:171, para 19.
61 Joined Cases C-159/91 and C-160/91, *Poucet and Pistre v AGF and Cancava*, EU:C:1992:358 paras 8–19; Case C-218/00, *Cisal*, EU:C:2001:448, paras 37–45; Case C-350/07, *Kattner Stahlbau*, EU:C:2008:631, paras 35–68; *EasyPay and Finance Engineering* (n 42), para 38.
62 Communication from the European Commission, 'Services of General Economic Interest' (n 57), para 19.
63 Ibid., para 20.
64 Joined Cases C-264/01, C-306/01, C-354/01 and C-355/01, *AOK Bundesverband and Others*, EU:C:2004:150, para 56.
65 Other cases include, *Kattner Stahlbau* (n 61); Case C-437/09, *AG2R Prévoyance*, EU:C:2011:112. For an analysis of the latter judgement, Christian Kersting, 'Social Security and Competition Law: ECJ Focuses on Art. 106(2) TFEU' (2011) 2 *Journal of European Competition Law and Practice* 473.
66 In the latter sense Volker Emmerich in Ulrich Immenga and Ernst-Joachim Mestmäcker (eds.), *Wettbewerbsrecht*, Vol. 1 EU/Part 1 (Beck, 2012); Article 101(1) TFEU, para 29.
67 ILO Convention No 87 on the Freedom of Association and Protection of the Right to Organize (1948) and ILO Convention No 98 on the Right to Organize and Collective Bargaining (1949).
68 Michael Doherty, 'W(h)ither Social Europe? Labour Rights in a Social Market Economy', in this volume. The right of collective bargaining in Article 28 of the Charter is subject to certain restrictions, i.e. it has to be exercised 'in accordance with Union law and national laws and practices' (Case C-341/05, *Laval un Partneri*, EU:C:2007:809, para 91); Article 156(1) TFEU, as well as the Declaration on Article 156 TFEU. Article 1(7) of the Services Directive (Directive 2006/123/EC of 12 December 2006 of the European Parliament and of the Council on services in the internal market, [2006] OJ L376/36) states that nor does the Directive 'affect the right to negotiate, conclude and enforce collective agreements and to take industrial action in accordance with national law and practices which respect Community law'. See also Articles 11–14 of the Community Charter of the Fundamental Social Rights of Workers alluded to in the fifth recital of the Preamble to the TEU as well as in Article 151 TFEU.
69 Doherty, 'W(h)ither Social Europe? Labour Rights in a Social Market Economy' (n 68), Section 3.
70 On the structural market failure in labour markets, Schiek *et al.*, 'EU Social and Labour Rights and EU Internal Market Law' (n 5), paras 1.3.3, 2.2.4 and 4.3.2.
71 Section 20 of the Clayton Act grants immunity to collective activities by employees. For more details, including the difference between the 'statutory' and the 'non-statutory' exemption for labour markets, Herbert Hovenkamp, *Federal Antitrust Policy: The Law of Competition and Its Practice* (West Publishing, 2016) 965–969. This author points to the fact that regarding the first thirteen antitrust violations found by American courts after the enactment of the Sherman Act in 1890, twelve regarded labour strikes while only one was directed against a restrictive agreement among manufacturers.
72 Case C-22/98, *Becu and Others*, EU:C:1999:419, para 26.
73 Ibid., para 27.
74 Doherty, 'W(h)ither Social Europe? Labour Rights in a Social Market Economy' (n 68), Section 3.
75 *Albany* (n 8), paras 59 and 60. See also Joined Cases C-115/97, C-116/97 and C-117/97, *Brentjens'*, EU:C:1999:434 and Case C-219/97, *Drijvende Bokken*, EU:C:1999:437. The EFTA Court takes the same view, Case E-14/15, *Holship Norge AS/Norsk Transportarbeiderforbund*, [2016], para 40.

76 See (n 72) and (n 73).
77 *Pavlov* (n 51), paras 68–70.
78 Case C-413/13, *FNV Kunsten Informatie en Media*, EU:C:2014:2411, paras 24–30; however, this reasoning does not apply to 'false self-employed' service providers who have to be treated like employees, ibid., paras 31–36.
79 Joined Cases T-217/03 and T-245/03, *FNCBV and Others v Commission*, EU:T:2006:391, para 100; confirmed by Joined Cases C101/07 P and C110/07 P, *Coop de France bétail and viande v Commission*, EU:C:2008:741.
80 Case C-309/99, *Wouters*, ECLI:EU:C:2002:98, para 97.
81 Ibid., paras 109 and 110.
82 Case C-519/04 P, *Meca-Medina and Majcen v Commission*, EU:C:2006:492, paras 42 and 45; Joined Cases C-184/13 to C-187/13, C-194/13, C-195/13 and C-208/13, *API and Others*, EU:C:2014:2147, para 47.
83 Case C-136/12, *Consiglio nazionale dei geologi and Autorità garante della concorrenza e del mercato*, EU:C:2013:489, para 54.
84 Opinion of AG Fennelly, Case C-222/98, *van der Woude*, EU:C:2000:226, paras 30 and 31.
85 Immenga and Mestmäcker (eds.), *Wettbewerbsrecht* (n 66), para 26.
86 Volker Emmerich in Schiek *et al.*, 'EU Social and Labour Rights and EU Internal Market Law' (n 5), para 2.2.4.
87 *Albany* (n 8), paras 191 and 192.
88 Ibid., para 193.
89 Ibid., paras 59 and 60.
90 *van der Woude* (n 84), para 22; *AG2R Prévoyance* (n 65), paras 28.
91 *Holship Norge AS v Norsk Transportarbeiderforbund* (n 75), paras 48–53.
92 Case C-438/05, *Viking*, EU:C:2007:772, paras 52–55.
93 Ibid., paras 56–61.
94 *Albany* (n 8), para 183.
95 Case C-41/90, *Höfner*, EU:C:1991:161.
96 Case C-341/05, *Laval*, EU:C:2007:809, para 105.
97 European Commission, 'Guidelines on the Method of Setting Fines Imposed Pursuant to Article 23(2)(a) of Regulation No 1/2003', [2006] OJ C210/2, para 35.
98 Commission Decision, Case C.38.359, *Electrical and Mechanical Carbon and Graphite Products*, 2004/420/EC [2004] OJ L125/45, paras 350 and 357.
99 This principle has been recognized since Joined Cases 40 to 48, 50, 54 to 56, 111, 113 and 114/73, *Suiker Unie*, EU:C:1975:174, paras 173–174. From recent case law, Case C-74/14, *Eturas*, EU:C:2016:42, para 27 ('requirement of autonomy').
100 On the distinction between object and effect, Richard Whish and David Bailey, *Competition Law* (OUP, 2015) 120.
101 Schiek *et al.*, 'EU Social and Labour Rights and EU Internal Market Law' (n 5), Section 1.5.1.
102 Ernst-Joachim Mestmäcker and Heike Schweitzer, *Europäisches Wettbewerbsrecht* (C.H. Beck, 2014), § 11 n 100.
103 Report of the Special Representative of the Secretary-General on the issue of human rights and transnational corporations and other business enterprises, John Ruggie, *Guiding Principles on Business and Human Rights* (2011) UN Document A/HRC/17/31. The 'responsibility to respect' refers to internationally recognized human rights. Firms should not infringe human rights themselves, and they should address adverse human rights impacts with which they are involved.
104 Thomas Ackermann, 'Corporate Social Responsibility und Kartellrecht' in Reto Hilty and Frauke Henning-Bodewig (eds.), *Corporate Social Responsibility* (Springer, 2014) 147.

105 John Ruggie, *Business and Human Rights: Towards Operationalizing the 'Protect, Respect and Remedy' Framework* (2009) UN Doc A/HRC/11/13, para 46.

106 Commission Decision, Case COMP/39579, *Consumer Detergents*, [2011] OJ C193/14.

107 AISE, *Code of Good Environmental Practice for Household Laundry Detergents* (16 January 1997). This Code was endorsed by the European Commission, Recommendation 98/480/EC of 22 July 1998 concerning good environmental practice for household laundry detergents, [1998] OJ L215/73.

108 European Commission, 'Guidelines on the Applicability of Article 101 TFEU to Horizontal Co-Operation Agreements', [2011] OJ C11/1.

109 Case 42/84, *Remia v Commission*, EU:C:1985:327, para 42. For an analysis of the case law, Witt, 'Public Policy Goals under EU Competition Law: Now Is the Time to Set the House in Order' (n 9).

110 Ioannis Lianos, 'Some Reflections on the Question of the Goals of EU Competition Law' in Ioannis Lianos and Damien Geradin (eds.), *Handbook on European Competition Law: Substantive Aspects* (Edward Elgar, 2013) 1, at 58–59; Christopher Townley, *Article 81 EC and Public Policy* (Hart, 2009); Giorgio Monti, 'Article 81 EC and Public Policy' (2002) 39 *Common Market Law Review* 1057 who proposes a new Article 81(4) (now Article 101(4) TFEU) providing for exemptions in favour of public policy goals subject to an authorisation by the European Commission, at 1097.

111 US antitrust law is comparable to EU law in this respect. In *Topco* (US Supreme Court, *United States v Topco Associates, Inc.*, [1972] 406 U.S. 596, 611–612), the US Supreme Court has refused a general balancing of social values and has reserved this right to Congress.

112 European Commission, 'Guidelines on the Application of Article 81(3) of the Treaty' (n 35), para 42; Joined Cases T-528/93, T-542/93, T-543/93 and T-546/93, *Métropole Télévision v Commission*, EU:T:1996:99, paras 118 and 123.

113 The focus on efficiency has been strengthened by the more economic approach of the European Commission and by the transition to the system of legal exception, Giorgio Monti, *EC Competition Law* (CUP, 2007) 113–123; Witt, 'Public Policy Goals under EU Competition Law: Now Is the Time to Set the House in Order' (n 9).

114 Heike Schweitzer, 'Competition Law and Public Policy: Reconsidering an Uneasy Relationship' in Josef Drexl, Laurence Idot and Joël Monéger (eds.), *Economic Theory and Competition Law* (Edward Elgar, 2009) 149–150. Šmejkal, 'Competition Law and the Social Market Economy Goal of the EU' (n 25), at 39, who evokes the possibility of an extended interpretation of Articles 101(3) and 106(2) TFEU because of the social objectives in the Lisbon Treaty.

115 This is the definition of market dominance given by the CJEU (Case C-27/76, *United Brands*, EU:C:1978:22, para 65).

116 European Commission, 'Guidance on the Commission's Enforcement Priorities in Applying Article 82 of the EC Treaty to Abusive Exclusionary Conduct by Dominant Undertakings', [2009] OJ C45/7, paras 1 and 6. Schiek *et al.*, 'EU Social and Labour Rights and EU Internal Market Law' (n 5), at 25, affirm that '[t]he prohibition on abusing a dominant market position aims at hindering large corporate actors from crushing smaller entrepreneurs'.

117 US Supreme Court, *Verizon Communications Inc. v Law Offices of Curtis v Trinko* [2004] 540 U.S. 398, III: Monopoly prices are tolerated as an incentive for risk-taking in the free market system.

118 Whish and Bailey, *Competition Law* (n 100), at 759–761.

119 Opinion of AG Wahl, Case C-177/16, *Biedrība 'Autortiesību un komunicēšanās konsultāciju aģentūra – Latvijas Autoru apvienība' v Konkurences padome*, EU:C:2017:286, para 48.

120 René Joliet, *Monopolization and Abuse of Dominant Position* (Martinus Nijhoff, 1970) 250–251.

121 Council Regulation (EC) 139/2004 of 20 January 200 on the control of concentrations between undertakings (the EC Merger Regulation) [2004] OJ L24/1.

122 According to Article 21(4) ECMR, this does not prevent Member States from taking measures to protect legitimate interests in other fields than competition law, for example regarding public security, plurality of the media and prudential rules.

123 Case T-12/93, *CCE Vittel v Commission*, EU:T:1995:78, para 38.

124 Article 18(4) EC Merger Regulation according to which the recognized representatives of the employees may be entitled to be heard in the procedure.

125 This seems to be a general insight from all jurisdictions having the possibility to refer to general policy arguments, OECD, 'Executive Summary of the Roundtable on Public Interest Considerations in Merger Control' (2006) DAF/COMP/WP3/M(2016)1/ANN5/FINAL, at 3: 'The discussion showed that OECD Member country competition authorities that are empowered to assess public interest considerations rarely rely on them, and, when they do, they usually interpret and apply them narrowly'.

126 Scepticism towards public interest arguments in merger control has been expressed by Torsten Körber in Immenga and Mestmäcker (eds.), *Wettbewerbsrecht* (Beck, 2012), Art. 2 FKVO (ECMR), para 212 and 400; Whish and Bailey, *Competition Law* (n 100), at 868–870.

127 Examples are Article L430-7-1 of the French *Code de commerce*, which mentions general interest, such as industrial development, international competitiveness, employment and the German *Gesetz gegen Wettbewerbsbeschränkungen*, which mentions overriding public interest, for example international competitiveness.

128 This question has been raised regularly, so far without success; Giuliano Amato, 'A European Cartel Office?' in *EUI Collected Courses of the Academy of European Law* (Kluwer Law International, 2001) 143.

129 The Rome Declaration of 25.3.2017 which pleads at the same time for a 'prosperous and sustainable Europe' based on the single market and for a 'social Europe' promoting the shared values.

130 Michael Sandel, *What Money Can't Buy: The Moral Limits of Markets* (Farrar, Straus and Giroux, 2012).

8 State aid law in a social market economy

*Delia Ferri and Juan Jorge Piernas López**

1 Introduction

State aid control is a distinctive feature of the European Union's (EU) competition law,[1] and was inserted in the founding Treaties with the intention of maintaining a level playing field for undertakings, and avoiding a 'subsidy race' among Member States that would undermine the creation and functioning of the internal market.[2] State aid law and policy is traditionally considered part of EU competition law,[3] and, as economic integration has become more established within the EU legal order, it has become more and more centred on competition concerns.[4]

Article 107(1) TFEU provides that any aid granted by a Member State or through State resources, which distorts, or threatens to distort, competition by favouring certain undertakings or the production of certain goods, is incompatible with the internal market, insofar as it affects trade between the Member States. State measures are prohibited if the cumulative criteria listed in Article 107(1) TFEU are satisfied. This provision has not been modified since its introduction in the EEC Treaty of 1957, save for the draftsman replacing the phrase 'common market' with 'internal market'. This blanket prohibition is however allayed by a set of exceptions laid down in Article 107(2) and (3) TFEU. These exceptions are premised on the assumption that markets are not entirely self-regulating, and do not always work properly if left alone. Consequently, some intervention from the State may be needed for markets to work more effectively. In addition, equity and social considerations may call for public intervention.[5]

Treaty rules are complemented by a composite system of guidelines issued by the Commission, as well as through regulations. Article 109 TFEU allows for the adoption of secondary legislation in the field of State aid. Under this provision, the Council adopted Regulation 994/98,[6] i.e. the Enabling Regulation, which has empowered the Commission to adopt individual regulations in which it declares certain types of aid to be lawful and exempts them from the obligation of prior notification of aid projects under Article 108(3) TFEU. Further to the Enabling Regulation, in 2006, the Commission adopted the first *De minimis* Regulation,[7] which was replaced by a new regulation in 2013.[8] The Commission does not need to be notified regarding measures that fulfil the criteria of the *De minimis*. From 2001 to 2006, the Commission also endorsed a series of exemption regulations,[9] consolidated in the 2008 General Block Exemption Regulation

(GBER),[10] which was subsequently replaced by a new GBER in 2014.[11] The GBER lays down the conditions under which aid can be considered compatible with the internal market, and exempted from prior notification. Unlike other competition provisions, this complex net of EU State aid rules is addressed to Member States and imposes strict limits on the ability of the Member States to pursue their own policy objectives. However, the Treaty, by virtue of the derogations laid down in Article 107(2) and (3) TFEU, allows Member States to protect and promote specific rights or values. In addition, the way in which the Commission has implemented State aid law has *de facto* nudged States to use their public spending towards identified common goals.[12]

Against this background, this chapter discusses the social dimension of EU State aid law and policy. Without engaging in a detailed analysis of the technicalities related to State aid control, it aims to locate State aid control in the realm of the 'social market economy'. Mirroring the analysis carried out by Heinemann on antitrust,[13] the remainder of this chapter is structured as follows. Section 2 discusses the extent to which social considerations may lead to EU State aid rules being inapplicable, leaving Member States free to pursue their own social policies. Section 3 succinctly examines whether the application of State aid rules to transfer pricing arrangements and corporate taxation can be framed within the pursuit of the social market economy objective, and are underpinned by a broader social justice concern. Sections 4 and 5 analyse whether and to what extent social considerations may lead to an aid measure being compatible with the internal market under the derogations provided by the Treaty. In particular, Section 4 focuses on aid having 'a social character' under Article 107(2)(a) TFEU. Section 5 discusses the social dimension of derogations under Article 107(3) TFEU. Section 6 includes some conclusions.

2 The definition of state aid and social considerations

2.1 The starting point: the notion of aid as an objective notion

Article 107(1) TFEU declares 'any aid' *a priori* incompatible with the internal market. However, it does not define what is an aid for the purposes of State aid law. The wording of this provision is intentionally broad and has allowed for a greater degree of flexibility when identifying what must be considered an aid for the purposes of the Treaty. The CJEU has clarified that the notion of aid requires the following criteria to be met.[14] There must be an intervention by the State or through State resources. The intervention must be liable to affect trade between Member States. It must confer an advantage on the recipient. The CJEU has also affirmed that the advantage conferred must be selective as it has to favour 'certain undertakings or the production of certain goods'.[15] Measures of general application, directed to all undertakings, do not give rise to State aid. The intervention must distort or threaten to distort competition.[16]

The concept of State aid is objective,[17] and the Commission has 'no margin of discretion' in the application of this concept.[18] Article 107(1) TFEU 'does not distinguish between the measures of State intervention concerned by reference to their causes or aims but defines them in relation to their effects. Consequently, the alleged fiscal nature *or social aim* of the measure in issue cannot suffice to shield it from the application of Article [107]' (emphasis added).[19]

In light of the foregoing, there is no apparent scope for social considerations under Article 107(1) TFEU. However, the way in which this provision has been implemented has left the door open for a social dimension to emerge, as it will be discussed in the following subsections.[20]

2.2 *The notion of undertaking and social considerations*

Just like with competition law rules, State aid provisions only apply where the beneficiary of a measure is an 'undertaking',[21] i.e. an entity engaged in economic activities within the meaning of the *Höfner* jurisprudence.[22]

Even though the interpretation of *undertaking* has been quite broad, the Commission has left the door open to State measures aimed at incentivizing social or environmental goals when directed at individuals. One of the most notable examples is that of incentivizing private persons to install and use renewable energy sources.[23] In addition, the way in which the CJEU opens up the scope for public funding to protect and promote certain activities that have a social value, such as healthcare and education should also be underlined.[24] For the purpose of this analysis, there are three fields in which, by carving out the notion of undertaking, the scope of application of EU State aid law seems to have been sensibly narrowed. First, that of social security. Even though social security schemes are generally considered to incorporate an economic activity, solidarity-based[25] schemes fall outside the remit of State aid as they are not considered undertakings when they meet certain criteria. These criteria have been identified over time by the CJEU.[26] Namely, that the scheme must be supervised by the State; it must be not be conducted for financial profits and therefore pursue exclusively social objectives; affiliation to the scheme must be compulsory; and the benefits for affiliated are independent of the contributions made and not necessarily proportionate to the earnings of the person insured. If these criteria are collectively met, the solidarity-based schemes are not undertakings, and national policies that support them fall outside the realm of State aid control. The scope of the 'exception' carved out by the Court is narrow, and despite the flow of case law and the attempt of the Commission to clarify the criteria, they remain quite blurred. The entry into force of the Lisbon Treaty has thus far not visibly influenced the scope of this exception. However, as Heinemann has argued earlier in this volume, the individual assessment carried out by the Commission can effectively reconcile social and economic goals.

A field within which the scope of State aid rules has been most significantly narrowed down is that of 'cultural activities'. Benefits that support cultural entities are generally considered to constitute State aid, but they can be allowed under Article 107(3)(d) TFEU, or exempted from notification under the GBER. The 2016 Commission Notice has further clarified that 'public funding of a cultural or heritage conservation activity accessible to the general public free of charge fulfils a purely *social* and cultural purpose which is non-economic in nature' (emphasis added). The Commission also explained that, even when visitors of a cultural institution or participants in a cultural or heritage conservation activity are required to pay a monetary contribution that only covers a fraction of the true costs, the non-economic nature of that activity is not altered. Mengozzi highlights the innovative character of the Notice in this respect.[27] Before 2016, the Commission had systematically taken the view that cultural activities were, in principle, to be considered economic in nature and capable of falling within the remit of the State aid rules, despite most of the aid measures being considered compatible with the internal market.[28] It might be argued that the new approach of the Commission and the emphasis on the social role of culture sits well in the realm of a 'social market economy' (yet not being a direct consequence of the entry into force of Article 3 TEU).

Finally, a field in which the scope for the application of State aid rules is limited is that of education. The CJEU has consistently held that public education organized within the national educational system, funded and supervised by the State, may be considered to constitute a non-economic activity, and that the State 'by establishing and maintaining such a system of public education [. . .] does not intend to become involved in activities for remuneration, but carries out its task towards its population in the *social*, cultural and educational areas' (emphasis added).[29] In the recent case *Congregación de Escuelas Pías*, the CJEU considered whether a tax exemption granted by Spanish authorities to the Catholic Church, in respect of educational activities, constituted State aid prohibited under Article 107(1) TFEU. The CJEU ultimately left to the national court to decide whether or not the tax exemption fell within the remit of application of Article 107(1) TFEU, as it was a preliminary ruling, but clearly stated that this provision would be applicable only if at least some of the educational activities are classified as 'economic activities' and the hall in question is used, at least in part, for such economic activities. This decision exemplifies that the line between economic and non-economic activities in the educational field is not always clear-cut. However, there is a clear scope for the State to subsidize educational activities without becoming caught within the prohibitions laid down in the Treaty.

In general, Article 3 TEU has thus far not displayed a visible influence on the way in which an undertaking is defined for the purposes of State aid rules. However, as noted by Sauter,[30] the test applied by the Commission to verify whether the activity is economic is continually being refined and diversified across different sectors. It seems that, *de facto*, this test leaves the door open to weigh social considerations, and consequently allows Member States a small space within which to manoeuvre for the purposes of subsidizing activities that fulfil social rights and pursue social goals.

2.3 Selectivity, general measures and social considerations

In *Maribel bis/ter*, the Court analysed whether a measure applicable only to some sectors of the Belgian economy could be considered as a general measure (not implying aid) in relation to the fact that the exclusion of some sectors from the application of the measure was due to its alleged social objective (i.e. promotion of employment of manual workers). In particular, the measure under review consisted of a reduction in social charges to some sectors that were particularly exposed to international competition and benefitted certain sectors of the Belgian economy explicitly listed in the legislation. Two companies referred the case to the Commission: one of them claimed that support for the sectors most exposed to international competition was incompatible with the State aid rules. The other claimed that this support was discriminatory (against Belgian undertakings not benefitting from the aid) and demanded to be afforded equal treatment. The Belgian Government submitted that the *Maribel bis/ter* scheme was a general measure. It submitted that a measure directed to 'all undertakings', is a measure directed to undertakings which are 'in an objectively similar position'[31] and not 'all undertakings' in a given Member State, otherwise it would be very difficult to adopt social, fiscal or economic policy measures, as they hardly apply simultaneously to all undertakings in a given Member State. In this regard, the Belgian Government noted that the Commission itself had conceded, in a Communication on the monitoring of State aid and reduction of labour costs, that measures favouring certain categories of workers, therefore benefitting only those undertakings employing those categories of workers, did not constitute State aid if they applied automatically and ¨without discrimination.[32] In fact, the Commission had already explicitly referred to 'companies which are in the same objective position' in a 1996 decision. The case ended in front of the CJEU and the Court confirmed (as the Commission did) that the measure was selective because it was restricted to certain sectors of the Belgian economy. The Court noted that

> Neither the high number of benefiting undertakings nor the diversity and importance of the industrial sectors to which those undertakings belong warrant the conclusion that the *Maribel bis/ter* scheme constitutes a general measure of economic policy, as the Belgian Government claims.[33]

However, the Court did not end the analysis at that point. Instead, the CJEU examined whether the exclusion of some sectors from the application of the measure was compatible with its alleged objective (i.e. promotion of employment of manual workers), and noted that the objectives of the measure at stake were compatible with the general social system in force in Belgium. The Court also held that Member States retained important powers in the field of social security systems and that they could, through the redistribution of social charges, pursue, among others, the objectives advanced by the Belgian authorities, namely, the maintenance of a high level of employment amongst manual workers and the maintenance of an industrial sector in order to balance the Belgian economy. However, according to the Court, the achievement of those objectives did not justify reducing the scope of application of the measure at stake only to some undertakings (those chosen by the measure).

Interestingly, the Court accepted the interpretation of the concept of 'all undertakings' given by the Belgian authorities even though, in the end, it found that some of the sectors excluded from the contested measures (as the tertiary or the building sector) were in a comparable situation to those sectors benefitting from the contested measures, and concluded that the measure was *prima facie* selective.[34]

Once this *prima facie* selectivity was established, the Court also analysed whether the contested scheme could be justified by the nature or general scheme of the Belgian social security system. In this regard, the Commission emphasized in its pleadings that the 'justification for the measures to reduce the burden of social security costs adopted under the *Maribel bis/ter* scheme should be sought in the internal logic of the general social welfare system existing in Belgium and not in the specific purpose of the scheme'.[35] The Commission's position was in fact coherent with the test that it had included in its notice on direct business taxation and State aid, published while this case was pending.[36] The Court, however, while admitting that the measure could only be justified by the general social security system applicable in Belgium (and not by the Maribel scheme), took into account the objectives pursued by the general social security system, not so much its internal logic, as requested by the Commission. Furthermore, the Court noted that the objectives of the general social security system were very close to the objectives pursued by the contested scheme,[37] and that Member States retained the power to organize their social security systems and to promote objectives of employment policy, such as those pursued by both the *Maribel bis/ter* scheme and the general social security system applicable in Belgium.[38] Nevertheless, the Court concluded that those objectives could not justify the selective character of the advantage under review.[39]

The CJEU confirmed the Commission's decision and endorsed its approach. It also implicitly supported the selectivity test contained in the notice on direct business taxation and State aids published while this judgement was pending by following the derogation-justification analysis proposed in that notice. However, the victory for the Commission in this case was a pyrrhic one. The Court also introduced some important qualifications to the discrimination-like test for selectivity defended by the Commission since the early 1990s by concluding that the concept of 'all undertakings' referred to those in a comparable position by reference to the objective pursued by the measure, and not to all undertakings in a given Member State, as the Commission had traditionally claimed. Secondly, contrary to the Commission's submissions, the CJEU took into consideration the social objectives pursued by the contested measure at the general systemic level and not, or at least not only, the internal logic of the general social welfare system. Therefore, the Court seems to have struck a balanced in this judgement between the application of the State aid rules, particularly the definition of aid under Article 107(1) TFEU, and the social objectives pursued by the measure under review. In sum, the social character of the measure under review, its social aim, seems to have been relevant to the Court in deciding this case, despite the traditional formula cited above, and according to which neither the fiscal character or social aim of a given measure are relevant for the definition of State aid under article 107(1) TFEU.

3 Transfer pricing rulings for multinationals and social justice

Section 2 discussed the way in which the definition of State aid might leave room for Member States to pursue their own policies outside the framework of State aid law. However, the application of State aid control is not *per se* devoid of social consideration. This seems well exemplified by the recent Commission decisions on transfer pricing and corporate taxation.

Any tax measure that is found to selectively benefit an undertaking or a group of undertakings can constitute State aid for the purpose of Article 107(1) TFEU. In the last few years, there has been an increase in more sophisticated corporate tax measures,[40] often deemed to attract foreign investment, that have been considered to fall within the realm of EU State aid rules. In fact, fiscal aid provided by way of tax reductions,[41] deferrals[42] or even outright waiving of taxes owed by a specific undertaking or group of undertakings,[43] accounted for nearly 40% of all EU aid between 2004 and 2013.[44]

In relation to the foregoing, in 2014, the Commission initiated several investigations into high profile multinational companies, suspected of being granted State aid from the States in which their European headquarters were located. The Commission argued that the aggressive tax planning of these multinationals allowed them to obtain tax rates which were more favourable than those based on normal market conditions.[45] In June 2016 an investigation was launched into Luxembourg's tax treatment of McDonald's.[46] On 30 August 2016, the Commission concluded that Ireland's tax benefits to Apple were illegal under State aid rules,[47] because they allowed Apple to pay substantially less tax than other businesses in a comparable situation. In a similar vein, one year later, in October 2017,[48] the Commission concluded that Luxembourg granted illegal tax benefits to Amazon of approximately €250 million. Similar decisions were taken on the Starbucks and Fiat cases against the Netherlands[49] and Luxemburg.[50] In general, the Commission found that multinationals were shifting their profit to holding companies in order to reduce their tax liabilities in the country. In all the decisions at stake, national authorities were considered responsible for having allowed and *de facto* endorsed a method used by multinationals to calculate their taxable profits in the State that was beneficial for these same companies, in breach of Art. 107(1) TFEU.

In all these cases, the assessments of the 'economic advantage' and 'selectivity requirement'[51] in relation to the tax measures were the core legal issues and the biggest bone of contention.[52] There is a general agreement that the Commission's approach to selectivity has been less 'formal' and characterized by 'a more effects based stance'.[53] In line with most recent case law of the CJEU[54] that put forward an effects-based analysis when it comes to detecting the selective economic advantage that the fiscal measure gives to the multinational at stake, the Commission is clearly concerned with the failure of multinationals to 'pay their fair share' of taxes.[55] These decisions embody a hard-line policy on harmful tax competition in the internal market.[56] On the other hand, there seems to be an underpinning social concern. The investigations were actually started under Commissioner Almunia, a member of the Spanish Socialist Workers' Party, who had underlined the relevance of the context in which these investigations took place, a context characterized by years of public budget constraints and cuts as a result of the economic crisis that has affected the EU.[57] In countries such as Ireland, hit by the crisis and where the slow recovery has created further inequalities, these Commission decisions might be seen as a way to counteract unjust market behaviours. In this vein, they might be seen as a way to realize the 'social market economy' envisaged by the Treaty. The approach of the Commission however remains problematic. There has been clearly a vast degree of discretion that the Commission has exercised in its application of State aid law to transfer pricing arrangements, impinging on national tax sovereignty and *de facto* overcoming the EU limited competence on taxation matters, as exemplified by the fact that Member States such as Ireland have elected to appeal the Commission decisions before the EU Courts.

4 *De Jure* derogations and social considerations: aid having 'a social character' under Article 107(2) TFEU

As mentioned previously, EU State aid control is based on a system of *ex ante* authorization. This means that State aids are prohibited unless the Commission has been notified of the aid, has assessed it under Article 107(2) or (3) TFEU, and has finally approved it. The former provision specifies a number of cases in which national support measures are permissible. The Commission has no discretion as to whether to authorize the aid when the criteria set forth in the provision are met.[58] This section deliberately focuses on social aid under Art. 107(2)(a) TFEU.[59] The latter provision exempts measures having 'a social character' granted to individual consumers, without discrimination in terms of the origin of the products. This derogation not only unequivocally allows and justifies a State intervention to protect certain disadvantaged segments of the populations, but also to protect and promote certain social rights.

In the past, the Commission had consistently argued that the term 'social character' should be interpreted narrowly and refer to aid 'addressing the needs of underprivileged population groups'.[60] This strict interpretation was in line with the general principle that 'the exceptions to the general rule of incompatibility of the aid with the [internal] market must be interpreted narrowly'.[61] Aid of a social character was interpreted as aid solely and directly for the disadvantaged sections of the population, and had primarily been applied in the air transport sector. In several decisions, the Commission argued that reduced airline fares must only benefit certain disadvantaged groups, such as the elderly, disabled or some other specific class (whilst the aid must not discriminately benefit a specific airline).[62] Still, a more flexible interpretation was carved out by the Commission when admitting aid to certain categories of consumers living in remote areas or disadvantaged regions[63] or islands[64] or regions underprivileged and in need of such aid.[65] The Commission argued that the eligible categories of disadvantaged groups do not constitute a *numerus clausus*. It affirmed that

> the aid must have a social character, that is, it must, in principle, only cover certain categories of passengers travelling on a route such as children, handicapped people, people with low income, etc. However in the case where the route concerned links an underprivileged region the aid could cover the entire population of this region.[66]

Art. 107(2)(a) is now the basis for the block exemption laid down in Article 51 of the GBER, which covers aid for air and maritime transport for the benefit of consumers resident in remote regions.[67]

Interestingly, the way in which 'social character' has been most recently interpreted creates an even greater flexibility over the notion of 'aid having a social character'. For example, aside from approving various measures to switch to digital television targeting certain specific disadvantaged groups (such as, e.g. people with disabilities),[68] in order to improve social inclusion, the Commission allowed measures that go in the direction of protecting social rights of the population beyond traditionally disadvantaged groups. This is the case of the UK Homeowners Mortgage Support Scheme or the Cyprus State Grant Scheme to borrowers and micro-companies,[69] which were considered compatible with the internal market under Art. 107(2)(a) TFEU. These schemes were meant to enable households experiencing a significant and temporary loss of income (because of the economic crisis), to defer principal repayments. They were explicitly designed to help borrowers avoid repossession. The Commission recognized that, and although these individuals may not be as such part of a disadvantaged group, the worsening economic crisis made them vulnerable, acknowledging the tensions between property rights, market values and social needs. The approval of these aid measures should be viewed within the broader context of policy measures to combat poverty. Since 2010, which was the European Year for Combating Poverty and Social Exclusion, and in line with European Strategy Europe 2020,[70] the Commission has launched various initiatives to promote an inclusive growth,[71] and tackle homelessness, housing exclusion, financial exclusion and high indebtedness.[72] The European Social Pillar (EPS), solemnly proclaimed on November 2017,[73] also goes in this direction. Principle 19 of the EPS affirms that 'vulnerable people have the right to appropriate assistance and protection against forced eviction', while stating that social housing and related services must be ensured.

All in all, Article 107(2)(a) TFEU has so far allowed State subsidies combating different forms of social exclusion and targeting both traditionally disadvantaged groups but also new forms of poverty, and has the potential to do so in the future.

5 Derogations under Article 107(3) TFEU and social considerations

Art. 107(3) TFEU affirms that some forms of aid may be considered compatible with the internal market. Among them, it lists aid to promote the economic development of areas where the standard of living is abnormally low or where there is underemployment (lett. a), aid to promote the execution of a project of common European interest or to remedy a serious disturbance in the economy of a Member State (lett. b), aid to facilitate the development of certain economic activities or of certain economic areas, where such aid does not adversely affect trading conditions to an extent contrary to the common interest (lett. c), aid to promote culture and heritage conservation (lett. d). While well-established case law has repeatedly stated that Article 107(3) must be interpreted strictly,[74] the Commission, when comparing and balancing the positive effects of the aid against its distortion of competition, enjoys a significant discretion in carrying out an assessment of economic, technical and policy considerations, and endorsing Member States policies aimed at protecting and promoting social rights. Without examining the technicalities pertaining to each of these categories of aid, this section focus on the extent to which some of these derogations allow Member States to pursue certain social policies and promote social rights.

5.1 Regional aid

Even though the Commission has adopted a quite cautious approach and performed a rigorous economic analysis, the horizontal category[75] of 'regional aid' provided for in Art. 107(3)(a)(c) TFEU has a clear 'social dimension'. It aims to support economic development and job creation in Europe's most disadvantaged regions. It has first and foremost a geographical scope, as it applies only to those areas that experience an economic or social disadvantage. The Guidelines on regional State aid for 2014–2020,[76] which define the regions eligible for aid and the criteria governing the assessment of regional aid, clearly state that 'through its equity or cohesion objective regional aid may contribute to the achievement of the Europe 2020 strategy delivering an inclusive and sustainable growth'.[77] Friederiszick and Merola note that, especially in the short term, these measures 'attempt to buffer political and social tension between or within Member States by equalising wages and income, increasing employment in lagging regions or reducing migration incentives'.[78]

Art. 107(3)(a) TFEU concerns areas where the economic situation is unfavourable in relation to the Union as a whole,[79] while Art. 107(3)(c) allows more flexibility in terms of identifying the areas in which the Member State can use the aid. The latter derogation has a wider scope, as it allows for aid to areas that do not satisfy the conditions set out by lett. a, the Commission has the power to authorize aid intended to further the economic development of areas of a Member State that are disadvantaged in relation to the national situation.

Although most of the regional aid is now block exempted, the economic approach endorsed by the General Court in *Hotel Cipriani* (long before the entry into force of the Treaty of Lisbon) appears to still be the rule when it comes to the assessment of regional aid. This implies that the Commission must carefully asses the anti-competitive effects of the aid. In *Hotel Cipriani*, the General Court rejected a teleological interpretation of Article 107(3)(c) TFEU which favours the goal of social cohesion. The applicant, Hotel Cipriani, had argued that the provision should have been interpreted in accordance with the objectives of economic and social cohesion laid down in the Treaty. It also put forward the view that 'the realisation of a [internal] market and the protection of competition do not constitute an end in themselves but are intended to realize the essential objectives of the Treaty', and that regional aid constituted 'an essential instrument in the pursuit of those objectives'. The General Court rejected this thesis and affirmed the fact that 'regional State aid promotes the economic, social and territorial cohesion of Member States and the [EU] as a whole cannot therefore have any bearing on the interpretation of the rules governing regional State aid'. It went on to affirm that 'the Commission is not required, in the exercise of its discretion, to apply those rules in a more flexible way so as to favour the objectives of the policy of economic and social cohesion over those of competition policy'. In a similar vein, the Guidelines on regional State aid for 2014–2020[80] specify that the Commission in its assessment must analyse 'whether the design of the aid measure ensures that the positive impact of the aid towards an objective of common interest exceeds its potential negative effects on trade and competition'. Nonetheless, the Guidelines suggest a variety of indicators to identify the positive effects of the aid the contribution to regional development, which, for the most parts, have a social nature. The number of direct and indirect jobs created by the investment, a commitment by the beneficiary to enter into training activities for the workforce and to put in place traineeships or apprenticeships for young people are considered important indicators of the development.

5.2 *Aid to remedy a serious disturbance in the economy and the financial crisis: a hidden social dimension?*

During the financial crisis that hit Europe after the dramatic fall of Lehman Brothers in the summer of 2008,[81] Art. 107(3)(b) TFEU was used to allow Member States to subsidize financial institutions, mainly through capital injection, in the attempt to stop the turmoil of the financial market and to avoid their collapse.[82] In this short chapter it is not possible to examine in detail the whole range of measures adopted by the Commission, or to discuss the flexible application of competition law to financial institutions. This subsection rather focuses on indirect social considerations which were nonetheless purported in these measures, to identify the potential for State aid to address economic crisis and limit the social cost they bear.

Before the crisis, the scope of application of Article 107(3)(b) TFEU was extremely narrow. The CJEU had clarified that 'aid cannot be benefiting only one company or one sector but must tackle a disturbance in the entire economy of a Member State',[83] and consistently held that aid measure approved under Article 107(3)(b) cannot 'resolve the problems of a single recipient [. . .], as opposed to the acute problems facing all operators in the industry'.[84] However, when the Commission adopted the first Banking Communication in 2008,[85] and then a series of other soft law documents to set forth criteria to assess aid to financial institution and coordinate Member States reaction to the crisis,[86] this Treaty provision was deemed the most appropriate derogation to allow Member States' action to curb the effects of the crash. The emergency State aid policy ushered during the financial crisis responded to the necessity to protect the integrity of the internal market. It was limited in a temporal sense, as well as clearly being targeted towards ensuring financial stability in Europe targeting the financial sector. However, an overall and broad social aim can be identified: that of supporting the real economy and with that the labour market and, even more obviously, access to finance. In the 2009 Communication on the 'Temporary framework for State aid measures to support access to finance in the current financial and economic crisis',[87] which expired in 2011, the Commission made it clear that

> While the situation on financial markets appears to be improving, the full impact of the financial crisis on the real economy is now being felt. A very serious downturn is affecting the wider economy and hitting *households*, businesses and *jobs*.
>
> (emphasis added)

The Commission's approach to the use of State aid during the financial crisis, though criticized in many respects,[88] eventually succeeded in containing the global threat to economic stability. Between 2008 and 2011 the Commission took over 200 decisions authorizing aid measures to the financial sector.[89] The improved market conditions since 2013 has signalled a return to a more restrictive approach to aid to financial institutions, but the Commission's measures between 2008 and 2011 signal, albeit indirectly and, probably quite partially, that the Treaty allows the use of State aid control to reduce the very high social costs of an economic and financial crisis.

5.3 *Aid to facilitate the development of certain economic activities and social considerations*

Under Article 107(3)(c) TFEU the Commission has, as discussed later in this volume by Mete and Heffron, aimed at the promotion of renewable energy and the increase of the energy supply.[90] Most interestingly for the purpose of this chapter, this provision has also allowed measures indirectly related to the protection and promotion of social rights and aimed at social inclusion of vulnerable groups. In most cases, the Commission recognized that positive effects offset the negative effects of the aid on competition. An example can be found on the approval of the Polish State aid scheme N 519/2007 for operators employing persons held in detention, and of its renewed version in 2017.[91] This aid scheme was aimed at providing aid to undertakings employing persons in detention to prepare them for work in the open labour market, after their release from prison. The Commission, in its assessment, found that 'the positive effects of the scheme, namely the promotion of inclusion of vulnerable and marginalised group' outweighed its negative effects.

A series of soft law documents have clarified the way in which the Commission carries out its assessment, and identified specific social related goals. For example, in 2009, the Commission set out the criteria to assess the compatibility of notified aid measures for disadvantaged and disabled workers (i.e. of individual aid targeted to combat unemployment of persons with disabilities, granted either *ad hoc* or as a part of a scheme where the grant exceeds 10 million euros).[92] This Communication, as noted elsewhere, while retaining an economic approach shows 'a renewed commitment by the Commission to the promotion of equality and full employment through EU state aid policy'.[93] Another notable example is the 2014 Communication on State aid for rescuing and restructuring non-financial undertakings in difficulty,[94] which build upon the previous guidelines,[95] but also take into account the Europe 2020 strategy goals, including that of inclusive growth. The Commission acknowledges that 'rescue and restructuring aid are among the most distortive types of State aid'. For this reason, this type of aid is seen as an *extrema ratio*, the conditions laid down in the guidelines are aimed to limit as far as possible the anti-competitive effects of the aid. Interestingly, for the purposes this analysis, the guidelines include a specific section on aid to cover the social costs of restructuring (i.e. social security payments and other benefits to redundant employees). Member States are generally allowed to provide for general social security schemes for redundant employees as these schemes fall outside the scope of Article 107(1) TFEU. However, since restructuring entails reductions in the workforce or abandonment of certain production activities, Member States are allowed to support restructuring in particular industries in relation to benefits to redundant workers, such as redundancy payments or measures to increase their employability. The guidelines also endorse the adoption of 'restructuring scheme for training, counselling and practical help with finding alternative employment, assistance with relocation, and professional training and assistance for employees wishing to start new businesses'. The guidelines explicitly state that:

> [g]iven that such measures, which increase the employability of redundant workers, further the objective of reducing social hardship, the Commission consistently takes a favourable view of such aid when it is granted to undertakings in difficulty.

In the last couple of years, the Commission assessed a few schemes under the guidelines, such as the Spanish (Basque) 'Restructuring aid scheme for SMEs "BIDERATU Berria"',[96] and in all these cases, while approving the aid, carefully assessed whether the aid would effectively mitigate the social and economic consequences that would otherwise occur.

Interestingly, none of the guidelines discussed, adopted at the time or after the entry into force of the Lisbon Treaty, mention or refer overtly to Article 3 TEU. Nonetheless, they are illustrative of social objectives being engrained and embedded in the assessment conducted under Art. 107(3)(c) TFEU.

6 Conclusion

This succinct analysis of the current State aid framework demonstrates that, in the last decade, the Commission has sought out, and potentially achieved, a more appropriate balance between the main objective of preserving competition in the internal market on the one hand, and social objectives on the other. It would appear that market goals have become more and more intertwined with social goals, and the way in which State aid rules in the Treaty have been implemented so far is deeply infused with a 'political dimension'.[97] Member States can now more easily pursue social goals without triggering Article 107(1) TFEU, and, perhaps most visibly, the Commission has strenuously nudged national economic policies towards social objectives that are of 'European interest', in view of the targets set forth in the Europe 2020 strategy.

It is not entirely clear whether Articles 3 TEU or 9 TFEU have displayed a visible effect on State aid policy, as none of the guidelines or regulations explicitly refer to them, and the Commission has thus far not evoked the overall objective of the 'social market economy'. It has rather referred to the Europe 2020 strategy and to its goals, often mentioning that of 'inclusive growth'. However, the GBER as soft law documents also refer to other sectoral provisions of the Treaty where relevant. This supports the assumption that State aid law and policy must be interpreted in light of all the other provisions of the Treaty and, first and foremost, in compliance with the overall EU objectives laid down in Article 3 TEU. While being careful not to overstate the social dimension of State aid control, it does seem evident that there has been a shift towards allowing public expenditure which can enhance social cohesion. In light of the financial and economic crisis that hit Europe after 2008 and its aftermath, the Commission has seemed inclined to a more flexible application of the rules at stake, and this might be seen as the realization of a 'social market' oriented State aid control.

Notes

* This chapter is the product of a joint reflection. However, Sections 1, 2.2, 4, 5 have been written by Delia Ferri, while sections 2.1, and 2.3 have been written by Juan Jorge Piernas López. Sections 3 and 7 have been written jointly.

1 Kelyn Bacon (ed.), *European Union Law of State Aid* (OUP, 2017) 4.

2 José Luis Buendía Sierra, 'Not Like This: Some Skeptical Remarks on the "Refined Economic Approach" in State Aid' *Proceedings of 4th EStALI Expert's Forum*, May 2006, Brussels

3 Case C-225/91, *Matra*, EU:C:1993:239.

4 Juan Jorge Piernas Lopez, *The Concept of State Aid Under EU Law: From Internal Market to Competition and Beyond* (OUP, 2015) 11.
5 Claus-Dieter Ehlermann, 'State Aid Control in the European Union: Success or Failure?' (1994) *Fordham International Law Journal* 1210, at 1216.
6 Council Regulation (EC) No 994/98 [1998] OJ L142/1.
7 Commission Regulation (EC) No 1998/2006 [2006] OJ L379/5.
8 Commission Regulation (EC) No 1407/2013 of 18 December 2013 [2013] OJ L352/1.
9 Commission Regulations (EC) No 68/2001 [2001] OJ L10/20, 70/2001 [2001] OJ L10/33, 2204/2001 [2002] OJ L337/3, and 1628/2006 [2006] OJ L32/29.
10 Commission Regulation (EC) No 800/2008 – General Block Exemption Regulation [2008] OJ L214/3.
11 Commission Regulation (EU) No 651/2014 [2014] OJ L187/1.
12 Michael Blauberger, 'From Negative to Positive Integration: European State Aid Control through Soft and Hard Law' (2009) *Paper to be presented at EUSA Eleventh Biennial International Conference* at <http://aei.pitt.edu/33031/1/blauberger._michael.pdf>.
13 Andreas Heinemann, 'Social Considerations in EU Competition Law: The Protection of Competition as a Cornerstone of the Social Market Economy', in this volume.
14 Commission Notice on the notion of State aid as referred to in Article 107(1) TFEU, [2016] OJ C 262/1.
15 *Inter alia* Case C-409/00, *Spain v Commission*, EU:C:2003:92.
16 Case C-280/00, *Altmark*, EU:C:2003:415, para 75.
17 Case C-83/98 P, *Ladbroke Racing*, EU:C:2000:248, para 25.
18 European Commission, *Report on the Implementation of the Commission Notice on the Application of the State Aid Rules to Measures*, C(2004)(434), at 6.
19 Case 173/73, *Italian Textiles*, EU:C:1974:71, para 13.
20 Non-economic activities fall outside the scope of Article 107(1) TFEU. There is, however, a third 'lieu' where the ordinary application of the State aid rules has been excluded under Article 106(2) TFEU: Services of General Economic Interest (SGEI). This will be discussed further by Piernas Lopez and Pellizzari. Juan Jorge Piernas López, 'Services of General Economic Interest and Social Considerations', in this volume; Silvia Pellizzari, 'Social Services, Services Providers and Non-Economic Activities in the Realm of the EU "Social Market Economy"', in this volume.
21 Case C-237/04, *Enirisorse*, EU:C:2006:197, paras 27–28.
22 Case C-222/04, *Cassa di Risparmio di Firenze SpA and Others*, EU:C:2006:8, para 107. Heinemann, 'Social Considerations in EU Competition Law the Protection of Competition as a Cornerstone of the Social Market Economy' (n 15); Niamh Dunne, 'Knowing When to See It: State Activities, Economic Activities, and the Concept of Undertaking' (2009–2010) *Columbia Journal European Law* 427.
23 Commission Decision No 241/04, Austria Viennese Aid Programme.
24 Commission Notice on the notion of State aid as referred to in Article 107(1) of the Treaty on the Functioning of the European Union (n 26); Wolf Sauter, 'The Notion of Undertaking' in Herwig Hofmann and Claire Micheau (eds.), *State aid Law of the European Union* (OUP, 2017) 74.
25 Alexander Winterstein, 'Nailing the Jellyfish: Social Security and Competition Law' (1999) *European Competition Law Review* 324.
26 European Commission, 'Notice on the Notion of State Aid as Referred to in Article 107(1) of the Treaty on the Functioning of the European Union' (n 26).
27 Pieralberto Mengozzi, 'Le attività culturali e la comunicazione della Commissione del 19 luglio 2016 sulla nozione di aiuto di Stato' (2016) *Il Diritto dell'Unione Europea* 741.

28 Delia Ferri, 'Cultural Diversity and State Aids to the Cultural Sector' in Evangelia Psychogiopoulou (ed.), *Cultural Governance and the European Union: Protecting and Promoting Cultural Diversity in Europe* (Palgrave Macmillan, 2015) 119.
29 Case C-318/05, *Commission v Germany*, EU:C:2007:495, para 68.
30 Wolf Sauter, 'The Notion of Undertaking' in Hofmann and Micheau (eds.), *State aid Law of the European Union* (n 27), 74, at 83.
31 C-75/97, *Belgium v Commission* ('Maribel'), EU:C:1999:311, para 17.
32 European Commission Notice, 'The Monitoring of State Aid and Reduction of Labour Costs', 97/C 1/05 [1997] OJ C 1, at 10.
33 Maribel (n 31), para 32.
34 AG La Pergola had held in point 8 of its Opinion to this case that 'it is obviously necessary to take account of the persons to whom the measures are addressed and to analyse whether the Maribel bis/ter scheme is directed at a category of undertaking [those employing manual workers] considered in its entirety without introducing exemptions from any general scheme which would otherwise apply to those undertakings'.
35 Maribel (n 31), para 18.
36 European Commission Notice, 'The Application of the State Aid Rules to Measures Relating to Direct Business Taxation', [1999] OJ C 384/3.
37 Maribel (n 31), para 36: 'It is true that an increased reduction of social security contributions, concerning only a limited category of employers owing to their belonging to certain industrial sectors, thus relieving them of certain social security charges, does not at first sight appear to derogate from the nature and scheme of the general system of social protection'.
38 Ibid., para 37.
39 Ibid., paras 38–39.
40 Georgios Matsos, 'Systematic Misconceptions of State Aid Law in the Area of Taxation' (2014) *European State Aid Law Quarterly* 491, at 491.
41 Case C-6/12 P, *OY*, EU:C:2013:525.
42 Wolfgang Schon, 'Tax Legislation and the Notion of Fiscal Aid: A Review of Five Years of European Jurisprudence' at <http://ssrn.com/abstract=2707049>.
43 Joined Cases C-78/08 and C-80/08, *Paint Graphos*, EU:C:2011:550.
44 Phedon Nicolaides, 'Grants Versus Fiscal Aid: In Search of Economic Rationality' (2015) *European State Aid Law Quarterly* 410, at 411.
45 Lisa Lovdahl Gormsen, 'EU State Aid Law and Transfer Pricing: A Critical Introduction to a New Saga' (2016) *Journal of Competition Law and Practice* 1, at 12.
46 European Commission, 'State Aid: Commission Opens Formal Investigation into Luxembourg's Tax Treatment of McDonald's' (2015) at <http://europa.eu/rapid/press-release_IP-15-6221_en.htm>.
47 Commission Decision of 30.8.2016 on State aid SA.38373 (2014/C) (ex 2014/NN). This decision has been challenged by the Irish government in front of the CJEU. For a comment, Eugene Stuart, 'Whether or Not to Bite the Apple: Some Implications of the August 2016 Commission Decision on Irish Tax Benefits for Apple' (2017) *European State Aid Law Quarterly* 209.
48 European Commission, 'State Aid: Commission Refers Ireland to Court for Failure to Recover Illegal Tax Benefits from Apple Worth Up to €13 Billion' (2017) at <http://europa.eu/rapid/press-release_IP-17-3702_en.htm>.
49 Commission Decision of 21.10.2015 on State aid SA.38374 (2014/C ex 2014/NN).
50 Commission Decision of 21.10.2015 on State aid SA.38375 (2014/C ex 2014/NN).
51 Dimitrios Kyriazis, 'Driving in the Wrong Direction? The Opening Decision in Fiat' (2011) *State Aid Hub* at <http://stateaidhub.eu/blogs/stateaid/post/803>.

52 Lisa Lovdahl Gormsen, 'EU State Aid Law and Transfer Pricing: A Critical Introduction to a New Saga' (2016) *Journal of Competition Law and Practice* 1, at 12.
53 Theodoros Iliopoulos, 'The State Aid Cases of Starbucks and Fiat: New Routes for the Concept of Selectivity' (2017) *European State Aid Law Quarterly* 263.
54 Joined Cases C-106/09 P and C-107/09 P, *Government of Gibraltar v Commission*, EU:C:2011:732. In this case the Court found that the proposed tax reform was materially selective in that it granted selective advantages to the offshore companies, which had no real physical presence in Gibraltar.
55 Joaquin Alumnia Comments in European Commission, 'State Aid: Commission Investigates Transfer Pricing Arrangements on Corporate Taxation of Apple (Ireland) Starbucks (Netherlands) and Fiat Finance and Trade (Luxembourg)' (2014) at <http://europa.eu/rapid/press-release_IP-14-663_en.htm>.
56 Juan Jorge Piernas Lopez, 'Tax Rulings and State Aid: Now or Never' (2014) *State Aid Hub* at <http://stateaidhub.eu/blogs/stateaid/post/801>.
57 Ibid.
58 Massimo Orzan, '*De Jure* Compatible Aid under Article 107(2) TFEU' in Hofmann and Micheau (eds.), *State aid Law of the European Union* (n 27), at 234.
59 Article 107(2)(b) TFEU list aid that 'makes good the damage caused by natural disasters or exceptional occurrences'. This provision also mentions at letter (c): 'aid granted to the economy of certain areas of the Federal Republic of Germany affected by the division of Germany, in so far as such aid is required in order to compensate for the economic disadvantages caused by that division'. This exemption is of limited practical relevance, and is now *ex lege* repealed.
60 State aid decision C 52/05, *Subsidy to Digital Decoders*, [2007] OJ L 147/1. Case T-177/07, *Mediaset*, EU:T:2010:233; Case C-403/10 P, *Mediaset*, EU:C:2011:533.
61 Ibid.
62 Johnathan Faull and Ali Nickpay, *The EU Law of Competition* (OUP, 2014) 1966.
63 A block exemption of aid for residents of remote regions was introduced through Commission Regulation (EU) No 651/2014, Article 51.
64 Commission Decision, Case SA-33966, *Aide à caractère social au bénéfice des résidents des îles de la Guadeloupe*, 3/5/EU [2012] OJ C128/2.
65 Commission Decision, Case SA-32888, *Befreiung von der Luftverkehrsteuer hinsichtlich Abflügen von Inselbewohnern und in anderen Fällen*, 8/3/EU [2001] OJ C70/3.
66 State aid No 27/2008 – United Kingdom. Aid of a social character Air Services in the Highlands and the Islands of Scotland, dated 14 November 2008 C(2008)685.
67 See *infra* section 6.
68 In 2010, the Commission approved an aid measure for the purchase of set of boxes for socially vulnerable people in Slovakia. In 2011, the Commission approved aid measures for the purchase of digital decoders by low income households in Lithuania and for the distribution of digital decoders to persons with visual disabilities in Spain. In 2012, the Commission approved an aid measure for socially disadvantaged households in Hungary.
69 SA.45004 (2016/N) – Cyprus State grant Scheme to borrowers and micro-companies.
70 Communication from the European Commission, 'A European Strategy for Smart, Sustainable and Inclusive Growth', COM(2010)2020.
71 Communication from the European Commission, 'The European Platform against Poverty and Social Exclusion: A European Framework for Social and Territorial Cohesion', COM(2010)758.
72 Ibid.

73 European Commission, 'Statement of President Juncker on the Proclamation of the European Pillar of Social Rights' (2017) at <http://europa.eu/rapid/press-release_STATEMENT-17-4706_en.htm>.
74 Case 730/79, *Philip Morris*, EU:C:1980:209.
75 Regional aid concerns in all sectors of economic activity, apart from the fisheries and aquaculture, agricultural and the transport sector, which are subject to special rules (European Commission, 'Guidelines on Regional State Aid for 2014–2020', [2013] OJ C209/1, para 10 and 30).
76 Ibid.
77 Ibid., para 7.
78 Hand Friederiszick and Massimo Merola, 'Regional State Aid Control in Europe: A Legal and Economic Assessment' (2015) *European School of Management and Technology Working Paper No 15-05* at <https://ssrn.com/abstract=2698053>.
79 Case 248/84, *Germany v Commission*, EU:C:1987:437. In particular, the CJEU has consistently held that the use of the words 'abnormally' and 'serious' in Article (107)(3)(a) shows that the exemption concerns only areas where the economic situation is extremely unfavourable in relation to the EU as a whole.
80 European Commission, 'Guidelines on Regional State Aid for 2014–2020' (n 82).
81 John Breslin, *Banking Law* (Thomson Round Hall, 2013) 8.
82 Christian Koenig, '"Instant State Aid Law" in a Financial Crisis, State of Emergency or Turmoil: Five Essential and Reasonable Requirements under the Rule of Law' (2008) *European State Aid Law Quarterly* 629.
83 Joined Cases T-132/96 and T-143/96, *Freistaat Sachsen and Volkswagen AG Commission*, EU:T:1999:326, para 167.
84 Case C-47/1996, *Crédit Lyonnais*, [1998] OJ L221/28, Point 10.1.
85 Communication from the European Commission, 'The Application of State Aid Rules to Measures Taken in Relation to Financial Institutions in the Context of the Current Global Financial Crisis', [2008] OJ C270/8. A new Banking Communications was issued in 2013 to replace the existing 2008 Communication (Communication from the European Commission, 'Application of State Aid Rules to Support Measures in Favour of Banks in the Context of the Financial Crisis', [2013] OJ C216/1).
86 Andrea Bomhoff, Anna Jarosz-Friis and Nicola Pesaresi, 'Restructuring Banks in Crisis: Overview of Applicable State Aid Rules' (2009) *Competition Policy Newsletter* 3.
87 Communication from the European Commission, 'Temporary Framework for State Aid Measures to Support Access to Finance in the Current Financial and Economic Crisis', [2011] OJ C6/5.
88 Hans Gilliams, 'Stress Testing the Regulator: Review of the State Aid to Financial Institutions after the Collapse of Lehman' (2011) *European Law Review* 3.
89 Ramona Ianus and Massimo Orzan, 'Aid Subject to Discretionary Assessment under Article 107(3) TFEU' in Hofmann and Micheau (eds.), *State aid Law of the European Union* (n 27), 240, at 275.
90 Gokce Mete and Raphael Heffron, 'The Social Dimension of EU Energy Law', in this volume.
91 State aid No SA.46134(2016/N) – Poland State aid scheme for operators employing persons held in detention (amendment to the aid scheme SA.33608 (2011/N)).
92 Communication from the European Commission, 'Criteria for the Compatibility Analysis of State Aid to Disadvantaged and Disabled Workers Subject to Individual Notification', [2009] OJ C188/6.
93 Delia Ferri and Mel Marquis, 'Inroads to Social Inclusion in Europe's Social Market Economy: The Case of State Aid Supporting Employment of Workers with Disabilities' (2011) *European Journal of Legal Studies* 4.

94 Communication from the European Commission, 'Guidelines on State Aid for Rescuing and Restructuring Non-Financial Undertakings in Difficulty', [2014] OJ C 249/1.

95 After the first guidelines adopted in 1994 and their revised version passed in 1999, the Commission adopted new guidelines in 2004 (European Commission, 'Community Guidelines on State Aid for Rescuing and Restructuring Firms in Difficulty', [2004] OJ C244/2), the validity of which was extended until their replacement by new 2014 rules.

96 State aid SA.47595 (2017/N) – Spain Restructuring aid scheme for SMEs 'BIDERATU Berria', C(2017)4984.

97 Bacon (ed.), *European Union Law of State Aid* (n 1), at 5.

9 Services of general economic interest and social considerations

Juan Jorge Piernas López

1 Introduction

This chapter aims to analyse the extent to which social rights are protected and promoted under Article 106(2) TFEU, in particular under the notion of Services of General Economic Interest (SGEI) included therein. For these purposes, the chapter focuses on the so-called Social Services of General Interest, particularly on those that have an economic nature, namely, the Social Services of General Economic Interest (SSGEI). It is well-known that Social Services of General Interest (SSGI) can be economic or non-economic in nature, but EU competition – including State aid – and free movement rules only apply to undertakings (entities engaged in an economic activity), as discussed by Heinemann and Ferri and Piernas Lopez in this volume.[1] In this regard, as the Commission has phrased it

> [s]ocial services of general interest (SSGI) [. . .] include social security schemes covering the main risks of life and a range of other essential services provided directly to the person that play a preventive and socially cohesive/ inclusive role. While some social services (such as statutory social security schemes) are not considered by the European Court as being economic activities, the jurisprudence of the Court makes clear that the social nature of a service is not sufficient in itself to classify it as non-economic. The term social service of general interest consequently covers both economic and non-economic activities.[2]

This chapter focuses only on those SSGI which are economic in nature, and aims to clarify what these services are, and whether their characteristics, *vis-à-vis* general SGEI, have warranted a different treatment under EU legislation, taking into account the Court of Justice of the European Union (CJEU) case law and the Commission's decisional practice, or whether they should warrant a different treatment in the future, for the sake of social protection. In this context, it should be kept in mind that under Article 14 TFEU, SGEI form part of the common values of the Union and promote social and territorial cohesion. Finally, similarly to Article 14 TFEU, Article 36 of the EU Charter of Fundamental Rights (EU CFR) states that the Union recognizes and respects access to SGEI with a view to promoting social and territorial cohesion of the EU.

Against this background, this chapter is structured as follows. Section 2 analyses the main tenets of the definition of SSGEI under Article 106 TFEU, namely, its economic nature and its social purpose, having regard to the relevant case law of the CJEU and to the applicable EU secondary law. Section 3 succinctly examines the advantages of defining a service as SSGEI in light of the 2011 Commission Decision and the relevant case law of the EU Courts. Section 4 analyses the decisional practice of the Commission on SSGEI in order to evaluate whether the entry into force of the social provisions included in the Lisbon Treaty has led to a different application of Article 106(2) TFEU in the case of social services. Section 5 includes some conclusions.

2 The definition of SSGEI: economic nature and 'social' purpose

Article 106 TFEU, the provision that warrants the existence of SGEI and SSGEI, is intended to reconcile the application of the Treaty rules on free movement and competition with the legitimate role of the State in the marketplace in mixed economies. This provision, introduced by the Treaty of Rome under Article 90 EEC, makes the conduct of public undertakings and public/private undertakings entrusted with special or exclusive rights subject to the competition rules of the Treaties, yet it provides for important exceptions in the case of public services, or services of general economic interest as the TFEU refers to them, that lead, if applied, to the non-applicability of the relevant Treaty provisions.[3]

Article 106 TFEU is divided into three parts. Article 106(1) TFEU prevents Member States from adopting, with regards to public undertakings or undertakings bearing special or exclusive rights, any measure that would lead to an infringement of another Treaty provision, including Articles 101 and 102 TFEU, Article 107 TFEU on State aid, and the free movement provisions.[4] Secondly, Article 106(2) TFEU provides for an exception to the application of the Treaty rules for Services of General Economic Interest to the extent that this exception is necessary for the achievement of the public service missions they are entrusted with. Three steps can be differentiated in the application of this provision. Firstly, it has to be determined whether the undertaking at stake has been entrusted with a genuine SGEI. Then, it has to be determined whether the application of the Treaty rules would obstruct the performance, in law or in fact, of the special mission assigned to the undertaking. Finally, the development of trade must not be affected to such an extent as would be contrary to the interests of the Union. Thirdly, Article 106(3) TFEU allows the European Commission to adopt directives and decisions in order to ensure the application of the application of this Article.[5]

2.1 *SSGEI as SGEI: the economic nature*

SSGEI are first and foremost SGEI. This means that they must be economic in nature. Therefore, having regard to the relevant case law of the CJEU, social security schemes based on solidarity,[6] the exercise of public prerogatives[7] or other activities under State control[8] do not fall within the realm of SSGEI. However, the notion of SGEI itself, which appears in Article 106(2) TFEU, is left undefined. The absence of a clear concept of SGEI has been recognized by the European Courts. The General Court in *BUPA* affirmed that:

> in [EU] law and for the purposes of applying the [. . .] Treaty competition rules, there is no clear and precise regulatory definition of the concept of a SGEI mission and no established legal concept definitively fixing the conditions that must be satisfied before a Member State can properly invoke the existence and protection of a SGEI mission.[9]

Notwithstanding, some constituent elements of the SGEI can be inferred from the analysis of the Treaties and secondary law. Protocol No 26 to the Lisbon Treaty on services of general interest underline the essential role and broad discretion of national authorities to define SGEIs, their diversity (geographical, social and cultural situations), and some of their features: a high level of quality, security and economic accessibility, equal treatment and promotion of universal access and user rights.[10]

Secondary law also provides some guidance as to what can be considered as a SGEI. In particular, the Directive 2006/123/EC (Services Directive),[11] provides that SGEI are services performed for an economic consideration, and therefore do fall within the scope of Article 50 TFEU.[12] In addition, it states that services may be considered to be SGEI only if they are provided in application of a special task in the public interest entrusted to the provider by the Member State concerned. In this regard, the Directive specifies that SGEI are entrusted with tasks relating to social and territorial cohesion. Examples of these include postal services and utilities. In this context, the Commission has defined SGEI as 'economic activities which deliver outcomes in the overall public good that would not be supplied (or would be supplied under different conditions in terms of quality, safety, affordability, equal treatment or universal access) by the market without public intervention'. The Public Service Obligation (PSO) is imposed on the provider by way of an entrustment and on the basis of a general interest criterion which ensures that the service is provided under conditions allowing it to fulfil its mission'.[13] Essentially, SGEI are provided for economic consideration in the execution of a specific task of public interest entrusted to the provider by a public authority of a Member State, and that they must promote social and territorial cohesion. In *BUPA*[14] the General Court has further clarified that there must be an act of public authority entrusting the operators concerned with a SGEI mission and this mission must be universal and mandatory. However, a universal service does not always require the service to be provided to the whole population or to the whole territory of a Member State. In addition, the mandatory nature of an SGEI does not exclude that the provider of the SGEI may have some scope for action. Member States must also clarify the reasons why the service in question differs from other economic activities and therefore deserves to be considered a SGEI.

The CJEU has traditionally affirmed that 'Member States have a wide margin of discretion when defining what they consider to be SGEI and the European institutions can only exercise limited control to investigate the existence of a manifest error of assessment in relation to that definition'.[15] In this regard, the Court has carried out a proportionality test between, on the one hand, the distortion of competition (general interest of the EU), and the Member State's (e.g. social) interests.[16] In the *Analir* judgement,[17] the Court seemed to conclude, within the scope of the fundamental freedoms, that Member States could only impose public service obligations if they demonstrate the existence of a real need for public service, in particular, if they prove that market forces are insufficient to meet the demand. The European Commission has also made reference to this judgement in a communication on SGEI, in relation to the conditions to be met in order to define a service as a SGEI.[18]

Recent judgements of the General Court seem to point in the direction of a further reduction of the discretion that Member States enjoy in defining certain services as SGEI. In particular, in three decisions of 16 September 2013 the General Court noted that the existence of a market failure is relevant in determining the existence of a SGEI,[19] and that the assessment of the existence of such a market failure is a prerequisite for the classification of an activity as an SGEI.[20] The Court added that the concept of market failure is an objective concept whose assessment is based on an analysis of the specific market situation.[21] Two of these judgements were appealed and confirmed by the CJEU, although no further reference was made to the concept of market failure.[22] Interestingly, the General Court did not refer to the *Analir* in its decisions. Indeed, although the rulings used general terms to refer to the relationship between the market failure criterion and SGEI, they were issued in the context of the application of State aid rules to the rapid deployment of broadband networks, in which the Commission has followed the criterion of market failure for the analysis of the legality of a SGEI, both in its decision-making practice and in its communications. Therefore, it may not be deduced straightforward from this decision that SGEI may only be defined in the presence of a market failure. This interpretation has been recently confirmed by the General Court in the *Andersen* judgement.[23]

In a nutshell, the brief analysis conducted above of relevant primary and secondary EU Law, as interpreted by the CJEU, provides some clear guidance as to what types of services can be defined as SGEI, even though the concept has not been defined with precision. The lack of a precise definition may even be considered positively, as SGEI may evolve over time (e.g. the deployment of broadband networks could not have been foreseen by the Treaty makers) and may vary according to the particular preferences of Member States, regions or municipalities.

The question to be then asked is whether SSGEI comply with the general SGEI criteria. The answer seems to be affirmative. In this regard, SSGEI may comply with the formal criteria enshrined in Article 106(2) TFEU, namely, an act of public authority entrusting the operators concerned with a SGEI mission and this mission must be universal and mandatory. To this extent, the requirement that the service is universal is also met in the case of assistance to vulnerable groups as the EU Courts have held, as mentioned before, that this requirement does not imply in all cases that the service be provided to the whole population, or to the whole territory of a Member State. In the same vein, SSGEI, as currently defined by the Commission, are special tasks in the public interest entrusted to operators that would probably not provide them, or not to the same extent, without public support. The next question could therefore be whether there is any added value in defining SSGEI differently from SGEI. We aim to address that question in the following section.

2.2 *The social purpose*

SSGEI are not mentioned in the Treaties. Neither are they defined in CJEU case law. EU Secondary law, in particular the Commission Decision of 20 December 2011 on the application of Article 106(2) TFEU to State aid in the form of public service compensation granted to certain undertakings entrusted with the operation of SGEI (2011 Decision), defines SSGEI as services of economic interest 'meeting social needs as regards health and long-term care, childcare, access to and reintegration into the labour market, social housing and the care and social inclusion of vulnerable groups'.[24]

This definition is the result of a compromise between a rigid formulation that would provide full legal certainty, as those included in block exemptions,[25] and one flexible enough to cover all types of social services across the Member States.[26] As it has been noted by Sinnaeve, the formula used by the Commission, and particularly its last sentence, i.e. the reference to 'the care and social inclusion of vulnerable groups', is quite broad and flexible and may cover many beneficiaries, including refugees, immigrants or persons with disabilities.[27] Interestingly, it has also been noted that the openness of the definition provided by the 2011 Decision, will lead to the Commission and the CJEU being called upon to define these services. This will necessarily result in a unified EU approach to these type of services and, arguably, to the definition of vulnerable groups, ultimately tracing the boundaries of the Member States 'welfare state'.[28] In this respect, the notion of SSGEI has already been criticized for creating legal uncertainty at the national level and for constraining the legitimate role of the State to provide social services under the Treaties.[29]

3 The advantages of defining some services as SSGEI

The qualification of a service as SSGEI has an immediate advantage *vis-à-vis* other SGEI, namely that there is no economic threshold to the compensation that the providers of these type of services can receive for their provision under the 2011 Decision.[30] Consequently, Member States can grant as much compensation as they consider necessary for the provision of these services without notifying the European Commission, provided that they define them properly and meet the rest of the criteria of the 2011 Decision (i.e. entrustment, parameters of compensation etc.).[31]

Secondly, the qualification of a service as a SSGEI may, and this chapter argues that it should, have an impact on the interpretation of Article 106(2) TFEU by the Commission and the CJEU, as the proportionality test that has to be carried out under this provision ought to take into account, as part of the EU general interest, the fact that the EU Treaties now include social protection objectives, alongside the competition and free movement objectives. To this extent, Baquero Cruz has noted that, in the so-called *Altmark* package, the Commission had already decided to apply a softer necessity test to try to reconcile social policy aims and competition.[32]

Article 3(3) TEU and the 'crosscutting' social protection clause[33] included in Article 9 TFEU could provide a bedrock for such an interpretation, which could be also backed by referring to Article 7 TFEU. Consequently, competition policy, as already argued by Heinemann in this volume,[34] should be applied in a consistent manner with other policies of the Treaty, such as social policy, and other objectives, values and rights such as social protection, the prevention of social exclusion or the access to SGEI that promote social cohesion. To this extent, in the context of the application of Article 106(2) TFEU to the hospital sector, closely related to social protection, the General Court has held that 'concerned must take account of respect for the responsibilities of the Member States for the definition of their health policy and the organisation and delivery of health services and medical care', and that such consideration stems from the Treaty itself.[35]

In this context, the CJEU has recently shown sensitivity as regards social services, somewhat highlighting the social element of a 'social market economy'.[36] Interestingly, the General Court has also recently distinguished between sectors as regards to the definition of SGEI.[37] It held that:

> the criteria laid down by the Court of Justice in the *Altmark* judgment [relevant for the purposes of defining a SGEI mission] concerning transport, which is unquestionably an economic and competitive activity, cannot be applied strictly to the hospital sector, which ***does not necessarily have such a competitive and commercial dimension***.[38]

This decision of the Court shows that not all sectors of the economy of the Member States have to be assessed under Article 106(2) TFEU, in accordance with the classical analysis enshrined in the case law of the CJEU, which was originally developed for ordinary commercial activities, such as transport, in the absence of any reference to the need to ensure social protection in the Treaty.

However, the traditional case law on Article 106(2) TFEU remains fully valid and applicable.[39] In particular, in a case related to the rejection by the Commission of a European citizens' initiative (ECI) entitled 'Right to Lifelong Care: leading a life of dignity and independence is a fundamental right!', which aimed to invite the EU to propose legislation ensuring the fundamental right to human dignity by guaranteeing adequate social protection and access to quality, sustainable long-term care beyond healthcare,[40] thereby related to SSGEI, the General Court held that 'the Commission cannot propose generally to exempt from the application of internal market rules services (in particular long-term care services) whose classification as an SGEI depends on the national policy pursued by each Member State'.[41]

Indeed, as the General Court rightly concludes, the Commission may not exclude the application of the fundamental freedoms and the competition rules to SSGEI, yet the Commission, in its role as guardian of the treaties could interpret those rules in a more flexible manner, particularly in the application of the proportionality test of Article 106(2) TFEU when SSGEI are involved, in order to combine the protection of fair competition within the Internal Market with the guarantee of adequate social protection and the fight against social exclusion, also enshrined in the Treaty. This view has been suggested by the current President of the CJEU, Koen Lenaerts, with reference to Article 9 TFEU.[42]

4 The decisional practice of the Commission on SSGEI

This section focuses on the decisions adopted by the European Commission on activities related to SSGEI in order to evaluate whether the entry into force of the social provisions included in the Lisbon Treaty has led to a different application of Article 106(2) TFEU in the case of social services. In particular, it focuses on two cases where the Commission has specifically referred to categories of SSGEI included in the 2011 Decision' definition, namely compensation for the provision of health and long-term care, and the provision of social housing.[43]

In this regard, in the last decision adopted by the European Commission in relation to the financial support granted by Belgian authorities to public hospitals belonging to the IRIS (*Interhospitalière Régionale des Infrastructures de Soins*) association in Brussels (IRIS hospitals),[44] the Commission did not clearly distinguish between SSGEI and other SGEI. In particular, it held that the range of hospital and social tasks performed by the IRIS hospitals either qualified as genuine services of general economic interest, or as activities purely ancillary thereto. In essence, the Commission concluded that 'all medical and social services at issue in this case exhibit special characteristics as compared with those of other economic activities, i.e. primarily their importance for the medical and social well-being of society'.[45] Furthermore, the Commission found that the activities of the IRIS hospitals under examination could be covered by Articles 2(1)(b), related to compensation granted to hospitals providing medical care, and Articles 2(1)(c), related particularly to SSGEI, without any further differentiation as to which activities belonged to one or the other categories. In this regard, it is worth noting that the Commission accepted the granting of compensation for the provision of ancillary activities, in particular ambulance transport of patients between hospitals; a nursery for the children of staff members; nursing and elderly homes; nursing schools; research; assisted living; and psychiatric care institutions; a little shop for patients and visitors; renting of TVs to patients, renting of rooms to third parties; and a canteen and parking facilities, which represented on average less than 2% of the IRIS hospitals' total revenues.[46] These activities may be compensated if they are indeed considered as ancillary to the provision of services of general economic interest by hospitals providing medical care under Article 2(1)(b) of the 2011 Decision, but not if they are ancillary to the provision of SSGEI, as Article 2(1)(c) does not provide for that possibility. Consequently, it would have been more correct to clearly distinguish between the activities of the IRIS hospitals that fall under Article 2(1)(b), and their ancillary activities, and those that fall under Article 2(1)(c).

A more substantial discussion on the definition and extent of SSGEI has been held between the European Commission and the Dutch Government in relation to social housing, one of the activities considered as SSGEI by the 2011 Decision. The discussion, which has lasted for more than 10 years and is still ongoing, has also involved the CJEU as well as the European Economic and Social Committee.[47]

Indeed, this particular debate dates back to the negotiations of the Rome Treaty, more than 60 years ago, as shown by the interpretative declarations made in relation to Article 92 EEC at the time of adopting the Treaty. In this regard, the Dutch Parliament held that aid to housing was not State aid under the Treaty due to the absence of, at least, one of its constitutive elements, i.e. the distortion of competition. Consequently, there was no need to consider whether this type of aid should be declared compatible State aid. Similarly, '*le Comité des Chef de delegation*' considered that aids to Social Security services were not covered by the prohibition laid down in then Article 92(1).[48] In the same vein, the French delegation informed that, in its view, aids to compensate the provisions of tasks of general interest carried out by public or private companies were compatible with the Treaty.[49]

In essence, the more recent discussion on 'aid to housing' started in 2002 with a notification by the Dutch authorities concerning State aid to housing corporations ('*woningcorporaties*' – *WOCOS*) that subsequently withdrew. The European Commission sent a letter in July 2005 under Article 17 of the applicable procedural regulation,[50] qualifying the financial support granted to *WOCOS* as State aid, particularly existing aid. The Commission considered that the Netherlands should amend the public service definition of *WOCOS* so aid to social housing would be provided to a clearly defined target group of disadvantaged citizens or socially less advantaged groups. In addition, any commercial activities by the *WOCOS* should be carried out on market terms and should not benefit from State aid, and the offer of social housing should be adapted to the demand from disadvantaged citizens or socially less advantaged groups.[51]

After receipt of the letter, which was very controversial in the Netherlands given that aid to social housing associations is well-established in this Member State, going back to 1901,[52] the Dutch authorities and the Commission negotiated over the way in which aid to housing in the Netherlands should be adjusted in order to bring it in line with EU law. As a result of these negotiations, the Dutch Government presented to the Commission on 3 December 2009 a number of commitments for amending the existing aid scheme and make it compatible with the treaty under Article 106(2) TFEU, as a SGEI.

In particular, the Dutch authorities agreed, *inter alia*, to define a target group of socially disadvantaged households (eligible for social housing) as individuals with an income not exceeding EUR 33,000, to limit the maximum rent in social housing to EUR 647.53, and to ensure that 90% of the dwellings in each *WOCO* are allocated to individuals belonging to the target group at the moment of allocation.

The Commission accepted these commitments and, in the same decision, also accepted a newly notified aid for the revival of declining urban regions to social housing associations.[53] This decision was challenged by 133 housing associations before the General Court in April 2010, which declared the action inadmissible for lack of standing, without analysing the merits in an order of December 2011.[54] This order was appealed before the CJEU, which set it aside in February 2014, declaring the appeal admissible and referring it back to the General Court.[55] This latter Court adopted a new order on 12 May 2015 dismissing the appeal for, in this instance, being manifestly unfounded.[56] This decision was again appealed by the housing associations, and the CJEU again ruled in their favour on 15 March 2017, referring back the case to the General Court, as the latter should have analysed the associations' arguments concerning the lawfulness of the appropriate measures proposed by the European Commission to the Dutch authorities.[57]

Consequently, the General Court, and presumably the CJEU at a later stage, will finally get to analyse the merits of the 2010 appeal, and principally one of the arguments that may be more relevant for the purposes of this chapter, namely, whether the Commission erred in law and abused its powers by demanding that the Netherlands State redefine 'social housing provision'. In particular, the EU courts will assess whether the Commission exceeded its powers by advancing its own definition of social housing provision as a service of general economic interest, currently a SSGEI, notwithstanding the fact that the Netherlands must be regarded as having a wide discretion to determine its own policy in that area.[58]

Indeed, as mentioned before, the Commission considered in its 2005 letter and in the 2009 Decision that provision of social housing may qualify as SGEI, something that the Commission has been doing since at least 2001.[59] However, it added that social housing could be considered as a SGEI

> if it is restricted to a target group of disadvantaged citizens or socially less advantaged groups, while Member States have a wide margin as regards the size of the target group and the exact modalities of applying the system based on a target group.[60]

This target group was finally set at the income ceiling of EUR 33,000 per year, that is, the lowest-earning 43% of the population.

It could be argued that the Commission showed some flexibility in this case, as it negotiated for over four years with the Dutch authorities the appropriate measures, probably accepting a higher income ceiling than that originally considered appropriate for the target group. Indeed, a member of the Commission has underlined that the Commission in this case adopted 'a very flexible definition of what constitutes a "social policy" measure and what are "socially less advantaged households" [giving social policy objectives] more weight than economic considerations'.[61]

However, the question remains whether it is legitimate for the Commission, in the absence of harmonisation at the EU level for the provision of social housing, to consider that social housing may only be granted to a target group of disadvantaged citizens, or socially less advantaged groups. In sum, the Commission's reasoning leads to affirm that the Dutch authorities would commit a manifest error if they were to define the SSGEI of social housing as available for, e.g. the low and the middle earning citizens, those having an income of up to EUR 38,000 or even EUR 43,000. In this regard, it should be noted, as underlined by the Economic and Social Committee, that the Netherlands, together with Denmark, have traditionally followed the so-called universal approach to social housing, intended to provide housing for anyone, whatever their income, complementing in this way the traditional property market.[62] The Committee also underlined that, as a result of the Commission Decision, nearly 400,000 households had been excluded from access to social housing. It thus concluded that the Commission should reconsider its decision-making practices for checking manifest errors in Member States classification of social housing as a SGEI.[63]

It seems that, in the absence of harmonization at the EU level of the appropriate target group for the provision of social housing, Member States should enjoy a large margin of discretion to define this group, which, in the case at hand, could entail the possibility of providing social housing to low and middle earning citizens, if the Netherlands Government would so decide. This interpretation would be backed by the above-mentioned Protocol No 26, which highlights the universal access to SGEI and the large margin of discretion of Member States to define them, a margin of discretion that could be considered even larger in relation to SSGEI in light of Articles 3(3) TEU, 7 and 9 TFEU, as well as Article 36 and 34 of the EU CFR, the latter stating that

> the Union recognizes and respects the right to social and housing assistance so as to ensure a decent existence for all those who lack sufficient resources, in accordance with the rules laid down by Community law and national laws and practices.

All these provisions became binding, with the entry into force of the Lisbon Treaty, a few days before the adoption of the Commission Decision in this case. In relation to Article 34 of the EU CFR, it could be argued that the reference to 'those who lack sufficient resources' would support a definition of the SSGEI of social housing as the one suggested by the European Commission in this case. However, the same provision stipulates that the right has to be applied in accordance with the rules laid down by Union law, which have not defined the provision of social housing, and national laws and practices, which in the case of the Netherlands had clearly done so.

5 Conclusion

In light of the analysis conducted, a number of conclusions can be drawn, going back to the questions raised at the beginning of this chapter.

Firstly, as to the question of what are SSGEI, EU secondary law provides an answer that has been considered as a compromise between the interests of precision and legal certainty, on the one hand, and the necessary flexibility to cover all social services across the Member States, and their evolution, on the other. SSGEI have been defined after the entry into force of the Lisbon Treaty as SGEI meeting social needs as regards health and long-term care, childcare, access to and reintegration into the labour market, social housing and the care and social inclusion of vulnerable groups. Consequently, SSGEI are, first of all, SGEI and therefore the traditional case law on Article 106(2) TFEU applies to them. In this regard, the chapter has argued that SSGEI do comply with the general criteria for the definition of SGEI provided for in the case law of EU Courts.

Secondly, the classification of certain SGEI as SSGEI has an added value. SSGEI has an immediate advantage *vis-à-vis* over SGEI, namely that there is no economic threshold to the compensation that the providers of these type of services can receive for their provision under the 2011 Decision. Additionally, and potentially more significantly, this chapter argues that the qualification of a service as a SSGEI should have an impact on the interpretation of Article 106(2) TFEU by the Commission and the EU Courts, as the proportionality test that has to be carried out should take into account, as part of the EU general interest, the fact that the EU Treaties now include social protection objectives, alongside the competition and free movement ones. However, it should be highlighted that any definition of SSGEI by the European Commission should be 'handled with care', as the definition of a service as a SGEI remains, in the absence of harmonization at Union level, a prerogative of the Member States, as the discussion over the lawfulness of the Dutch social housing Commission decisions reveals.

Finally, as to whether the classification of certain services as SSGEI has already had an impact on the CJEU case law and the decisional practice of the European Commission, the answer must be nuanced. On the one hand, there seems to be a tendency, both in the Commission and the Courts, towards a higher flexibility in the application of Article 106(2) TFEU in the case of social services. In this regard, the General Court has even accepted that the application of Article 106(2) TFEU may vary from one sector to another, being less strict in sectors closely related to social protection such as healthcare. However, although the entry into force of the Lisbon framework has marked a shift towards the inclusion of social protection considerations while applying Treaty rules, neither the Commission nor the Courts have (yet) fully exploited the potential of the post-Lisbon legal framework in relation to social protection, and particularly the role of Article 9 TFEU, in conjunction with Article 3(3) TEU, Article 7 TFEU, and Article 36 EU CFR in the application of the proportionality test under Article 106(2) TFEU.

Notes

1 Andreas Heinemann, 'Social Considerations in EU Competition Law: The Protection of Competition as a Cornerstone of the Social Market Economy', in this volume; Delia Ferri and Juan Jorge Piernas Lopez, 'State Aid Law in a Social Market Economy', in this volume; Case C-172/03, *Heiser v Finanzamt Innsbruck*,

EU:C:2005:130, para 26; Case C-237/04, *Enirisorse SpA*, EU:C:2006:197, paras 26–29.

2 Communication from the European Commission, 'A Quality Framework for Services of General Interest in Europe', COM(2011)900, at 3–4.

3 José Luis Buendía Sierra, *Exclusive Rights and State Monopolies under EC Law* (OUP, 1999).

4 See for the definition of 'public undertakings', with reference to the Transparency Directive, Case C-188–190/80, *French Republic, Italian Republic and United Kingdom of Great Britain and Northern Ireland v Commission*, EU:C:1982:257, para 25.

5 In relation to Article 106(2) TFEU, Marise Cremona (ed.), *Market Integration and Public Services in the European Union* (OUP, 2011); Erika Szyszczak and Johan Willem Van de Gronden (eds.), *Financing Services of General Economic Interest: Reform and Modernization* (Asser Press, 2013).

6 Joined Cases C-159/91 and C-160/91, *Poucet and Pistre*, EU:C:1993:63, paras 17–19; Case C-67/96, *Albany*, EU:C:1999:430, paras 77–87, Joined Cases C-115 to C-117/97, *Brentjens*, EU:C:1999:434, paras 77–87; Case C-219/97, *Drijvende Bokken*, EU:C:1999:437, paras 67–77; Joined Cases C-180/98 to C-184/98, *Pavlov*, EU:C:2000:428, paras 67–77; Case C-218/00, *Cisal*, EU:C:2002:36, paras 31–42; Joined Cases C-264/01, C-306/01, C-354/01 and C-355/01, *AOK Bundesverbandand Others*, EU:C:2004:150, paras 45–66, and Case C-350/07, *Kattner Stahlbau GmbH v Maschinenbau- und Metall-Berufsgenossenschaft*, EU:C:2009:127, paras 44–59.

7 Case C-364/92, *SAT Fluggesellschaft v Eurocontrol*, EU:C:1994:7, paras 24–30.

8 *Cisal* (n 6), paras 31–42. José Luis Buendía Sierra, 'An Analysis of Article 86(2) EC' in Michael Sanchez Rydelski (ed.), *The EU State Aid Regime* (Cameron May, 2006) Part IV, 548.

9 Case T-289/03, *BUPA*, EU:T:2008:29, para 165.

10 Article 1 of the Protocol.

11 Directive 2006/123/EC of the European Parliament and of the Council of 12 December 2006 on services in the internal market, [2006] OJ L376, at 36–68.

12 Case C-250/06, *United Pan-Europe Communications Belgium*, EU:C:2007:783, para 38.

13 Communication from the European Commission, 'A Quality Framework for Services of General Interest in Europe', COM(2011)900, at 3.

14 *BUPA* (n 9), paras 167–189.

15 Case C-265/08, *Federutility*, EU:C:2010:205, para 29.

16 Koen Lenaerts, 'Defining the Concept of "Services of General Interest" in Light of the "Checks and Balances" Set Out in the EU Treaties' (2012) *Jurisprudence* 1255.

17 Case C-205/99, *Analir*, EU:C:2001:107, para 71.

18 Communication from the European Commission, 'Application of the European Union State Aid Rules to Compensation Granted for the Provision of Services of General Economic Interest', [2012] OJ C 8/02, para 48.

19 Case T-258/10, *Orange*, EU:T:2013:471, Case T-325/10, *Iliad*, EU:T:2013:472 and Case T-79/10, *Colt Télécommunications France*, EU:T:2013:463.

20 *Colt Télécommunications France* (n 19), para 154.

21 *Iliad* (n 19), para 185.

22 *Orange* (n 19) and *Iliad* (n 19).

23 Case T-92/11, *Andersen*, EU:T:2017:14, paras 69 and-70–72; Case T-162/13, *Magic Mountain Kletterhallen*, EU:T:2016:341, paras 78–79.

24 Commission Decision of 20 December 2011 on the application of Article 106(2) of the Treaty on the Functioning of the European Union to State aid in the form

of public service compensation granted to certain undertakings entrusted with the operation of services of general economic interest (notified under document C(2011) 9380), [2012] OJ L7, 3–10, at Recital 11 and Article 2(1)(c).

25 Article 109 TFEU allows the Council, on a proposal from the Commission and after consulting the European Parliament, to adopt regulations for the application of Articles 107 and 108 TFEU, and in particular to determine the conditions in which Article 108(3) [the formal notification procedure of State aid projects to the European Commission] shall apply and the categories of aid exempted from this procedure. In this regard, Article 108(4) TFEU allows the Commission to adopt regulations relating to the categories of State aid that the Council has, pursuant to Article 109, determined may be exempted from the procedure provided for by Article 108(3) TFEU. Consequently, some State aid measures are considered compatible with the internal market and exempted from the obligation to notify State aid projects to the European Commission. These measures are currently included in Commission Regulation (EU) No 651/2014 of 17 June 2014 declaring certain categories of aid compatible with the internal market in application of Articles 107 and 108 of the Treaty, [2014] OJ L187, at 1–78. Ferri and Piernas Lopez, 'State Aid Law in a Social Market Economy' (n 1).

26 Elisabetta Righini, 'The Reform of the State Aid Rules on Financing of Public Services Paving the Way towards a Clearer, Simpler and More Diversified Framework' (2012) *European State Aid Quarterly* 1, at 13–14.

27 Adinda Sinnaeve, 'What's New in SGEI in 2012? An Overview of the Commission's SGEI Package' (2012) *European State Aid Quarterly* 354; Lenaerts, 'Defining the Concept of "Services of General Interest" in Light of the "Checks and Balances" Set Out in the EU Treaties' (n 16), at 1264, with reference to Sinnaeve.

28 Caroline Wehlander, *Services of General Economic Interest as a Constitutional Concept of EU Law* (Asser Press, 2016) 263, referring in this regard to Johan Willem Van de Gronden and Catalin Stefan Rusu 'The *Altmark* Update and Social Services' in Erika Szyszczak and Johan Willem Van de Gronden (eds.), *Financing Services of General Economic Interest: Reform and Modernization* (n 5), 185.

29 Jean-Claude Barbier, 'Legal Uncertainty in Social Services: A Threat to National Social Protection Systems?' in Jean-Claude Barbier, Ralf Rogowski and Fabrice Colomb (eds.), *The Sustainability of the European Social Model: EU Governance, Social Protection and Employment Policies in Europe* (Edward Elgar, 2015) 255.

30 Article 2(1)(c).

31 Julio Baquero Cruz, 'Social Services of General Interest and the State Aid Rules' in Ulla Neergaard *et al.* (eds.), *Social Services of General Interest in the EU* (Asser Press, 2013) 307.

32 Ibid., at 304–305 and 312. The author highlights in this regard that this test 'only rules out the overcompensation of the concrete company entrusted with the service, not the compensation of inefficient providers [and that] This element of the package gives precedence to social policy aims over economic considerations. It accepts sub-optimal schemes for the provision of economic services of general interest, including social services, thereby enhancing the discretion of the Member States in this area'.

33 Opinion of AG Cruz Villalón, Case C-515/08, *de Santos Palhota and Others*, EU:C:2010:589, para 51. Lenaerts, 'Defining the Concept of "Services of General Interest" in Light of the "Checks and Balances" Set Out in the EU Treaties' (n 16), at 1262.

34 Heinemann, 'Social Considerations in EU Competition Law: The Protection of Competition as a Cornerstone of the Social Market Economy' (n 1).

35 Case T-137/10, *CBI*, EU:C:2011:280, para 92.

36 Case C-197/11, *Libert and Others*, EU:C:2013:288, paras 97–98.

37 *BUPA* (n 9), para 160, where the Court held that, in the light of the particular nature of the SGEI mission in certain sectors, it is appropriate to show flexibility with regard to the application of the *Altmark* judgement. The General Court has also stated that, in applying Article 106(2) TFEU, it is necessary to take into consideration the lack of a commercial dimension to the public service in question, its classification as an SGEI being explained more by its impact on the competitive and commercial sector; Case T-442/03, *SIC v Commission*, EU:T:2008:228, para 153.
38 *CBI* (n 35), para 89.
39 Case T-44/14, *Costantini*, EU:T:2016:223, para 26.
40 The main objectives of the ECI and the Commission's reply stating the reasons for refusal of registration can be consulted in the following link at <http://ec.europa.eu/citizens-initiative/public/initiatives/non-registered/details/1654?lg=en>.
41 *Costantini* (n 39), para 26.
42 Lenaerts, 'Defining the Concept of "Services of General Interest" in Light of the "Checks and Balances" Set Out in the EU Treaties' (n 17), at 1264. In a similar vein, Baquero Cruz suggests that the Commission has already given a relative precedence to social policy aims over economic and efficiency considerations. Baquero Cruz, 'Social Services of General Interest and the State Aid Rules' (n 31), at 311.
43 For a detailed overview of Commission Decisions on SSGEI in the healthcare provided by hospitals and other entities operating in the frame of national health systems of universal cover, social security and social housing, Danielle Gallo, 'Social Services of General Interest' in Leigh Hancher, Tom Ottervanger and Pieter Jan Slot (eds.), *EU State Aids* (Sweet and Maxwell, 2016) 295.
44 Commission decision of 5.7.2016 on state aid sa.19864–2014/c (ex 2009/NN54) implemented by Belgium Public financing of Brussels public IRIS hospitals, Brussels, 5.7.2016 C(2016)4051 final. In relation to this case, the Commission adopted a first decision in October 28 2009 (NN5409, C74/1) upon a complaint lodged by two associations of private hospitals (i.e. the *Coordination bruxelloise d'institutions sociales et de santé* (CBI) and the *Association bruxelloise des institutions de soins privées* (ABISP)) and also individually by several hospitals that were members of these associations, raising no objections at the end of the preliminary investigation under Article 108(3) TFEU. This decision was appealed before the General Court by CBI. The GC annulled the Commission decision by its judgement of 7 November 2012 in case *CBI* (n 36), concluding that this decision had been adopted in violation of the procedural rights of the complainants. Subsequently, the Commission initiated on 1 October 2014 the procedure laid down in Article 108(2) TFEU in respect of the public financing measures in favour of the Brussels public IRIS hospitals, that concluded with the decision of 5 July 2016.
45 Commission decision of 5.7.2016 on state aid sa.19864, cit., at 154.
46 Ibid., at 155.
47 The Opinion entitled 'Issues with Defining Social Housing as a Service of General Economic Interest', adopted in December 2012, reference number TEN/484 EESC-2012–597.
48 The submission of the Italian delegation to the Common Market Group, S. Neri, at 230 and the *Note présentée* on 11/9/1956 (Doc. MAE 257/56) S. Neri, op. cit., at 230–233.
49 S. Neri, op. cit., at 231.
50 The applicable procedural regulation was still Council Regulation (EC) No 659/1999 of 22 March 1999 laying down detailed rules for the application of Article 93 of the EC Treaty.

51 Commission Decision State aid No E 2/2005 and No 642/2009 – The Netherlands Existing and special project aid to housing corporations, Brussels, 15.12.2009 C(2009)9963, para 38.
52 Els Sol and Mara van der Vos, 'Services of General Interest, State Aid and Social Housing in the Netherlands' in Jean-Claude Barbier, Ralf Rogowski and Fabrice Colomb (eds.), *The Sustainability of the European Social Model: EU Governance, Social Protection and Employment Policies in Europe* (Edward Elgar, 2015) 276. For an analysis of this case, Johan Willem Van de Gronden, 'Social Services of General Interest and EU Law' in Erika Szyszczak *et al.* (eds.), *Developments in Services of General Interest* (Asser Press, 2011) 144.
53 Commission Decision State aid No E 2/2005 and No 642/2009 (n 51). A formal modification of this decision was adopted on 30 August 2010 as Decision C(2010)5841. The new decision concluded, in essence, that one of the measures considered as aid under the 2009 decision, related to the right to obtain loans from the *Bank Nederlandse Gemeenten*, should not be finally considered as such.
54 Case T-202/10, *Stichting Woonlinie and Others v Commission*, EU:C:2013:336.
55 Case C-133/12P, *Stichting Woonlinie and Others v Commission*, EU:C:2014:105.
56 Case T-202/10 RENV, *Stichting Woonlinie and Others v Commission*, EU:T:2015:287.
57 Case C-414/15P, *Stichting Woonlinie and Others v Commission*, EU:C:2017:215.
58 Action brought on 29 April 2010 – *Stichting Woonlinie and Others v Commission* (n 57), fourth argument. The Sixth argument in this regard: 'the Commission disregarded Decision 2005/842/EG 2 in that it demanded a specific description of the service of general economic interest. According to the applicants, the Commission erroneously decided that a Member State must define the service of general economic interest on the basis of an income threshold'.
59 State aid No 209/2001 – Ireland, Guarantee for borrowings of the Housing Finance Agency; Brussels, 03.07.2001 SG (2001) D/289528; Amendments of the Commission's proposal for appropriate measures on State guarantees for the public credit institutions in Germany, [2002] OJ C-150 (see II/4 measures with a purely social character); State Aid No 395/2005 – Ireland Loan Guarantee for social infrastructure schemes funded by the Housing Finance Agency, Brussels, 07.XII.2005, C(2005)4668 final.
60 Commission Decision State aid No E 2/2005 and No 642/2009 (n 51), para 55.
61 Baquero Cruz, 'Social Services of General Interest and the State Aid Rules' (n 32), at 306.
62 Opinion entitled 'Issues with Defining Social Housing as a Service of General Economic Interest' (n 48), at section 2.8.
63 Ibid., at sections 4.2 and 7.2. The ECSC added that 'Member States should be given the discretion to set access conditions and prices for housing in a way that takes account of local needs and local preferences, as well as the real needs of disadvantaged citizens or socially less advantaged groups, in accordance with the provisions of Protocol No 26 on services of general interest', at 7.2.

10 Social services, services providers and non-economic activities in the realm of the EU social market economy

Silvia Pellizzari

1 Introduction

It is well-established within the academic literature that the notion of economic or non-economic activity is extremely important in determining the applicability of EU free movement, competition and public procurement rules.[1] That is especially true with regard to the provision of services which Member States used to qualify as public and that, at the EU level, are considered to be 'services of general interest' (SIG). Once EU law, and especially the CJEU, has established that a national public service can be, in the abstract, an economic activity, the Member States' rules and public measures are necessarily assessed in accordance with the relevant EU market regulations. Otherwise, the national initiatives might constitute an unjustified restriction of the freedoms and rights guaranteed by EU law. However, the implementation of this approach in the field of welfare and social services has been quite problematic.

After the publication of the Commission Communication on the implementation of the Lisbon programme,[2] these so-called 'Social Services of General Interest (SSGI)' can be considered either economic or non-economic depending on the specific characteristics of the activities actually involved. Moreover, the fact that an activity is designated as *social* – or pursuing a *social interest* – is not *per se* sufficient to rule out its economic nature under EU law. In other words, as discussed by Piernas Lopez,[3] a SSGI whose nature is economic needs to be automatically deemed as a Social Service of General Economic Interest (SGEI).

Despite the assertion that EU law does not prevent Member States from organizing their welfare systems as they see fit, there is an inevitable limitation of national sovereignty and discretion resulting from the duty to justify public decisions capable of affecting the structure and functioning of the market. Consequently, it is not surprising that the implementation of EU law at the Member State level has triggered a conflict between the Union's regulatory model based on trade liberalization and free competition, on the one hand, and social rights typically protected by the national welfare state, on the other.

This tension between social and economic values remains evident in spite of the integration of the 'social market economy' clause within Article 3(3) TFEU. As both Civitarese and Heinemann outlined earlier in this volume,[4] the concept of a 'social market economy' can be quite complicated and hard to define. However, overall, it aims – within the competences and powers attributed to the EU legal system – to strike a balance between the existence of an effective body of competition rules and other social principles/objectives, which pursue an increased social inclusion and an improved consideration of social rights and protection measures. From a theoretical standpoint, such an approach could lead to multiple, and often quite compelling, outcomes with reference to the rules and principles applicable to services of social general interest, so long as such activities also have an economic characterization and are, therefore, subject to the applicability of the EU Treaties rules. In this respect, social services are reconcilable with the market-based principles enshrined elsewhere within the EU legal system.[5]

This chapter, which focuses on non-economic activities excluded from the application of market rules, aims to ascertain whether the concept of the 'social market economy' creates a tangible effect in terms of the criteria traditionally utilized to establish the economic or non-economic nature of a given social service. As far as the criteria used in defining a social activity as economic or non-economic are concerned, it is necessary to establish that there are not clearly enshrined rules set down in law in this respect and it therefore becomes necessary to rely on the relevant case law of the CJEU.

As some scholars have highlighted,[6] 'a number of Member States [. . .] argued that for services to be economic the provider had to seek to make a profit'. This kind of assertion has been supported by a well-known case regarding third-level education, which established, *obiter dictum*, that the service at hand could be considered economic under the following conditions: 1) that the system is financed by private funds (such as students' fees); and 2) that the institution providing the service pursues a profit.[7] However, the 'profit argument' is quite controversial, in addition to being potentially misleading.

Whether or not a private entity seeks profit in performing its activity is in principle irrelevant for competition law and free market principles.[8] Many private operators, regardless of the legal form they take, could be considered incompatible with the objective of turning a profit,[9] but entirely compatible with market-oriented behaviours within the system of service providing. In other words, the conscious decision on the part of the service provider to assume a 'non-profit' status is distinct from the nature of the service itself, whose qualification is usually determined through the analysis of the elements which characterize the 'contractual' transactions under analysis.[10]

For the purpose of this chapter, and hereinafter, the concept of 'social services' conforms with the definition established within Communication No 177/2006, where the Commission has identified two main categories of SSGI, in addition to health and medical services. The first group includes social security schemes, which usually cover the main risks of life, such as illness, old age, disability, unemployment and, more recently, pregnancy, childhood or educational needs which may occur at different stages of an individual's continuous development. The second group refers to other fundamental services provided directly to people in order to satisfy what is today known as the right to *social assistance* enshrined in Article 34 of the EU Charter of Fundamental Rights (along with the right to social security). These services play a role in ensuring social cohesion and facilitating social inclusion of the most vulnerable individuals within society. Finally, these services support families in taking care of dependent relatives of various ages, facilitate the inclusion of people with long-term health problems and disabilities, as well as providing (social) housing for disadvantaged citizens and groups.[11] SSGIs are indeed an essential part of the SGEI and, according to Article 14 TFEU, aim at 'promoting social and territorial cohesion'. They are, as such, of fundamental importance to citizens.[12]

Against this background, the chapter is structured as follows. Section 2 analyses the criteria the CJEU has utilized in order to define the economic or non-economic relevance of a given social service. Section 3 focuses on the 'solidarity principle' typical of several welfare states in light of the 'social market economy' concept and on the role that such a principle plays in order to qualify a given activity as non-economic. Sections 4 and 5 deal with the applicability of EU public procurement and internal market rules relating to social activities and services, highlighting the lack of relevance given to the 'profit' or 'non-profit' making status of the service providers in order to single out the specific scope of application of EU law. Such an applicability, indeed, follows the economic nature of the activities concretely carried out and not the legal form or status of the service providers, pursuant to the pragmatic and functional approach embraced by the CJEU. Finally, section 6 will draw some brief conclusions in light of the arguments previously developed.

2 Social services as economic activities: the criteria to assess their market relevance for the purpose of the Treaty

Some scholars[13] have recently highlighted how the CJEU case law has progressively followed a common criterion in recognizing the economic nature of a particular activity for the purpose of applying Treaty rules regarding competition (including State aid),[14] as well as those concerning the internal market freedoms and public procurement.

As discussed at length by Heinemann in this volume,[15] in order to establish whether an organization is an undertaking for the purposes of EU law, the Court applies its long-standing objective and functional test, under which it is relevant: 1) whether or not the activity is already provided on the market; and 2) whether or not the establishment of a dominant market position potentially distorts competition. The settled case law of the CJEU states that an activity can be considered economic when it consists of offering goods and services on a given market. Therefore, even if the activity involved pursues a social aim, the applicability of competition rules is not in principle ruled out. In *AG2R*, which dealt with the healthcare sector,[16] it was established that the 'social aim of an insurance scheme is not by itself sufficient to preclude the activity in question from being classified as an economic activity' within the meaning of Article 102 TFEU.

A natural consequence of this kind of determination is that every entity engaged in an economic activity is subject to EU market rules, regardless of its legal status (public, private or non-profit making) and the way in which it is financed.[17] In *Ambulanz Glockner v Landkreis Sudwestpfalz*[18] for example, a public health organization which operated as a non-profit organization and provided services in the market for emergency and ambulance services was considered an ***undertaking*** for the purposes of applying EU competition law, since 'such activities have not always been, and are not necessarily, carried out by such organisations'. The CJEU has attempted to specifically develop its case law in this area with reference to national legal actions concerning social security systems or social insurance schemes established and regulated following principles and organizational models potentially inconsistent with the EU market rules.

Obviously, the Court of Justice's stance depends on how social security and welfare systems are organized at the national level, and takes into account that the schemes can vary significantly among the Member States. As noted by Heinemann, there is no general exemption from competition law for the social security sector, and the CJEU adopts a 'case-by-case' approach.

The most basic and traditional social security measures are usually based on broad social insurance programmes, which provide mechanisms for guaranteeing a lasting income to individuals, citizens or families when their earnings are interrupted due to various different events, and pension schemes.

In many Member States, social security is provided on a contributory basis, frequently through institutions which are independent from the general State budget and rely on contributions from both employees and employers. Conversely, other Member States provide social security entirely independent of the labour market. In such instances, they are administered or supervised by the State, and are often funded by fiscal contributions and require a compulsory participation. These more 'universal' systems may also be funded through national insurance payments which tend to be absorbed by the general State budget.

One significant example of this second model, for which it has been quite easy to rule out the economic nature of the scheme, is the Italian system regulating the compulsory insurance scheme against accidents at work and occupational illnesses. This is managed by INAIL (the National Institute for Insurance against Accidents at Work), a public service institutional player subject to the supervision of the Ministry of Employment and Social Security.

Such a decision has been issued before the Lisbon Treaty came into effect and so, at that time, the EU did not pursue the aim of realizing a highly competitive social market economy. Nevertheless, the reasoning carried out by the judges in order to rule out the economic nature of the activities considered is still relevant and useful.[19]

The main question proposed by the national judge in its reference for preliminary ruling concerned whether:

> a public non-profit making insurance body, such as the INAIL, to which is entrusted, on the basis of sound economic and business practice, the operation as a monopoly of a scheme of insurance against risks deriving from accidents at work and occupational diseases, based on a system of compulsory registration which pays benefits on a partially automatic basis [. . .], even

> in the event of non-payment of premiums by the employer, and calculates the premiums on the basis of risk categories to which the insured work is assigned, constitute[d] an undertaking within the meaning of the [then] Article 81 of the EC Treaty.[20]

In its judgement, the CJEU pointed out that, generally speaking, under EU competition law the concept of undertaking covers any entity engaged in an economic activity, irrespective of its legal status and the way in which it is financed. The CJEU defined an economic activity as offering a good or service within a given a market. However, the CJEU did not believe INAIL was capable of being considered an undertaking based on two primary factors, as these factors were capable of confirming the non-economic essence of the activity carried out by INAIL. First of all, the insurance scheme was 'financed by contributions the rate of which is not systematically proportionate to the risk insured'.[21] Secondly, the amount of benefits paid was 'not necessarily proportionate to the insured persons' earnings, since, for the calculation of pensions, only salaries situated between a minimum and a maximum corresponding to the average nationwide salary [. . .] may be taken into consideration'.[22]

These elements demonstrate that the social security or the insurance scheme did not satisfy the so-called 'market participation test'[23] and was instead based on the principle of solidarity, as conceived in the *Poucet and Pistre* ruling.[24] The key element of such a conclusion was the lack of any direct link between the contributions paid by the members and the benefits granted, which clearly responded to the principle of solidarity between better paid workers and those who, given their low earnings, would have been otherwise deprived of an adequate, if not comparable coverage. In the estimation of the CJEU, it was also clear that the Italian Insurance Institute did not have an autonomous decision-making power comparable with the one of a private entity operating in the market, since INAIL was indeed 'subject to supervision by the State' and the amount of benefits and contributions was ultimately established by the State, which was implementing an exclusively social function without an economic motive. Finally, the law required a compulsory affiliation to the insurance scheme in question, which was essential for the financial sustainability of the system and for the pursuit of the solidarity principle, according to which the benefits paid to the insured persons were not strictly proportionate to the contributions they had previously paid. Accordingly, the activity was considered as non-economic in nature for the purpose of interpreting and applying EU competition rules and INAIL did not constitute an undertaking within the meaning of the Arts. 101 and 102 TFEU.

3 The principle of solidarity and its relevance to assess the non-economic nature of an activity

The principle of solidarity as referenced by the CJEU is a milestone of the welfare state regimes developed across Europe after the Second World War. The welfare state utilizes many different forms and categories of social insurance in order to promote a real and substantial equality among individuals.[25]

For these reasons, in the CJEU case law, the notion of solidarity has been defined as a 'social solidarity' rooted in civil society which, on the basis of political and legislative explicit decisions, facilitates the transfer of public resources from one social group to another.

In most cases, social solidarity implies redistributive policies, which represent the core of welfare states.[26] In this respect, the principle of solidarity refers to a welfare state model which is inherently different from 'the historical and also current interpretation of the social market economy', which is fully compatible with a strenuous enforcement of competition and other market rules.[27]

As a limit to the application of the EU market rules, the solidarity argument can be quite vague and essentially political. Indeed, it seems to imply that a service is not economic in nature when the State performs in favour of its population a social functional which is constitutionally binding and responds to the fundamental rights and needs of its constituents. This line of reasoning can quickly come into conflict with the traditional functionalistic approach used by the CJEU, which places a strong emphasis on the economic nature of the (social) service provided. The current definition and implications of the solidarity principle have concretized over time in the case law of the CJEU on the freedom of movement within the EU internal market.

In general, it seems easier to recognize the implementation of a solidarity-based welfare state when the financing of a specific service or benefit cannot be considered as a payment within a given transaction. This may be the case of a service provided by an institution (regardless of whether it is public or private), which receives a comprehensive budget, in so far as the actual number of users and the amount of their possible contributions are not crucial and decisive factors but are instead merely one element of appraisal among several other ones. On the contrary, a market-like relationship is more evident in many social insurance schemes against risk, so long as they are related to certain professions and funded from their members' contributions in the absence of additional public subsidies. These kinds of insurance mechanisms feature a much clearer economic structure where there is a direct correlation between the premiums paid and the benefits granted and this is relatively easy to establish.

4 Economic activities, social services providing and free movement rules

With regard to the free movement of services (Articles 56–62 TFEU) and the freedom of establishment (Articles 49–55 TFEU), the relevant EU Treaty rules and secondary legislation (such as the Services directive 2006/123/EC on the services in the Internal Market)[28] are applied where the social importance of the activity as well as of the final aims or the status of the providers are considered immaterial. What are instead emphasized are the behaviours of the parties and the economic and commercial nature of the relationship between them for the purpose of supplying the final service.

It is worth noting that the parties involved can vary in individual cases. Moreover, the relationships which must be considered and evaluated are those of the users and the providers, and those of the providers and the State (or, more generally, the competent public authority). That is especially true when public bodies decide to outsource some services to private operators.

In order to establish to what extent many activities are subject to the free movement rules enshrined into the EU Treaties, the preliminary element to evaluate is whether or not they can be considered as services according to Article 57 TFEU. The latter provisions states that services are considered to be 'normally provided for remuneration', and will include activities of a commercial character. On a number of occasions[29] the Court has recalled that the definition of what constitutes a service within EU law may not be interpreted restrictively. As it will subsequently be shown, the essential characteristic of remuneration lies in the fact that it should constitute a *consideration* for the service in question.[30] However, it must also be noted that this interpretation as contained in Article 57 TFEU has been progressively improved and extended.

In the early cases the Court embraced a more political approach. In the well-known *Humbel*[31] decision which concerned university education, the Court found that the activity at issue was not a service within the scope of the Treaty, since 'the State, in establishing and maintaining such a system' was not seeking 'to engage in gainful activity'; rather, it was fulfilling 'its duties towards its own population in the social, cultural and educational fields'. Furthermore, the system in question was 'funded from the public purse and not by pupils or their parents'.[32]

The arguments utilized by the Court build on some of the fundamental values and principles of the welfare state. According to such values, social services, and particularly educational ones, are run by the State in order to guarantee the principles of equality and equivalent opportunities to everybody with specific reference to social rights.

The judicial attitude started to change in the mid-1990s and, in this respect, the decision on the *Sodemare* case is quite symbolic.[33] The question submitted to the CJEU concerned a provision contained in Italian legislation adopted at a regional level which allowed only non-profit institutions to provide healthcare services within the overall umbrella of social welfare provision. The private parties' involvement depended on the conclusion of contracts, which included exclusively the reimbursement of the costs incurred by the providers. To summarize the case, the law had the effect of reserving the provision of social services to non-profit organizations, in so far as the non-profit requirement could be contrary to the freedom of establishment. On this point, the Court firstly stated that the principle of solidarity implies that Member States retain a broad discretion to organize their social welfare systems in whichever manner they see fit, which should take into account, as a matter of priority, the right of assistance guaranteed to those who have needs due to insufficient income, total or partial lack of independence, or the risk of being marginalized. For these reasons, the non-profit condition mentioned in the Regional Legislation forms an essential part of the social welfare system, which seeks in particular to promote and protect the health of the population through social welfare and health services and to operate in the interests of dependent persons, who have no family or whose family is not in a position to look after them, by bringing about or encouraging their reintegration into suitable families or environments within the community. However, and more specifically, the social services system laid down by the law was not considered to be incompatible with EU internal market law, since the non-profit requirement was inherent in the statutory scheme and confirmed by the mere reimbursement of the costs (mandatorily set forth by the contracts). In other words, the confinement to non-profit making private bodies of the status to conclude contracts was not relevant *per se*, but as a sign of a system inherently inconsistent with a profit making relation between the public and the private parties. The payment from the Region therefore could not be considered remuneration within the meaning of Article 57 TFEU. Above all, the decision shows that the profit-aim could be helpful factually and objectively to identify the element of consideration in an economic exchange.

This particular test has subsequently been applied in a number of other cases, albeit with different outcomes. In *Geraets-Smits*,[34] two Dutch citizens challenged the national sickness fund which provided insurance to the benefit of individuals with low income, and on terms and contributions (i.e. a premium) regulated by the law. The scheme was managed by a private not-for-profit organization, and was funded through individual premiums as well as through other subsidies from employers, the State and persons with non-sickness private insurance funds. The system provided benefits-in-kind and reimbursed the costs incurred by insured beneficiaries for healthcare services and treatments carried out in another Member State, subject to prior authorization. In the case at hand, the claimants received health treatments abroad and the fund refused to reimburse the expenses they had incurred for the same. For this reason, they argued that the system in force was in violation of the rules regulating the free movement of services under the EU Treaties. With regard to the benefits under examination in the case at hand, the Court underlined that the fund paid the providers directly. For the purposes of the Treaties, the relation between the parties involved was economic, since the remuneration entailed unquestionably the consideration for the service provided, in the end, to the citizens. Furthermore, the fact that hospital medical treatments and benefits were financed directly by the sickness insurance funds on the basis of pre-set scales of fees was not enough to remove such treatments from the scope of application of Article 60 TFEU.

Similarly, with reference to the reimbursement mechanism, the CJEU stated that a medical service provided in one Member State and refunded to the patient in his home country, cannot be excluded from the scope of the freedom to provide services guaranteed by the Treaty. In this case, the relevant transaction is the one between the foreign provider and the recipients.[35] To summarize, the decisive factor bringing an activity within the scope of the Treaty provisions regulating the freedom to provide services and, accordingly, of those relating to the freedom of establishment, is its economic character. In the absence of an express and clear provision imposing the mere reimbursement of costs or expenses incurred by the provider, it becomes difficult to exclude a profit- making relationship for the service's supply. Therefore, in this respect, there is no need for the person providing the service to be a for-profit organization, and it is in reality immaterial who pays the provider for the service.[36]

It is worth noting that, also in its most recent cases, the CJEU makes reference to the above-described arguments without explicitly mentioning the concept of a social market economy.

5 Social services, social providers and non-economic activities in EU public procurement law

A peculiar *trait d'union* between social services, social providers and the specific type of activity involved can be found in the field of public procurement, which is discussed extensively by Bovis earlier in this volume. According to the Public Sector Directive, amended in 2014 by Directive 2014/24/EU,[37] public contracts concluded for the provision of social services acquire a specific regime given their limited cross-border relevance.[38] In particular, this is part of a wider and new *light-touch regime*, which includes *inter alia* a higher EU-relevance threshold (equal to EUR 750,000) compared to those fixed for all the other services.

In this respect, the 2014 Directives implement – with a more conscious approach than before – the objectives of the 'social market economy', trying to balance social interests with the economic and market ones.[39]

However, in order to make such a balancing possible, the Directives themselves should be legally applicable and such an outcome is possible only when an economically relevant contract is concluded and signed by a public administration. Therefore, even in this context, the presence of a non-economic activity excludes the applicability of the European legislation and the (consequent) adaptation of the market structure to the principles enshrined into Article 3(3) TEU.

The notion of a public contract is crucial in determining the scope of applicability of the relevant EU public procurement rules. The CJEU has usually given a broad interpretation of the expression 'public contract' for the purpose of the EU directives, recognizing an 'economic transaction' as one of the essential elements relevant to single out a public contract. It is well-known that the public procurement directives apply when a contract between one or more contracting authorities and one or more economic operators is concluded for pecuniary interest.[40] This element has been further developed by the case law of the CJEU, underlining that a public contract shall consist of: 1) an agreement between two autonomous wills and 2) an offer of remuneration in exchange for services, goods or works. With regard to the latter condition, the judicial reasoning in public procurement cases is similar to the one previously analysed under the free movement rules. It is assumed that the interest of the private provider is to pursue some form of profit in the transaction, regardless of the legally binding reinvestment of the profits in order to achieve the organization's objective.[41] The fact that, in specific circumstances, the clearing price could be, *ex post*, a mere reimbursement of the costs or the expenses incurred by the provider does not *ex ante* exclude a contract's pecuniary interest and therefore the existence of a public contract. The crucial point is once again that the ability to prove a clear and objective not-for-profit motive capable of qualifying the exchange as a non-economic activity. This issue has been raised in cases concerning the transport of patients by ambulance services. In *Commission v Italy*,[42] the European Commission brought an action for the failure of the Italian Republic to fulfil its obligations under the EU public procurement directives. The Region of Tuscany and the local health agencies had awarded some framework agreements for the ambulance service to several voluntary associations without a previous call for tenders. According to the Member State's defence, the direct award was justified by the nature of the private parties involved which, as non-profit organizations, played an essential role in adhering to the solidarity principle and achieving a degree of social cohesion. Moreover, the payments received for the services provided were a mere reimbursement of the expenses incurred in providing them, without any additional remuneration.

The CJEU emphasized that the absence of a profit motivation cannot exclude volunteers' associations from carrying out an economic activity and being considered as private economic operators under the Treaties. With reference to the reimbursement of expenses, the Court pointed out that in the case at hand, the agreements were proper contracts for services, delivered against remuneration and consequently subject to the relevant EU rules. The payments budgeted by the public authorities were higher than the expenses incurred to provide the service; such amounts were previously fixed in lump sums based on tables annexed to a framework agreement and not determined after the analytic evidence of the expenditures.

The reasoning supporting the decision of the Court has been partly adapted and developed in *San Lorenzo*.[43] In this instance, legislation laid down by another Italian Region obligated local health authorities to entrust ambulance services to voluntary associations and to other approved public institutions or bodies on a preferential basis with the aim of ensuring that the public service in question was provided in an economically balanced manner for budgetary purposes. In this respect, the Act permitted the direct award of the right to provide the service to the voluntary associations, and the other institutions mentioned above, on the condition that the payments corresponded to the mere reimbursement of the expenses actually sustained, according to criteria decided by the regional council and based on the principles of economic efficiency, effectiveness and absence of any overpayment beyond the costs incurred. The CJEU found the national regime compatible with articles 49 and 56 TFEU and with the principles governing public procurement procedures.

The judicial reasoning on this issue has been quite interesting. First of all, the Court specified that the exclusive reimbursement of costs was not in general a decisive factor to exclude the existence of a public contract.[44] On the contrary, the direct award should have been justified on a different basis. The Court considered that the organization of the ambulance service at issue was 'grounded in the principles of universality, the good of the community, economic efficiency and suitability'. Hence, the entrustment of the service to the voluntary associations on a preferential basis sought specifically 'to ensure that the public service is provided in an economically balanced manner for budgetary purposes'.

As already specified in the settled case law of the CJEU, EU law does not prevent Member States from organizing their public health and social security systems as they see fit. However, on the one hand, the risk of seriously undermining the financial balance of a social security system *may* constitute an overriding reason in the general interest capable of justifying an obstacle to the freedom to provide services; on the other hand, the objective of maintaining, on the basis of the protection and promotion of public health, a balanced health or social service may fall within one of the derogations provided that it contributes to the attainment of a high level of individual and social protection.

This recent ruling is noteworthy because it has demonstrated that, for the purpose of public procurement law, it is crucial to combine the economic analysis of the parties' relationships and the demonstration of a public aim of guaranteeing, at the national level, a 'sufficient and permanent access' to a 'balanced range of high-quality' social benefits, ensuring the 'control of costs and prevention, as far as possible, of any wastage of financial, technical and human resources'. Given this framework, voluntary associations can play a significant role, since the Member State's choice to outsource to them 'is consistent with the social purpose of the emergency ambulance services and may help to control costs relating to those services'.[45]

Despite the discretion extended to Member States, they must demonstrate that endowing voluntary organizations with the power to provide public services will supplement the pursuit of social objectives, promote the well-being of the community, and contribute to the budgetary efficiency on which a specific social scheme is based. Hence, the CJEU confirmed that

> it is essential that [. . .] the voluntary associations do not pursue objectives other than those mentioned [. . .], do not make any profit as a result of their services, apart from the reimbursement of the variable, fixed and ongoing expenditure necessary to provide them, and do not procure any profit for their members.[46]

It is worth noting that ultimately the provision of the mere reimbursement is, once again, the factor which contributes to justifying a derogation to the EU general principles and rules.

6 Conclusions

The analysis conducted in the foregoing sections allows for some overall conclusions to be drawn. The notion of 'economic' or 'non-economic' activity, relevant to determine the applicability of EU rules on competition, free movement and public procurements, is quite problematic, especially when applied in the field of welfare and social services. According to Heinemann,[47] the somewhat blurred line between economic and non-economic activities and the case by case approach of the CJEU attempts to reconcile social and general economic goals. He contends that, on the one hand, a general social security exemption would endanger the application of EU competition law, and on the other, a general application of competition law to social activities would interfere with the competence of Member States to organize their social systems as they see fit, especially if we consider that Member States have traditionally been quite protective of their power to organize their national welfare systems in order to promote the social rights of citizens. This discretion has often been expressed through measures which derogate from EU law, including derogatory mechanisms (i.e. direct award) justified by the intent to support some private operators among others, particularly when they have a non-profit making status.

Despite the CJEU on several occasions stating that EU law does not limit the powers of the Member States to organize their welfare systems as they see fit, national prerogatives have inevitably been limited by the duty to justify their decisions where they intersect with the EU rules regulating the functioning of the internal market and its economic structure. The analysis carried out, though, shows that there are not decisive elements to argue that considering an activity as non-economic necessarily implies a clear will to balance social and economic objectives with the final aim of promoting a highly competitive social market economy.

It is worth noting that the CJEU's approach has remained unchanged even after the integration of this value within the Lisbon Treaty. Article 3(3) TEU might overcome the tension between social and economic values, insofar as market rules are applicable to the activity at hand, which should therefore be qualified as economic. The relationship between the economic and non-economic nature of a given service is rather based on a restrictive interpretation of the solidarity principle as the cornerstone of a welfare model incompatible with the market rules. That is rather evident considering the link between social services and social providers.

In defining if the activity performed is economic or non-economic in nature, this chapter has highlighted the principle, established in the CJEU's settled case law, according to which it is irrelevant and immaterial, under competition and free market rules, whether or not a private entity seeks profit in performing its activities. The will of a service provider to assume a non-profit making status is therefore kept apart from the nature of the service itself, whose classification is usually determined through the analysis of different elements, which show a sort of balance between objective economic factors and policy arguments. First of all, the application of the EU rules is limited by the identification of a principle of solidarity in the national system. In doing so, the Court seems to imply that a service, or more generally an activity, is not economic when the State performs a sort of essential social duty. This notion of solidarity can be defined as 'social solidarity' which, on the basis of a political and legislative clear decision, imposes to transfer public resources from a social group to another. In most cases, social solidarity implies redistributive policies which represent one of the main focus points of several welfare states.

The traditional functionalistic approach of the CJEU comes into play in order to complete this line of reasoning. According to such a pragmatic approach, what matters is the economic nature of the relation between parties located in the market of providing services. As it is clear from the free movement cases analysed, an implementation of the solidarity-based welfare state is recognized when the financing of a specific social service or benefit cannot be interpreted as the remuneration which identifies an economic transaction. In this respect, the essential characteristic of remuneration lies in the fact that it should constitute a consideration for the service in question. Such an expression should be intended as referred to an economic value included in the parties' transaction as a compensation for the provision of services, which is assumed to exceed the costs incurred by the operator. The recent ruling *San Lorenzo* demonstrates that both elements – the one based on the principle of solidarity and the one based on the non-economic nature of the activity – should combine each other at the same time.

For the purpose of EU market rules, a Member State should exercise its discretion in organizing a social service demonstrating the specific public aim of guaranteeing a 'sufficient and permanent access' to a 'balanced range of high-quality' social treatments able to ensure the 'control of costs and prevention, as far as possible, of any wastage of financial, technical and human resources'. In this context, a non-profit organization can play a significant role in providing the services entrusted to it through a direct award decided by the administration, which excludes competition with other operators, only as long as the economic relationship between the parties involved is limited to the reimbursement of costs without a margin profit. This aspect indicates once more the clear prevalence of a solidarity-based approach over an economic one.

Notes

1 For further references, Juan Jorge Piernas López, 'Services of General Economic Interest and Social Considerations', in this volume; Christopher Bovis, 'The Social Dimension of EU Public Procurement and the 'Social Market Economy', in this volume; Andreas Heinemann, 'Social Considerations in EU Competition Law', in this volume.

2 Communication from the European Commission, 'Implementing the Community Lisbon Programme: Social Services of General Interest in the European Union', COM(2006)177; Communication from the European Commission, Accompanying the Communication on 'A Single Market for 21st Century Europe', 'Services of General Interest, Including Social Services of General Interest: A New European Commitment', COM(2007)725; Communication from the European Commission, 'A Quality Framework for Services of General Interest in Europe', COM(2011)900, at 3–4.

3 Piernas Lopez, 'Services of General Economic Interest and Social Considerations' (n 1).

4 Heinemann, 'Social Considerations in EU Competition Law' (n 1) and Stefano Civitarese Matteucci, 'Social Rights, Social Market Economy, and the European Social Model: Tracing Conceptual Boundaries', in this volume.

5 The values typical of a 'sustainable development based on a highly competitive social market economy' may have a significant value resulting in the 'exemptions'

of 'certain activities or entities from the scope' of the full application of market rules (Václav Šmejkal, 'Competition Law and the Social Market Economy Goal of the EU' (2015) *International Comparative Jurisprudence* 33, at 37).

6 Gareth Davies, 'Welfare as a Service' (2002) *Legal Issues of Economic Integration* 29.

7 Case C-109/92, *Wirth v Landeshauptstadt Hannover*, EU:C:1993:916. The case concerned a system of university education financed and organized by the State, which was considered by the CJEU as a non-economic service.

8 Alison Jones and Brenda Sufrin, *EC Competition Law* (OUP, 2011) 90–92.

9 On the relevance of private intention in EU law and in particular in free movement law, Chris Hilson, 'Discrimination in Community Free Movement Law' (1994) *European Law Review* 445.

10 Vassilis Hatzopoulos, 'Recent Developments in the Free Movement of Services' (2000) *Common Market Law Review* 59.

11 Pierre Bauby, 'Unity and Diversity of SSGIs in the European Union' in Ulla Neergaard *et al.* (eds.), *Social Services of General Interest in the EU* (Asser Press, 2013) 25.

12 For these reasons, they must be available at an affordable price which would not be the case on a competitive market. Communication from the European Commission, 'The Application of the European Union State Aid Rules to Compensation Granted for the Provision of Services of General Economic Interest', C(2012)8/02.

13 Caroline Wehlander, *Services of General Economic Interest as a Constitutional Concept of EU Law* (Asser Press, 2013) 38. For a different point of view, Okeoghene Odudu, 'Economic Activity as a Limit to EU Law' in Catherine Barnard and Okeoghene Odudu (eds.), *The Outer Limits of European Union Law* (Hart, 2009) 225.

14 Delia Ferri and Juan Jorge Piernas López, 'State Aid Law in a Social Market Economy', in this volume.

15 Heinemann, 'Social Considerations in EU Competition Law' (n 1).

16 Case C-437/09, *AG2R*, EU:C:2011:112.

17 The principle has been stated in many CJEU's decision and particularly in Case C-41/90, *Höfner and Elser*, EU:C:1991:161. In Case C-118/85, *Commission v Italy*, EU:C:1987:283, the Court recognized that even 'the State may act either by exercising public powers or by carrying on economic activities of an industrial or commercial nature by offering goods and services on the market'; Case C-280/06, *ETI and Others*, EU:C:2007:775.

18 Case C-475/99, *Ambulanz Glockner v Landkreis Sudwestpfalz*, EU:C:2001:577.

19 Case C-218/00, *Cisal v INAIL*, EU:C:2002:36.

20 Ibid., para 15.

21 Ibid., para 39.

22 Ibid., para 40.

23 In Case C-205/03 P, *FENIN v Commission*, EU:C:2006:453, AG Maduro opines that the approach for establishing whether or not a public body is an undertaking is based on two separate stages.

24 Joined cases C-159/91 and C-160/91, *Poucet and Pistre*, EU:C:1993:63.

25 Gøsta Esping-Andersen, *Three Worlds of Welfare Capitalism* (Princeton, 1990) clarified how equality has always been the crucial element and objective of the welfare state which can vary depending on the different type of welfare states and the specific of social solidarity they pursue.

26 Gautier Busschaert, 'Revisiting the Fundamentals of Internal Market Law: Civil Society as a Third Sector between the State and the Market' (2011) *European Business Law Review* 725, at 726. For the notion of solidarity in EU law, Tamara Hervey, 'Social Solidarity: A Buttress against Internal Market Law?' in Jo Shaw (ed.), *Social Law and Policy in an Evolving European Union* (Hart, 2000); Catherine Barnard, 'EU Citizenship and the Principle of Solidarity' in Eleanor Spaventa

and Michael Dougan (eds.), *Social Welfare and EU Law* (Hart, 2005); Catherine Barnard, 'Solidarity and New Governance in Social Policy' in Gráinne De Burca and Joanne Scott (eds.), *Law and New Governance in the EU and the US* (Hart, 2006); Christopher Newdick, 'Citizenship, Free Movement and Health Care: Cementing Individual Rights by Corroding Social Solidarity' (2006) *Common Market Law Review* 1645; Malcolm Ross, 'Promoting Solidarity: From Public Services to a European Model of Competition?' (2007) *Common Market Law Review* 1057; Nina Boeger, 'Solidarity and EC Competition Law' (2007) *European Law Review* 319.

27 Václav Šmejkal, 'Competition Law and the Social Market Economy Goal of the EU' (2015) 1 *International Comparative Jurisprudence* 33, at 35.

28 Directive 2006/123/EC of the European Parliament and of the Council of 12 December 2006 on services in the internal market, [2006] OJ L376/36.

29 Joined Cases C-51/96 and C-191/97, *Deliège*, EU:C:2000:199, case law cited at para 52.

30 Case C-281/06, *Jundt*, EU:C:2007:816.

31 Case C-263/86, *Belgium v Humbel*, EU:C:1988:451.

32 Ibid., para 18; Busschaert, 'Revisiting the Fundamentals of Internal Market Law: Civil Society as a Third Sector between the State and the Market' (n 27), at 729.

33 Case C-70/95, *Sodemare*, EU:C:1997:301.

34 Case C-157/99, *Geraets-Smits*, EU:C:2001:404.

35 The CJEU stated a similar position in many other occasions, such as in Case C-444/05, *Aikaterini Stamatelaki v NPDD OAEE*, EU:C:2007:231, para 21; Case C-385/99, *Müller-Fauré and van Riet*, EU:C:2003:270.

36 *European Commission v Hungary* (n 30).

37 Directive 2014/24/EU of the European Parliament and of the Council of 26 February 2014 on public procurement and repealing Directive 2004/18/EC, [2014] OJ L94/65.

38 Ibid., Recital 114.

39 Even though there is not an explicitly reference to the social market recital (2) states that 'Public procurement plays a key role in the Europe 2020 strategy, set out in the Communication from the European Commission, 'Europe 2020, a Strategy for Smart, Sustainable and Inclusive Growth', COM(2010)2020 final (Europe 2020 strategy for smart, sustainable and inclusive growth), as one of the market-based instruments to be used to achieve smart, sustainable and inclusive growth'.

40 Article 2(5) EU Directive 2014/24/EU.

41 The notion of 'private operator' is quite broad at the EU level. For further details, Case C-357/06, *Frigerio*, EU:C:2007:818 and Case C-305/08, *CoNisma*, EU:C:2009:807.

42 Case C-119/06, *Commission v Italy*, EU:C:2007:729.

43 Case C-113/13, *San Lorenzo*, EU:C:2014:2440.

44 Case C-159/11, *Ordine degli Ingegneri della Provincia di Lecce and Others*, EU:C:2012:817.

45 Ibid., para 59.

46 'As regards the reimbursement of costs, it must be ensured that profit making, even indirect, cannot be pursued under the cover of a voluntary activity and that volunteers may be reimbursed only for expenditure actually incurred for the activity performed, within the limits laid down in advance by the associations themselves', Ibid., paras 60–62.

47 Heinemann, 'Social Considerations in EU Competition Law' (n 1).

11 Cross-border healthcare and the social market economy

*Lucia Busatta and Tamara Hervey**

1 Introduction: the predicted disaster

Cross-border healthcare is a classic example of the tight relationship between market and social rights within European Union (EU) law, and the sometimes contradictory tensions involved in these two areas of EU action. Cross-border healthcare encompasses the right of individual patients to obtain medical treatment in a Member State (MS) different from their home country (or the country in which they are socially insured) and to receive reimbursement for medical expenses incurred abroad from their home institution. It also includes the right of health service providers (natural persons and professionals, as well as legal persons of all types – public, private and 'third sector') to provide services across internal EU borders. Such cross-border health service provision could be in any of the following modes: the service moves across a border (such as telemedicine services); the patient moves across a border (for instance, to access a clinic in another Member State); a foreign-owned and controlled provider has a commercial presence (through a subsidiary or affiliate) in another Member State; or a national of another Member State provides a service either as an independent professional (for example, dentist) or as an employee of a health service supplier (such as a hospital). This chapter focuses on the second mode, i.e. on the movement of a patient across borders.

For the purpose of this volume, cross-border healthcare is a paradigmatic field as it shows one way in which the EU has handled the tensions inherent in the EU's 'social market economy' thus far. After one of the most crucial decisions of the Court of Justice of the European Union (CJEU) on cross-border healthcare, the *Watts* decision,[1] several legal scholars predicted nothing short of a disaster resulting from the emerging set of rights to cross-border healthcare, based on Article 56 TFEU. The *Watts* ruling was understood to have signalled the inception of an uncontrolled flow of (rich) patients, travelling from one Member State to another, to get the best and quickest treatment possible and applying afterwards for reimbursement by their competent national healthcare authority.[2] This fear had already been raised following the CJEU's *Smits and Peerbooms* decision in 2001.[3] The then English Secretary of State for Health announced an initiative to recommend patients from South-Eastern England to go to France or Belgium for some low-risk medical procedures, in order to reduce NHS waiting lists.[4] At that time, it had been assumed that the earlier decisions on patient mobility did not apply to 'NHS-type' healthcare systems, such as that in England and Wales. *Watts* confirmed that they did in fact apply. The second fear to emerge after *Watts* was a direct consequence of the first. An uncontrolled flow of patients was feared as a serious threat to the sustainability of Member States' healthcare systems, based on social solidarity models, especially those of lower income countries.[5]

In fact, the evolution of the EU's legal framework on cross-border healthcare, as an exemplar of the EU's 'social market economy', and its regulation, was not so simple. The way the EU legal framework evolved, both before and after the *Watts* ruling, demonstrates the tight relationship between social phenomena such as increased attention to patient autonomy and choice, their economic impact and the EU's ability to adopt laws that accommodate *both* social *and* market-based rights. Following *Watts*, the EU legislature began working on a Directive which was specifically intended to give legislative shape to the principles progressively established by the CJEU, and to secure the preferences of the governments of the Member States, their national health systems and of the European Parliament. The 'Patients' Rights Directive' was finally adopted in 2011.[6]

Following an outline of the evolution of EU law on cross-border healthcare (section 2), this chapter explains that the 'predicted disaster' of cross-border healthcare did not occur (sections 3 and 4). The reasons that it did not are found in the ways in which EU law manages the tensions inherent in its 'social market economy'. EU law allows MS to place restrictions on principles of free movement law, which are at the heart of the EU's 'market economy'. Those restrictions may embody 'social market economy' principles, such as the solidarity implicit in national health systems in the MS. They take legal form in procedural, rather than substantive, entitlements. However, the chapter goes further, to consider a much more serious challenge from EU law to national health systems, that of economic governance within the Eurozone (section 5). The chapter concludes with some reflections on how the lessons learned from embodying the EU's 'social market economy' in EU law on cross-border healthcare could be applied in the EU's economic governance competences (section 6).

2 The evolution of EU law on cross-border health care

Cross-border healthcare in the EU was first addressed in general terms by the EU Regulation on the coordination of social security systems, which provides for measures to facilitate the free movement of workers and their families in the EU.[7] The relative stability of movement of patients based on this EU Regulation was disrupted, however, by the reliance on directly effective Treaty provisions (in particular, what is now Article 56 TFEU) by patients seeking to secure cross-border healthcare entitlements. Based not only on these 'constitutional' rules, but also as a result of the development of the internal market in services, in and around the turn of the century, the circulation of EU citizens across the EU increased significantly, bringing with it the development of the new social phenomenon of cross-border healthcare.[8]

In this context, the CJEU was called upon to respond to the demands of individual patients to access the healthcare market in other Member States. The solidaristic nature of healthcare provision in the Member States, expressed in their State-based restrictions to accessing national systems, came into conflict with these individual 'market' rights. However, rather than simply allowing the unrestrained assertion of market rights, patient choice and autonomy, the CJEU began to set (and progressively specify) a series of criteria, rules and causes for lawful market restrictions in this specific area.[9] After almost ten years of litigation on the matter, the EU legislative institutions stepped in. They began drafting a Directive which would harmonise the very different national legislation concerning the possibility to obtain a medical treatment in another Member State at the expense of the home healthcare institution,[10] and which would protect the solidaristic basis of European healthcare. Despite its name, the content of the Directive has little to do with patients' rights. Rather, it outlines the (many) circumstances in which MS may lawfully restrict cross-border healthcare. In so doing, the Directive expresses the 'rule' of autonomous free movement of patients receiving services across borders within the EU, while at the same time articulating in legislative form the (many) exceptions to that rule, exceptions which *de facto* operate to protect national health systems and their social solidarity basis. The Directive, therefore expresses a legal arrangement that cements the EU's 'social market economy'.

The fears surrounding cross-border healthcare, already underlined in the introduction to this chapter, highlight the tight bond between the EU's push towards a continuous implementation of market freedoms, on the one hand, and the general concern for social rights and for the maintenance of a wide understanding of social solidarity across Europe, among Member States (and, indirectly, even within 'mere' internal social policies), on the other hand. The integration of the 'market' and the 'social' in the healthcare field is also reflected in Article 9 TFEU, which obliges the EU to pursue the goal of promoting a high level of human health in all its policies and activities – including free movement of services within the internal market.

3 The fear of free movement: the nature of the predicted disaster

The logic of the EU's internal market law, as applied in the context of healthcare, potentially has significant implications for the EU's 'social market economy', and for matters which belong within national competence, such as public health ethics. As Newdick put it,

> EU Institutions have misconceived the relationship between the economics of free market individualism and the politics of social welfare in the EU. The consequence of this misconception is especially serious with respect to cross-border access to health care because of the risk of damaging public health ethics.[11]

The fears of a disaster for national health systems have two interrelated aspects: the fear of uncontrolled flows of patients, and the fear of progressive erosion of social solidarity-based healthcare systems. However, in fact, neither fear has materialised, for the reasons explained below.

3.1 *The fear of an uncontrolled flow of patients and its critique*

As to the first fear of an uncontrolled flow of patients as a consequence of cross-border healthcare, a socio-economic approach suggests that the possible impact of this risky phenomenon is significantly less than initial legal assessments feared. In fact, the decision to travel abroad for healthcare, for a sick person, is generally an *extrema ratio* option. In other words, patients are likely to go abroad for medical treatments only if this is the last choice they have to be properly treated in a timely manner. In most cases, ill individuals would prefer to be treated at home for a number of reasons. Firstly, the linguistic gap: healthcare services do not automatically provide for interpretation services.[12] Secondly, the potential difficulties that an ill person may incur when travelling: patients might need care or assistance and their next of kin, relatives or caregivers might not be able to travel with them. Third, under the Treaty rules, as consolidated by the Patients' Rights Directive, patients travelling abroad would also have to pay in advance for the required medical treatment. This implies that only patients who have the necessary available resources (for instance, through savings or borrowing) to pay in advance for the healthcare service they will receive can *de facto* move. Taking these socio-economic factors into account, cross-border healthcare takes place in much narrower situations than one might expect. Firstly, cross-border healthcare is appropriate for highly specialised healthcare. In this regard, it is no coincidence that the Directive includes a provision expressly dedicated to this specific issue, and that a similar provision had already been incorporated within the older Regulation. Within the parameters laid down by the latter Regulation, some bilateral or specific agreements on highly specialised medical treatments both between Member States and between Member States and third countries had been set up. These 'European Reference Networks' for rare diseases have been supported for decades by EU funding.[13] In addition, cross-border healthcare has an added value in cross-border areas, such as across the Alps at the Italo-French border, the border between the Republic of Ireland and Northern Ireland, the Austrian-Italian border, or around the Pyrenean watershed. In these areas, neighbouring countries could set specific agreements on cross-border healthcare. Moreover, some successful experiments have been already implemented: a well-known example is represented by the cross-border hospital in Cerdanya, in the Pyrenees (for French and Spanish patients).[14]

3.2 *The fear of a progressive erosion of social solidarity systems and its critique*

As for the second, related, fear of a progressive erosion of national social solidarity systems, some legal scholars attempted to demonstrate that this fear was unfounded by focusing on the EU's competences in the field of healthcare.[15] The competence that EU legislative institutions indirectly have in the field of healthcare (narrowly speaking, as opposed to public health, where EU competence is more significant) is based on the EU's internal market competence, which is shared with the Member States. Article 168(7) TFEU explicitly provides that Member States are responsible for the delivery of healthcare. However this provision only allows the EU to set a series of procedural rights for individuals wishing to access healthcare in a Member State different from the one in which they are socially insured (or covered by taxation) at the expense of that national healthcare system. These procedural rights – as we will see *infra* – limit the power of Member States to restrict the freedom to provide services under the Treaty provisions, and are instrumental to the creation of the internal market in services. The legal basis for such EU intervention is Article 114 TFEU.

To go beyond a merely procedural rights-based approach, and protect and promote substantive rights, is to act outside the EU's competences. As Newdick put it:

> This means that any future EU regime should acknowledge the choices endemic to this area and generate transparent, procedural rights. This is the fairest way of balancing the interests of all patients. To adopt the contrary proposals of the European Parliament, by promoting market-individualism and letting the devil take the hindmost, will disrupt and divide the community and present an impoverished view of citizenship and the common good.[16]

Newdick also pointed out that the CJEU must consider the competence provisions, when exercising its interpretative jurisdiction:

> [I]nvestment in health care has to be the product of well-formulated public policy committed to promoting public interests. If health authorities are obliged to divert finite resources to some individuals without regard to the impact on others, public policy will be undermined. The CJEU must address the arguments for promoting citizenship and social welfare in the EU by confronting candidly who wins and who loses when judges direct how scarce resources should be allocated.[17]

4 The Patients' Rights Directive as a legislative expression of the social market economy

After the *Watts* decision, the EU legislature was caught in a situation that appeared impossible to resolve. Legislation was clearly necessary to secure certainty in the light of the CJEU's rulings. But what should the focus of that legislation be? EU legislation on free movement of medical services in the internal market (the 'market' in the social market economy) would present a risk to the stability of national healthcare services and social security systems and would undermine social solidarity and the sustainability of the social right to healthcare. But EU legislation focused on the social aspects of healthcare services (the 'social' in the 'social market economy') would have presented an equally disruptive laying of the foundations of a 'European Union-wide market for healthcare services'. If the EU had done so, the effects on the social, economic, medical and fiscal aspects of domestic healthcare provision would have been 'complex and politically difficult', with consequent effects on broader European integration.[18]

4.1 A balanced approach

The approach adopted by the EU legislature was to choose neither of these unappealing options. Rather, the Patients' Rights Directive (not a 'Directive on Free Movement of Medical Services') has a dual legal basis (i.e. Article 168 and Article 114 TFEU). This dual basis highlights the twofold nature of the Directive and – more widely – is representative of the EU law's approach to the right to healthcare – and, we argue, emblematic of its approach to the 'social market economy', even though there is no explicit reference to that concept in the text of the Directive.

On the one hand, several Recitals clarify the main objective of the Directive which justifies the EU legislative institutions' intervention: ensuring the functioning of the internal market and the free movement of goods, persons and services.[19] The preservation of the internal market is a dominant rationale for the Directive, in line with the long-standing CJEU's interpretation of health treatments as 'services' under the Treaty provisions, which dates back to the 1980s,[20] and this undoubtedly affects the overall approach of the EU.

But on the other hand, the preamble of the Directive expressly states that the EU seeks to pursue a 'high level of human health protection'.[21] Furthermore, Recital 3 of the Directive states that

> The health systems in the Union are a central component of the Union's high levels of social protection, and contribute to social cohesion and social justice as well as to sustainable development. They are also part of the wider framework of services of general interest.

This focus on human health protection is also confirmed by several provisions of the Directive that recall the importance of patients' safety.[22] Moreover, it must be noted that much of the substantive content of the Directive actually concerns protecting the healthcare policy choices taken by each Member State.[23] In this regard, the Directive respects the legislative settlement reached in the older Regulations on social security, which preserve the unique social arrangements in each Member State, but secure coordination between them so that people can move within the internal market without suffering a reduction of their social security (including healthcare) protections.

The Directive and its relationship with the Regulations on social security are thus valuable indicators of how the EU resolves the enduring tension between the

EU commitment for the protection and promotion of health, and of social rights, welfare and social justice in the EU on the one hand, and the EU's traditional liberal approach to market policies, on the other.

4.2 *Confirmation that the 'disaster' was avoided*

Six years after the Directive was approved and four years after the deadline for its transposition into national legislation, it is evident that the predicted disaster for national social solidarity systems of the EU's Member States did not take place. As provided for in Article 20 of the Directive, the Commission shall periodically report on the operation of the Directive to the European Parliament and to the Council. In September 2015, the Commission presented its first report. It collected data on Member States' transpositions and on the most relevant provisions, such as the procedures for prior authorisation, the levels of patients' mobility, the practices for reimbursement and other related matters. A second report was published in October 2016.[24] To follow up on the transposition of the Directive, a questionnaire was distributed to the relevant Member States institutions. The Commission received a response from 23 countries, while some other countries had difficulties in collecting the requested data.[25]

The data collected concerns some of the most relevant provisions of the Directive and, in particular, the number of requests for information; the number of requests for health treatments subject to prior authorisation; the number of requests for reimbursement related to healthcare not subject to prior authorisation; and the amount of payments. The report illustrates that, as a rather 'young' instrument, there is still a long way to make reporting obligations an effective tool to verify and understand the complicated phenomenon of cross-border healthcare.

Nevertheless, the report shows that patients' flows affect only a very small number of European citizens.[26] If the main goal was to boost patient mobility and raise the exchange of healthcare services among Member States, data show that this goal was not achieved. Alternatively, if, as it seems more plausible, the main intended goal of the Directive was an attempt to limit patient autonomous ability to cross internal EU borders in order to receive healthcare as market actors, this has been fully achieved. The drafters of the Directive were cognisant of the 'fear' that arose after *Watts* of an uncontrolled flow of patients. By providing for a number of procedural rules, they aimed to rationalise the phenomenon, and to enable Member States to reassert control.

4.3 *The indirect consequences of the legal framework*

A first indirect result of the current legal framework (under the Directive, the Regulation and the residual Treaty rules) is a general harmonisation of a minimal level of national healthcare services' procedures. As a consequence of the setting of procedural rules for patients and for healthcare administrations, state authorities are now required to organise their healthcare services in an adequate way.

One of the reasons that makes cross-border healthcare eligible for reimbursement is the impossibility to get the treatment required within a

> time limit which is medically justifiable, based on an objective medical assessment of the patient's medical condition, the history and probable course of the patient's illness, the degree of the patient's pain and/or the nature of the patient's disability at the time when the request for authorisation was made or renewed.[27]

This obligation means that Member States healthcare services must intervene to properly organise waiting lists and to set appropriate criteria to prioritise patients' needs, as well as requiring an individual assessment of such needs. This kind of planning goes a long way to avoiding uncontrolled flows of patients. In other words, by referring to the concept of 'undue delay' as a legitimate reason for granting reimbursement to patients who travelled abroad for medical treatments, the EU indirectly forces national healthcare authorities to avoid 'unjustified' delays in treating patients. As Gareth Davies pointed out, 'if healthcare system offered operations within a time corresponding to patients' medical needs, *Watts* would have no effect'.[28]

Similarly, the concept of availability of a medical treatment within a justifiable time limit has been interpreted by the CJEU to include the provision of adequate medical supplies and infrastructures, as stated in the *Petru* decision in 2014.[29] The reference to waiting lists also applies to the list of medical treatments granted by healthcare systems. However, these lists should be reasonably updated to current technological development, as specified by the CJEU in the *Elchinov* decision in 2010.[30] Put differently, if a healthcare system works well, there is no need for a patient to travel.

Of course, the Patients' Rights Directive represents only one example of the ways in which EU law embeds both the 'market' and the 'social' dimensions of the EU's 'social market economy'. The most recurrent criticism of cross-border litigation concerned the progressive extension of individual autonomous patients' rights to obtain medical treatment abroad at the expense of national healthcare systems, disrupting social settlements embodied in European healthcare systems. The legal argument to support this thesis was based in the CJEU's approach to free movement of services and to the increasing phenomenon of patients' consumerism.[31] However, as discussed earlier, this is too simplistic a legal argument. Healthcare does not involve consumer-based dimensions only. Rather, it is twofold, presenting also the features of a social right which requires States' active role in making it fully accessible to patients. EU law recognises this binary characteristic of healthcare. The 'predicted disaster' was therefore *already* prevented by the ways that health and healthcare are embodied within EU health law. The Treaty provisions on the internal market envisage legitimate restrictions that Member States may introduce on the exercise of the Treaty freedoms. The EU is obliged to consider health in all its policies. The EU's legal system recognises the objective of promoting fair and accessible healthcare, as a 'right to healthcare'.[32]

Nevertheless, we are currently facing another type of socio-economic catastrophe which is profoundly affecting healthcare systems in the EU. The following section will focus on this 'real disaster' for healthcare systems in some EU Member States, and consider the extent to which the concept of 'social market economy' could alleviate this disaster.

5 The real catastrophe for MS healthcare systems: EU austerity measures

The Patients' Rights Directive is an example of the EU's approach to the granting of social rights, and the ways in which EU law balances such rights, either in opposition to or in cooperation with market imperatives or entitlements of autonomous market actors.

However, national health systems in the EU are currently facing a genuine potential (and in some cases actual) catastrophe. This stems from the global economic crisis, the related Eurozone crisis and the EU's economic governance instruments, in particular those which have led to the adoption of austerity measures. EU economic governance is based on controlling government deficits, through coordinating national macroeconomic and fiscal policies via the Stability and Growth Pact. The 'six pack' of EU legislation supporting these processes, which entered into force in December 2011,[33] is aimed at reducing state public deficits. The process of economic policy coordination takes place within the 'European Semester', which is an instrument of 'soft' or 'new' governance. The intergovernmental Treaty on Stability, Coordination and Governance in the Economic and Monetary Union (the so-called Fiscal Compact), adopted in January 2012,[34] obliges Member States to balance their national budgets. And for Eurozone countries which need financial assistance from the EU and the IMF, in the wake of the crisis, economic governance goes further. The conditionality of financial assistance is secured through 'Memorandums of Understanding', which operate outside of the formal instruments of EU law. All of these instruments involved important changes in political decisions around the EU.[35] One important question for the concept of the EU's 'social market economy' is therefore the extent to which it is embedded in these EU economic governance, and 'non-EU law', mechanisms.

The effects and impact of EU austerity measures on Member States' healthcare systems, the general health status of the population and on healthcare services have been, and continue to be, significant.[36] The politics of austerity has led to a 'rethinking' of all aspects of health policy.[37] Some economic studies also suggest that the correct way to deal with fiscal austerity is to intervene in organisation and procedures in order to increase efficiency. Efficiency could be regarded as a key component of the 'social market economy': the disciplines of the market secure efficient provision of social entitlements. On the other hand, however, health policy studies argue that it is not recommended to make arbitrary and short-term cuts to essential services. Eroding financial protection, equitable access to care on the basis of medical need, or quality standards within health systems all involve destabilising effects which increase costs in the longer term.[38] This insight suggests that 'social market economy' considerations would support *justified* efficiency provisions in healthcare systems, *but only those* which also factor in long-term effects on population health. Short-term or arbitrary austerity provisions cannot be part of a well-functioning 'social market economy'.

EU austerity measures have deeply influenced the level of Member States' ability to finance social rights in general and healthcare treatments in particular. For example, as a consequence of the urgency to put in place austerity-driven measures, some Member States decided to remove some health treatments from the benefit package provided through their national health system. This is the case for in-vitro fertilisation in the Netherlands.[39] Other Member States provided for an increase in already provided co-payment fees[40] or for new fees: in Italy, for example, the already existing fee for secondary care (diagnostic examinations or specialised medical care) was increased by ten Euros, whereas a new co-payment fee of 25 Euros was introduced for emergency room treatments (applicable only where the patient is assigned a low priority access code).[41] Some other Member States introduced new and more restrictive criteria for access to some healthcare treatments: as an effect of a general rationing procedure carried on in the NHS, for instance, some local health authorities around England lowered female age for IVF funding or restricted access to IVF up to less than three cycles.[42] Other countries restricted migrants' access to healthcare services: in Spain, by Royal Decree 16/2012 irregular immigrants were denied access to healthcare services (with the sole exception of emergency treatments, pregnancy and maternity assistance and access to medical treatments for minors). Before 2012, irregular immigrants in Spain had been granted the same level of health benefits as Spanish citizens.[43]

Several of these provisions were subject to legal challenges. In some cases they even ended up before constitutional courts. The constitutional legitimacy of the Spanish exclusion of irregular migrants from healthcare services was recently upheld by the Constitutional Tribunal,[44] which stated that it stands within the powers of the legislature to set criteria for access to healthcare services for foreigners in Spain, given that a constitutionally imposed minimum standard is respected. Similarly, the Italian Constitutional Court upheld the legitimacy of the provision on the increase of co-payment fees, as it was considered to be an appropriate instrument to guarantee the balancing of the needs of the national healthcare service with equality of access to treatments for all.[45]

When considering the right to healthcare in the context of the EU 'social market economy', we cannot disregard the huge impact that the global and Eurozone crises have had on Member States' budgets and, therefore, on the granting of what have come to be seen as 'costly' rights (such as the right to healthcare) at a national level. So far, national courts have been unwilling to consider whether these policies are justified, taking into account not only their effects in terms of meeting economic governance imperatives in the short term (the European semester cycle is one year), but also their long-term effects on the population's health, particularly on vulnerable people, such as migrants or persons with disabilities. National courts have so far been unprepared to take into account the imperative of an EU 'social market economy' when determining the constitutionality of fiscal austerity measures. Likewise, the CJEU has declined to be involved,[46] even though it is at least arguable that the EU's 'social constitution' applies in interpretation and review of the relevant measures.[47]

Despite the lack of a EU competence in healthcare, measures adopted by the EU since the economic crisis are undoubtedly interfering with Member States' responsibility in organising and granting healthcare coverage and the efficient functioning of healthcare systems. These EU legal and governance interventions are significantly more important than EU internal market litigation or legislation like the Patients' Rights Directive. Social rights seem relatively invisible in the EU's fiscal governance framework. In that context, no counterbalancing measures have yet emerged in EU law that secure the 'social' of the 'social market economy'. Merely reasserting lack of EU competence is an inadequate response to this real disaster. EU austerity policies are no longer marginal in their effects on national healthcare. By contrast, they are deeply influencing state discretion.

Rather than substantive deficit rules, the granting of procedural rights (as the Directive attempts to do) would better secure the realisation of the EU 'social market economy'. Alternatives, such as rationing, organisational interventions, procedural rationalisations, and setting appropriate criteria to give priorities to healthcare treatments and requirements to access them, both secure the objective of reducing public expenditure and can at the same time maintain an adequate level of guarantee of healthcare rights. For instance, Member States could be required to account for whether they need to maintain national capacity in certain rare disease treatment, or containment of contagious diseases, or whether EU level collaborative activities would be a more effective deployment of scarce resources. As discussed previously, the Patients' Right Directive steers Member States towards these kinds of activities securing greater efficiency through economies of scale. For instance, it proposes a framework for cooperation and coordination among Member States to guarantee mutual acknowledgement of medical and pharmaceutical prescriptions among Member States; a European network for health technology assessment; and more broadly, it seeks to secure mutual assistance and cooperation among Member States in healthcare.[48] This approach would allow scrutiny – including through judicial review by the courts – of Member States' decisions over healthcare, adopted as a result of fiscal austerity measures. Rather than accepting reductions to healthcare benefits as an inevitable consequence of the conditionality imposed under the European Stability Mechanism, or other economic governance measures, an alternative approach could have been adopted. Such an alternative would better express the EU's 'social market economy' in the context of the real disaster for national healthcare systems that emerges from the threat of unbridled EU market law.

6 Conclusion

The European Commission's *White Paper on the Future of Europe*[49] reminds us that the EU's economy has been profoundly transformed by the global financial and economic crisis. The new dynamics of globalisation also present challenges (as well as opportunities) for the EU.[50] Although the EU's economy may be slowly recovering, these effects are not felt equally among all members of society.[51] If the most vulnerable are not to be left behind from the benefits of the European integration project, EU action is necessary to secure their inclusion. The TEU's 'social market economy' is the legal and constitutional embodiment of this necessity.

The European Commission has carried out a public consultation (March–December 2016) on a 'European Pillar of Social Rights'. The consultation confirms that the 'market' and the 'social' challenges facing the EU are inextricably intertwined. Under President Juncker, the European Commission seeks to 'build a more inclusive and fairer European Union'.[52] All elements of EU law and governance should be deployed to this end: the social *acquis*, the internal market *acquis*, EU level social dialogue between the social partners, economic policy coordination, measures concerning sustainability of the Eurozone, and EU structural funding. A future EU modelled on limiting the social dimension of the EU's economy to free movement (one of the five models under consideration in the Commission's White Paper on the Future of Europe) would secure the cross-border mobility aspects of the *acquis*, but would involve a significant reduction in its social aspects. In healthcare policy, for instance, the cooperation aspects of EU involvement, such as those outlined previously, would cease. On the other hand, a future EU modelled on greater EU action in the social field could move towards greater health system efficiencies, such as common pricing of medicines and vaccines, or joint healthcare workforce planning and training. But this model would *de facto* leave some Member States behind, with the consequences that the EU law derived rights of some EU citizens would be greater than those of others.

The 'European Pillar of Social Rights' includes among its key principles equality of opportunities and instruments for a basic social protection. Healthcare is considered in this context, by recalling that everyone should have access to affordable healthcare of good quality, as already established by Article 35 of the EU Charter of Fundamental Rights. The driving force behind the 'European Pillar of Social Rights' is the general objective 'to protect the dignity and autonomy of individuals as well as social justice'.[53] The economic crisis demonstrated that dignity and autonomy are in danger if states lack resources to grant a minimum level of benefits concerning social rights in general, and the right to healthcare in particular. Dignity is the foundational principle of the EU Charter of Fundamental Rights; moreover the rights proclaimed in the Charter are often framed as specification of the central role of human dignity in all EU commitments. The concept of dignity is also related to the idea of 'social market economy' enshrined in Article 3 TFEU, whereby the latter is intended as instrumental to fight against 'social exclusion and discrimination', and to 'promote social justice and protection'. This aspect of the place of health in the EU's social constitution has also been recognised by the CJEU, or at least its Advocate General, who has confirmed that the fundamental asset of citizens' right to healthcare 'cannot be considered solely in terms of social expenditure and latent economic difficulties'.[54]

To gain traction, the European Commission's proposals now need political leadership among the governments of the Member States. The election of Macron in France and the UK leaving the EU may well provide the impetus for a more socially focused phase of European integration: it is too soon to tell. What is clear – and what we have exemplified in this chapter – is that the formal competence constraints in the EU's constitutional settlement are insufficient to protect European healthcare systems, and the people whose dignity they protect, from indirect and negative effects of certain economic EU and EU-led laws and policies. While the cross-border mobility of patients turned out not to involve the 'disaster' predicted, the EU's economic governance measures constitute a serious threat to the sustainability of healthcare systems in some EU Member States. A fair and equitable society cannot be secured within an EU whose constitution fails to resolve the enduring tension between market and social rights.

As argued above, the example of the Patients' Rights Directive and the litigation based on Article 56 TFEU suggest that one way to secure the EU's 'social market economy' in such an area of tension is to provide procedural, rather than substantive rights. These types of rights provide a national level mechanism for scrutiny of national policies and approaches, but one that is mandated, and secured, by EU law. Whether such an approach could be effectively deployed in the context of Eurozone or fiscal governance remains to be seen, but it at least holds some potential. Procedural review might help to secure minimum standards for basic social rights, such as the right to healthcare.[55] Furthermore, this approach could contribute to the realisation of the general objectives of the EU, to secure a high level of human health protection.

Notes

* The chapter is the product of joint reflections by the two authors. However, sections 1, 2, 3 and 4 could be attributed to Lucia Busatta and sections 5 and 6 to Tamara Hervey.

1 Case C-372/04, *Watts*, EU:C:2006:325.

2 One of the strongest voices in this regard, Christopher Newdick, 'Citizenship, Free Movement and Health Care: Cementing Individual Rights by Corroding Social Solidarity' (2006) 43 *Common Market Law Review* 1645, at 1663 argues that 'health authorities and insurance funds will have less discretion than has been imagined to restrict the numbers of those seeking treatment abroad. As a result, it will be more difficult to contain the numbers of those entitled to obtain treatment elsewhere in the EU with the consequent draining effect on finite health budgets at home'.

3 Vassilis Hatzopoulos, 'Killing National Health and Insurance Systems But Healing Patients? The European Market for Health Care Services after the Judgments of the ECJ in Vanbraekel and Peerbooms' (2002) *Common Market Law Review* 683.

4 Jean McHale, 'Law, Patient's Rights and NHS Resource Allocation: Is Eurostar the Answer?' (2006) *Health Care Analysis* 169, at 182; Jean McHale, 'Framing a Right to Treatment in English Law? Watts in Retrospective' (2007) *Maastricht Journal of European and Comparative Law* 263, at 279.

5 Uncontrolled and unplanned patient movement, based on enforceable legal rights to reimbursement, would result in sub-optimal resource allocation, as only those

patients wealthy enough to pay in advance and healthy enough to travel could avail themselves of the ability to move.

6 Directive 2011/24/EU of 9 March 2011 on the application of patients' rights in cross-border healthcare [2011] OJ L88/45.

7 Originally Council Regulation (EEC) 1408/71 of 14 June 1971 on the application of social security schemes to employed persons and their families moving within the Community [1971] OJ L149/2. The 1971 Regulation has now been replaced by the European Parliament and Council Regulation (EC) 883/2004 of 29 April 2004 on the coordination of social security systems, [2004] OJ L166/1.

8 Dorte Sindbjerg Martinsen and Juan Mayoral, 'A Judicialisation of Healthcare Policies in Denmark and Spain? The Universalist Healthcare Model Meets the European Union' (2017) *Comparative European Politics* 414; Dorte Sindbjerg Martinsen, 'Conflict and Conflict Management in the Cross-Border Provision of Healthcare Services' (2009) *West European Politics* 792; Dorte Sindbjerg Martinsen, 'Social Security Regulation in the EU: The De-Territorialisation of Welfare?' in Grainne de Burca (ed.), *EU Law and the Welfare State: In Search of Solidarity* (OUP, 2005) 89. While cross-border healthcare has always existed, it has been the preserve of the very few wealthy enough to rely on entirely private healthcare. The novelty of EU law is the use of cross-border healthcare at the expense of social insurance systems or national health systems based on taxation.

9 These were progressively established in the quite intense CJEU litigation on cross-border healthcare, which constitutes about twenty decisions which influenced both EU law and national legal frameworks. Case C-158/96, *Kohll*, EU:C:1998:171; Case C-120/95, *Decker*, EU:C:1998:167; Case C-368/98, *Vanbraekel*, EU:C:2001:400; Case C-157/99, *Smits* e *Peerbooms*, EU:C:2001:404; Case C-385/99, *Müller-Fauré* e *van Riet*, EU:C:2003:270; Case C-56/01, *Inizan*, EU:C:2003:578; Case C-8/02, *Leichtle*, EU:C:2004:161; Case C-145/03, *Keller*, EU:C:2005:211; Case C-193/03, *Bosch*, EU:C:2004:630; *Watts* (n 1); Case C-444/05, *Stamatelaki*, EU:C:2007:231; Case C-466/04, *Herrera*, EU:C:2006:405; Case C-208/07, *von Chamier-Glisczinski*, EU:C:2009:455; Case C-211/08, *Commission v Spain (Major Medical Equipment)*, EU:C:2010:340; Case C-336/08, *Reinke*, EU:C:2010:604; Case C-173/09, *Elchinov*, EU:C:2010:581; Case C-255/09, *Commission v Portugal (Non-Hospital Medical Care)*, EU:C:2011:695; Case C-490/09, *Commission v Luxembourg (Medical Laboratory Tests)*, EU:C:2011:34; Case C-562/10, *Commission v Germany (Care Equipment)*, EU:C:2012:442; Case C-430/12, *Luca*, EU:C:2013:467; Case C-268/13, *Petru*, EU:C:2014:2271; Joined Cases E-11/07 and E-01/08, *Rindal*, [2008] EFTA Ct. Rep. 320.

10 On the framing of the Directive, Stephane De La Rosa, 'The Directive on Cross-Border Healthcare or the Art of Codifying Complex Case Law' (2012) *Common Market Law Review* 15. On the process of adopting the Directive, Dorte Sindbjerg Martinsen, 'Governing EU Health Law and Policy: On Governance and Legislative Politics' in Tamara Hervey, Calum Young and Louise Bishop (eds.), *Research Handbook on EU Health Law and Policy* (Edward Elgar, 2017) 36, at 45–55.

11 Christopher Newdick, 'Disrupting the Community: Saving Public Health Ethics from the EU Internal Market' in Johan Willem van de Gronden *et al.* (eds.), *Health Care and EU Law* (Asser Press, 2011) 211.

12 Gabriella Berki, 'Lightning or Lightning Bug: The Role of the Language Gap and the Access to Proper Information on Entitlements in Cross-Border Patient Mobility' (2017) *European Journal of Health Law* 1.

13 European Commission, 'European Networks of Reference for Rare Diseases' at <http://ec.europa.eu/health/rare_diseases/european_reference_networks/

erf_en>. For discussion, Teresinha Evangelista *et al.*, 'The Context for the Thematic Grouping of Rare Diseases to Facilitate the Establishment of European Reference Networks' (2016) *Orphanet Journal of Rare Diseases* 17.

14 European Commission, 'A Cross-Border Hospital in Cerdanya Improves Healthcare for French and Spanish Citizens' (2014) at <http://ec.europa.eu/regional_policy/en/projects/france/a-cross-border-hospital-in-cerdanya-improves-healthcare-for-french-and-spanish-citizens>.

15 As it is well-known, despite the general understanding of health as a general objective for all EU policies and actions, the European Union does not have any competence in organising healthcare and the Treaties leave to the member states' responsibility the granting of healthcare to their residents.

16 Newdick, 'Disrupting the Community' (n 6), at 236.

17 Newdick, 'Citizenship, Free Movement and Health Care' (n 3), at 1668.

18 Gareth Davies, 'The Effect of Mrs Watts' Trip to France on the National Health Service' (2007) *King's Law Journal* 158, at 167.

19 Recital 2 of the Directive 2011/24/EU: 'Article 114 TFEU is the appropriate legal basis since the majority of the provisions of this Directive aim to improve the functioning of the internal market and the free movement of goods, persons and services. Given that the conditions for recourse to Article 114 TFEU as a legal basis are fulfilled, Union legislation has to rely on this legal basis even when public health protection is a decisive factor in the choices made. In this respect, Article 114(3) TFEU explicitly requires that, in achieving harmonisation, a high level of protection of human health is to be guaranteed taking account in particular of any new development based on scientific facts'.

20 Joint cases C-286/82 and C-26/83, *Luisi and Carbone*, EU:C:1984:35.

21 Recital 1 of the Directive 2011/24/EU: 'According to Article 168(1) [TFEU], a high level of human health protection is to be ensured in the definition and implementation of all Union policies and activities. This implies that a high level of human health protection is to be ensured also when the Union adopts acts under other Treaty provisions'.

22 For example, Articles 4 and 8.

23 Articles 7(1), 8 and 9 of the Directive 2011/24/EU, which provide that the Directive applies only to the 'basket of care' available in the paying Member State; and which outline a list of circumstances in which Member States may control cross-border patient movement by requiring prior authorisation. This list is significantly longer than that developed by the CJEU.

24 European Commission, 'Member State Data on Cross-Border Healthcare: Year 2015' (2016) at <http://ec.europa.eu/health/cross_border_care/policy_en>.

25 As reported in the document, Austria, Finland, France, Iceland, Latvia, Lithuania and Portugal did not reply, at 4; some others provided some specific comments to the questionnaire, at 26.

26 European Commission, 'Member State Data on Cross-Border Healthcare' (n 24) point out that 'A majority of the Member States received less than 100 requests for prior authorisation during year 2015' and that on average the half of them was authorized. Most requests were aimed at seeking healthcare in bordering Member States.

27 Article 8(5) of Directive 2011/24/EU.

28 Davies, 'The Effect of Mrs Watts' Trip to France on the National Health Service' (n 19), at 166.

29 *Petru* (n 9).

30 *Elchinov* (n 9).

31 Tamara Hervey and Jean McHale, *European Union Health Law* (CUP, 2015) 74; William Andereck, 'From Patient to Consumer in the Medical Marketplace' (2007) *Cambridge Quarterly of Healthcare Ethics* 109.

32 Article 35 EU Charter of Fundamental Rights.
33 The Six Pack is composed of five regulations and one directive: European Parliament and Council Regulation (EU) 1175/2011 of 16 November 2011 amending Council Regulation (EC) 1466/97 on the strengthening of the surveillance of budgetary positions and the surveillance and coordination of economic policies [2011] OJ L306/12; Council Regulation (EU) 1177/2011 of 8 November 2011 amending Regulation (EC) No 1467/97 on speeding up and clarifying the implementation of the excessive deficit procedure, [2011] OJ L306/33; European Parliament and Council Regulation (EU) 1173/2011 of 16 November 2011 on the effective enforcement of budgetary surveillance in the euro area, [2011] OJ L306/1; Council Directive 2011/85/EU of 8 November 2011 on requirements for budgetary frameworks of the Member States, [2011] OJ L306/41; European Parliament and Council Regulation (EU) 1176/2011 of 16 November 2011 on the prevention and correction of macroeconomic imbalances, [2011] OJ L306/25; European Parliament and Council Regulation (EU) 1174/2011 of 16 November 2011 on enforcement measures to correct excessive macroeconomic imbalances in the euro area, [2011] OJ L306/8.
34 The Treaty was signed by all EU member States, with the exception of the Czech Republic and the UK. Croatia did not sign it either, as it entered the EU in 2013.
35 Scott Greer and Holly Jarman, 'European Citizenship Rights and European Fiscal Politics after the Crisis' (2016) *Government and Opposition* 1, at 9.
36 Marina Karanikolos *et al.*, 'Financial Crisis, Austerity, and Health in Europe' (2013) 381 *The Lancet* 1323; Philipa Mladovsky *et al.*, 'Health Policy Responses to the Financial Crisis in Europe' (2012) *Policy Summary* 5. World Health Organisation on behalf of the European Observatory on Health Systems and Policies, Copenhagen, Denmark.
37 Helena Legido-Quigley and Scott Greer, 'Austerity, Health, and the Eurozone' (2016) *International Journal of Health Services* 203.
38 Mladovsky *et al.*, 'Health Policy Responses to the Financial Crisis in Europe' (n 36), at V.
39 Ibid., at 17.
40 A co-payment fee is a contribution made by a patient (unless exempted) for her/his healthcare, for instance a payment for medicines. Co-payments may be made to the public healthcare service or to the insurance company at the point of delivery of a specific healthcare treatment. In public healthcare services the introduction of these fees has been quite disputed because it seems to be in contrast with the general principle of universality that drives these services, given that the individual is supposed to participate to the financing of public healthcare by paying taxes.
41 These fees were already provided by the 2007 Annual Budgetary Law, but they were never applied as they were immediately suspended by law. A further legislative intervention introduced these fees again (Law decree No 98/2011) and since then they were never reduced nor modified.
42 This resulted in a real postcode lottery in the local application of NICE guideline on IVF. Emily Cornish, 'IVF Funding: A Postcode Lottery?' (2015) at <www.omsg-online.com/ivf-funding-a-postcode-lottery/>.
43 Legido-Quigley and Greer, 'Austerity, Health, and the Eurozone' (n 39), at 204; Amets Suess *et al.*, 'The Right of Access to Health Care for Undocumented Migrants: A Revision of Comparative Analysis in the European Context' (2014) 24 *European Journal of Public Health* 712; Pedro Gallo and Joan Gené-Badia, 'Cuts Drive Health System Reforms in Spain' (2013) 113 *Health Policy* 1; Joaquin Cayon-De Las Cuevas and Tamara Hervey, 'A Place in the Sun? Healthcare Rights of Retired UK Citizens in Spain Post Brexit' (2017) *Health Economics Policy and Law* 297.

44 Spanish Constitutional Tribunal, decision STC No 139/2016 of 21 July 2016.
45 Italian Constitutional Court, decision No 187/2012, which also recalled its previous decision No 203/2008.
46 Paivi Leino Sandberg, 'An Overview of the Legal Aspects of Risk Sharing' (2016) *A Dynamic and Economic Monetary Union Working Paper* 37. Even though in Case C-370/12, *Pringle*, EU:C:2012:756, the CJEU held that the ESM Treaty was valid in EU law, it also pointed out that intergovernmental action by Member States must comply with their obligations in EU law, para 101. Logically, those obligations include obligations pertaining to the EU's 'social market economy'.
47 Claire Kilpatrick, 'Are Bailouts Immune to Social Challenge Because They Are Not EU Law?' (2014) *European Constitutional Law Review* 393.
48 Articles 10–15.
49 European Commission, 'White Paper on the Future of Europe: Reflections and Scenarios for the EU27 by 2025', COM(2017)2025 final.
50 European Commission, 'Reflection Paper on Harnessing Globalisation', COM(2017)240 final.
51 European Commission, 'Reflection Paper on the Social Dimension of Europe', COM(2017)206 final.
52 Communication from the European Commission, 'Establishing a European Pillar of Social Rights', COM(2017)250.
53 Claire Kilpatrick, Elise Muir and Sacha Garben, 'From Austerity Back to Legitimacy? The European Pillar of Social Rights: A Policy Brief' (2017) at <http://eulawanalysis.blogspot.it/2017/03/from-austerity-back-to-legitimacy.html?utm_source=feedburner&utm_medium=email&utm_campaign=Feed:+EuLawAnalysis+(EU+Law+Analysis)>.
54 *Stamatelaki* (n 9), para 40.
55 Greer and Jarman, 'European Citizenship Rights and European Fiscal Politics after the Crisis' (n 37), at 7.

12 Social considerations in EU consumer law

The legislator, the court and a rhapsody in blue

Vanessa Mak

1 Introduction

EU consumer law generally refers to rights which facilitate the economic participation of EU citizens in the internal market.[1] Social rights, which extend to other aspects of consumers' lives such as employment, social inclusion, and environmental protection, are perceived to fall outside the realm of European consumer law,[2] although they have received more attention in the wake of the economic crisis.[3] Does that mean that they are of a secondary nature,[4] and exist solely in the shadow of the EU's internal market goals? While the answer to that question might still in essence be 'yes', this chapter aims to show that the EU has progressively come to express a greater commitment to the social rights of consumers. This development has not been linear, and the outcomes of it are not settled. A careful examination of the instances in which social considerations have persuaded the legislator or, more recently, the Court of Justice of the EU (CJEU) to strengthen the position of consumers is the starting point for identifying where social rights reside in relation to economic rights within European consumer law. This analysis takes into account the political and economic thoughts that underlie legislative and court action in this area. The chapter therefore aims to unveil not only the position of social rights in the EU's internal market project, but also to discuss how those rights are embedded in the political and economic context of the market. Consistent with the approach taken within this volume,[5] this chapter is underpinned by the traditional dichotomy between social rights and economic rights, noting that these terms here are only used for analytical purposes and, in EU consumer law, do not bear intrinsic normative weight.[6] Social rights are thus defined as all rights with a non-economic objective, exemplified by rights that pursue the protection of weaker parties in society, such as workers and consumers.[7]

The structure of the chapter is as follows. Section 2 describes the emergence of consumer law as part of the EU 'social market economy'. In order to establish what position was attributed to social rights in the early days of European consumer law, this section will seek to analyse the legislative action taken by the European institutions, taking into account the internal market itself, and the ideological bases on which it operated. Section 3, will assess how social rights are currently being balanced with economic rights in EU consumer law: the Treaties, the EU Charter of Fundamental Rights, free movement(s) regulation and harmonized consumer law. Soft law is not of great relevance to social rights in consumer law and, therefore, will not be discussed in this chapter.[8] While social rights appear to have gained recognition in some of these legislative texts, it is submitted that the primary support for consumers' social position has instead come from the CJEU. Section 4 examines these 'glimmers of social justice' and evaluates what meaning they have in the broader fabric of European market regulation. Section 5 concludes by evaluating the position of the Court within the wider framework of lawmaking in EU consumer law, and puts the primary responsibility for the promotion of social rights in this field back with the EU legislature. This development, with alternating roles for the legislator and the Court and inspired by the wish to protect consumers from harm, can be compared to a rhapsody – a free instrumental composition in one extended movement, typically one that is emotional in character – and in keeping with the EU colour, a rhapsody in blue.[9]

2 Foundations of consumer law in the internal market

In order to understand what position social rights hold in European consumer law, it is helpful to first consider the economic and political context within which consumer law developed. This part provides a brief overview of that development. Two preliminary points require clarification, namely: what is encompassed by the term 'European consumer law', and who are its addressees.

2.1 Tracing the boundaries: European consumer law

Consumer law is not defined as such in the EU Treaties but the term is conventionally understood to include internal market regulation through the rules on free movement of goods and services aimed at removing legal barriers to trade (negative harmonization), and regulation through legislative harmonization in the form of directives and regulations that seek to lay down a uniform set of minimum rules for consumer protection (positive harmonization).[10] Positive harmonization of consumer law has primarily been given effect through secondary legislation in the field of private law, i.e. consumer contract law and (product) liability law.

The addressees of consumer law are, primarily, consumers and businesses.[11] Consumers are generally defined as natural persons not acting in the course of a trade, business or profession.[12] Businesses (or traders, or suppliers), in an almost mirror image, are natural or legal persons acting in the course of a trade, business or profession.[13] Consumer law, it should be noted, is concerned with final consumers. That is a significant difference with competition law, which often includes a much wider range of buyers affected by business behaviour, whether they are indirect or direct users, small or large, natural or legal persons (including businesses), intermediate buyers or final consumers.[14]

2.2 *Four ages of European consumer law*

The substance of European consumer law often acknowledges the social rights of consumers; however, social rights tend to be considered secondary to economic rights. The underlying rationale for that distinction can be found within the economic and political foundations of consumer law in the internal market. Looking at the development of the EU internal market, four 'ages of consumer law' may be identified. While the first three – the founding of the internal market, its completion on the basis of the Single European Act of 1985 and its submergence into a broader, political order after the founding of the EU – can be relatively well-defined, the fourth – post-crisis and post-*Aziz* –[15] is harder to assess. How meaningful are the examples of 'social justice' in European consumer law in the European market? The prevailing view,[16] substantiated in the following analysis, suggests that the primary ideology underlying the market is still a liberal one, even if the market has been driven by variations of liberalism over time.

Firstly, the foundations of the internal market can be traced to the development of 'ordoliberalism' by legal and economic thinkers in Freiburg from the 1930s and in particular the late 1940s onwards. As further discussed by Heinemann earlier in this volume, ordoliberalism, also referred to as 'social liberalism', was conceived in post-war Germany as a model that can ensure that a free market reaches its theoretical potential in terms of production and growth by ensuring economic freedom for all market participants.[17] In this model, the role of the government is to ensure that there is free competition. The protection of individual liberty and equality therefore are values in themselves. That sets the model apart from neoclassical economics, in which the pursuit of economic efficiency is the primary goal.[18] From a viewpoint of political philosophy, the model must be distinguished from neoliberalism, since it does not in principle plead for a 'small' government. Instead it regards the government as an important guardian of economic freedom and holds that regulation of the market is needed to secure free competition between individuals. The government, for example through protection against cartels, must ensure that there are no legal obstacles to the functioning of the free market.[19]

Secondly, the idea of a free market that can sustain economic growth and – as the EC and EU Treaties expressly state as an aim – enhance the welfare of peoples across Europe appears to have worked well in the post-war era, when economic growth in the developed capitalist world experienced a 'Golden Age' in which wages and living standards more than doubled.[20] However, the boom of capitalist economies was due to a particular set of circumstances – including investment and an expansion of government spending to support post-war recovery and rebuilding – and came to an end when economic growth halted in the late 1970s. National governments across Europe turned towards neoliberal politics in response.[21] Privatization of public services and a move towards deregulation followed, both with an eye to managing the economy (and society) in the interest of private business. In this time when individual liberty pushed social policies to the side, the idea of a free market extending beyond national borders found fertile ground. The actions towards completion of the European internal market initiated by the Delors Commission in the 1980s lent support to the establishment of economic freedom for all – but primarily for businesses – across the European Member States. The ordoliberal model of EC law at that time coincided with national neoliberal politics, albeit that the EC model aimed to reach its goals through a wave of regulation, rather than through deregulation.[22] Part of this regulation related to consumer law. The first Directive in this field was the Product Liability Directive of 1985.[23] It was followed by some twenty other directives and regulations concerning consumer rights in contract and tort, all adopted on the basis of the internal market competence of the European legislator. They include Directive 1993/13/EEC on unfair terms in consumer contracts, Directive 1999/44/EC on consumer sales, Directive 2005/29/EC on unfair commercial practices and Directive 2011/83/EU on consumer rights.[24] This body of legislation is considered to have made a substantial impact on consumer protection in Europe. The recent 'Fitness Check' of European consumer and marketing law confirms that the key directives introduced in the 1990s and 2000s, when effectively applied, tackle the most important problems encountered by consumers in the EU, also in online markets.[25] Those problems, in line with the focus on the internal market, are considered primarily of an economic nature.

In the meantime, however, the political constellation within which European consumer law developed went through another transformation. The central position of ordoliberal thought in Europe fit less well with the addition of European goals for cooperation that went beyond market integration. The Maastricht Treaty of 1992 by some is viewed as the end of the 'European economic constitution' that was solely focused on market integration through free competition. Maastricht 'demoted' the internal market to one part of a larger, political cooperation. In the same movement, ordoliberal thought became part of the opposition, rather than a supporting ideology for internal market policies.[26] While that seems an accurate assessment for the post-1992 era,[27] it does not mean that the EU market has since then evolved towards a 'social model'.[28] The balance between liberal and social values in internal market regulation, as exemplified in private law, continues to be a matter of debate.[29] Until now, liberal motives appear to be stronger – e.g. reflected in the strong emphasis in contract law on party autonomy – and indications of a more socially oriented approach limited to specific rules or (lines of) case law, sometimes in the field of European consumer law.[30] Notably, even in the field of EU consumer law the objective of ensuring a 'high level of consumer protection' throughout the EU appears primarily a corollary of internal market policy.[31] Nonetheless, alternative readings of the socio-economic underpinnings of EU law are also emerging. Kaupa has, for example, posed that 'while neoliberalism continues to shape the Union's law and policies, the Treaty is yet not fully determined by it . . . the Treaty allows for different readings in the light of competing socio-economic paradigms'.[32] The question is whether the tide may be turning in some areas of European consumer law. The CJEU's judgement in the *Aziz* case of 14 March 2013 can be seen as a radical support of social rights, in this case the right to housing, brought about through an active, socially inspired interpretation of consumer contract law by the Court.[33] Some authors have suggested that there may be a 'hidden constitutionalization' in the Court's judgement,[34] meaning that the Court is giving effect to constitutional rights (of consumers) through contract law. That would mean that social rights, in particular those laid down in the Charter, which fall within the definition of constitutional rights,[35] are of direct influence on the, otherwise economic, rights laid down in European consumer law. Whether the *Aziz* judgement is indeed such a turning point remains to be seen.

3 European consumer law: the state of play

Having regards to the succinct overview conducted in Section 2, it does not seem surprising that social rights are secondary to economic rights in the EU's free movement regulation (negative harmonization) and mostly also in its harmonized consumer law (positive harmonization). Nevertheless, the CJEU's actively social interpretation of consumer contract law in *Aziz* suggests that there is a legal basis for the balancing of economic rights with social rights in European consumer law. In light of the secondary nature of social rights in free movement regulation and in harmonized contract law, however, a question arises: what legal basis is this, and where can it be found in EU law?

The answer to that question is not straightforward. The legal basis for a social rights-based approach in EU consumer law is seldom clarified in the case law of the CJEU and has received limited attention in the literature.[36] Nonetheless, a closer look at the EU Treaties reveals that the legal basis for a social rights-based approach in EU law can be identified which, it is submitted, comes from the values and objectives laid down in the EU Treaty – in particular the objectives of Article 3(3) TEU – and the Charter of Fundamental Rights. These will be discussed first, before reflecting on their relationship to free movement regulation and harmonized consumer law. The general line that will become apparent is that EU legislation gives expression to economic rights of consumers but, in line with its liberal underpinnings, does relatively little to pursue the social goals of Article 3(3) TEU. That role, as will be discussed in Section 4, is left to the Court of Justice.

3.1 Social considerations in the values and objectives of the EU

The basis for social rights in EU consumer law can be discerned in Article 3(3) TEU, although it does not refer to the field explicitly and does not even refer to the 'consumer' or 'consumer protection'. The provision refers to the establishment of the internal market as an aim of the Union. It goes on to set out a number of other objectives of EU law, some of which can encompass consumer protection goals. These include that the Union shall work for 'a highly competitive social market economy' and 'a high level of protection and improvement of the quality of the environment'. The Union shall also 'combat social exclusion and discrimination, and shall promote social justice and protection, equality between women and men, solidarity between generations and protection of the rights of the child'. While these objectives relate to broader societal goals, they provide the context within which the EU's consumer policy can further take shape. A more concrete specification of the Union's consumer policy objectives is laid down in the TFEU, in particular in Articles 12, 114(3) and 169(1).[37] Those provisions can be read as an elaboration of the values expressed in Articles 2 and 3 TEU, in particular the 'social market economy' mentioned in Article 3(3) TEU.[38] Article 169(1) TFEU is the most elaborate of these three. It provides that

> [i]n order to promote the interests of consumers and to ensure a high level of consumer protection, the Union shall contribute to protecting the health, safety and economic interests of consumers, as well as to promoting their right to information, education and to organize themselves in order to safeguard their interests.

Interestingly, the provision defines the interests of consumers as much broader than purely economic, referring to health and safety, as well as to a 'right to information' and to education. All of these could be regarded as non-economic, and therefore social, rights.[39] Other, specific bases for the protection of social rights are laid down in Articles 151 and 168(1) TFEU, which respectively concern employment and social protection, and health protection.

The practical usefulness of these Treaty provisions for consumers, however, is limited. Rather than providing a direct cause of action, as constitutional rights in certain national systems or fundamental rights in the European Convention for Human Rights (ECHR) do,[40] these provisions can in general not be invoked by individual citizens in litigation against other parties. Citizens only have standing before the CJEU in cases where they have been directly affected by an EU regulatory act that did not require implementing measures[41] or in cases where a question is referred to the Court for a preliminary ruling on the basis of Article 267 TFEU.

These Treaty provisions could however, at least in theory, give ground to other legal actions. They might form the basis for an allegation that an EU legislative measure is invalid, in case of consumer protection if the measure is thought to fail to meet the requirements stipulated in Article 169(1) TFEU with regard to a high level of protection.[42] The likelihood that the Court will find such a violation is however low. It would mean that the Court has to establish that there has been a manifest legislative neglect on the part of the EU legislature to take into consideration the protective quality of the harmonized rule or a manifest error of appraisal regarding the applicable conditions.[43] The Court will not soon be inclined to reach that conclusion. It would furthermore seem that the EU legislature can easily prevent (the impression of) that kind of neglect from arising by simply citing Article 169(1) TFEU in the impact assessment and in the Preamble to the adopted legislation.[44] As practical examples often illustrate, the EU legislature is prone to including generous references to the 'pursuit of a high level of consumer protection' in its proposals in the field of consumer law, and in the subsequent legislation. Impact assessments also, seeking to gather the political momentum needed for legislation to be adopted, tend to emphasize the proposed legislations importance for the pursuit of consumer protection.[45]

The relevance of Article 3(3) TEU, therefore, lies primarily in its expression of social rights as part of the EU's objectives. It can be read as ancillary to Article 2 TEU, which establishes the values on which the Union is built. These values are common to the Member States in a society in which pluralism, non-discrimination, tolerance, justice, solidarity and equality between women and men prevail. Together, Articles 2 and 3 TEU make clear that the Union, although it started out as a market building project, has in its primary legislation firmly adopted values and objectives that go beyond an economic cooperation. The question is then whether these provisions are more than a kind of mission statement for the Union. As subsequent sections will demonstrate, other EU legislative measures give rise to stronger legal effects.

3.2 The EU charter of fundamental rights

Although likely seen as tangential to consumer rights laid down in EU Directives and Regulations, the EU Charter of Fundamental Rights has proven to become increasingly influential in consumer cases. The *Aziz* case has already been mentioned as a potential harbinger for the 'constitutionalization' of European contract law,[46] even if that case did not actually cite the Charter directly. The case concerned the potential unfairness of terms included in the mortgage agreement between Mohamed Aziz, a Moroccan national who lived and worked in Spain, and Spanish bank Catalunyacaixa. After the financial crisis hit Spain, Aziz, like many other borrowers, was unable to repay the instalments of his mortgage loan. The bank ordered repayment of the debt and, after Aziz failed to pay, obtained a court order for a judicial auction and eviction of Aziz and his family from the residence. Shortly before the eviction, however, Aziz had instigated proceedings at the court of first instance in Barcelona with the aim of obtaining a declaration that certain terms in the mortgage contract were unfair. Importantly, the aim of these proceedings was also to establish that while the case on the potential unfairness of terms in the mortgage agreement was pending, the parallel proceedings for auction and eviction should be stalled. As Spanish legislation did not attach suspensory effect to such declaratory proceedings, the judge at first instance referred the case to the CJEU with the question whether that legislation constituted a limitation of consumer protection, since it involves a clear impediment to the consumer's exercise of rights of action or judicial remedies of such a kind as to guarantee the effective protection of his rights.[47] The CJEU gave an affirmative answer to this question, thereby making it possible to protect consumers from eviction procedures during the time that proceedings on unfair terms in mortgage contracts are pending. In response, the Spanish legislator has amended the relevant legislation.[48] Follow up case law has cited the Charter,[49] as have other cases in the field of consumer law, as it will be discussed later in this chapter.

The most obvious consumer law provision is Article 38, which states that 'Union policies shall ensure a high level of consumer protection'. The added value of this provision alongside Articles 114 and 169 TFEU however seems limited. It seems somewhat anachronistic to conceive of 'consumer protection' as a fundamental right in the classical sense, and therefore the general consensus appears to be that the provision does nothing more than consolidate the EU's commitment to consumer protection within the Treaties and as observed in internal market and free movement regulation.[50] Of greater relevance is Article 47 of the Charter.[51] This provision stipulates that '[e]veryone whose rights and freedoms guaranteed by the law of the Union are violated has the right to an effective remedy before a tribunal'. The CJEU has discovered this provision as a mechanism through which to give effect to consumer rights laid down in EU legislation, emphasizing the obligation that it places on the Member States to ensure that citizens have effective remedies that allow them to enforce rights derived from EU law in national courts. Article 47 can therefore be seen as the embodiment of the principle of effectiveness of EU law, which through its elevation to a 'fundamental right' has given the Court an impetus to appeal to it in consumer cases, in particular in those that are closely related to other, perhaps more classical fundamental rights.[52] The protection achieved through Article 47 in the Spanish mortgage cases, heralded by *Aziz*,[53] for example, have enhanced the protection of citizens against the loss of their family home, which is laid down in Article 7 of the Charter as: '[e]veryone has the right to respect for his or her . . . home'. In sum, the Charter, like the EU Treaties, contains rights that reflect that consumer protection encompasses more than solely the economic interests of consumers. It can provide a legal basis also for cases in which social rights, such as the right to housing, are at stake.

3.3 Free movement regulation and harmonized consumer law

Despite the firm footing that social rights appear to have in the Treaties and in the EU Charter of Fundamental Rights, they are less visible in more specific applications of EU consumer law. The two legs of EU law that concern the regulation of the consumer market, free movement regulation and harmonized consumer law, seem to focus primarily on economic rights. That is not surprising, as both are tied to the internal market goals of the Union. Their aim is, either through negative or through positive harmonization, to bring the laws of the EU Member States closer and thereby to eliminate barriers to trade. For consumers this means that the underlying aim of the regulatory approach of EU consumer law is to ensure that they can pass the threshold for taking part in, and benefitting from, the internal market. In the words of Micklitz, EU consumer law pursues 'access justice' (*Zugangsgerechtigkeit*).[54] Nonetheless, social rights or policies are recognized as factors that may potentially restrict market integration objectives. The balance for now, however, appears to lean towards economic rights and market integration.

In free movement regulation the internal market objective is clearly paramount. On the basis of free movement rules – laid down in Article 26 TFEU, with further provisions for goods laid down in Articles 28–37 TFEU and for services in Articles 56–62 TFEU[55] – regulations at Member State level that form a real or potential barrier to trade in the internal market can be set aside. There is some room for limiting the free movement, as can be seen in particular in relation to goods, but that space is narrowly demarcated. An exception exists for non-discriminatory prohibitions or restrictions on the free movement of goods that are equivalent to quantitative restrictions, if they can be justified

> on grounds of public morality, public policy or public security; the protection of health and life of humans, animals or plants; the protection of national treasures possessing artistic, historic or archaeological value; or the protection of industrial and commercial property.[56]

Justifications for such restrictions also stem from the case law of the CJEU, where an exception has been recognized for provisions that are 'necessary in order to satisfy the mandatory requirements relating in particular to the effectiveness of fiscal supervision, the protection of public health, the fairness of commercial transactions and the defence of the consumer'.[57] In practice, however, cases in which national measures are set aside appear to be more numerous than cases in which prohibitions or restrictions to the free movement of goods are deemed justified. An explanation for that trend may be that the CJEU by setting aside national legislation that restricts trade gives a boost to the integration of the internal market. Economic concerns therefore often trump social considerations.

In harmonized consumer law the balance between economic and social rights is largely similar, but not completely the same. The legal basis for harmonization in EU consumer law, the aim of which is to approximate the laws of the Member States in specific areas of consumer (private) law, has in practice always been Article 114(3) TFEU. That means that the harmonization of consumer law is tied to the goal of integration of the internal market. The content of harmonizing legislation largely reflects this underlying market ideology. Directives in the field of consumer contract law are often aimed at empowerment of consumers through information rights. Examples are Directive 2011/83/EU on consumer rights, Directive 90/314/EEC on package travel, Directive 2008/48/EC on consumer credit, Directive 2014/17/EU on consumer mortgage credit,[58] as well as Directive 93/13/EEC on unfair terms and Directive 2005/29/EC on unfair commercial practices that seek to ensure that consumers receive information that is clear, intelligible, fair and not misleading.[59] The idea that information on the characteristics of products and services can empower consumers by helping them make sound purchase decisions is connected to neoclassical economic theory, in which consumers are perceived as rational actors. That paradigm is leading in EU consumer legislation.[60] Still, sometimes stronger consumer protection rights are included, for example, in the form of warnings, prohibitions or other measures that aim to support social policies. The most prominent example is the restriction placed on the availability of credit with an eye to protecting consumers against over-indebtedness.[61] A little more remote is the potential effect of the remedies laid down in Directive 1999/44/EC on consumer sales:[62] by making repair a primary remedy for non-conformity, the Directive contributes to sustainability goals.[63] Express provision is therefore made for consumer protection rights in specific instances. Nevertheless, the overall picture that emerges in relation to harmonized consumer law is that, at least on paper, it is concerned with economic rights more than with social rights. The survey of the EU Treaties, the Charter of Fundamental Rights, and secondary legislation in EU consumer law made in this section thus confirms two things. Firstly, it has revealed that there is a legal basis for social policies in EU consumer law. That legal basis follows from Article 3(3) of the EU Treaty, in combination with the consumer law provisions laid down in Articles 12, 114(3) and 169(1) TFEU. The Treaties however, because they can only in limited circumstances be directly invoked by consumers, are not the main source for social rights in EU consumer law. More direct causes of action can be based on the Charter, in particular on Article 47, and on social rights laid down in consumer law Directives. The second conclusion, nonetheless, is that social rights take up a secondary position in relation to economic rights in the legislation. To see how these rights have in recent years gained importance, we need to turn to the case law of the European Court of Justice.

4 The CJEU and social justice

The *Aziz* case of 2013 could represent a turning point for the protection of social rights through EU consumer law.[64] Whether the case is indeed the first step in that direction is of course something that we cannot oversee at this time. The case law of the Court in consumer law does, however, carry the seeds of an approach that promises more in terms of the pursuit of social rights and policies in the future. Two elements are important, one substantive, the other relating to the position of the Court in the institutional framework of the Union. Firstly, on the substantive point, the Court appears sometimes to promote social justice over economic goals in consumer contract law cases. Secondly, the position of the Court in relation to national courts and legislators enables 'strategic litigation' by consumers or others who seek to pursue social goals. It should be noted that the term 'social justice' in relation to the CJEU's case law is used in a specific context, and is narrower than that of 'social rights' more generally discussed in this chapter.[65] It has, in EU consumer law, primarily emerged in relation to consumer contract law, which deals with the rules applicable to business-to-consumer transactions. Generally speaking, social justice is concerned with redistributive effects that may be achieved through private law, or more specifically contract law. Social justice objectives can frame the autonomy of contracting parties beyond economic interest.[66] Autonomy might for example be restricted on grounds of equality or non-discrimination, or in the rare circumstance of 'social *force majeure*'.[67]

The CJEU's judgement in the *Aziz* case and related follow up judgements can be regarded as instances in which the Court has let social justice concerns intervene with the autonomy of the contracting parties.[68] In *Aziz* the Court held that a Spanish procedural rule allowing eviction on the grounds of non-payment of mortgage instalments should be set aside in cases where a consumer had instigated proceedings against the mortgage lender to challenge unfair terms in the mortgage agreement.[69] *Sánchez Morcillo* confirmed that ruling, with explicit reference to Art. 47 of the Charter, and established that the Spanish legislator needed to do yet more work to ensure that its procedural law offered effective judicial remedies for consumers to enforce their rights derived from Directive 1993/13/EEC on unfair terms.[70] In a round-about way, therefore, the Court lent support to the right to housing which, although not referred to in the judgement, is laid down in Article 7 of the EU Charter of Fundamental Rights. Article 7 enshrines the right to respect of private and family life, including respect of one's home.[71] The case therefore goes beyond what might have been expected on the basis of Directive 93/13/EEC on unfair terms.

One explanation for the prominent position of the CJEU in the social justice debate may be that the institutional framework in which the Court operates enables 'strategic litigation'. The Court's role has been attributed to the possibilities that EU law provides to consumers who have run out of options for protection in their own legal systems, either because of a lack of protective rights or – in practice more important – the inability to enforce them. Micklitz posits that the absorption of consumer law into mainstream private law has led to an expulsion of protection from consumer law, a process reinforced by EU law's choice for an average consumer who is rational, autonomous and self-confident.[72] However, there is room within the system of EU law to find other ways of achieving just outcomes, namely by using the reference procedure of the CJEU. That route could lead to outcomes that are unavailable in national law but, if the Court is willing to take a proactive stance, can be introduced through a conceptualization of social justice values in European contract law. In the words of Micklitz:

> [f]rom a theoretical point of view, the European-inspired "consumer law without protection" provides an open goal-mouth for the conceptual design of a modern European contract law, of which the civil law scholars in Germany and throughout Europe are taking advantage.[73]

The premises for an active or perhaps even activist role of the CJEU in relation to social rights in EU consumer law therefore are present. Of course, this rather bold idea of the role of the CJEU raises the question *how* the Court should approach cases in which market values and social justice values influence the outcome of the case. The lack of methodological transparency in the Court's reasoning in private law cases has been amply documented, for example in relation to general principles, but also more specifically in relation to the 'constitutionalization' of European contract law.[74] The general gist of analyses of the CJEU's case law in the field suggests that there are examples of cases in which the Court explicitly pursues social justice goals through private law, but that it is hard to discern a consistent line or even a theoretical framework underlying the Court's approach. Rather than attributing an active role to the Court for bringing in social values into EU market regulation,[75] the status quo seems to point to a more hesitant take on that role. It might well be that the Court, through limitations to the rights existing in EU law that it gets to rule on, is simply not in a position to set out a consistent social justice response in European market regulation.[76] Instead, the cases can probably only be considered 'glimmers' of social justice in a market otherwise informed by liberal values.[77]

5 Conclusion

The discussion conducted in this chapter leads to the conclusion that EU consumer law is still mainly concerned with the economic rights of EU citizens, although it contains openings for the pursuit of social rights and policies. The foregoing has shown that there is a legal basis, or that there are perhaps several, for balancing economic and social rights in EU consumer law. Articles 2 and 3(3) TEU include social rights firmly within the values and objectives of EU law. More specific consumer protection rules laid down in Articles 12, 114(3) and 169(1) TFEU confirm that social rights, in the sense of non-economic rights, are part and parcel of the EU's internal market project. At least symbolically, therefore, the Treaties lend support to social rights in consumer law. Nonetheless, for now the legislator has remained fairly inactive in promulgating social rights in this field. That might be explained by the difficulty of moderating legislative competences between the EU and its Member States, in particular in areas that go beyond market building.[78] As noted earlier in this book,[79] social policy is still primarily determined at Member State level. EU consumer legislation, such as harmonized rules of contract or tort law, therefore primarily deals with issues related to facilitating business-to-consumer transactions in the internal market. Information rights for consumers, aiming to 'empower' consumers as rational market actors, are more prominent in this legislation than other, more protective rules that support social goals, such as the protection of consumers against over-indebtedness through consumer credit law.

The CJEU, at the same time has stepped into the void left by the legislator and in recent case law has achieved the protection of social rights of consumers through contract law. That development, fuelled by a growing reliance on the EU Charter of Fundamental Rights, could provide a useful route for the integration of social considerations in EU consumer law. The Court, moreover, is of great practical significance for the protection of consumers' social rights, as it provides a judicial route for the protection of individual rights even in cases where consumers (or traders) cannot obtain that protection within their national legal system. The *Aziz* case is rightfully seen as an example of 'strategic litigation', where the possibility to submit a preliminary reference to the CJEU was used by the national court to obtain an outcome that national, Spanish legislation did not allow. The decision effectively led to the protection of consumers against eviction from their home during the time that proceedings on the potential unfairness of terms in their mortgage agreement were pending. The broader reach of this judgement lies in the question whether it signals a move towards the greater protection of social or constitutional rights through private law. The

CJEU may have paved the way for such a development in EU consumer law. At the same time, the Court is constrained in what it can achieve, since it only rules on a case-by-case basis and is dependent on the cases that come before it. While the CJEU can be an important recourse for individual rights protection, therefore, the baton will have to be returned to the EU legislator to promote the further development of social rights in European consumer law. The recent Fitness Check of the major consumer law Directives appears to be a missed opportunity in this regard, but perhaps future initiatives from the legislature will put social rights in a more prominent place. That would do justice to the values and objectives laid down in the EU Treaties.

Notes

1 The terms 'EU consumer law' and 'European consumer law' are used as synonyms. Both refer to the body of consumer law developed through EU legislation and the case law of the Court of Justice of the EU. National consumer laws are not included in the term and are not discussed in detail in this chapter, apart from one or two instances where some knowledge of the national context is necessary in order to understand a judgement of the Court.

2 This was a main criticism of a group of scholars involved in the harmonization debate in European private law; Study Group on Social Justice in European Private Law, 'Social Justice in European Contract Law: A Manifesto' (2004) *European Law Journal* 653.

3 Hans Micklitz and Irina Domurath, *Consumer Debt and Social Exclusion in the EU* (Ashgate, 2015).

4 Iris Benöhr, *EU Consumer Law and Human Rights* (OUP, 2013) 53.

5 Delia Ferri and Fulvio Cortese, 'Introduction', in this volume.

6 Kaupa rightly points out that these terms, similar to other dichotomies, are otherwise not neutral. Deeming one set of rights economic and another not implies a certain worldview that can have normative implications. Clemens Kaupa, *The Pluralist Character of the European Economic Constitution* (Hart, 2016) 11–12.

7 That definition is in line with Scharpf's, who speaks of rights and policies aimed at social protection and equality. Fritz Scharpf, 'The European Social Model: Coping with the Challenges of Diversity' (2002) *Journal of Common Market Studies* 645.

8 Soft law has had only a limited impact on social aspects of the consumer market, for example in projects concerning corporate social responsibility (CSR), where non-binding guidelines and codes of conduct have been developed (Andreas Heinemann, 'Social Considerations in EU Competition Law', in this volume, section 5.1).

9 That title is a reference to Gershwin's famous composition of that name.

10 Stephen Weatherill, *EU Consumer Law and Policy* (Edward Elgar, 2013) 8.

11 One might also consider consumer organizations as addressees, albeit that their role is secondary, as guardians of consumer interests from a collective perspective.

12 The definition in Article 2(1) of Directive 2011/83/EU on consumer rights, [2011] OJ L304/72 (Consumer Rights Directive), which is broadly reflective of other definitions used in European consumer legislation.

13 The trader definition in Article 2(2) of the Consumer Rights Directive (n 12).

14 Albertina Albors-Llorens and Alison Jones, 'The Images of the "Consumer" in EU Competition Law' in Dorota Leczykiewicz and Stephen Weatherill (eds.), *The Images of the Consumer in EU Law: Legislation, Free Movement and Competition Law* (Hart, 2016) 43, at 56.

15 Case C-415/11, *Aziz*, EU:C:2013:164.
16 Kaupa also acknowledges that the hegemonic narrative conceives of the EU as a legal order based on liberal ideology; Kaupa, *The Pluralist Character of the European Economic Constitution* (n 6), at 11.
17 The term 'ordoliberalism' was first coined by Möller (Horst Möller, 'Liberalismus' (1950) *Jahrbücher für Nationalökonomie* 24, at 224), who added 'ordo' in reference to the *ORDO* journal – a leading economic journal at that time, founded by Franz Böhm and Walter Eucken (David Gerber, 'Constitutionalising the Economy: German Neo-Liberalism, Competition Law and the "New" Europe' (1994) *American Journal of Comparative Law* 25, at 31–32); Heinemann, 'Social Considerations in EU Competition Law' (n 8), section 2.
18 Compare Pilar Akman, 'Searching for the Long-Lost Soul of Article 82 EC' (2009) *Oxford Journal of Legal Studies* 276, at 276–277; Georgio Monti, *EC Competition Law* (CUP, 2007) 24.
19 Ordoliberalists referred to this as *Ordnungspolitik* or 'indirect regulation', which means that the government does not direct the processes of the economy but merely establishes structural conditions within which those processes can function effectively. For a broader account, Gerber, 'Constitutionalising the Economy: German Neo-Liberalism, Competition Law and the "New" Europe' (n 7), at 47 and Monti, *EC Competition Law* (n 18), at 23–24.
20 Jim Stanford, *A Short Guide to the Economics of Capitalism* (Pluto Press, 2015) 46.
21 Ibid., at 47–48.
22 According to Majone, privatization in national systems did not imply an end to all regulation, but rather a changed role of the state: from producer of goods and services to an umpire whose function it is to ensure that economic actors play by the agreed rules of the game (Giandomenico Majone, 'The Rise of the Regulatory State in Europe' (1994) *West European Politics* 77, at 80).
23 Council Directive 85/374/EEC on the approximation of the laws, regulations and administrative provisions of the Member States concerning liability for defective products [1985] OJ L210/29.
24 Council Directive 93/13/EEC of 5 April 1993 on unfair terms in consumer contracts, [1993] OJ L95/29; Directive 1999/44/EC of the European Parliament and of the Council of 25 May 1999 on certain aspects of the sale of goods and associated guarantees, [1999] OJ L171/12; Directive 2005/29/EC of the European Parliament and of the Council of 11 May 2005 concerning unfair business-to-consumer commercial practices in the internal market, [2005] OJ L149/22; Directive 2011/83/EU of the European Parliament and of the Council of 25 October 2011 on consumer rights, [2011] OJ L304/64.
25 Directive 2011/83/EU on consumer rights was assessed separately. The results of the Fitness Check as well as the supporting studies, can be accessed online at <ec.europa.eu/newsroom/just/item-detail.cfm?item_id=59332>. For a discussion of the position of social rights in these directives, Section 3.3.
26 Christian Joerges, 'What Is Left of the European Economic Constitution?' (2005) *European Law Review* 461, at 474.
27 Some authors doubt the influence of ordoliberal thought on EU market integration altogether: Jacobien Rutgers, 'The DCFR and the EC-Treaty' in Martijn Hesselink, Chantal Mak and Jacobien Rutgers, 'Constitutional Aspects of European Private Law' (2009) *Centre for the Study of European Contract Law Working Paper Series* 62 at <http://ssrn.com/abstract=1413089>.
28 Although some social rhetoric is reflected in the Treaty (Article 2 EC Treaty as inserted by the Treaty of Amsterdam) and the promotion of social values continues to be pushed by those on the political left (Hugh Collins, *The European Civil Code: The Way Forward* (CUP, 2008) 96).

29 Martijn Hesselink, 'Five Political Ideas of European Contract Law' (2011) *European Review of Contract Law* 295; Martijn Hesselink, 'Democratic Contract Law' (2015) *European Review of Contract Law* 81. Instructive comparisons have also been made by US legal theorists, Aditi Bagchi, 'The Political Economy of Regulating Contract' (2014) *American Journal of Comparative Law* 687.

30 Whilst Hesselink, 'Five Political Ideas of European Contract Law' (n 29) proposes a pluralist view on the political foundations of European private law, that view seems normative rather than empirical in nature. It is commonly accepted that European private law, and the broader field of market integration, is governed by liberal thought, often at the expense of consumer protection and other social values; Simon Deakin, 'The Lisbon Treaty, the Viking and Laval Judgments and the Financial Crisis: In Search of New Foundations for Europe's "Social Market Economy"' in Niklas Bruun, Klaus Lörcher and Isabelle Schömann (eds.), *The Lisbon Treaty and Social Europe* (Hart, 2012) 19. For a critical analysis, Marija Bartl, 'Internal Market Rationality, Private Law and the Direction of the Union: Resuscitating the Market as the Object of the Political' (2015) *European Law Journal* 572, at 580–581.

31 Hannes Unberath and Angus Johnston, 'The Double-Headed Approach of the ECJ Concerning Consumer Protection' (2007) *Common Market Law Review* 1237, at 1242.

32 Kaupa, *The Pluralist Character of the European Economic Constitution* (n 6), at 6.

33 *Aziz* (n 15). For the facts of the case, see below at 15.

34 Hans Micklitz and Norbert Reich, 'The Court and Sleeping Beauty: The Revival of the Unfair Contract Terms Directive (UCTD)' (2014) *Common Market Law Review* 771, at 800.

35 For a survey of social rights in European constitutions, Cécile Fabre, 'Social Rights in European Constitutions' in Gráinne de Búrca, Bruno de Witte and Larissa Ogertschnig (eds.), *Social Rights in Europe* (OUP, 2005) 15.

36 For general explorations of social rights, Stephen Weatherill, *Law and Values in the European Union* (OUP, 2016) 136–137; Benöhr, *EU Consumer Law and Human Rights* (n 4), at 98; Filip Dorssemont 'Values and Objectives' in Bruun, Lörcher and Schömann (eds.), *The Lisbon Treaty and Social Europe* (n 30), at 47, which focuses on labour law. Relevant to the argument set out here is also Kaupa's study of pluralism in the European economic constitution, which proposes that the Treaty leaves room for multiple, i.e. pluralist socio-economic interpretations. Kaupa, *The Pluralist Character of the European Economic Constitution* (n 6), at 6–7 for the main premises of his argument.

37 Formerly both contained in Article 153 EC Treaty.

38 Weatherill, *Law and Values in the European Union* (n 36), at 136–137.

39 The reference to a right to organize themselves, on the other hand, would be a fundamental right, which is found also in many national constitutions.

40 Article 43 ECHR.

41 Article 263 TFEU, which also states that a natural or legal person may institute proceedings against an act addressed to that person or which is of direct and individual concern to them. The term 'act' here is intended to refer not to regulatory acts but to individual acts of EU institutions.

42 Weatherill, *Law and Values in the European Union* (n 36), at 137.

43 Ibid.

44 Ibid.

45 For a critique of the way in which impact assessments have been used in European private law, Esther van Schagen, 'The Hidden Potential of Regulatory Impact Assessments (RIAs) in the Private Law *Acquis*' (2014) *European Review of Private Law* 69, who concludes that RIAs have much potential to improve the quality of

private law but only if shortcomings, such as unsubstantiated assumptions and a lack of neutrality, are addressed.

46 *Aziz* (n 15).

47 Ibid., para 31.

48 Although the initial legislation, as it turned out, did still not comply with the effectiveness principle of EU law; Case C-169/14, *Sánchez Morcillo I*, EU:C:2014:2099.

49 Ibid., para 35. In a Slovakian case with similar facts to the Spanish cases, the Court ruled that the national legislation at issue in the proceedings did comply with the requirements of Article 47 of the Charter; Case C-34/14, *Kušionová*, EU:C:2014:2189.

50 Stephen Weatherill, 'Article 38: Consumer Protection' in Steve Peers *et al.* (eds.), *The EU Charter of Fundamental Rights: A Commentary* (Hart, 2014), para 38.04, who states that 'Article 38 draws on existing material in EU law, and is not a leap into the unknown or the little known.'

51 For early explorations on the potential of Article 47, Norbert Reich, 'The Principle of Effectiveness and EU Contract Law' (2013) *Osservatorio del diritto civile e commerciale* 337; Chantal Mak, 'Rights and Remedies: Article 47 EUCFR and Effective Judicial Protection in European Private Law Matters' in Hans Micklitz (ed.), *Constitutionalization of European Private Law* (OUP, 2014) 236.

52 Article 47 is however also used in cases involving traders. The CJEU's decision in *Biuro podróży 'Partner'* confirmed that traders, when rights derived from Directive 1993/13/EEC on unfair terms are enforced against them, also are entitled to judicial safeguards, based on *their* right – rather than the consumer's – to an effective remedy grounded in Article 47 of the Charter; Case C-119/15, *Biuro podróży 'Partner'*, EU:C:2016:987.

53 *Aziz* (n 15).

54 Hans Micklitz, 'The Visible Hand of European Regulatory Private Law: The Transformation of European Private Law from Autonomy to Functionalism in Competition and Regulation' (2009) *Yearbook of European Law* 3, at 13.

55 Article 49–55 TFEU (freedom of establishment), Article 63–66 TFEU (free movement of capital), and Article 21 and Titles IV and V TFEU (free movement of persons) are less relevant for consumer law and are therefore not discussed here.

56 Article 36 TFEU.

57 Case 120/78, *Cassis de Dijon*, EU:C:1979:42, para 8.

58 Directive 2011/83/EU on consumer rights (n 24); Council Directive 90/314/EEC of 13 June 1990 on package travel, package holidays and package tours, [1993] OJ L158/59; Directive 2008/48/EC of the European Parliament and of the Council of 23 April 2008 on credit agreements for consumers, [2008] OJ L133/66; Directive 2014/17/EU of the European Parliament and of the Council of 4 February 2014 on credit agreements for consumers relating to residential immovable property, [2014] OJ L60/34.

59 Directive 1993/13/EEC on unfair terms (n 24); Directive 2005/29/EC on unfair commercial practices (n 24).

60 For an account of the influence of neoclassical and behavioural economics on EU consumer law: Alberto Alemanno and Anne-Lise Sibony (eds.), *Nudge and the Law: A European Perspective* (Hart, 2015).

61 See the obligation laid down in Article 18 of Directive 2014/17/EU on consumer credit, which holds that credit providers must refuse mortgage loans if the consumer does not pass the creditworthiness assessment. This requirement is new in comparison to Directive 2008/48/EC on consumer credit.

62 Directive 1999/44/EC on consumer sales (n 24).

63 Sustainability is covered on a more general level by the reference to 'improving the quality of the environment' in Article 3(3) TEU.
64 For the facts of the case, see above at 15.
65 That general distinction is between social and economic rights, in which social rights are defined as all non-economic rights.
66 Thomas Wilhelmsson, 'Varieties of Welfarism in European Contract Law' (2004) *European Law Journal* 712; Study Group on Social Justice in European Private Law, 'Social Justice in European Contract Law: A Manifesto' (n 2).
67 An example is the universal service obligation laid down in Directive 2009/72/EC concerning the supply of electricity, which prohibits disconnection of electricity to vulnerable consumers in critical times [2009] OJ L211/55; Norbert Reich, *General Principles of EU Civil Law* (Intersentia, 2014) 82–83. Gokce Mete and Raphael Heffron, 'The Social Dimension of EU Energy Law', in this volume.
68 *Aziz* (n 15); *Kušionová* (n 49). Compare Joined Cases C-154/15 and C-307/15, *Francisco Gutiérrez Naranjo v Cajasur Banco SAU*, EU:C:2016:980.
69 *Aziz* (n 15).
70 *Sánchez Morcillo* (n 48). On the particularities of the new Spanish legislation, see also joined Cases C-482/13, C-484/13, C-485/13 and C-487/13, *Unicaja Banco SA*, EU:C:2015:21; Case C-8/14, *BBVA*, EU:C:2015:731; Case C-421/14, *Banco Primus*, EU:C:2017:60.
71 Another legal basis might potentially be found in Article 34(3) of the Charter, which concerns the right to social housing and housing assistance. In both cases, however, it is important to realize that the provisions do not provide a legal basis for individual actions by consumers, as Article 47 can. The provisions rather seem to have the character of principles, or of fundamental rights to be guaranteed and protected by public authorities. Compare Micklitz and Reich, 'The Court and Sleeping Beauty: The Revival of the Unfair Contract Terms Directive (UCTD)' (n 34), at 800 and the Opinion of AG Cruz Villalón, Case C-176/12, *Association de médiation sociale*, EU:C:2013:491, para 45, referring to the distinction between 'rights' and 'principles' included in Article 52(5) of an earlier version of the Charter.
72 Hans Micklitz, 'The Expulsion of the Concept of Protection from the Consumer Law and the Return of Social Elements in the Civil Law: A Bittersweet Polemic' (2012) *Journal of Consumer Policy* 283, at 289.
73 Ibid., at 290. Van Duin emphasizes that Article 47 of the Charter promotes individual rights protection for both parties, therefore also for traders. Anna van Duin, 'Metamorphosis? The Role of Article 47 of the EU Charter of Fundamental Rights in Cases Concerning National Remedies and Procedures under Directive 1993/13/EEC' (2017) *Journal of European Consumer and Market Law* 190, at 197.
74 Chantal Mak, 'The One and the Many: Translating Insights from Constitutional Pluralism to European Contract Law Theory' (2013) *European Review of Private Law* 1189; Carla Sieburgh, 'A Method to Substantively Guide the Involvement of EU Law in Private Law Matters' (2013) *European Review of Private Law* 1156.
75 For an 'optimistic' view, Hans Micklitz, 'The ECJ between the Individual Citizen and the Member States: A Plea for a Judge Made European Law on Remedies' in Hans Micklitz and Bruno de Witte (eds.), *The European Court of Justice and the Autonomy of the Member States* (Intersentia, 2012) 349, at 392.
76 On effective remedies in EU law, Dorota Leczykiewicz, '"Where Angels Fear to Tread": The EU Law of Remedies and Codification of European Private Law' (2012) *European Review of Contract Law* 47, at 58.
77 Other authors have been bolder in suggesting that a coherent approach might be developed. Hugh Collins, 'The Revolutionary Trajectory of EU Contract Law

towards Post-National Law' (paper presented at the Final Workshop: European Regulatory Private Law. 'A European Advantage in Transnational Lawyering?', EUI, Florence, 26–27 May 2016), who suggests that fundamental rights of EU law can provide a new 'rule of recognition' (in the vein of Hart's concept of law) for European private law.

78 Klaus Lörcher, 'Social Competences' in Bruun, Lörcher and Schömann (eds.), *The Lisbon Treaty and Social Europe* (n 30), 165, at 166, who emphasizes 'the desire of Member States to limit the extension of the Union's [social] competences as much as possible'.

79 Delia Ferri and Fulvio Cortese, 'Introduction', in this volume.

13 Towards a more socially oriented EU copyright law

A soft paradigm shift after Lisbon?

Caterina Sganga

1 Introduction

Intellectual property (IP) is a heterogeneous category of exclusive rights. Since their relatively late creations, intellectual property rights (IPRs) have been strictly territorial in scope. In spite of their monopolistic nature and potential negative effects as a barrier to trade, primary EU law sources did not attribute any competence to the European legislator in the field until the Lisbon Treaty. A deference towards national IP systems emerged from Article 30 EC, which admitted derogations to the freedom of circulation of goods and services when required to protect industrial and commercial property, and in Article 243 EC, which stated that the Treaty left unprejudiced the Member States' systems of property ownership.[1]

Due to the lack of competence, most of the acts have been adopted on the basis of former Article 95 EC (now Article 114 TFEU). This has also been the case for copyright, a field heavily regulated by ten harmonization Directives, two Regulations and two recasts from 1991 to 2017, with an additional important directive in the pipeline. Whereas the market-based foundation of the EU legislative interventions had a limited impact on the commercial-oriented genetic code of industrial property rights, its effects on authors' rights have been much more revolutionary. Compared to national copyright laws, which are only partially inspired by economic normative theories, EU copyright has evolved into a hybrid model, whose predominant market inspirations have overshadowed other copyright functions, more closely related to cultural and social policies.[2] The market emphasis has also attributed more relevance to the protection of industrial intermediaries, to the detriment of individual authors. The very same reasons are the root cause of non-authors being often defined as mere consumers of cultural products, rather than holders of potentially conflicting non-economic rights. The situation did not change substantially after the Lisbon Treaty, despite the new emphasis put on cultural policies and on the social nature of the EU market economy. In fact, Article 118 TFEU gives now full competence to the Parliament and the Council to create European IPRs, but it does it only 'in the context of the establishment and functioning of the internal market', without further connotations. At the same time, the EU legislator may still intervene on national IP laws under Article 114 TFEU, in pursuance of internal market goals.[3]

Assuming the complete extraneousness of non-economic considerations to the realm of EU IP law would be imprecise, though. Signs of an increasing attention towards its impact on cultural and social rights emerge between the lines of legislative preambles, soft law documents and from the decisions of the CJEU. Such epiphanies are particularly visible in copyright law, due to the relevance of its subject-matter for the enjoyment of a broad range of non-economic rights. For this reason, and especially in light of the necessarily concise nature of this contribution, authors' rights will be the main focus of this analysis.

The chapter is structured in five sections. Section 2 provides an overview of the CJEU's application of EU primary law provisions in the field of copyright, with the aim to understand whether and with which impact non-market considerations have found their way in the Court's decisions. Sections 3 and 4 propose a diachronic overview of soft law and secondary legislation that have intervened on national copyright laws respectively from 1991 to the advent of the Lisbon Treaty, and from the Lisbon Treaty to today, focusing on the interplay between market and non-market rationales. Section 5 conducts the same assessment on the CJEU's case law, searching for references to social and cultural rights and policies, and evaluating their impact on copyright rules. The overall aim is to verify whether the 'social market economy' principle has caused any paradigm shift in the approach to the harmonization of EU copyright law and, if yes, with which results.

2 Copyright and social considerations before Lisbon: the Treaties through the lenses of the CJEU's case law

2.1 Copyright vs fundamental freedoms?

Although primary EC law did not make any express reference to IPRs, it did not take long for these territorial, non-harmonized legal monopolies to clash with the four fundamental freedoms protected by the Treaty. Already from the 1970s, national courts referred to the Court questions related to the interpretation of Article 30 EC in cases where rightholders exercised their IPRs with the aim of segmenting the internal market in several national monopolies, hindering parallel import and blocking second-hand markets[4] through territorially limited license agreements that leveraged the principle of national exhaustion, which terminated the distribution right after the first sale of the work only if it happened within the territory of the state where the right was granted and the protection sought.[5] Forced to face conducts that altered the balance set by Article 30 EC between the incentivizing functions of IP monopolies and the Treaty's principles and goals, the CJEU circumvented the exception set by the provision by distinguishing between existence and exercise of IPRs. In *Deutsche Grammophon*, it argued that the Treaty left to Member States the competence to regulate their creation, ownership and features, but it did not exclude the Court's power to intervene when the rightholders' exercise of their prerogatives violated any Treaty provision, going beyond what was necessary for the rights to perform their essential function, and for the legal system to protect their specific subject-matter.[6] Through the existence-exercise dichotomy, the Court could use the Treaties to develop the doctrine of Community exhaustion, which extended the principle to any first authorized sale of the work anywhere in the Community,[7] putting an end to forms of copyright misuses that negatively affected the internal market. Market arguments, however, justified also opposite decisions, where exhaustion was excluded because the type of work or right protected required a territorially segmented exploitation for copyright to perform its essential function of rewarding and incentivizing creators.[8]

2.2 *Beyond the 'essential function of copyright'*

The introduction of the notion of essential function of copyright brought forward two important considerations. First, the protection of IPRs was not absolute and idiosyncratic, but functionalized to the pursuance of specific goals. Second, and despite the exception enshrined in Article 30 EC, national IP rules had to respect the Treaties.[9] This holding gave the CJEU ample margin to intervene on Member States' IP laws much before the EU legislator found creative grounds to support its harmonization agenda, and introduced the idea that IP could yield *vis-à-vis* countervailing rights and interests when its exercise would go beyond what is necessary for the right to reach its systematic objectives.

A similar path was followed in another strain of decisions, issued in the 1990s and tackling the interplay between copyright and competition law. The application of antitrust provisions on copyright matters has long been excluded for two concurrent reasons. On the one hand, since copyright covers expressions and not ideas, the possibility for its holder to exercise full control over raw data and to block the creation of new works is theoretically excluded. On the other hand, copyright, as every other IPR, is a monopoly purposefully created by law to pursue innovation goals, making the application of competition law inherently contradictory.[10] The situation changed when copyright started stretching to apply to technical and informational works such as software and databases, thus allowing rightholders to monopolize ideas, and increasing the risk of abusive behaviours. As it happened in the 1970s with fundamental freedoms, unbalanced anti-competitive practices of copyright owners reached the CJEU,[11] requiring it once again to determine whether and to what extent a violation of Treaty provisions should have been tolerated to protect IPRs.

Excluding the equation between IP monopoly and dominant position, and considering the barrier to entry against competitors as a necessary component of IPRs, the Court ruled that an exercise of copyright could be defined as abusive for EU competition law purposes only in 'exceptional circumstances', where the right-holder's use of her exclusive rights went beyond their essential function, 'which was to protect the moral rights in the work and ensure a reward for the creative effort'.[12] With a clear emphasis on market mechanisms, the CJEU identified such circumstances in conducts that hinder the offering of a new product, without an objective justification, and with the aim of excluding all competition from the secondary market.[13]

Despite the potential of this interpretative theory, the internal market focus of both case law strands prevented the Court from developing a general conceptual framework that could provide an effective balancing tool also for instances of abuse and misuse of copyright that challenged the realization of its non-economic goals, hindered the fulfilment of general socio-cultural policies, or violated fundamental rights of non-IP owner. With the exception of *Metronome Musik*[14] and its isolated reference to the cultural development of the Community as key function of copyright, no other traces of such kind can be found, not even after the entry into force of the Lisbon Treaty.

3 Social considerations in EU copyright law before the Lisbon Treaty

Social and cultural rights and policies are often intertwined in their positive and negative relationships with copyright. Protecting authors is necessary to grant them a reward for their creative work, thus ensuring them an adequate standard of living. At the same time, copyright works as incentive for authors to produce cultural products, which is vital to cultural diversity – a backbone of EU cultural policies.[15] Similarly, protecting the investments of producers and distributors is essential for cultural industries to strive, which is conductive to economic growth and higher employment rates. These intermediaries are also responsible for the dissemination of copyright products, which is fundamental to ensure cultural diversity and access to culture. However, a strict protection of copyright may clash against a wide and intertwined array of cultural and social rights. The freedom of art and science and the right to take part in cultural life, often constrained by copyright enforcement, are closely linked to the right to education, while the rights of people with disabilities to equal treatment and equal opportunities can hardly be respected, protected and fulfilled without granting disabled individuals the fullest enjoyment of their cultural rights.[16] For this reason, any assessment of the inclusion of social market considerations in secondary EU copyright law should necessarily consider both cultural and social policies and rights. This section provides an overview of the emersions of socio-cultural arguments in soft law and legislation before the Lisbon Treaty, laying the groundwork for the comparison with more recent trends.

3.1 Soft law

Interestingly, the first soft law documents referring to copyright in the 1970s and 1980s[17] mention the need to harmonize the field in order to protect the European cultural heritage and foster cultural production, but ground the intervention on cultural matters on the protection of fundamental freedoms.[18] The real debut of internal market arguments in the field is marked, instead, by the 1988 Green Paper 'Copyright and the Challenge of Technology',[19] which emphasizes the 'growing importance of copyright to industry and commerce',[20] and centres its attention on the need to strengthen the internal market and ensure its proper functioning,[21] incentivize the competitiveness of European industries and stimulate investments from producers and distributors of creative works.[22] Predictably, the subsequent papers[23] set as goals for the future harmonization the reinforcement of exclusive rights and the intervention on every rule that may have an impact on the development of the internal market.[24] The chief example comes from the Green Paper 'Copyright and Related Rights in the Information Society',[25] according to which copyright should be protected as incentive for European cultural industries to invest in creative endeavours, become more competitive and create more employment.[26] Similarly, the harmonization of copyright is justified by the need to allow the free circulation of cultural goods and services, and offer to cultural industries the broad market they need to make their investments profitable.[27]

3.2 EU copyright legislation

Most of the EU harmonization of national copyright laws took place in the period that goes from 1991 to the entry into force of the Lisbon Treaty. Directive 91/250/EC on the protection of computer programmes[28] justifies its enactment with the need to remove the obstacles to the functioning of the internal market created by non-harmonized national rules,[29] and to protect the investments of software producers,[30] in light of their fundamental role for the industrial development of the Community.[31] The same two goals underline Directive 92/100/EC on rental, lending and related rights.[32] The new exclusive rights are introduced to provide an 'adequate' income to rightholders, and thus to foster creations and investments.[33] Even the provision of an unwaivable equitable remuneration for authors and performers, usually anchored to social considerations such as the goal to ensure a decent standard of living to creators, is based on neutral economic arguments.[34]

The necessity to remove obstacles to the free circulation of goods and services is the basis of Directive 93/98/EC on the harmonization of terms of protection.[35] For the first time, the use of the term 'consumers' to identify the individuals enjoying copyright products contextualizes both the functions of the discipline and the balance between conflicting interests in a framework where authors, producers, users and new potential creators are all treated as market players, rather than as individual holders of (also) non-economic rights.[36] Directive 96/6/EC on the protection of databases[37] epitomizes the rationales that characterize this first phase of EU harmonization, such as the protection of investments, the incentive for the development of an industry sector,[38] and the fostering of the competitiveness of European companies in the information market,[39] with a consequent loss of centrality of the personal link between the author and her work. To reach these goals, the Directive aims at providing an appropriate level of protection to secure the remuneration of the database maker,[40] which should be 'stable and uniform' enough to stimulate and protect their investments.[41] This represents the foundation of the *sui generis* right,[42] which is attributed on the content of the database on the mere ground of the investment, without any further requirement.[43]

When in 2001 the EU legislator decided to grant authors of graphic and plastic artworks the resale right,[44] one could have expected to find explicit social arguments in the preamble. Instead, the 'share in the economic success of their original works of art' is given to guarantee the competitiveness of the market in modern and contemporary art,[45] while harmonization serves to realize the internal market and avoid discrepancies between national laws that may distort competition.[46]

The Information Society Directive (2001/29/EC)[47] – EU's first attempt to standardize the main pillars of national copyright laws – reiterates the same objectives with a much more articulated narrative. In its preamble, the high level of protection of authors' rights is indicated as the only solution to stimulate investments in creativity and innovation, which are linked to economic growth, industrial competitiveness and higher employment rates.[48] The EU legislator justifies its intervention as necessary to foster the development of the European information society in Europe,[49] which is based on the presence of a well-functioning internal market for new copyright products.[50] Nothing else in the recitals suggests a consideration of the author as an individual, save for a cursory reference to the need to safeguard 'the independence and dignity of artistic creators and performers' by means of an adequate economic reward.[51] The production and distribution of cultural products is linked to industrial policies, and only secondarily to cultural or social goals, while the intervention on copyright is only timidly justified also under Article 167 TFEU, which requires the EU 'to take cultural aspects into account in its action'.[52]

One would have expected this to be the premise of a more prismatic approach to the field, embedding also non-economic considerations. Signs of this trend appear, in fact, in Recital 14, which indicates the need to promote learning and culture through copyright, and provides exceptions for education and research, and in Recital 31, which calls for a 'fair balance of rights and interests' between different categories of rightholders, and between rightholders and users, significantly not labelled as 'consumers'. However, their potential impact is minimized by Recital 22, which states that the goal of dissemination of culture 'must not be achieved by sacrificing strict protection of rights', and by Recital 32, which emphasizes that the harmonization of exceptions should be guided by the consideration of 'their impact on the smooth functioning on the internal market'. Also the recitals commenting on specific limitations do not elaborate on their social or cultural policy rationale, focusing more on their potential impact on the market of the work.[53] Similarly, the exhaustive nature of their list provided by the Directive and their strict reading are motivated by the need to 'duly reflect the increased economic impact [they] may have in the context of the new economic environment'.[54] Since exceptions are the natural gateway for social and cultural rights to penetrate within the tangles of copyright, this is probably the most evident indication of the almost unidirectional market focus of EU copyright law.

Similar references to the functioning of the internal market,[55] competitiveness and employment[56] feature the second horizontal act, the Enforcement Directive, where a high level of proprietary protection is deemed necessary to maintain the confidence of business circles in the internal market, as precondition for their engagement in highly risky investment.[57] The call for a balance between IP enforcement, the widest access and dissemination of IP-protected works possible, the circulation of information and the protection of privacy are confined to a minor side reference;[58] and the same can be said for the respect of potentially conflicting fundamental rights.[59]

4 EU copyright law: the state of play after the Lisbon Treaty

4.1 Soft law

Starting from 2004, the cultural dimension of copyright has assumed a more relevant – albeit still secondary – role in a number of soft law documents.[60] Still, the market emphasis returns strongly every time the Commission looks at the challenges posed by the digital environment to the circulation of creative content.[61]

Signs of a soft paradigm shift emerge in the key consultative document of the period, the 2008 Green Paper 'Copyright in the Knowledge Economy',[62] where the Commission discusses the measures that may be necessary to ensure the circulation and access to research and educational materials.[63] Despite cultural policies are in the spotlight, however, there is no real departure from the classic market approach, since a 'high level of copyright protection' is still 'crucial for intellectual creation',[64] and necessary to foster investments and ensure 'the maintenance and development of creativity'.[65] Specific access problems are targeted with narrowly defined exceptions, and a focus limited to the digitization of libraries and archives collections, the creation and protection of user generated content (UGC), and the easier access and dissemination of materials for teaching and research.[66]

Economic arguments dominate subsequent documents, which are all based on market studies and follow exclusively a market logic. For instance, the issue of access to cultural goods is analysed under the perspective of the evolving consumers' expectations on the accessibility of digital content, which prompt the Commission to plan an intervention on national collective management organizations (CMOs) and on cross-border licenses.[67] In a similar vein, the problem of the creation of cultural materials is addressed by focusing on creative industries and entrepreneurship,[68] and IP law is defined as a framework 'that incentivizes investment by rewarding creation, stimulates innovation in an environment of undistorted competition and facilitates the distribution of knowledge', and as catalyst to growth, competitiveness and job creation.[69] At the same time, however, it demands flexible rules that avoid abuses of IPRs or their enforcement as an end in themselves,[70] as they are not only incentives for innovation, but also tools to promote development and address 'some of today's global challenges'.[71]

The economic approach finds its peak in the Communication 'A digital single market strategy for Europe', where copyright is 'one of the main drivers of the growth' of the creative sector.[72] Due to the very specific goals, however, the Commission plans only narrow interventions on EU copyright,[73] as illustrated in the Communication 'Towards a modern, more European copyright framework'.[74] The focus is again on market regulation: the Communication targets rules that are a precondition for 'a well-functioning marketplace for copyright',[75] are necessary to ensure a fair sharing of revenues among the different market participants,[76] facilitate the sustainable financing of the production of creative content,[77] and guarantee its dissemination through reliable, transparent and cross-border contractual arrangements.[78] However, for the first time the Commission seems to perform an assessment of the balance between copyright and social and cultural goals struck by previous legislative acts,[79] emphasizing how inadequate the lack of harmonization of exceptions and the restrictive approach taken by some national legislators are, and proposing the introduction of a set of narrow but mandatory limitations.[80] Differently than in the past, when the harmonization of exceptions was mostly justified by the need to remove obstacles to the internal market, here the arguments used in support merge social and cultural policy objectives with internal market, leadership and competitiveness goals.[81] This more holistic approach does not result in revolutionary changes, though. While it is true that the Commission challenges the traditional EU reliance on stakeholders' agreements and market-led solution,[82] the economic model remains dominant, as proven by the fact that the need to protect authors and performers against commercial intermediaries is justified by their weak bargaining power, and is tackled with solutions such as collective management and unwaivable remuneration rights.

The same approach is reiterated in the Communication 'Promoting a fair, efficient and competitive European copyright-based economy in the digital single market', which introduces the most recent EU copyright reform package (September 2016).[83] Its wording testifies to the conflictual interaction of two souls in EU copyright law, particularly accentuated by the post-Lisbon broadening of EU competences, which have now set on almost equal foot economic and cultural policies and goals. As a glaring example, it explicitly states that creative industries 'constitute a significant economic sector but are also a primary source of learning and entertainment and are crucial to maintaining and nurturing Europe's cultural diversity', and that copyright law should contribute to make them competitive 'so they can reach out to larger audiences and ultimately provide more choices to citizens'.[84] The measures proposed show the same hybrid characteristics. Market tools such as license agreements and hubs are heavily relied on 'to increase availability of works for citizens, provide new distribution channels for creators, promote cultures of Members States and bring the EU's common cultural heritage to the fore'.[85] They are the preferred instrument also for the realization of wider public goals, such as the digitization and dissemination of out-of-commerce works by cultural heritage institutions.[86] Also the more central role regained by authors and performers is coloured by market nuances, since the Communication focuses on the need to ensure that they receive fair compensation and their weaker bargaining power is rebalanced.[87] Then, to complete the picture, no reference is made to the need for a more comprehensive, less patchworked harmonization in order to ensure the contextual pursuance of economic, social and cultural objectives. On the contrary, the problem-based approach is reaffirmed by the plan to continue assessing 'a number of other issues related to exceptions' in light of the outcome of cases pending in front of the CJEU.[88]

4.2 *Legislative texts*

As indicated by the preparatory documents, the harmonization efforts of the EU legislator in the field of copyright witnessed a partial shift in focus after the entry into force of the Lisbon Treaty. The 'social market economy' of Article 3 TEU is never directly mentioned, but translates into the greater consideration the legislator shows for non-economic goals, and the use of market regulations to pursue not only efficiency, competition and growth, but also a blend of social and cultural goals.

The first example of the new trend comes from the Orphan Works Directive (OWD),[89] which aims at facilitating the digitization of works of authors who cannot be traced and reached, through the provision of a specific exception to the benefit of cultural heritage institutions. The Preamble contextualizes the measure in the framework of EU cultural and social policies, by stating that the mass digitization and dissemination of works that the Directive wants to achieve is 'a means of protecting Europe's cultural heritage' and to ensure the citizens' access to it.[90] However, the market-based rationales still remain central. Other recitals ground the intervention on the need to remove obstacles to the free circulation of cultural content, created by the diverging national standards on the recognition of the orphan work status.[91] The strong link between copyright and EU industrial policies is highlighted by Recital 5, which defines the former as a tool to reward the 'creative sector', for its function of 'economic foundation for the creative industry' is to stimulate innovation, creation, investment and production. The economic rationale appears also in the provisions that allow cultural heritage institutions to generate revenue from their use of orphan works in order to finance the digitization.[92] Yet, the post-Lisbon blend of market arguments with social and cultural considerations leads to a more hybrid approach than in the past, as shown, *inter alia*, by the range of criteria suggested for calculating the fair compensation due to authors who redeem their work from the orphan status, which take into account the cultural promotion objectives of the institutions that have benefitted from the exception, their public interest mission and the non-commercial nature of the use, while only at last the harm caused to rightholders.[93]

Compared to this, the second post-Lisbon intervention is significantly more market-oriented, but still featuring hybrid traits. Directive 2014/26 on collective management organizations (CMOs) and multi-territorial licensing of musical works for online use[94] aims at tackling the fragmentation of the digital market for creative content[95] through the creation of a single level playing field of common rules to foster an undistorted competition between CMOs. As usual, the declared ultimate goal is to encourage investments in creativity and innovation.[96] Still, the market-based nature of the Directive is balanced by the inclusion, among the grounds of the intervention, of Article 167 TFEU, which obliges the Union to consider and promote cultural diversity.[97] In this sense, the harmonization effort on CMOs is justified by their role as 'promoters of the diversity of cultural expression', for they provide social, cultural and educational services for rightholders and the public, and enable 'the smallest and less popular repertories to access the market'.[98]

From 2012 on, the Commission launched a number of public consultations to set policy priorities in the revision of EU copyright rules. As a result of this, a new reform package was unveiled in 2016, which was composed of three main elements: the first one (a Directive[99] and a Regulation, approved in July 2017)[100] implements the Marrakesh Treaty and its measures to increase access to copyright materials for people with disabilities; the second (a Regulation, approved in June 2017)[101] ensures cross-border content portability, and the third (a proposed Directive, still under discussion) introduces a set of targeted measures in the context of the Digital Single Market strategies.[102]

The three actions are all part of the Digital Single Market agenda,[103] and connected through an evident *fil rouge*. A greater and fairer access to online content is deemed important to fulfil the social rights of consumers,[104] while the adoption of the Marrakesh exception is fundamental for persons with disabilities to enjoy on an equal basis with others their rights to education and access to cultural goods.[105] Along the same line, some of the key innovations of the proposed CDSM Directive respond to the protection of other social rights, such as the right to education – and the connected research –, and to cultural diversity goals.[106] The different inspiration emerges also in the text of their preambles and explanatory memoranda.

In the Regulation on cross-border portability the beneficiary of the measure is the digital subscriber who is 'temporarily present in a Member State other than their Member State of residence'. No reference is made to individual rights, but only to consumer demand,[107] internal market potential[108] and the need to remove contractual barriers to the cross-border availability of lawfully subscribed digital content,[109] without affecting the high level of protection guaranteed to copyright and related rights.[110] On the contrary, and inevitably, the Directive and Regulation implementing the Marrakesh Treaty are the only texts whose inspiration is fully centred on cultural rights. By introducing a mandatory exception to copyright, the Directive aims at allowing the making of accessible format copies of otherwise non-accessible works for visually impaired people,[111] while the Regulation ensures the cross-border exchange of accessible format copies between the Union and third countries that have adhered to the Treaty, in order to increase their availability and reduce duplicate costs. Interestingly, and despite the Union's obligation to abide by the Marrakesh Treaty and the UN Convention for the Rights of People with Disabilities (UNCRPD),[112] the explanatory memorandum to the Directive identifies the legal basis for the proposal in Article 114 TFEU. The blend of rationales emerges in Recital 1, which states that EU copyright directives 'contribute to the proper functioning of the internal market and stimulate innovation, creation, investment and the production of new content', while aiming 'to promote access to knowledge and culture by protecting works [. . .] and by permitting exceptions or limitations that are in the public interest'. Yet, the preamble never mentions explicitly the rights of people with disabilities, but consistently frames the goal of the intervention as that of improving 'the availability of works and other protected subject-matter in accessible formats',[113] and to substantially remove the discrimination between visually able and visually impaired individuals as to the accessibility to books, journals, newspapers and alike.[114]

4.3 New legislative proposals

Also the proposal of a CDSM Directive identifies its legal basis in Article 114 TFEU. As in the case of the OWD, much of the emphasis of the text is put on exceptions and the social and cultural policies underlying their introduction. However, the economic model and the central role played by internal market rationales still dominate the explanatory memorandum and the preamble. The modernization of copyright rules is justified by the need to respond to the evolution of digital technologies, the emersion of new uses, actors and business models, the impact they had on the creation and distribution of protected works, and the new access opportunity for digital consumers.[115] Some exceptions and limitations have to be recast not only to make sure that they keep on achieving their public policy objectives (research, education and cultural diversity) and ensuring the fair balance between the rights and interests of rightholders and users, but also – and mainly – to avoid that differences in national legislations hamper cross-border uses of protected works.[116] In fact, particular attention is put on 'uses and works where clearance of rights is complex', implicitly identifying the primary goal of exceptions as that of tackling market failures,[117] and framing the achievement of socio-cultural objectives as a consequence of the better market regulation.

The double inspiration of the proposal appears evident in the contextual use of the term 'consumer' and 'citizen' to refer to the final beneficiaries of the improved access to European cultural heritage and copyright-protected content.[118] Similarly, it emerges in the double aim of the related right attributed to publishers to address the problems they face in 'licensing the online use of their publications and recouping their investments',[119] and of the measures introduced to tackle the so-called 'value gap', which is the remuneration generally not provided to rightholders by online platforms hosting user-uploaded content. Both are meant to solve a remuneration problem caused by a market failure. Yet, the first is also deemed necessary to foster a 'free and pluralist press', ensure quality journalism and citizens' access to information, and so bringing a 'fundamental contribution to the public debate and the proper functioning of a democratic society';[120] while the second is – as usually – linked to the need to make sure that copyright keeps on performing its incentivizing function for the creation of new works.[121] Also the proposal to introduce measures to rebalance the weak bargaining position of authors and performers *vis-à-vis* industrial intermediaries aims at the same time at 'achieving a well-functioning marketplace for copyright' and at increasing the production and availability of content, with positive effects on media pluralism and 'to the ultimate benefit of consumers'.[122]

The preamble follows the same approach. Several recitals identify the functions of copyright[123] and the justification for the mandatory nature of exceptions in the need to ensure the good functioning of the internal market and avoid distortion in competition.[124] The same can be said for the exception provided to allow the digitization of collections by cultural heritage institutions, which strives to prevent that different national rules 'hamper cross-border cooperation and the sharing of means of preservation in the internal market, leading to an inefficient use of resources'.[125] Similar arguments support the creation of a related right for publisher.[126] In line with the blended social market approach typical of this phase, the rightholders' remuneration in case of text and data mining exception is excluded for lack of real harm, while the decision on whether or not to subordinate the granting of the educational exception to the availability of affordable commercial licenses is left to Member States.[127] Recital 2 connects the better functioning of the copyright marketplace to consumer welfare, media pluralism, greater cultural diversity, better education and research, and the improvement of the dissemination of Member States' and EU cultural products, in line with the Union's policies.[128] In fact, all these cultural and social objectives are meant to be reached through a great reliance on market mechanisms, as proven by the choice of contractual arrangements between CMOs and cultural heritage institutions as the preferred regulatory tool to achieve the preservation of cultural heritage through the digitization of out-of-commerce works.[129] And the same applies to the intervention on the contractual relationships between authors, performers and industrial intermediaries, with the introduction of transparency obligation to avoid information asymmetry, remuneration adjustment mechanism for license agreements, and ADR paths to solve smoothly and cheaply controversies between the parties.[130]

In their diachronic evolution from the early 1990s to today, both preparatory documents and legislative texts and proposals in the field of copyright show a clear and unequivocal tendency towards a progressively more pronounced merging of market-based rationales and objectives with socio-cultural considerations. Social and cultural policies, instead of being merely external constraints justifying the presence of exceptions to exclusive rights, move to the core of the discipline and become, even if often only secondarily, objectives of EU copyright law. A similar phenomenon can be traced, albeit with more blurred contours, in the copyright case law of the CJEU.

5 Social and cultural considerations in the case law of the CJEU

From the very early days, the CJEU has played a major role in advancing the harmonization of EU copyright law, exercising little self-restraint and expanding the scope of EU law principles and rules much beyond the borders set by the EU legislator.[131]

Save for the already mentioned *Metronome Musik*, there is no sign of consideration of the interferences between copyright law and conflicting rights and interests until 2008, when the notion of 'fair balance' between copyright and fundamental rights makes its first appearance in *Promusicae*.[132] The case questioned the existence of an EU law obligation on national legislators to impose injunctions against ISPs forcing the disclosure of users' information in civil proceedings on copyright infringement. At stake there was the interplay between the right to (intellectual) property, the right to an effective remedy and the right to privacy and respect for private life. Unfortunately *Promusicae* did not provide clear criteria to guide the balance, but only one general indication, the highly cited recital 68, which states that 'Member States must [. . .] rely on an interpretation of the directives which allows a fair balance to be struck between the various [EU] fundamental rights', and does not conflict 'with those fundamental rights or with the other general principles of Community law'.[133] The precedent could have opened the gate to the horizontal application of fundamental rights in EU copyright law, but its vagueness and Solomonic remittance of the assessment to Member States, with no further indications, led instead to a strain of swinging decisions. Ruling on a similar fact pattern, *Bonnier Audio* judged proportionate and balanced a Swedish provision that allowed courts to issue the same type of injunctions contested in *Promusicae*, arguing that the benefits for the investigation 'outweigh the nuisance [. . .] which the measure may entail'.[134] Later, *Scarlet Extended* and its twin decision *Netlog* judged disproportionate an injunction directed to oblige an ISP to install a general preventive filter against infringements for all its electronic communications, stating that 'nothing whatsoever in the wording of that provision or in the Court's case law [. . .] suggest that that right is inviolable and must for that reason be absolutely protected'.[135] In fact, the measure was considered too burdensome on the ISP's freedom to conduct business (Article 16 EUCFR), and too much harmful of user's privacy and freedom of information (Articles 8 and 11 EUCFR).[136] Then, decisions such as *UPC Telekabel*[137] and *McFadden*[138] circumscribed the fundamental right check to the mere role of one of the prongs of the legitimacy assessment of the injunction, and weakened its cogency even more, by remitting its evaluation to the ISP in case of open injunctions, with no clear guidelines.

Even after the entry into force of the Lisbon Treaty, the Court's case law has not witnessed substantial changes.[139] No reference has been made, for instance, to Articles 3 and 9 TFEU, mostly due to the existence of subject-specific general clauses already enabling the horizontal application of fundamental rights and the consideration of public policy goals, such as the notion of 'fair balance'. However, some isolated sparks suggest a growing sensitiveness of the Court towards the blended, social market economy approach that currently characterizes EU copyright law. Four examples may suffice to offer a glimpse on this recent shift.

In *Deckmyn*,[140] the Court defined the notion of parody as autonomous concept of EU law, and excluded that Member States could provide a more restrictive interpretation of its scope and requirement, not to create undue obstacles to the realization of the function of the exception, which is to protect freedom of expression. For the first time, the CJEU's harmonizing intervention on a limitation was not directed to avoid distortions in the internal market, but to ensure that its implementations lead to the uniform respect of the fair balance between copyright and fundamental right, as concurrent goal of the EU copyright harmonization.

Similarly, in *Ulmer*,[141] the Court extended the exception to the right of communication to the public provided under Article 5(3)(n) InfoSoc, which allowed libraries to offer the digital version of their collections on dedicated terminals, ruling that the provision included also the possibility to digitize the libraries' printed collections, and therefore entailed also an additional exception to the right of reproduction, even if rightholders offered a license agreement for the correspondent electronic edition. The CJEU justified the reading on the basis of a functional argument: without this ancillary right, Article 5(3)(n) InfoSoc would not be able to perform its cultural promotion role to foster 'research and private study, through the dissemination of knowledge, which constitutes [. . .] the core mission of publicly accessible libraries'.[142]

The same socio-cultural consideration supported the application of the public lending exception to e-books in *Vereniging Openbare Bibliotheken* (VOB).[143] Against the common interpretation that excludes the extension of the notion of 'copy' to intangible supports, based on the systematic reading of several EU and international provisions,[144] the CJEU ruled that

> given the importance of the public lending of digital books, and in order to safeguard both the effectiveness of the [. . .] public lending exception and [its] contribution [. . .] to cultural promotion, it cannot [. . .] be ruled out that Article 6(1) of Directive 2006/115 may apply where the [lending of electronic books] by a publicly accessible library [. . .] has essentially similar characteristics to the lending of printed works.[145]

With a remarkable change of approach, objectives of cultural promotion justify a new extensive reading of exceptions, even against opposite literal and systematic indications.

Another partial shift, which turns the spotlight from industrial rightholders to authors, and thus from the market to the individual, found recently its confirmation in *Soulier and Doke*,[146] a decision that declared contrary to EU law the French law on out-of-commerce works, which introduced an automatic mechanism through which a selected collecting society could license the right to digitize and commercialize works published before January 2001 and no longer distributed. Authors and successors in title could have opposed the process upon compliance with specific requirements, and under the obligation to commercialize the work. The CJEU recognized the public interest goal underlying the measure and did not believe that the explicit right-holder's consent is always needed to authorize the exercise of an exclusive right. Still, it required that authors are informed of the envisaged use of their works and of the measures to be taken to oppose it, and that their capability to terminate the license is not subordinated to the concurrent will of the original publisher or subject to other formalities.[147] In this sense – and this represents the most important statement for our analysis – the Court stressed how the InfoSoc Directive does not prohibit Member States 'from granting certain rights or certain benefits to third parties, such as publishers',[148] but that 'those rights and benefits' should not 'harm the rights which that directive gives exclusively to authors'.[149] Albeit implicitly, the decision puts back the author to the centre of the stage, emphasizing one of the most neglected functions of EU copyright law, that is protecting the author's interest in controlling the use of her work and enjoying the fruits of her efforts, which translates in her capability to exercise some of her basic social and cultural rights, such as the right to an adequate standard of living and to benefit from the protection of the material and moral interests resulting from her artistic or scientific productions.

6 Conclusions

Screening EU copyright sources in search for mentions to the 'highly competitive social market economy' enshrined in Articles 3 TEU is an exercise that leads to no results. Primary EU law did not make any direct reference to IPRs until the Lisbon Treaty, save for listing their protection as an exception to the freedom of circulation of goods and services. The harmonization of national IP laws has been consistently based on Article 114 TFEU, which gives to the EU the competence to intervene on Member States' legislations when necessary to ensure the proper functioning of the internal market. After Lisbon, a two-tier system was created: Article 118 TFEU attributes to the EU legislator the competence to create and regulate unitary European IP titles 'in the context of the establishment and functioning of the internal market'; parallel to this, Article 114 TFEU still remains the legal basis to justify the harmonization of national IP laws. Notably, both provisions are grounded on internal market goals. As a natural consequence, early days CJEU decisions that applied primary EU provisions on national copyright laws also focused on matters related to the correct functioning of the internal market, and namely on the clash between copyright and fundamental freedoms, and copyright and competition law.

A diachronic overview of soft law and legislative texts show a market-based definition of the functions of copyright and of its harmonization, with considerations of economic efficiency, industrial growth, competitiveness and incentives to be given for innovation, creativity and investments prevailing over any other policy goals. Authors lose their centrality *vis-à-vis* industrial rightholders, while non-authors are defined as 'consumers', and only rarely as 'citizens' or individuals who also carry rights and interests. Green Papers, Communications and Directives' recitals qualify the EU copyright harmonization as a market regulation pursuing specific industrial policies, where cultural and social goals are only by-products. With a soft paradigm shift, however, documents and acts published after 2009 show a more blended approach, with social and cultural rights and policies mentioned more often among the objectives of the discipline, albeit always merged with internal market goals. Some Directives have cultural and social policies as main goals, as in the case of the OWD and the Directive implementing the Marrakesh Treaty, yet with market arguments still playing a significant role. Other texts reiterate the traditional market-based functions of the EU copyright harmonization, but also due to Article 167 TFEU cultural considerations are always embedded in the legislative exercise. For instance, the intervention on CMOs, which is mostly a market regulation, is justified also in light of their role of 'promoter of the diversity of cultural expressions', and the cultural and educational services they provide to the public. Social and cultural rights support also the most recent proposals for the modernization of copyright rules.

Despite this change, Article 114 TFEU remains the legal basis of EU copyright law; market tools are still the preferred regulatory option to increase the availability of works, promote cultures and bring the EU's common cultural heritage to the fore; the intervention on exceptions is still depicted as a solution to market failures; the term 'consumer', 'individual' and 'citizen' are used interchangeably; and industrial, cultural and social policies are very closely intertwined.

The CJEU's copyright case law follows the same evolutionary path. Social and cultural considerations and the need to strike a fair balance between copyright and conflicting rights appear for the first time only in 2008 (*Promusicae*). Although the Court's decisions still tend to provide a broad reading of exclusive rights and a restrictive application of exceptions, recent precedents seem to open the gate to different interpretations. The need to pursue specific social and cultural objectives, or to ensure the respect of fundamental rights, supports the definition of a minimum mandatory content for specific exceptions, such as parody (*Deckmyn*), or their extensive interpretation (*Ulmer* and *VOB*); for similar reasons, albeit implicitly, authors gain back their place under the spotlight against the favour traditionally granted to industrial rightholders (*Soulier and Doke*).

How much of these trends can be understood as the product of the 'highly competitive social market economy' principles enshrined in the Lisbon Treaty, it is hard to establish. However, the positive 'contamination' of the dry market-based regulation of copyright matters with broader non-market, more social considerations is undeniable, and indicates an evolutionary path that now seems to be consistently followed by EU sources, and which leaves hopes for a more inclusive, balanced EU copyright law in the years to come.

Notes

1 Daniela Caruso, 'Private Law and Public Stakes in European Integration: The Case of Property' (2004) *European Law Journal* 751. A more inclusive reading is offered by Bram Akkermans and Eveline Ramaekers, 'Article 345 TFEU (Article 295 EC Treaty), Its Meanings and Interpretations' (2010) *European Law Journal* 292.

2 Giuseppe Mazziotti, *EU Digital Copyright Law and the End-User* (Springer, 2008) 45; Herman Cohen Jehoram, 'European Copyright Law: Even More Horizontal?' (2001) IIC 532, at 537.

3 Ana Ramalho, *The Competence of the European Union in Copyright Lawmaking: A Normative Perspective of EU Powers for Copyright Harmonization* (Springer, 2016) 14.
4 Alain Strowel and Hee-Eun Kim, 'The Balancing Impact of General EU Law on European Intellectual Property Jurisprudence' in Justine Pila and Ansgar Ohly, *The Europeanization of Intellectual Property Law: Towards a European Legal Methodology* (OUP, 2012) 121; Christine Godt, 'Intellectual Property and European Fundamental Rights' in Hans Micklitz (ed.), *Constitutionalization of European Private Law* (OUP, 2014) 213.
5 Guido Westkamp, 'Emerging Escape Clause? Online Exhaustion, Consent and European Copyright Law' in Jan Rosen (ed.), *Intellectual Property at the Crossroad of Trade* (Edward Elgar, 2012) 43–44.
6 Case C-78/70, *Deutsche Grammophon*, EU:C:1971:59.
7 Ibid., paras 11–13.
8 Case C-62/79, *Coditel I*, EU:C:1980:84; Case C-262/81, *Coditel II*, EU:C:1982:334; Case C-158/86, *Warner Bros*, EU:C:1988:242.
9 Peter Oliver, *Free Movements of Goods in European Community* (Hart, 2003) 315.
10 Josef Drexl, *Copyright, Competition and Development, Report to the World Intellectual Property Organisation* (2016) at <www.wipo.int/export/sites/www/ip-competition/en/studies/copyright_competition_development.pdf> at 41; Estelle Derclaye, 'Abuses of Dominant Position and Intellectual Property Rights: A Suggestion to Reconcile the Community Courts Case Law' (2003) 4 *World Competition* 685.
11 Jerome Reichman, 'Legal Hybrids between the Patent and Copyright Paradigms' (1994) *Columbia Law Review* 2432.
12 Joined Cases C-241/91P and C-242/91P, *Magill*, EU:C:1995:98, para 28.
13 Ibid., para 30.
14 Case C-200/96, *Metronome Musik*, EU:C:1998:18, para 23.
15 Council Resolution of 16 November 2007 on a European Agenda for Culture, [2007] OJ C 287/1, Articles 2 and 3(b).
16 The literature on the difficult interplay between copyright and human rights is immense. Paul Torremans, *Copyright and Human Rights* (Kluwer Law International, 2004); Christophe Geiger, *Research Handbook on Intellectual Property and Human Rights* (Edward Elgar, 2015).
17 Parliament Resolution on the protection of Europe's cultural heritage, [1974] OJ C 62/5, 6, and Communication from the European Commission, 'Community Action in the Cultural Sector', COM(1977)560, at 5.
18 Ibid. This position is reiterated in the Communication from the European Commission, 'Stronger Community Action in the Cultural Sector', COM(1982)590, at 2.
19 European Commission, 'Green Paper on Copyright and the Challenge of Technology: Copyright Issues Requiring Immediate Action', COM(88)172.
20 Ibid., para 1.2.
21 Ibid., para 1.3.2.
22 Ibid., para 1.2.2–3.
23 European Commission, 'Follow-Up to the Green Paper: Working Programme of the Commission in the Field of Copyright and Neighbouring Rights', COM(90)584.
24 Ibid., at 3.
25 European Commission, 'Green Paper on Copyright and Related Rights in the Information Society', COM(95)382.
26 Ibid., paras 13–15.
27 Ibid., paras 11–12 and 47–48.

28 Council Directive 91/250/EEC of 14 May 1991 on the legal protection of computer programmes [1991] OJ L122/42, now Directive 2009/24/EC of 23 April 2009 on the legal protection of computer programmes [2009] OJ L111/22.
29 Ibid., Recitals 4–5.
30 Ibid., Recital 2.
31 Ibid., Recital 3.
32 Council Directive 92/100/EEC of 19 November 1992 on rental right and lending right and on certain rights related to copyright in the field of intellectual property, [1992] OJ L346/61.
33 Ibid., Recital 7.
34 Ibid., Recital 15.
35 Council Directive 93/98/EEC of 29 October 1993 harmonizing the term of protection of copyright and certain related rights, [1993] OJ L290/9, Recital 2.
36 Ibid., Recital 10.
37 Directive 96/9/EC of 11 March 1996 on the legal protection of databases, [1996] OJ L77/20.
38 Ibid., Recital 9.
39 Ibid.
40 Ibid., Recital 48.
41 Ibid., Recitals 7 and 11.
42 Ibid., Recital 40.
43 Ibid., Recital 41 and Article 7.
44 Directive 2001/84/EC of 27 September 2001 on the resale right for the benefit of the author of an original work of art, [2001] OJ L272/32.
45 Ibid., Recitals 3 and 13 and Article 11.
46 Ibid., Recitals 11, 14, 15.
47 Directive 2001/29/EC of 22 May 2001 on the harmonization of certain aspects of copyright and related rights in the information society, [2001] OJ L167/10 (InfoSoc Directive) Recital 20.
48 Ibid., Recital 4.
49 Ibid., Recital 2.
50 Ibid., Recital 6.
51 Ibid., Recital 11.
52 Ibid., Recital 12.
53 As in Recital 32 ('this list takes due account of the different legal traditions in Member States, while (. . .) aiming to ensure a functioning internal market').
54 Ibid., Recital 44.
55 Directive 2004/48/EC of 29 April 2004 on the enforcement of intellectual property rights, [2004] OJ L157/32 Recital 8.
56 Ibid., Recital 1.
57 Ibid., Recital 9.
58 Ibid., Recital 2.
59 Ibid.
60 Communication from the European Commission, 'Management of Copyright and Related Rights in the Internal Market', COM(2004)261, at 6; Communication from the European Commission, 'A European Agenda for Culture in a Globalizing World', COM(2007)242; Communication from the European Commission, 'Scientific Information in the Digital Age: Access, Dissemination and Preservation', COM(2007)56.
61 Communication from the European Commission, 'Creative Content Online in the Single Market', COM(2007)836.
62 European Commission, 'Green Paper on Copyright in the Knowledge Economy', COM(2008)466.
63 Ibid.

64 Ibid., para 1.2.
65 Ibid.
66 Ibid.
67 Communication from the European Commission, 'A Digital Agenda for Europe', COM(2010)245, at 7–10.
68 As in the European Commission, 'Green Paper on the Online Distribution of Audiovisual Works in the EU: Opportunities and Challenges towards a Digital Single Market', COM(2011)427, at 15–16.
69 Communication from the European Commission, 'A Single Market for Intellectual Property Rights', COM(2011)287, at 4; Communication from the European Commission, 'Trade, Growth and Intellectual Property', COM(2014)389, at 11.
70 Ibid., at 5.
71 Ibid., at 2.
72 Communication from the European Commission, 'A Digital Single Market for Europe', COM(2015)192, at 6.
73 Ibid., at 2.
74 Communication from the European Commission, 'Towards a Modern, More European Copyright Framework', COM(2015)626, stating that the intervention on EU copyright rules is justified by the need 'to overcome fragmentation and frictions within a functioning single market', and thus to 'inject more single market [. . .]into the current EU copyright rules' (Ibid., at 1).
75 Ibid., at 2.
76 Ibid.
77 Ibid.
78 Ibid., at 5.
79 Ibid., at 2.
80 Communication from the European Commission, 'Towards a Modern, More European Copyright Framework' (n 74), at 7.
81 Ibid.
82 Ibid., at 5.
83 Communication from the European Commission, 'Promoting a Fair, Efficient and Competitive European Copyright-Based Economy in the Digital Single Market', COM(2016)592, 3, at 6–7.
84 Ibid., at 10.
85 Ibid., at 3.
86 Ibid.
87 Ibid., at 7.
88 Ibid.
89 Directive 2012/28/EU of 25 October 2012 on certain permitted uses of orphan works, [2012] OJ L299/5.
90 Ibid., Recitals 22–23.
91 Ibid., Recital 14.
92 As introduced in ibid., Recital 21.
93 Ibid., Recital 18.
94 Directive 2014/26/EU of 26 February 2014 on collective management of copyright and related rights and multi-territorial licensing of rights in musical works for online use in the internal market, [2014] OJ L84/72.
95 Ibid., Recital 38.
96 Ibid., Recital 1.
97 Ibid., Recital 3.
98 Ibid.
99 Directive 2017/1564/EU on certain permitted uses of works and other subject-matter protected by copyright and related rights for the benefit of persons who are blind, visually impaired or otherwise print disabled, [2017] OJ L242/6.

100 Regulation (EU) 2017/1563 on the cross-border exchange between the Union and third countries of accessible format copies of certain works and other subject-matter protected by copyright and related rights for the benefit of persons who are blind, visually impaired or otherwise print disabled, [2017] OJ L242/1.
101 Regulation (EU) 2017/1128 of 14 June 2017 on cross-border portability of online content services in the internal market, [2017] OJ L168/1.
102 European Commission, 'Proposal for a Directive on Copyright in the Digital Single Market', COM(2016)593 (Proposal for a CDSM Directive).
103 Communication from the European Commission, 'Towards a Single Market Act: For a Highly Competitive Social Market Economy', COM(2010)608, at 1.
104 Cross-Border portability Regulation (n 101), Recital 1.
105 Marrakesh Directive, Recitals 3 and 5.
106 Proposal for a CDSM Directive (n 102), Recitals 5, 8, 15, 18 and 31.
107 Ibid., Recital 3.
108 Ibid., Recitals 1–2.
109 Ibid., Recital 10.
110 Ibid., Recital 12.
111 As reported in the Explanatory Memorandum of the European Commission 'Proposal for a Directive of the European Parliament and of the Council on Copyright in the Digital Single Market' (n 102), at 2.
112 Particularly Article 30 on the right to take part in cultural life, and the obligation to make sure that IP laws do not constitute a discriminatory barrier to access to cultural materials for persons with disabilities. The EU has been bound by the UNCRPD since January 2011 (Council Decision 2010/48/EC [2010] OJ L23/35). On the obligations arising from the Convention, Caterina Sganga, 'Disability, Right to Culture and Copyright: Which Regulatory Option?' (2015) 29 *International Review of Law, Computers and Technology* 88; Abbe Brown and Charlotte Waelde, 'Human Rights, Persons with Disabilities and Copyright' in Christophe Geiger (ed.), *Research Handbook on Human Rights and Intellectual Property* (Edward Elgar, 2015) 577.
113 Marrakesh Directive, Recital 4.
114 Ibid., Recital 5.
115 Explanatory Memorandum of Proposal for a CDSM Directive (n 111), at 2.
116 Ibid.
117 Ibid.
118 Ibid., at 3.
119 Ibid.
120 CDSM Directive (n 106), Recital 31.
121 Explanatory Memorandum of the Proposal of a CDSM Directive (n 111), at 3.
122 Ibid.
123 CDSM Directive (n 102), Recital 2.
124 Ibid., Recitals 2 and 5.
125 Ibid., Recital 19.
126 Ibid., Recitals 3 and 36.
127 Ibid., Recital 13.
128 Explanatory Memorandum of the Proposal of a CDSM Directive (n 111) at 4.
129 CDSM Directive (n 102), Article 7.
130 Explanatory Memorandum of the Proposal of a CDSM Directive (n 111), at 3.
131 The CJEU's interventions have been defined a sort of 'harmonization by stealth' by Lionel Bently, 'Harmonization by Stealth: Copyright and the ECJ' (20th Annual IP Law and Policy Conference, Fordham Law School, 2012).
132 Case C-275/06, *Promusicae*, EU:C:2007:454.
133 Ibid., para 68.

134 Case C-461/10, *Bonnier Audio*, EU:C:2012:219, para 58.
135 Case C-70/10, *Scarlet Extended*, EU:C:2011:255, para 43; Case C-360/10, *Netlog NV*, EU:C:2012:85, para 41.
136 *Scarlet Extended* (n 135), paras 43 and 53; *Netlog* (n 135), paras 45 and 51.
137 Case C-314/12, *UPC Telekabel*, EU:C:2014:192, paras 50–54.
138 Case C-484/14, *McFadden*, EU:C.2016:689, paras 148–149.
139 Matthias Leistner, 'Europe's Copyright Law decade: Recent Case Law of the European Court of Justice and Policy Perspectives' (2014) 2 *Common Market Law Review* 559.
140 Case C-201/13, *Deckmyn*, EU:C:2014:2132.
141 Case C-117/13, *Ulmer*, EU:C:2014:2196.
142 Ibid., para 27.
143 Case C-174/15, *Vereniging Openbare Bibliotheken v Stichting Leenrecht*, EU:C:2016:856.
144 WIPO Agreed Statement on Articles 6 and 7 WCT at <www.wipo.int/treaties/en/text.jsp?file_id=295456>. Similarly, Case C-135/10, *Società Consortile Fonografica*, EU:C:2012:140, para 55.
145 *VOB* (n 148), para 51.
146 Case C-301/15, *Soulier*, EU:C:2016:878.
147 Ibid., paras 49–50.
148 The statement is in line with the 'author principle' expressed in Case C-277/10, *Martin Luksan*, EU:C:2012:65, para 69.
149 Case C-572/13, *Hewlett-Packard Belgium*, EU:C:2015:750.

14 The social dimension of EU energy law

Gokce Mete and Raphael Heffron

1 Introduction

Energy is a vital resource fuelling our economy and daily lives. This extends from the micro level of heating and cooking to the macro level of transport and traffic management. Consequently, the extent to which energy is available, affordable and accessible is a fundamental issue for States, particularly due to its uneven distribution across the world. Energy infrastructure is capital and technologically intensive. It is also often immovable and considered a high-risk investment. Therefore, creating the economic conditions for the sector to consistently develop and effectively function is of paramount concern. Creating this infrastructure will however have additional consequences, and raise ancillary, but no less important issues. For example, building a hydroelectric dam may often require the resettlement of local communities, and ultimately lead to human rights abuses if carried out without fair compensation and transparent communication with residents. This will also have significant implications on the environment, human health and natural habitats, which occur at a different rate for each energy source (oil, gas, coal, wind, solar, biomass etc.), but in almost all cases, some degree of adverse impact will be registered by citizens. Hence, energy law and policy need to address environmental and human rights concerns, or, more broadly, social concerns, while ensuring security of energy supply and sustainable economic development.

Within the EU, energy is regulated at three distinct but entrenched levels: the national, European and international (i.e. EU, Energy Community[1] and international agreements/treaties). At the national level, according to Article 194 TFEU, Member States have the right to decide on the specific modalities of their energy usage, which could include unconventional or conventional hydrocarbons such as oil, gas, coal and/or low carbon energy sources such as nuclear energy and/or renewable energy. National legislation largely follows EU directives, as well as guidelines, which were introduced in the energy field starting from late 1990s, covering electricity and gas markets and the renewables sector. At the regional level, energy has been a central aspect of economic integration since the establishment of the European Coal and Steel Community in 1951. Nowadays, the TFEU allows the EU to adopt legislative measures, *inter alia*, on the functioning of the energy markets, energy security, energy efficiency and promotion of the interconnection of energy networks. At the international level, energy is regulated under international agreements that the EU and Member States have signed with non-EU countries, either to establish a cooperation framework such as under International Energy Agency,[2] Energy Charter Treaty[3] and International Atomic Energy Agency[4] or to implement a multi-jurisdictional energy project such as a cross-border hydrocarbon pipeline or transmission line. These three legislative levels are supported by soft law instruments, such as the Strategy for a Resilient Energy Union (Energy Union),[5] which has been launched to give consistency to the different spread of actions in the energy sector, and aims to ensure affordable, secure and sustainable energy for Europe and its citizens.

Against this background, this chapter aims to discuss the challenge of reconciling economic and social concerns in the EU energy law and how the continuing imbalances and injustices could be addressed in future energy policy and legislation in the realm of the EU 'social market economy'. This chapter focuses on social and economic rights regulated within the sphere of EU energy law. It addresses the energy-specific provisions of the Treaties, secondary legislation, international agreements in the field of energy and relevant soft law instruments. It is structured as follows. Section 2 will examine the EU's competences in the field of energy; section 3 will detail the way in which different socio-economic aspects of the energy sector are regulated in EU secondary legislation. Section 4 will provide a synopsis of relevant soft law instruments, laying down relevant policy frameworks for the functioning of European energy markets. Section 5 will conclude by discussing to what extent social and economic concerns are included in the field of EU energy law and how the EU pursues the objective of creating a 'highly competitive social market economy', while attempting to balance the competing aims of energy security, protection of the environment and respect for market economy principles.

2 The EU competences in the energy field: setting the scene

2.1 The energy provisions in the TFEU

Although an energy-specific provision was not included within the Treaties until the adoption of the Lisbon Treaty, the EU has exercised extensive powers in the energy field prior to this. Pre-Lisbon, the EU justified its actions in relation to energy based on alternative legal basis, such as provisions on the internal market, trans-European networks, competition and environmental protection, and this allowed the EU to develop a far-reaching framework of energy legislation.[6] Competition law, in particular, had been employed as a tool by the Commission to influence the functioning of the energy industry. Articles 101 and 102 TFEU, have been invoked on a number of cases against European energy companies, such as GDF, ENI and ENEL.[7] The first Electricity[8] and Gas Directives[9] were adopted relying on the competences on the internal market and environment in the late 1990s.

The coming into force of the Lisbon Treaty marked a new era of shared competences between the EU and Member States in the field of energy.[10] Article 194 TFEU grants powers to the EU to develop a pan-European energy policy and EU-wide energy legislation aimed at the establishment and functioning of the internal market.[11] However, it is not clear whether these powers extend to the external sphere and allow the EU to conduct a 'foreign energy policy'.[12] This may be challenging, as the existence of an external Union competence in the energy field would arguably allow for the balancing environment and climate change concerns with security of supply within the EU. While both Member States and the EU negotiated and ratified the Paris Agreement in 2016,[13] the EU could not set renewable energy targets for Member States. When it comes to security of supply, as it will be discussed further in section 5.3, the Commission exerts influence on external energy producers through an 'information exchange mechanism' which was adopted in 2012.[14]

2.2 *Social elements of energy provisions of the TFEU*

The energy provisions in the Treaty aim to balance environmental protection and related rights of EU citizens on the one hand, and to respect the national policies of Member States aimed at the security of energy supply on the other. Article 194(2) TFEU does not provide an absolute right to the Member States to determine their own energy extraction, use and supply policies, as these must align with Article 192(2)(c) TFEU on environmental protection. The latter provision requires the Council to act by unanimity when adopting environmental measures 'significantly affecting a Member State's choice between different energy sources and the general structure of its energy supply'. It is unclear whether this reference is enough to allow the EU to prohibit fossil fuel production, transport and consumption in Member States. This remains an open question, which has not been fully addressed within the case law of the CJEU to date.[15] However, Article 192 TFEU is nonetheless the legal basis for the promotion of renewable energy in the EU.

Article 107(3) TFEU, which provides for exemptions to the general prohibition of State aid.[16] In particular, Art. 107(3) allows aid 'to facilitate the development of certain economic activities within the European Union, where such aid does not adversely affect trading conditions to an extent contrary to the common interest', facilitating renewable energy projects by extension. The Guidelines on State aid for environmental protection and energy[17] set out the conditions under which aid for energy and environment may be justified as is explained later. State aid exemptions have helped renewable energy to penetrate the market and to achieve EU environmental targets to date, but as will be discussed below, the varied implementation of the Commission's guidelines by Member States have resulted in a number of conflicts brought before the CJEU. In fact, in some instances, national renewable energy support schemes have created market barriers for renewables, and undertakings complained that such schemes are implemented in a way that is inconsistent with the free movement of goods principle.[18] One of the most relevant cases was *Ålands Vindkraft AB v Energimyndigheten*,[19] in which the CJEU decided that a wind-farm investor located in Finland was not allowed to receive a green certificate in Sweden for the electricity exported there. The Court found that, despite being connected to the Swedish grid, the wind-farm in Finland could not benefit from the Swedish green energy subsidies as it did not extend beyond the Member State border. As it will be analysed later in this chapter, another concern arising from the application of Article 107(3) TFEU, is that, in Member States where the cost of subsidies are passed onto the consumers, energy prices have increased beyond the market price.

3 Social elements of the secondary legislation

3.1 Preliminary remarks

The development of the EU energy market mirrors the development of the internal market. In the energy sector, the free movement translates into the objective of energy freely flowing without barriers across borders, and consumer services delivered in an open and competitive environment to the benefit of European citizens. The EU legislative and policy objectives in the energy sphere, since the early 1990s, focused on opening up markets, the creation of a single energy market and providing uninterrupted, affordable and sustainable energy to consumers.

The current energy policy places consumers at the centre of the energy system in a more robust way than ever before.[20] The 2011 'Third Energy Package' deepens the organisation of the EU internal energy market, including the reinforcement of national regulatory authorities and introduces a new set of measures to tackle market concentration, which brings greater transparency and coordination, and equal access to energy facilities.[21] The package consists of two Directives and three Regulations.[22] The Gas and Electricity Directives make reference to the Member States objectives of social and economic cohesion, with respect to public service requirements, which is a fundamental tenet of these Directives. The preambles acknowledge the need for Member States to create adequate economic incentives and tools to include liability mechanisms to guarantee the necessary investment, while at the same time providing common minimum standards in delivering public service obligations. These common standards include objectives of common protection, security of supply, environmental protection and equivalent levels of competition in all Member States. However, each Member State retains the right to interpret what it considers to be its own national public service requirements as per its national circumstances.[23] The preambles confirm the rights of EU consumers to access to energy at reasonable, non-discriminatory and transparent tariffs.[24] The Electricity Directive calls Member States to integrate social policies and energy efficiency improvements for housing in measures adopted in order to achieve the energy legislation's objectives.[25] Consumers should also have the right to be properly informed regarding the cost of energy and their energy consumption in an effective and timely manner, in order to encourage energy savings and to allow them to choose from a range of competitive suppliers.

3.2 Social 'elements' in the 'Third Energy Package'

After the brief overview provided above, the following subsections discuss the 'social elements' included in the 'Third Energy Package' and focus on specific aspects related to the pursuit of non-market goals or directly connected to the protection of rights which can be broadly qualified as 'social rights'.[26]

3.2.1 Unbundling

In order to open the electricity and gas wholesale markets to new entrants, the 'Third Energy Package' requires companies to unbundle along vertical and horizontal lines. Unbundling supply from transportation/transmission and production/generation creates distinct markets, where participants can minimise price and supply risks. Unbundling does, however, increase transaction risks due to increased number of stakeholders along the energy value chain, but ultimately spot markets act as intermediaries to promote efficient pricing and minimise transaction costs, which ultimately favour consumers.

Unbundling is exercised in practice through a certification procedure for transmission system operators (TSOs),

Ownership unbundling has been subject to legal debate within the case law of the CJEU since its inception in 2012. In a number of cases, it was alleged that OU breaches Article 345 TFEU on the right to peaceful enjoyment of property in Member States and Article 63 TFEU (on the free movement of capital).[27] The Court's position is that restrictions to the free movement of capital are justified by public interest in achieving transparency in energy markets and the prevention of distortions of competition, provided that these measures are appropriate and proportionate.[28]

3.2.2 Third party access

Separating generation and supplier interest from transmission functions creates a level playing field for different supply companies. A competitive market requires network access to be non-discriminatory, transparent and fairly priced. Article 32 of both the Electricity and the Gas Directives aim to ensure that the access regime, including circumstances that tolerate denial of access to the transmission/transport network, is non-discriminatory and based on published tariffs to EU citizens.[29] The TSOs are required to provide access to the available capacity in the network for eligible suppliers/shippers. According to Article 13 of the Gas Regulation, Member States may elect to apply market-based tariffs or empower their National Regulatory Authorities (NRAs) to approve tariffs proposed by relevant TSOs.

This access regime is mandatory in principle and covers electricity transmission and distribution systems, gas transport and distribution pipelines, LNG facilities, gas storage facilities and line-pack.[30] Companies from third countries acquiring control of the transmission system or the TSOs should also comply with the unbundling, tariffs and third party access rules.[31] Access to the network can only be denied on the basis of lack of capacity, public service obligations, force majeure or serious economic and financial difficulties with a take-or-pay contract.[32] Undertakings can apply for an exemption from these rules, for major new infrastructure and for significant increases of existing capacity.[33]

3.2.3 Protection of vulnerable consumers

As the disciplines of unbundling and third party access demonstrate, consumer interests are at the heart of the secondary legislative packages, which impose a central responsibility on energy undertakings to provide quality of service.[34] Public service requirements are a vital part of the Electricity and Gas Directives.[35] Member States can determine the scope of public service obligations to be delivered in their jurisdiction at the national level. However, they should provide common minimum standards taking into account the objectives of consumer protection, security of supply, environmental protection and equivalent levels of competition.[36] Public service obligations should be performed in a transparent and non-discriminatory manner and shall comply with the requirements of State aid.[37]

The preamble of the Electricity and Gas Directives also highlights the importance of consumers' access to their rights in relation to the energy sector, and requires general consumer rights be clearly set out in the national laws of the Member States.[38] This is particularly important for the protection of vulnerable consumers, who are living in energy poverty, and those who find it difficult to obtain or assimilate information and report problems when comparing and switching deals. The 'Third Energy Package' also requires governments to develop national action plans to ensure the necessary energy supply for vulnerable consumers.[39] The latter are defined differently in each Member State, due to the diverse national circumstances, and only less than a quarter of these national legislations explicitly acknowledge the concept of energy poverty.[40] A 2015 study undertaken by the Commission found that around 11% of the EU's population (circa 54 million people) are not able to adequately heat or provide other required energy services in their homes at an affordable cost, 'due to rising energy prices, recessionary impacts on national and regional economies, and poor energy efficient homes', particularly in Central Eastern and Southern Europe.[41] This study found that increased liberalisation might counterweight energy poverty and enhance protection of vulnerable consumers, as it leads to more transparency in terms of price comparisons, consumption and cost of energy.[42] Indeed, the purpose of 'promoting fair competition and easy access for different suppliers' is defined as enabling consumers to take full advantage of the opportunities of a liberalised internal market in energy.[43]

3.2.4 *Subsidies and cost of energy*

Information on energy prices and the cost of energy is also vital for the protection of consumers. Today, around three quarters of the EU's energy consumption comes from fossil fuels,[44] which are used in the generation of electricity, space heating and transport and within the industry. Consumers may be aware of the price of fossil fuels but are often poorly informed about the subsidies applied to them, which alter the actual cost of energy.[45]

In the EU, up to €200 billion is spent on fossil fuel subsidies per year.[46] Removal of such subsidies would lift the strain on their budgets, lead to lower CO2 emissions and rebalance inequalities in the society as subsidies benefit the wealthy, while limiting access to affordable energy sources by vulnerable consumers. Subsidies also stand against market competitiveness for low carbon industries such as renewable energy and energy efficiency. Thus, the transition to a low carbon economy is slowed down by subsidies, resulting in adverse impact on public health due to increased air pollution.[47] The EU legislation requires State aid for uncompetitive coal mines to be phased-out at the end of 2018,[48] and the EU position is to support phasing-out of all subsidies for environmentally harmful fossil fuels by 2020. However, there is no binding legislation to achieve the latter objective. The targets are set out merely in soft law instruments.[49] This is because energy pricing is a sensitive issue for most governments. Significant increases in energy prices as a result of overnight removal of subsidies could have a detrimental impact on low income groups of the society. There may also be considerations of international competitiveness and effects on inflation. Therefore, governments have been wary of the potential electoral implications of subsidy reform.[50] In the current setting, sceptics do not expect European economies to switch to a low carbon economy without some financial support from the public budget.[51] However, fossil fuels will be the target of an upcoming revised version of the EU Energy Taxation Directive, which is expected to propose minimum tax rates on energy and CO2 content across the EU.[52] The issue of the removal of subsidies has also been referred in the Clean Energy Package of 2016,[53] which aims to step up the Union's action in removing inefficient fossil fuel subsidies in line with international commitments under G7 and G20 and in the Paris Agreement.[54]

3.2.5 *Security of supply*

Since its inception, EU energy policy has evolved around three interrelated pillars: energy security, efficiency and sustainability,[55] with energy security being at the core of long-term market planning and lawmaking. This is due to the EU's dependency on imported energy, with 90% of its crude oil and 66% of its natural gas being imported. Most of the world's largest hydrocarbon resources are located in politically unstable regions and there have been major supply cuts in the past, *inter alia*, as a result of inter-State conflict in producing and/or transit countries, political tensions, commercial disputes, infrastructure failure and terrorist attacks.

The traditional meaning of energy security, hence, implies supply security. Nowadays, the definition of energy security has expanded to encapsulate demand-side measures, such as energy conservation measures capable of achieving significant energy savings. The principle of supply security within the Gas Directive is focused on maintaining a spirit of solidarity between the Member States and the establishment of greater regional cooperation, both of which require further integration of national markets through physical interconnections and price convergence.[56]

A specific Security of Gas Supply Regulation[57] was adopted in 2010 to implement the above-mentioned objectives of the Gas Directive. This Regulation establishes an infrastructure requirement known as the N-1 standard. This requires Member States to demonstrate that they can ensure security of supply in the event of disruption of supply of its larger single gas infrastructure. Furthermore, Member States are compelled to enable physical reverse flows in pipeline interconnections between them, to adopt emergency plans and identify risk mitigation measures. In addition, their national competent authorities and natural gas undertakings have to ensure protected consumers are supplied with natural gas even under severe conditions.[58]

In the electricity sector, 'security' means both security of supply and provision of electricity, and technical safety.[59] Security of electricity supply is fundamental for the development of European society, the implementation of a sustainable climate change policy and the fostering of competitiveness within the internal market.[60] Member States are required to adopt measures that create adequate economic incentives for the maintenance and construction of the necessary network infrastructure, including interconnection capacity in order to secure the supply of all energy sources at the most competitive prices to consumers.[61] They have to implement policies that balance the objectives of demand-side management measures to combat climate change and of objectives of investment facilitation to send right signals for network capacity development to meet the demand.[62]

A stress test carried out in 2014 found that a prolonged supply disruption would have a substantial impact on the EU.[63] In a strategy document developed in response to the stress test, the Commission recommended, *inter alia*, increasing energy efficiency and reaching the proposed 2030 energy and climate goals through developing renewable energies as long-term measures to address these security of supply challenges.[64] Diversification of energy supplies is also a long-term strategy of the EU to prevent another energy supply crisis.

3.2.6 Environmental protection

The relationship of security of supply and environmental protection and sustainability, which can be considered at the core of a 'social market economy',[65] is problematic. The policy objectives are contradictory, even though interrelated. As such, the environmental dimension of the EU's energy policy and law is gaining increasing importance. It is acknowledged that enduring strategies need to be adopted to establish and to withstand a sustainable, resource efficient and low carbon economy.[66] In 2010, the Commission set the 2020 EU agenda for competitive, sustainable and secure energy.[67] This Communication stipulated that a new set of rules needed to be adopted to clearly identify the essential energy infrastructure with European interest to achieve the objectives of these three pillars. The proposed rules include an improved permitting procedure in line with the environmental legislation.

The Commission also updated the 2008 Guidelines on State aid for environmental protection in 2014, as part of the European agenda to modernise State aid and to take environmental protection and sustainability objectives one-step further.[68] These revised Guidelines integrate environmental protection measures with the public financing of energy sector. It specifies under which conditions State aid for energy and environment may be considered compatible with Article 107(3)(c) TFEU. The purpose of the Guidelines is, *inter alia*, to mitigate potential distortions to competition caused by previous support schemes for renewable energy sources, hence as a first step it obliterates the feed-in tariffs (purchase guarantee at fixed price) to encourage renewable energy producers to participate in the market.[69] The aid is still allowed but as a premium added to the market price and such State aid could only be granted based on a competitive bidding procedure.[70] The Guidelines facilitate the 2020 objective of promotion of sustainable, smart and inclusive growth in a competitive internal market and streamlines the administrative process for decision-making.[71]

3.2.7 The fight against climate change

Energy and climate change legislation has existed in Europe in some form since the 1990s.[72] However, more robust action has been taken since the launch of the 'Climate and Energy Package' in 2009.[73] This package introduces legally binding 20–20–20 targets for gradual reduction of greenhouse gas (GHG) emissions. The three key targets of the package are: 20% cut in GHG emissions (from 1990 levels); 20% of EU energy from renewables; and 20% improvement in energy efficiency. Currently, the EU is determining the 2030 energy and climate targets. The 'Clean Energy for All' legislative package proposed a new set of legislation to take the climate change agenda a step further post-2020, and to place gradual targets for reduction of GHG emissions up to 2050.[74]

The Energy and Climate Change package also introduced an EU emissions trading system (ETS), as an instrument for the reduction of GHG emissions from large industrial facilities, aviation sector and power plants. The EU ETS places a monetary value on carbon to create incentives for these industries to revert to the most effective emission reductions and to invest in lower carbon technologies.[75]

There are national commitments by Member States, under the 'Efforts Sharing Decision', to reduce emissions from housing, agriculture, waste and transport sectors. These targets vary as per national welfare of each country and their progress is monitored very closely by the Commission through a reporting mechanism.[76] Furthermore, as part of this package, Member States have agreed to binding national targets for raising the share of renewables in their energy consumption by 2020. The Renewable Energy Directive stipulates that these targets are determined as per each Member State's national starting point for renewable energy production and ability to raise its share.[77]

3.2.8 *Energy efficiency*

The EU's 20% energy savings target will broadly equate with the closure of 400 power stations. To facilitate this objective, measures for increasing energy efficiency are adopted at the EU level as part of the 2020 agenda. Energy efficiency has benefits beyond energy savings and the reduction of GHG emissions. It is a fundamental resource for economic and social development. Energy efficiency fuels sustainability of the energy system, makes indoor environments healthier, fosters industrial productivity, leads to growth in employment and betters public balance sheets.[78] However, the benefits of energy efficiency must outweigh the costs. Therefore, the EU energy efficiency policy focuses primarily on sectors where these efficiencies can be more readily achieved and show a demonstrable impact, such as buildings. The Energy Efficiency Plan[79] of 2011 identifies the EU strategy for promotion of a low carbon system, which improves the EU's supply security by decreasing its energy dependency. The EU Energy Efficiency Directive stipulates that of binding measures are to be set in order to help the EU meet its 20% energy efficiency target.[80] There rules require the Member States to establish tri-annual National Energy Efficiency Action Plans (NEEAPs), which are to demonstrate their estimated energy consumption, planned energy efficiency measures and the improvements achieved. These individual energy efficiency targets could be calculated on the basis of primary or final energy consumption, primary or final energy savings, or energy intensity.[81]

In 2016, the Commission proposed a revision of the Energy efficiency Directive to reset the target for 2030.[82] Previously, the European Council agreed to a 27% energy efficiency target for 2030. The proposals recommend a 30% binding target for 2030 which could result in a €4.5–8.3 billion reduction in the cost of pollution control and health damage, 12% decline in gas imports and an approximately €70 billion increase in GDP. Other proposals on energy efficiency include improving the energy performance of products, informing consumers and a smart finance for buildings proposal.

3.3 *New perspectives: the 'Clean Energy Package'*

In November 2016, the Commission released the 'Clean Energy for All Europeans' proposals,[83] which provide the principles of post-2020 regulatory framework. This 'Clean Energy Package' was presented to the Parliament and Council as a political priority, in order to follow up the Paris Agreement. These proposals are notable in the context of this analysis and of this volume because they inextricably integrate market and non-market objectives. They put forward a strong and robust push for energy transitions and, *inter alia*, include: a revision of the Renewable Energy Directive,[84] particularly the design of support schemes and administrative procedures; a revision of the Energy Efficiency Directive,[85] aimed at setting up a 30% energy efficiency target by 2030 and simplify calculation of energy savings; a revision of the Energy Efficiency of Buildings Directive,[86] to lift electric vehicle uptake, fast-track building renovation and decarbonisation of housing stock. The package also includes a Communication on Accelerating Clean Energy Innovation,[87] which highlights the contribution of financial instruments on lowering new technology risks and how to better target research and innovation funding and a revised Electricity Market Design and Security of Supply,[88] setting out principles, *inter alia*, for balancing markets, priority dispatch, network access chargers and national capacity mechanisms.

The 'Clean Energy Package' proposals give signals on the Commission's objective to lead the energy transition for all European citizens and at a global level. Consumers are placed firmly at the centre of this package, and fighting energy poverty is among its primary objectives. The whole bulk of the proposals aim to increase transparency and improve the current regulatory framework to provide a fair deal for consumers, allowing a better choice of supply, access to reliable energy price comparison tools and the possibility to produce and sell their own electricity.[89] Full participation of consumers in the market will necessitate a better connection between retail and wholesale markets and an attractive investment climate to provide incentives for development of new technologies by both producers and consumers.[90]

4 Social elements in soft law instruments

The EU energy policy objectives are pursued not only through legislation, but also through soft law instruments. These are considered in this section, focusing on how social concerns have been addressed by them.

4.1 The 'Energy Union'

The Energy Union project, which is 'A Framework Strategy for a Resilient Energy Union with a Forward-Looking Climate Change Policy', was launched in 2015. It has five pillars; energy security, solidarity and trust, a fully integrated internal energy market, energy efficiency, climate action, decarbonising the economy, research, innovation and competitiveness.[91] This Energy Union package promotes access to affordable energy, effective regulation, and increased competition, building investor confidence, the identification of long-term energy needs and exploration of advanced energy technologies. It aims to remove market barriers, terminating isolation of small energy islands and increase the coordination of national policies. The underlying motivation from an energy security perspective is to reduce the susceptibility of Member States and their citizens to external shocks, interruptions and disruptions.[92] The underlying philosophy that is repeatedly stressed is 'working together on security of supply'.[93] Innovation, technology, competitiveness, research and development are elements of energy security that are intertwined in the Energy Union package.

Above all, the ultimate goal of the Energy Union is to accelerate the transition and modernisation of the European economy towards a low carbon, efficient and socially fair system, and which ultimately benefits Europe's citizens and businesses. Consumer empowerment and protection is placed at the centre of this energy transition. Since the launch of the Energy Union, there had been some progress, with an increasing number of consumers actively participating in the market, a rise in solar photovoltaic capacities on private houses, a greater number of renewable energy companies and higher switching rates.[94] However, energy prices remained high in 2017, and the need to introduce new measures to address energy poverty and the protection of vulnerable consumers persists. The New Electricity Market Design Proposal mentioned earlier aims to tackle this growing problem.

The Energy Union opens up opportunities for European companies by virtue of its strong support for new technologies and business models aimed at realising a low carbon economy. Boosting European companies' international competitiveness requires a robust external dimension in terms of energy diplomacy, in order to expand exports of European low carbon technology solutions. A resilient external dimension is also important in fostering climate change diplomacy, as well as leading the global energy transition. Security of supply is also a key ingredient of the external aspect of the Energy Union, by building a strong solidarity and trust among the Member States.

4.2 The Energy Trilemma

As the previous section has shown, the objectives of EU energy policy and law include multiple, interrelated and sometimes contradictory, aims arising from the economic-environment-energy security nexus. Finding the appropriate balance between these different goals for the benefit of European consumers is not an easy task. This is a challenge faced not only by the EU level but at the global level. The World Energy Council therefore came up with terminology to define these dimensions and a methodology to tackle them in its Energy Trilemma Index.

The Energy Trilemma Index ranks countries' energy performance to achieve energy sustainability around the world and provides a framework to benchmark progress. Energy sustainability is considered to be based on three core tenets: energy security, energy equity and environmental sustainability.[95] The 2016 Energy Trilemma Index found that the key to success is in balancing efforts to resource productivity and manage energy demand growth. Member States of the EU had the highest scores in the 2016 assessments; however, energy transitions carry the risk of disrupting energy security and the affordability of energy in Europe if not managed appropriately. A particularly worrisome concern is higher prices on energy. This has to be addressed through strong policies which improve the energy market design, the establishment of regional markets, development of demand management and design of an effective carbon price.[96]

The Third Energy Package does not incorporate conflicting aims of the economic-environment-energy security nexus properly.[97] The Commission instead brings a greater focus on the nexus via policy instruments such as the Energy Union strategy. Currently, just one of those three issues – economics, politics and the environment – dominates the energy agenda; and more often than not, it is economic market-driven policy that has dominated. However, the environmental dimension has gained greater traction in recent times. In essence, effective and efficient energy law and policy will balance these three aims to deliver the best outcome for society.[98]

5 Concluding remarks and future developments

The analysis conducted in this chapter has attempted to highlight that achieving sustainable, competitive and yet 'socially conscious' energy markets requires the balancing of different economic, environmental and political issues. While the analysis contained in the earlier sections portrays a variety of mixed messages emanating from the EU, there are several developments that have the potential to introduce a more social approach to the EU energy market, which has yet to be fully realised.

5.1 The transition to a low carbon economy

The transition to a low carbon economy, which ensures a sustainable development, is already happening within the EU. The 'Clean Energy Package' proposal underlines the EU's commitments to accelerate the transition and implementation of the Paris Agreement. This is a welcome step, as data from 2015 shows that 72.5% of all energy in the EU-28 was still produced from fossil sources.[99] The switch to low carbon technologies is not easy, as the ultimate benefits will be felt in the long term and may not display immediate benefits for either producers or the consumer. Often governments fear electoral reprisal over rising costs and the risk of lights going out. Leadership and tailor-made support and assistance to regions in transition are therefore key to make it a reality. The EU's support includes providing funds and technical assistance on research on the economic strengths of Member States in making the transition.

The 'Transition' focuses on energy use across the entire energy value chain. There is global consensus that the circular economy (i.e. from cradle to grave) perspective should be an integral part of low carbon transitions and the climate change agenda.[100] The circular economy keeps materials and products in the system through regeneration and restoration until they lose their highest value. Recycling and waste prevention can lead to significant energy savings and the reduction of GHG emissions, as recycling of materials produces less energy than the production of raw materials. The Commission adopted an EU Action Plan for the Circular Economy[101] and a recent Communication on the Role of

Waste-To-Energy, the latter of which provides measures that could lead up to 29% energy savings, recovered from waste.[102]

Empowering people is the engine of the Union's energy transitions strategy. The Clean Energy Package facilitates consumers taking an active role within the Energy Market, or to produce energy directly through local communities, for instance through crowdfunding.[103] The Communication, 'Accelerating Clean Energy Innovation', supports European businesses, start-ups and public entities in boosting their research into additional clean energy solutions. Employment linked to the green economy is already above 4 million full-time equivalents. The business case for transformative results of low carbon economy is, in many respects, already proven.[104]

As the EU modernises and digitalises its economy ensuring the cyber-security and privacy of smart-metering systems is a challenge.[105] The Communication on the second State of the Energy Union acknowledges the imminent need for robust data protection rules and strengthening synergies between the Energy Union and the Digital Single Market.[106] Ultimately, it is the citizens who should take ownership of the energy transition process, as today the policy and legislative framework at large provides the recipe for a successful and socially fair transformation.[107]

5.2 *Energy justice in a 'social market economy'*

Energy justice is a concept that could align the EU energy sector to the goal of a 'social market economy' envisaged in Article 3(3) TEU. In essence, energy justice seeks to apply human rights across the energy life-cycle and it is feeding slowly into policy making.[108] It aims to address the inequalities that exist in the energy sector. For example, there are still over 50 million people in Europe who live at the risk of energy poverty and high energy prices persist. In fact, electricity prices for household consumers have increased continuously from the first half of 2010 to date.[109] Energy justice informs on society's decision on which energy source would be more just for a society to build. It provides a decision-making and policy toolkit, the Energy Justice Metric (EJM), to enable energy policy makers to balance the competing aims of economics, politics and the environment (energy trilemma).[110] This relatively new concept provides for an interdisciplinary framework to identify when and where injustices occur and how best law and policy can respond.[111] By applying EJM into energy policy, decision-makers are able to measure, allocate and distribute the full costs and benefits of new energy infrastructure in a just and equitable method for current and future generations. The principled approach of energy justice is based on eight core principles: availability, affordability, due process, transparency and accountability, sustainability, intra-generational equity, inter-generational equity and responsibility.[112] Advocates of the energy justice concept foresee its practical application particularly in the course of environmental impact assessment and their monitoring and when a social-license-to-operate is sought. This goes beyond the strictly legal license but refers to the principle that energy projects should provide support to, or encourage, beneficial externalities while mitigating or offsetting any negative externalities and address national plans and priorities once these emerge to demonstrate responsiveness to the legitimate interests of the citizens.[113] The EJM captures the energy sector as it moves throughout the energy life-cycle with an aim to restore equality in eventual outcomes in the energy sector.

The 2008 European Security Strategy referred to energy as 'artery of the European economy'.[114] Indeed, social and economic impacts of EU law in the field of energy are felt strongly by EU citizens and will continue to be so in particular in relation to the transition to a low carbon economy, due to the benefits attached to the transformation (enhanced quality of life, job creation and social inclusion) and the magnitude of risks of failure. In order to reap the full advantages, the transition has to happen swifter, cheaper and be powered by people[115] and the energy sector is in need of a fundamental shift to promote a more social dimension to energy activities and operations.

Notes

1 The Energy Community is an international organisation consisting of the EU and the countries of Albania, Bosnia and Herzegovina, Georgia, the former Yugoslav Republic of Macedonia, Kosovo, Moldova, Montenegro, Serbia and Ukraine.
2 The International Energy Agency (IEA) is an autonomous organisation that works to ensure reliable, affordable and clean energy for its 29 member countries.
3 The Energy Charter Treaty is an international agreement that establishes a multilateral framework for cross-border cooperation in the energy industry.
4 The International Atomic Energy Agency is an international organisation that seeks to promote the peaceful use of nuclear energy, and to inhibit its use for any military purpose, including nuclear weapons at <www.iaea.org/>.
5 Communication from the European Commission, 'A Framework Strategy for a Resilient Energy Union with a Forward-Looking Climate Change Policy', COM(2015)80.
6 For instance, Articles 81–88, 95, 154–156 and 175 of the Treaty of Nice, Amending the Treaty on European Union, the Treaties Establishing the European Communities and Certain Related Acts, [2001] OJ C 80/01.
7 Case COMP/38.662, *Gas De France v ENI* and *ENEL*.
8 Directive 96/92/EC of the European Parliament and of the Council of 19 December 1996 concerning common rules for the internal market in electricity, [1997] OJ L 027.
9 Directive 1998/30/EC of the European Parliament and of the Council of 22 June 1998 concerning common rules for the internal market in natural gas, [1998] OJ L 204.
10 Article 4(2)(i) TFEU.
11 ClientEarth, 'The impact of the Lisbon Treaty on Climate and Energy Policy: An Environmental Perspective January' (2010) at <www.clientearth.org/reports/clientearth-briefing-lisbon-treaty-impact-on-climate-and-energy-policy.pdf>.
12 Johann-Christian Pielow and Britta Lewendel, 'The EU Energy Policy after the Lisbon Treaty' in André Dorsman *et al.* (eds.), *Financial Aspects in Energy* (Springer, 2011) 147.
13 Paris Agreement signature status at <https://treaties.un.org/Pages/ViewDetails.aspx?src=TREATY&mtdsg_no=XXVII-7-d&chapter=27&lang=_en&clang=_en>.
14 Decision No 994/2012/EU of The European Parliament and of The Council of 25 October 2012 establishing an information exchange mechanism with regard

to intergovernmental agreements between Member States and third countries in the field of energy.

15 For a detailed debate on the relationship between Article 194 and 192 TFEU, Thea Sveen, 'The Interaction between Article 192 and 194 TFEU' (2014) *MarIus* 157.

16 Article 107(1) TFEU; Delia Ferri and Juan Jorge Piernas Lopez, 'State Aid Law in a Social Market Economy', in this volume.

17 Communication from the European Commission, 'Guidelines on State Aid for Environmental Protection and Energy 2014–2020', [2014] OJ C 200/1.

18 Stephen Tindale, *State Aid for Energy: Climate Action Is More Important Than the Single Market*, Centre for European Reform (2015) at <www.cer.eu/sites/default/files/publications/attachments/pdf/2015/State_aid_for_energy_sct_22.02.15-10650.pdf>.

19 Case C-573/12, *Ålands Vindkraft*, EU:C:2014:2037.

20 European Commission, 'Fact Sheet, State of the Energy Union: Questions and Answers' (2015) at <http://europa.eu/rapid/press-release_MEMO-15-6106_en.htm>.

21 Inge Bernaerts, 'The Internal Energy Market: Practical Priorities for the Commission' in Jean-Michel Glachant, Adrien de Hauteclocque and Nicole Ahner (eds.), *EU Energy Law & Policy Yearbook 2012* (Claeys and Casteels, 2013) 37.

22 Directive 2009/72/EC of the European Parliament and of the Council of 13 July 2009 concerning common rules for the internal market in electricity and repealing Directive 2003/54/EC, [2009] OJ L211 (Electricity Directive), Directive 2009/73/EC of the European Parliament and of the Council of 13 July 2009 concerning common rules for the internal market in natural gas and repealing Directive 2003/55/EC, [2009] OJ L 211 (Gas Directive), Regulation (EC) No 714/2009 of the European Parliament and of the Council of 13 July 2009 on conditions for access to the network for cross-border exchanges in electricity and repealing Regulation (EC) No 1228/2003, [2009] OJ L 211 (Electricity Regulation), Regulation (EC) No 715/2009 of the European Parliament and of the Council of 13 July 2009 on conditions for access to the natural gas transmission networks and repealing Regulation (EC) No 1775/2005, [2009] OJ L 211 (Gas Regulation) and Regulation (EC) No 713/2009 of the European Parliament and of the Council of 13 July 2009 establishing an Agency for the Cooperation of Energy Regulators, [2009] OJ L 211.

23 Gas Directive (n 22), Preamble paras 44–47; Electricity Directive (n 22), Preamble paras 46–48.

24 Gas Directive (n 22), Preamble para 23; Electricity Directive (n 22), Preamble para 32.

25 Electricity Directive (n 22), Preamble para 53.

26 Delia Ferri and Fulvio Cortese, 'Introduction', in this volume.

27 Kim Talus, *Introduction to EU Energy Law* (OUP, 2016) 100.

28 Joined Cases C-105/12 to C-107/12, *Staat der Nederlanden v Essent NV (C-105/12), Essent Nederland BV (C-105/12), Eneco Holding NV (C-106/12) and Delta NV (C-107/12)*, EU:C:2013:677, para 68.

29 Gas Directive (n 22), Articles 32–35.

30 Ibid., Article 34.

31 Ibid., Article 11.

32 Ibid., Article 35; Electricity Directive (n 22), Article 32(2).

33 Gas Directive (n 22), Article 36.

34 Gas Directive (n 22), Preamble para 48; Electricity Directive (n 22), para 51.

35 Ibid., Articles 3.

36 Case C-439/06, *Energy Management Proceedings Citiworks AG*, ECLI:EU:C:2008:298, para 26.

37 Communication from the European Commission, 'European Union Framework for State Aid in the form of Public Service Compensation', [2011] OJ C 8, at 15–22; Case C-280/00 *Altmark*, EU:C:2002:188.
38 Gas and Electricity Directives (n 22), Preamble para 46.
39 Gas Directive (n 22), Preamble para 50; Electricity Directive (n 22), para 53.
40 Steve Pye *et al.*, *Energy Poverty and Vulnerable Consumers in the Energy Sector Across the EU: Analysis of Policies and Measures* (Report Commissioned by the European Commission in 2015) at <www.innoenergy.com/wp-content/uploads/2016/03/INSIGHT_E_PR2_Energy-Poverty-Main-Report.pdf> at 5.
41 Ibid.
42 Ibid., at 55.
43 Gas Directive (n 22), Preamble para 54.
44 European Commission, 'Fossil Fuels' (2015) *Eurostat data* at <http://ec.europa.eu/eurostat/web/environmental-data-centre-on-natural-resources/natural-resources/energy-resources/fossil-fuels>.
45 European Commission, *Energy Prices and Costs in Europe*, SWD(2016)420 at <https://ec.europa.eu/energy/sites/ener/files/documents/com_2016_769.en_.pdf>.
46 Frans Oosterhuis *et al.*, *Enhancing Comparability of Data on Estimated Budgetary Support and Tax Expenditures for Fossil Fuels: Final Report* (2014) at <http://ec.europa.eu/environment/enveco/taxation/pdf/201412ffs_final_report.pdf>.
47 Directorate General for Internal Policies Policy Department A, 'Economic and Scientific Policy Fossil Fuel Subsidies In-Depth Analysis' (2017) at <www.europarl.europa.eu/RegData/etudes/IDAN/2017/595372/IPOL_IDA(2017)595372_EN.pdf>.
48 Council Decision of 10 December 2010 on State aid to facilitate the closure of uncompetitive coal mines, 2010/787/EU, [2010] OJ L 336/24.
49 Joint Statement by the Council and the Representatives of the Governments of the Member States, 'New European Consensus on Development, "Our World, Our Dignity, Our Future"' (2017) at <https://ec.europa.eu/europeaid/sites/devco/files/european-consensus-on-development-final-20170626_en.pdf> at 23; Communication from the European Commission, 'Europe 2020 Strategy', COM(2010)2020.
50 Directorate General for Internal Policies: Policy Department A, 'Economic and Scientific Policy Fossil Fuel Subsidies In-Depth Analysis' (n 47).
51 Stephen Tindale, 'State Aid for Energy: Climate Action Is More Important Than the Single Market' (2015) at <www.cer.eu/sites/default/files/publications/attachments/pdf/2015/State_aid_for_energy_sct_22.02.15-10650.pdf> at 3.
52 European Commission, 'Revision of the Energy Taxation Directive: Questions and Answers' (2011) *Press Release Database MEMO/11/238* at <http://europa.eu/rapid/press-release_MEMO-11-238_en.htm?locale=en>.
53 Communication from the European Commission, 'Clean Energy for All Europeans', COM(2016)0860.
54 Directorate General for Internal Policies: Policy Department A, 'Economic and Scientific Policy Fossil Fuel Subsidies In-Depth Analysis' (n 53).
55 Communication from the European Commission, 'Second Strategic Energy Review: An EU Energy Security and Solidarity Action plan', COM(2008)0781.
56 Gas Directive (n 22), Preamble para 55–58.
Regulation (EU) No 994/2010 of the European Parliament and of the Council of 20 October 2010 concerning measures to safeguard security of gas supply and repealing Council Directive 2004/67/EC Text with EEA relevance, [2010] OJ L 295; Gas Directive (n 22), Preamble paras 55–58.
57 Regulation (EU) No 994/2010 of the European Parliament and of the Council of 20 October 2010 concerning measures to safeguard security of gas supply and

repealing Council Directive 2004/67/EC Text with EEA relevance, [2010] OJ L 295 (Security of Gas Supply Regulation).

58 Severe conditions are defined as either a 7-day temperature peak (statistical probability of once in 20 years); or at least 30 days of exceptionally high demand (same statistical probability); or at least 30 days without the single largest infrastructure working, under average winter conditions, Article 8 of Gas Security of Supply Regulation (n 57).

59 Electricity Directive (n 22), Article 2.

60 Ibid., Preamble para 5.

61 Ibid., Article 3.

62 Ibid., Preamble para 10 and Article 6.

63 European Commission, 'Gas Stress Test: Cooperation Is Key to Cope with Supply Interruption' (2014) *Press Release Database* at <http://europa.eu/rapid/press-release_IP-14-1162_en.htm>.

64 Communication from the European Commission, 'European Energy Security Strategy', COM(2014)0330.

65 Ferri and Cortese, 'Introduction' (n 26).

66 Emanuela Orlando, 'The Evolution of EU Legislation and Policy in the Environmental Field: Achievements and Current Challenges' in Christine Bakker and Francesco Francioni (eds.), *The EU, the US and Global Climate Governance* (Ashgate, 2014) 61.

67 Communication from the European Commission, 'Energy 2020: A Strategy for Competitive, Sustainable and Secure Energy', COM(2010)639.

68 Communication from the European Commission, 'Guidelines on State Aid for Environmental Protection and Energy 2014–2020' (n 17).

69 Ibid., para 124.

70 Ibid., para 20.

71 European Network of Environmental Law Organisations, 'New Guidelines on Environmental and Energy State Aid for 2014–2020' (2014) *Justice and Environment* at <www.justiceandenvironment.org/_files/file/2014/New%20Energy%20State%20Aid%20Guidelines.pdf> at 4.

72 Concerto, 'Timeline of EU Energy and Climate Legislation' at <http://smartcities-infosystem.eu/sites/default/files/EU_policy_timeline.pdf>.

73 Climate and Energy Package is a set of legislation which consist of: Directive 2009/29/EC of the European Parliament and of the Council of 23 April 2009 amending Directive 2003/87/EC so as to improve and extend the greenhouse gas emission allowance trading scheme of the Community, [2009] OJ L 140/63; Directive 2009/28/EC of the European Parliament and of the Council of 23 April 2009 on the promotion of the use of energy from renewable sources and amending, [2009] OJ L 140/16 (Renewable Energy Directive); Directive 2009/31/EC of the European Parliament and of the Council of 23 April 2009 on the geological storage of carbon dioxide and amending Council Directive 85/337/EEC, European Parliament and Council Directives 2000/60/EC, 2001/80/EC, 2004/35/EC, 2006/12/EC, 2008/1/EC and Regulation (EC) No 1013/2006, [2009] OJ L 140/114; Decision No 406/2009/EC of the European Parliament and of the Council of 23 April 2009 on the effort of Member States to reduce their greenhouse gas emissions to meet the Community's greenhouse gas emission reduction commitments up to 2020, [2009] OJ L 140/131.

74 Communication from the European Commission, 'Energy Roadmap 2050', COM(2011)885.

75 European Environmental Agency, 'Energy and Climate Change' (2017) at <www.eea.europa.eu/signals/signals-2017/articles/energy-and-climate-change>.

76 European Commission, 'Progress Made in Cutting Emissions' at <https://ec.europa.eu/clima/policies/strategies/progress_en>.
77 Renewable Energy Directive (n 73), Preamble 13 to 15; European Commission, 'Progress towards Member States' Renewable Energy Targets' (2016) at <www.eea.europa.eu/themes/climate/trends-and-projections-in-europe/trends-and-projections-in-europe-2016/5-progress-towards-member-States>.
78 International Energy Agency, 'Capturing the Multiple Benefits of Energy Efficiency' (2014) at <www.iea.org/publications/freepublications/>.
79 Communication from the European Commission, 'Energy Efficiency Plan 2011', COM(2011)109.
80 Directive 2012/27/EU of the European Parliament and of the Council of 25 October 2012 on energy efficiency, amending Directives 2009/125/EC and 2010/30/EU and repealing Directives 2004/8/EC and 2006/32/EC, [2012] OJ L 315.
81 European Commission, 'National Energy Efficiency Action Plans and Annual Reports' at <https://ec.europa.eu/energy/en/topics/energy-efficiency/energy-efficiency-directive/national-energy-efficiency-action-plans>.
82 European Commission, 'Proposal for a Directive of the European Parliament and of the Council Amending Directive 2012/27/EU on Energy Efficiency', COM(2016)761.
83 Ibid.
84 European Commission, 'Proposal for a Directive of the European Parliament and of the Council on the Promotion of the Use of Energy from Eenewable Sources (Recast)', COM(2016)0767.
85 European Commission, 'Proposal for a Directive of the European Parliament and of the Council Amending Directive 2012/27/EU on Energy Efficiency' (n 82).
86 European Commission, 'Proposal for a Directive Amending Directive 2010/31/EU on the Energy Performance of Buildings', COM(2016)0765.
87 Communication from the European Commission, 'Accelerating Clean Energy Innovation', COM(2016)763.
88 Commission Staff Working Document, 'Evaluation Report covering the Evaluation of the EU's regulatory framework for electricity market design and consumer protection in the fields of electricity and gas Evaluation of the EU rules on measures to safeguard security of electricity supply and infrastructure investment (Directive 2005/89), Accompanying the document Proposal for a Directive of the European Parliament and of the Council on common rules for the internal market in electricity (recast), Proposal for a Regulation of the European Parliament and of the Council on the electricity market (recast), Proposal for a Regulation of the European Parliament and of the Council establishing a European Union Agency for the Cooperation of Energy Regulators (recast), Proposal for a Regulation of the European Parliament and of the Council on risk preparedness in the electricity sector', SWD(2016)0412.
89 European Commission, 'Clean Energy for All Europeans: Unlocking Europe's Growth Potential' (2016) *Press Release Database* at <http://europa.eu/rapid/press-release_IP-16-4009_en.htm>.
90 European Commission, 'Fact Sheet, State of the Energy Union: Questions and Answers' (2015) at <http://europa.eu/rapid/press-release_MEMO-15-6106_en.htm>.
91 Communication from the European Commission, 'A Framework Strategy for a Resilient Energy Union with a Forward-Looking Climate Change Policy', COM(2015)80 (Energy Union Communication).
92 Communication from the European Commission, 'Short Term Resilience of the European Gas System Preparedness for a Possible Disruption of Supplies from the East during the Fall and Winter of 2014/2015', COM(2014)654.

93 Energy Union Communication (n 91), at 5–6.
94 Ibid., at 8.
95 World Energy Council, 'World Energy Trilemma Index' (2016) at <www.worldenergy.org/wp-content/uploads/2016/10/Full-report_Energy-Trilemma-Index-2016.pdf>.
96 Ibid.
97 Raphael Heffron, *Energy Law: An Introduction* (Springer, 2015).
98 Ibid.
99 Eurostat, 'Energy Trends' at <http://ec.europa.eu/eurostat/statistics-explained/index.php/Energy_trends>.
100 Circle Economy and Ecofys, 'Implementing Circular Economy Globally Makes Paris Targets Achievable' (2016) at <www.circle-economy.com/wp-content/uploads/2016/06/ircle-economy-ecofys-2016-implementing-circular-economy-globally-makes-paris-targets-achievable.pdf.pdf>.
101 Communication from the European Commission, 'Closing the Loop: An EU Action Plan for the Circular Economy', COM(2015)0614.
102 Communication from the European Commission, 'The Role of Waste-to-Energy in the Circular Economy', COM(2017)34.
103 Thomas Pellerin-Carlin *et al.*, *Making the Energy Transition a European Success Tackling the Democratic, Innovation, Financing and Social Challenges of the Energy Union* (2017) *Jacques Delors Institute* at <www.institutdelors.eu/media/makingtheenergytransitionaeuropeansuccess-study-pellerincarlinfernandesrubio-june2017-bd.pdf?pdf=ok> at 11.
104 Communication from the European Commission, 'Report on the State of the Energy Union', at 2.
105 Ibid., at 10.
106 Ibid.
107 European Commission, 'The Energy Union on Track to Deliver' (2015) *Press Release Database* at <http://europa.eu/rapid/press-release_IP-15-6105_en.htm>.
108 Raphael Heffron and Darren McCauley, 'The Concept of Energy Justice across the Disciplines' (2017) *Energy Policy* 658.
109 Eurostat Statistics, 'Development of Electricity Prices for Household Consumers, EU-28 and EA, 2008–2017' (2017) at <http://ec.europa.eu/eurostat/statistics-explained/index.php/File:Development_of_electricity_prices_for_household_consumers,_EU-28_and_EA,_2008-2017_(EUR_per_kWh).png>.
110 Raphael Heffron, Darren McCauley and Benjamin Sovacool, 'Resolving Society's Energy Trilemma through the Energy Justice Metric' (2015) *Energy Policy* 168.
111 Ibid.
112 Benjamin Sovacool *et al.*, 'Energy Decisions Reframed as Justice and Ethical Concerns' (2016) *Nature Energy* 1.
113 Heffron and McCauley, 'The Concept of Energy Justice across the Disciplines' (n 108).
114 Communication from the European Commission, 'Second Strategic Energy Review: An EU Energy Security and Solidarity Action Plan', COM(2008)0781.
115 Thomas Pellerin-Carlin, *Making the Energy Transition a European Success Tackling the Democratic, Innovation, Financing and Social Challenges of the Energy Union* (2017) *Jacques Delors Institute* at <www.institutdelors.eu/media/makingtheenergytransitionaeuropeansuccess-study-pellerincarlinferndesrubio-june2017-bd.pdf?pdf=ok> at 10.

15 The social dimension of the common commercial policy

*Vivian Kube and Luigi Pedreschi**

1 Introduction

The tensions between economic integration and social concerns are a recurrent theme in European Union ('EU') law. As discussed in the Introduction to this volume,[1] the extent to which the two are capable of co-existing on equal terms has been extensively examined, with recent contributions suggesting that social concerns have given way to those of the market.[2] However, little attention has been paid to the role that Article 3 TEU has played since its inclusion by the Lisbon Treaty. Similarly, the impact of the general objectives and principles of Article 3(5) and 21 TEU included as part of the Lisbon reforms, which cover all foreign policy making and thereby explicitly link EU trade policy to social concerns, is also unclear.

Although the relevance of human rights and sustainable development for the Common Commercial Policy ('CCP') has been recognised for some time by the Court of Justice of the European Union ('CJEU'), the recent *Opinion 2/15* can be seen as a landmark decision in that it elevated the integration of sustainable development into trade policy to a constitutional obligation and sheds some light (and adds some uncertainty) as to the limits of such integration.[3] This contribution attempts to clarify the consequences of the recent constitutional changes beyond the current literature.[4] More concretely, it charts the place the EU constitution grants to social interests within the CCP and traces their operationalisation within two specific fields: sustainable development and public services.

The chapter begins by introducing the architecture of CCP competences and the pre-Lisbon relationship between trade and social interests that was based on a different constitutional structure before inclusion of the stated general principles and objectives (section 2). Thereafter, the chapter examines the CJEU's *Opinion 2/15* and proposes three possible options for the relationship between liberalisation of trade and social interests in the CCP (section 3). It then proceeds to analyse the fields of sustainable development (section 4) and public services (section 5). Respectively, each section explains why sustainable development and public services represent a dimension of the 'social market economy'. The concluding section demonstrates how the EU and its institutions balance and reconcile the tensions which may arise between trade liberalisation and social interests and, consequently, how the constitutional requirements are operationalised. This chapter ultimately argues that the EU envisions a liberalisation of trade embedded in and constrained by social interests.

2 Tracing the boundaries: the EU common commercial policy and the trade-development nexus

From its beginning, the EU was tasked with pursuing a common commercial policy (CCP) as a corollary to the internal market.[5] The scope of the CCP was aimed at what today still constitutes the core of Articles 206 and 207 TFEU: the harmonious development of world trade and the progressive abolition of restriction on international trade and the lowering of customs barriers.[6] At the outset, and as a consequence of the connections between European countries and former colonies, the CCP was connected strongly to development,[7] albeit based on a different constitutional setting. Through case law and subsequent treaty changes, the CCP has expanded in scope to include trade in goods and services, as well as intellectual property and foreign direct investment with regard to access barriers, and to some extent, the regulation of non-tariff-barriers.[8]

Prior to Lisbon, the protection and promotion of human rights was a specific objective of development cooperation,[9] Common Foreign and Security Policy[10] and economic, financial and technical cooperation.[11] Nevertheless, as indicated previously, sustainable development and human rights have been linked to EU trade policies for quite some time,[12] and this has been backed-up by the CJEU.[13] However, due to competence fragmentation, the integration of human rights and sustainable development was only possible to a limited extent. One may categorise the human rights policies that emerged as being part of the trade and development nexus, or as part of agreements aimed at the approximation of standards.[14]

As part of the trade and development nexus, trade was used as a conditionality instrument for developing countries through instruments such as the General System of Preferences ('GSP'),[15] 'GSP +'[16] and 'Everything but Arms' initiative for least developed countries.[17] Further, sustainable development and human rights issues were part of the approximation requirements when closer economic and political cooperation or accession to the EU of other States was envisioned. For this reason, the provisions relating to human rights are more elaborate in economic cooperation agreements (Articles 207, 211, 212 and 218 TFEU), association agreements (Article 217 TFEU) or agreements that are part of the European Neighbourhood Policy (Article 8 TEU) than in 'pure' trade agreements (Articles 207 and 218 TFEU).[18]

A direct link between trade and human rights was only established by human rights clauses or so called 'essential element clauses' which, since 1995, have been included in all EU trade agreements with third countries.[19] However, like other trade-related human rights instruments, human rights clauses did not overtly attempt to constrain EU trade policies in the name of social interests or to fulfil EU constitutional requirements. By contrast, these trade policies conceived trade as an instrument for the promotion of social development. Conflicts (and their resolution) with social development that stem directly from EU trade policies were not envisaged.

The following part of this chapter therefore explores whether the link between trade and social interests established by the general policy objectives gradually brings about a change of focus of such policies and suggests that, particularly in light of *Opinion 2/15*, they ought to do so.

3 The CCP and social interests: the EU Treaties

Following the Lisbon Treaty, the CCP is subject to two groups of potentially competing objectives and principles.[20] The first are its trade policy objectives (Articles 206 and 207 (1) TFEU). The second are the general EU principles and values which must inform its external action (Article 3(5) and 21 TEU, Article 205 TFEU). The latter embed the CCP's social dimension and provide a basis for the pursuit of a 'highly competitive social market economy' within the CCP. This section briefly discusses the basis of each set of objectives and principles, and thereafter considers three ways in which these competing objectives and principles can be balanced in instances of conflict.

3.1 The objective of the liberalisation of trade

As indicated above, Article 206 TFEU lays down the objectives of the CCP and focuses on trade, by providing:

> [t]he Union shall contribute, in the common interest, to the harmonious development of world trade, the progressive abolition of restrictions on international trade and on foreign direct investment, and the lowering of customs and other barriers.

It transpires from this provision that the 'liberalisation' of global trade and investment is a primary objective of CCP.[21] This includes the regulation and assimilation of non-tariff barriers. Echoes of the WTO's General Agreement on Trade in Services or the North American Free Trade Agreement underlie such a statement of intent.[22] Both emphasise the need to and benefits of reducing barriers to cross-border trade and are firmly focused on advancing this. It is clear that a specific CCP objective is to contribute to the continued development of global trade.[23] Article 207 TFEU first confirms the transfer of key trade policy competences to the EU in services, commercial aspects of intellectual property and foreign direct investment. Second, it requires uniformity of action in relation to the CCP. To protect the integrity of the internal market, the uniformity principle requires the adoption of common rules throughout the EU and in the field of CCP.[24] Third, it provides a bridge to the broader goals of the EU's external action by stating that the CCP is to be conducted in the context of those principles and objectives (discussed further below).

3.2 *The legal consequences of the general principles and objectives of EU external action*

The requirement that trade policy objectives are pursued within the framework of general principles of EU external action is found in Articles 205 and 207(1) TFEU and Article 21(3) TEU. They stipulate that the Union external policies and the CCP shall be guided by the principles and objectives laid down in the TEU. Consequently, the EU's trade policy is situated within its value-laden constitutional structure that both enables and restricts its capacity to enter trade agreements. This is significant because, unlike many of its trading partners, the EU does not have *carte blanche* to negotiate an agreement as it sees fit.[25] Instead, its external trade policy must reflect the values on which the community is based. This includes 'the sustainable development of the Earth, solidarity and mutual respect among peoples, free and fair trade, eradication of poverty and the protection of human rights'.

Article 21 TEU further states that the EU's international action must be 'guided by the principles which have inspired its own creation, development and enlargement, and which it seeks to advance in the wider world'. This explicitly mentions 'democracy, the rule of law, the universality and indivisibility of human rights and fundamental freedoms, respect for human dignity, the principles of equality and solidarity, and respect for the principles of the United Nations Charter and international law' as core EU values.

By reading Article 206 TFEU in light of these provisions, it can be argued that the CCP must advance non-economic goals, such as the supporting of democracy, the rule of law and human rights (including social rights) and sustainable development. The importance of these values was stated in the mentioned *Opinion 2/15*.[26] The opinion was requested by the EU Commission to bring clarity to the much-disputed scope of the CCP competence to cover all trade and investment-related aspects that were meant to be included in the new generation of trade agreements.[27]

The Opinion addressed the question of whether the EU has the competence to integrate social concerns into its free trade agreements on the basis of its exclusive CCP competence. This is the first opinion on the EU's competence regarding its new generation of trade agreements. Whilst denying that there was an exclusive competence to cover all aspects of the new agreement, the CJEU forcefully reiterated the legal relevance of non-economic goals within the Union's trade policy. The Court held that the EU has an obligation to integrate the general foreign policy objectives and principles according to Article 21 TEU and Articles 205 and 207(1) TFEU into its trade and investment policies. These general objectives are 'new aspects of contemporary international trade'[28] and 'form an integral part of the CCP'.[29] The Court added that the cross-cutting social clause (Article 9 TFEU) 'must be taken into account' within trade policy making, referring to the *AGET Iraklis* case.[30]

As a result, the Court has made it easier for the EU to incorporate mechanisms for the protection of social concerns into trade agreements; particularly so, given the Court did not follow the conclusions of the Advocate General Sharpston who inferred from the pre-Lisbon case law that sustainable development must be ancillary to trade in order to fall within the CCP.[31] This implied that those measures necessary to make the liberalisation of trade compatible with sustainable development must sufficiently demonstrate the required link between more social goals and trade and therefore fall under the Union's exclusive competence. However, some uncertainties remain. To delineate trade-related social protection from harmonisation of internal social policies, which would fall under the shared competence of Articles 151 and 153(1) TFEU, the Court also set some limits to the integration of social protection into trade measures. The Court stressed that the trade agreement does not impose new social standards on either of the parties, but only refers to existing ones and allows each trade partner to maintain their own levels of protection.[32]

Further, the Court highlights that the provisions on labour rights and environmental protection are disconnected from any dispute resolution mechanisms established by the agreement.[33] If the latter is to be understood as a condition for the inclusion of social protection under CCP and not requiring an additional legal base, the establishment of stronger enforcement mechanisms might be discouraged. EU trade policy makers may refrain from integrating means for enforcing labour rights and environmental protection in order to remain within the exclusive competence. However, the Court did not have to decide on the compatibility of the agreement with EU law and, hence, gave no concrete guidance as to how potentially substantive conflicts between the liberalisation of trade and social goals were to be solved, an issue discussed in Section 3.3.

3.3 Options on how to reconcile the tensions

Whilst the CCP fails to mention the objective of a 'social market economy', it is evident that the non-economic values underpinning the sphere of EU external action advance key elements of this concept. This raises the question of how the two may be balanced against one another when they conflict. In the absence of case law on the hierarchy between trade liberalisation and social protection after the Lisbon Treaty, this section posits that there are three possible options as to how the CCP could strike a balance while categorising and discussing the opinions advanced in legal scholarship accordingly.

The first option is that post-Lisbon the mandate to liberalise trade has increased in significance and enjoys primacy over social concerns.[34] In support of this interpretation is Article 206 TFEU that tasks the EU with the progressive abolition of restrictions on international trade and on foreign direct investment. Further, the general external principles and objectives include progressive abolition of restrictions on international trade (Article 21 (2)(e) TEU) as well as free and fair trade (Article 3(5) TEU). In view of this potentially stronger mandate to liberalise, previous case law, in which the Court ruled that the CCP did not entail such an obligation, should be reconsidered.[35] Further, it has been argued that the enhanced liberalisation objective requires that the burden of justification is reversed and to assimilate the test for legitimate restrictions to those of internal market freedoms.[36] This argument may find support in the reference, within *Opinion 2/15*, to *AGET Iraklis*, as this concerned a restriction of the freedom of establishment aimed at ensuring the protection of workers and of employment (hence, social rights *strictu sensu*) which was ultimately considered disproportionate.[37]

A second option is a constrained form of trade liberalisation. Article 21(2)(e) TEU, as well as Article 206 TFEU, speaks of '*progressive* abolition of restrictions on international trade'. Additionally, the latter emphasises the 'the *harmonious* development of world trade'. These references describe a gradual and more nuanced vision of trade liberalisation that is in some way subservient to or limited by other objectives. Further, Article 21(2)(e) TEU describes gradual liberalisation as one means of achieving the aim of integrating all countries into the global economy. The reference to free and fair trade in Article 3(5) TEU makes the constraints on trade policy and the relevance of considerations other than the elimination of trade barriers most explicit. In *Opinion 2/15*, the CJEU interpreted the term 'fair trade' as referring to sustainable development,[38] and not merely adherence to WTO standards, as it has been proposed in the literature.[39] It is important to note that trade liberalisation never stands alone in the Treaties. On the contrary, one may argue that the Treaties clearly envision a form of trade liberalisation which is embedded in and constrained by considerations of sustainable development and social protection.

A final option is that rather than supersede one another, the two are placed on an equal footing.[40] As all objectives are of equal value, they should be pursued on a mutually reinforcing basis where possible. In the case of conflicts between these different objectives they would need to be balanced based on the principle of proportionality.[41] These readings require policy makers to justify their decision in light of these constitutional mandates and set limits on their political discretion. At the very least, these constitutional mandates should discipline policy makers to consider the different objectives in a transparent and objectively justifiable manner. In the following section, this chapter will explore two fields of CCP in order to see how such conflicts are solved and which of these readings is used to resolve the dispute.

4 The enhancement of sustainable development as an example for the EU 'social market economy'?

This section analyses what role the pursuit of sustainable development plays within the making of EU trade agreements, their implementation and enforcement. By looking at the inclusion of sustainable development in the process of making trade agreements as well as in the treaties' texts, it aims to identify how the relationship between the constitutional values of the social and the commercial is operationalised within the CCP. As explained, other trade-related sustainable development instruments which emerged in pre-Lisbon times perceived trade as a tool for promoting development. This analysis focuses on the treatment of the 'social' within trade agreements and identifies instances of conflicting objectives being pursued within one instrument.

4.1 *Sustainable development as the social dimension of the global market*

First, it is necessary to discuss the extent to which sustainable development can be linked to the notion of a 'social market economy', and therefore the extent to which it embodies the social dimension of a global market. The Union's concept of sustainable development emerged in connection with international summits, conferences and subsequent declarations and agendas.[42] In essence, the concept comprises the three pillars of economic, social and environmental development based on solidarity across generations and nations.[43] Since the adoption of the human rights-based approach to sustainable development ('HRBA') at the UN level,[44] the EU has increasingly stressed the importance of basing sustainable development strategies and their assessments on the normative framework of human rights.[45] This means that the social pillar of sustainable development should be based on an authoritative catalogue of social rights. Next, the Commission has emphasised that sustainable development is closely linked to solidarity[46] and inclusiveness.[47] As mentioned, the principles of solidarity, equality and universality of human rights also form part of the principles and objectives governing EU external relations. The EU acknowledges that the realisation of sustainable development requires strengthening governance structures and institutions to constrain global market forces accordingly.[48] The principle of non-discrimination features prominently in all policy documents on the implementation of human rights in the context of external relations. Therefore, although the objective of a 'highly competitive social market economy' does not specifically refer to external relations, the concept of sustainable development that the EU promotes exhibits similar features as found in the notion of the internal EU 'social market economy'. The concept of sustainable development that the EU promotes is the overarching concept for the social dimension of global trade.

4.2 *Integration of sustainable development concerns in the making of trade agreements*

The major mechanisms for incorporating social concerns into trade policy choices and into the making of trade agreements are Sustainability Impact Assessments ('SIAs'). Since the 1990s, large-scale protests were levelled against the newly established WTO and its allegedly negative social and environmental impact on the developing world. The EU, alongside other major trading states, responded by beginning to systematically incorporate sustainable development objectives into the assessment of future trade policies.[49] The methodology of SIAs has undergone significant reform in recent years. In its 2012 and 2015 Action Plan on Human Rights and Democracy, the Council tasked the Commission with the insertion of human rights into the assessment of trade measures and the improvement of the method used to carry out SIAs.[50] Based on the 2015 Better Regulation Agenda,[51] the Commission published a revised handbook on SIAs[52] as well as Guidelines for the integration of human rights into the Trade SIAs (EU Guidelines on HRIA).[53]

The normative content of the SIAs is comprehensive. In terms of social rights, these soft law instruments necessitate that the EU assesses every trade agreement against its impact on all core UN human rights conventions, ILO conventions on international labour standards, the European Convention on Human Rights ('ECHR') and other regional human rights conventions, as well as customary international law.[54] An additional social analysis is meant to take into consideration internationally agreed principles on corporate social responsibility ('CSR') and responsible business conduct ('RBC').[55] Further, every trade instrument has to be assessed in light of the EU Charter of Fundamental Rights ('EU CFR') that constitutes a binding legal requirement.[56] The handbook and the guidelines acknowledge that to capture discriminatory impacts attention must be paid to effects on vulnerable and marginalised groups. Gender equality and discrimination should be treated as a cross-cutting issue.[57] These self-imposed guidelines consequently establish an ambitious programme for the assessment of trade agreements.

These instruments are less clear on the consequences of conflicts between social objectives and trade policy, e.g. when an SIA concludes that specific trade measures will negatively impact social rights. More importantly, there is no secondary legislation that links the outcome to the policy choices or that would set procedural rules for the decision-making on trade-offs. The guidelines do describe the outcome of the HRIA as being capable of setting restraints on policy options with regards to absolute rights. They make clear that no restrictions and limitations of absolute rights are acceptable.[58] Further, the referred Tool #28 'Fundamental Rights & Human Rights'[59] makes clear that absolute rights cannot be limited, whereas interference with the remaining rights requires strict compliance with the proportionality principle laid out in Article 52 EU CFR. As far as absolute rights are concerned, it seems that the guidelines conceive the outcome of an HRIA as having the potential to obligate the Commission to refrain from a certain trade measure. Apart from the clear stance on absolute rights, the SIA handbook, as well as the guidelines, says relatively little on the consequences of the outcome and the obligations that follow. The guidelines do state that the HRIA should 'warn decision-makers of any identifiable risks of a significant negative impact on human rights and also of the type of response which is warranted by those risks'.[60] It remains unclear whether adopting such responses or even considering them is mandatory. The guidelines only foresee the adoption of a response paper by the Commission. However, the response papers published so far rarely justify the ultimate policy choices and the accepted trade-offs. Typically, they do not include any transparent balancing of the competing interests involved or consideration of alternatives. On the contrary, mitigating measures that are recommended by the SIAs are often perceived as falling outside CCP competence.[61] Hence, the influence of these SIAs on decision-making seems limited. This is partly because they are conducted at a very late stage of the policy making cycle, when major policy choices are already made.[62] Finally, although EU trade policy makers have committed themselves to taking into account a wide range of social concerns during the drafting of trade agreements, the actual effects on policy choices remains unclear. It seems that in the absence of clear rules on conflict-resolution trade policy makers enjoy a wide margin of discretion.

4.3 *Sustainable development in the implementation of trade agreements*

Since the announcement of the new generation of trade agreements, sustainable development has been systematically integrated into the substance of trade agreements and combined with an institutional monitoring framework. A cornerstone of this new approach is a reformulated preamble that places stronger emphasis on social goals and objectives. In CETA, the preamble includes the recognition of fundamental and human rights, sustainable development, domestic and international commitments on labour and environmental rights together with CSR. However, it does not give any instructions to resolve conflicts between these social objectives. Moreover, the first three objectives are economic in nature aimed at strengthening the already close economic relationship between the EU and Canada by reducing barriers to trade and investment and establishing clear, transparent and predictable rules to govern trade and investment. It is difficult to predict the influence of the preamble. In terms of its influence on enforcement through dispute settlement mechanisms, it is noteworthy that within investment arbitration, tribunals arrived at diverging conclusions when faced with preambles containing potentially conflicting objectives.[63] The existence of such conflicts has been interpreted as providing insufficient guidance for the interpretation of specific provisions.[64]

Since the EU-Korea Free Trade Agreement ('FTA'), a Trade and Sustainable Development chapter ('SD chapter') is included in every trade and investment agreement in combination with a monitoring and advisory body.[65] Substantively, these SD chapters, with slight variations, contain the following social provisions: encouragement of the use of voluntary CSR mechanisms,[66] adherence to the ILO fundamental principles such as the freedom of association,[67] recognition of the ILO Decent Work Agenda[68] and the ILO Declaration on Social Justice for a Fair Globalization of 2008.[79] Further, an SD chapter usually stipulates the right of the parties to maintain their own protection standards.[70] This makes sure that the trade agreement is not imposing new obligations on the parties and, from an EU perspective, not harmonising the EU's social policy.[71]

Transparency clauses normally require parties to the agreement to publish or make available any information on envisaged state action that affects sustainable development issues to enable interested persons to comment on it and to examine any resulting feedback.[72] Additionally, non-derogation clauses are included which prohibit the parties from reducing their domestic social protection standards in a way that affects trade, i.e. in a protectionist manner.[73]

These clauses are however of limited enforceability. First, all social provisions are explicitly excluded from any dispute settlement mechanisms.[74] Instead, the SD chapter creates its own monitoring and advisory mechanisms. It consists of intergovernmental bodies and domestic advisory groups. The latter are supposed to include independent civil society organisations representing in a balanced manner social, economic and environmental interests. In cases of disagreement over social provisions, these monitoring bodies can be involved in the governmental consultations or Panel of Experts. Apart from involvement in the dispute resolution mechanisms, their main task is to meet regularly and to submit opinions and recommendations to parties directly or to intergovernmental bodies.[75] However, the parties are under no obligation to respond in any way or react to the submission made by the public or civil society organizations. In the absence of procedural rules, claims of breaches of social provisions (that are likely to come mainly from civil society) might be without any practical effect.[76] In *Opinion 2/15*, the Court made a novel remark by stating that, in accordance with the rule of customary international law codified in Article 60(1) of the Vienna Convention on the Law of the Treaties,[77] 'a breach of the provisions concerning social protection of workers [give the parties the right] to terminate or suspend liberalisation'.[78] However, the effectiveness of the right to suspend the agreement, which was previously explicitly only linked to human rights, has been criticised for its infrequent and arbitrary enforcement.[79] Further, they only stipulate a right to suspend but not an obligation to act or activate any kind of response-mechanism.[80]

In sum, the new generation of trade agreements are equipped with more comprehensive provisions on social protection, which feature within the framework of the objective to advance sustainable development. However, they do not include any mechanism capable of resolving cases of actual conflict between trade measures and social protection, or of sanctioning parties for their lack of compliance with the agreement. The formulations suggest that usually synergies are anticipated. A hierarchy does however become visible at the enforcement level. Whereas the economic objectives are implemented as legally enforceable commitments, breaches of the social provisions give at most a right to the party to suspend, which is in practice rarely used, or are being diverted to cooperative mechanisms that lack rules for sanctioning or accountability.

5 Public services in EU trade agreements

5.1 Public services in the 'social market economy'

The concept of public services has no universal definition. Broadly speaking, the concept can be said to refer to those services provided and regulated for non-commercial public interests based on societal need and in a way the market cannot achieve.[81] They are aimed at the provision of a service in a uniform or regulated manner that is accessible at either no direct cost or at an affordable price.[82] In deciding whether a service should be provided publicly, two different rationales are commonly adopted to distinguish them from other services. The first is based on the economic concept of public goods. This is a service that will not be produced privately in the free market due to unprofitability or because its price cannot be effectively fixed even though it is in society's interest to have such a service available.[83] For instance, universal access to telecommunications is a public good which requires some form of special regulatory arrangement because it can only be achieved through collective coordination and not through wholly private means.[84]

The second is based on a broader political understanding of the concept. This considers public services as those services provided in the general interest, and to fulfil individuals' fundamental rights, e.g. universal healthcare.[85] In this way, their goals are distinguishable from private ones which justifies their special treatment.[86] Once a particular collective need is determined, intervention through the use of a public service can be undertaken.[87] Consequently, public services are those services aimed at meeting societal needs that will not be addressed by market mechanisms or cannot be to a suitable degree.

The provisions of the Treaties dealing with the CCP do not mention public services. As discussed by Piernas Lopez and Pellizzari earlier in this volume,[88] the TFEU includes general references to Services of General Economic Interest (SGEI) in Articles 14 and 106, and Protocol No 26 on services of general interest ('SGI'). Taken together, they can be considered to recognise the role and wide discretion of national, regional and local authorities in operating SGEIs, and their diversity.[89] The Lisbon Treaty gave legal effect to Article 36 EU CFR which recognises the right of access to SGEI 'to promote social and territorial cohesion of the Union'. These legal provisions are concerned with the EU internal sphere; however, they cannot but have an external reflection and an influence on EU trade agreements.[90]

Arguably, *Opinion 2/15* has strengthened the argument for public services to be reflected in EU trade agreements. As stated earlier, the CJEU made clear that the cross-cutting social clause of Article 9 TFEU 'must be taken into account' within trade policy making.[91] At its lowest, this has the potential to cover many areas of public service provision and may be interpreted as strengthening the need for consideration of public services in trade agreements. Such references make clear that public services are a value of the CCP that requires expression in EU trade agreements.[92] Accordingly, trade objectives should be balanced with space for public service provision through restrictions on the overall scope of an agreement.

5.2 *Social services in trade agreements concluded under the CCP*

In its trade agreements, the EU uses a patchwork of overarching exemptions, reservations and justified derogations to carve out space for public services. Two types of overarching exemption are used in its agreements: sectoral and functional. With regard to the former, there are five sectors that are always excluded from the scope of application of its provisions on services and establishment, specifically: 1) mining, manufacturing and processing nuclear weapons; 2) production of trade or trade in arms, munitions and war materials; 3) audio-visual services; 4) national maritime cabotage; and, 5) domestic and international air transport services.[93] Obviously, such exemptions cover only those public services associated with the fulfilment of sovereign activities, rather than those of a social nature. So functional exemptions are those which are more useful. The EU adopts the GATS Article I:3(b) exemption for services supplied under governmental authority in both its second generation[94] and newer agreements.[95] It is accompanied by a supplementary definition which clarifies that the limitation applies to services provided neither on a commercial basis nor in competition with one or more suppliers.[96] The EU has frequently incorporated this supplementary definition into its agreements.[97]

From a public services perspective, the advantage of this clause is that it is not limited to any particular sector. Provided its cumulative conditions are satisfied, it can serve to exempt, and therefore create space for, a wide breadth of services including those of a social nature. However, application of the two conditions will likely restrict the provision of public services in any sector where they compete with private providers or provide services for some sort of remuneration. If so, this would restrict the scope of the exemption to monopoly services that are provided for free which are currently a relatively uncommon form of public service provision.

Turning to the use of reservations, most past agreements have followed the positive listing approach of the GATS. This means that the core trade disciplines of market access and national treatment apply to an economic sector only when it has been listed in a party's schedule and subject to any reservations set out. Recent negotiations suggest a shift away from this practice towards to a negative listing approach, where such core disciplines automatically apply to an economic sector unless it is explicitly reserved, or a hybrid of the two practices.[98] The EU has used the same horizontal public utilities reservation widely in its schedules of commitments on the establishment rules of a service provider. This means that it applies to the rules on temporary presence of natural persons for business purposes. As a result, it restricts only services provided by service suppliers with an established presence or natural persons that have entered to provide a service. Whilst not always the same, generally it reads as follows:

> Economic activities considered as public utilities at a national or local level may be subject to public monopolies or to exclusive rights granted to private providers.[99]

In the majority of agreements (including those with Korea, Columbia and Peru, Ecuador, Central America, the CARIFORUM States and CETA), this is supplemented with an explanatory footnote that reads:

> Given that public utilities often exist at sub-central level, detailed and exhaustive sector-specific listing is not practical. To facilitate comprehension, specific

> footnotes in this list of commitments will indicate in an illustrative and non-exhaustive way those sectors where public utilities play a major role.[100]

More recently in the draft-Vietnam agreement and in the CETA the following footnote is found:

> Public utilities exist in sectors such as related scientific and technical consulting services, R&D services on social services and humanities, technical testing and analysis services, environmental services, health services, transport services and services auxiliary to all modes of transport. Exclusive rights on such services are often granted to private operators, for instance operators with concessions from public authorities, subject to specific service obligations.[101]

As the term 'public utilities' has no specific meaning in international trade or EU law,[102] the scope of this provision is not immediately clear.[103] The terms themselves are suggestive of service or supply of network industries such as energy, water or transport. This is a point noted by the Commission who has previously equated it with SGEI.[104] Additionally, for the sectors of Education and Health and Social Services, it has consistently, in its schedules of commitments, defined the sector as applying to *only privately funded services.* Frequently, the definition for Health and Social Services in the establishment schedules is supplemented by a footnote explaining that the sector is also covered by the public utilities exemption.[105] This definition suggests that all publicly funded services in these sectors are outside the application of the core disciplines. This approach has been criticised on the basis that it is unclear whether this would exempt services with any sort of public funding or only those that were 100% or predominantly publicly funded.[106] On the EU's part, it argues that this allows Member States the space to regulate certain services in whatever way they choose, even if it means treating EU suppliers or investors differently from foreign-based providers.[107]

Finally, there are justified derogations which provide total relief from the scope of application of the agreements so long as the measure in question meets the stated threshold for justification. The relevant derogations which are identifiable in all EU agreements are those necessary: 1) to protect public morals or public order; 2) to protect human, animal or plant life; and, 3) to secure compliance with laws and or regulations not inconsistent with the provisions of that particular agreement.[108] Such clauses apply generally, provided they do not constitute 'arbitrary or unjustified discrimination' or a 'disguised restriction of trade'. Whilst these have yet to be interpreted at the Union level, their almost exact replication of the GATS suggests that their interpretation follow that of the WTO jurisprudence.

In this context, it has been found that States have a broad margin of appreciation in defining what constitutes health and their desired level of protection.[109] It has been accepted that the aims of protecting human, animal and plant life health take priority over trade liberalisation commitments so long as they are deemed necessary.[110] Both exceptions contain the 'necessity' test which is determined through a 'weighing and balancing of a series of factors'.[111] This requires consideration of how the measure contributes to the realisation of its stated ends and also the restrictive impact of the measures on international commerce.[112] This has been interpreted by the Appellate Body as requiring a balance between members' intervention 'rights' and liberalisation 'duties'.[113] In this exercise, the validity of the level of protection a particular state considers appropriate must not be questioned.[114] This exercise will involve an understanding of the relevant domestic values and principles together with an evaluative judgement of their relative importance.[115]

5.3 Observations and preliminary conclusions

In sum, the EU does not have an overarching exemption for public services. Rather, it has adopted a piecemeal approach that is centred around three layers of clauses deployed at different junctures of its trade agreements. What is observable is that the level of protection for public services (and more broadly the social rights associated with such services) provided by these clauses is high. Any service that comes within their scope is given full exemption. However, that scope fluctuates significantly depending on the nature of the particular clause. Given their imprecise and seemingly narrow coverage, it appears that only a small range of public services will fall completely outside the scope of application of the EU's agreements. Returning to our starting point, this suggests that public services are not viewed as a value to be promoted but rather are considered an exception to the general rules and objectives of trade liberalisation.

6 Conclusion

After Lisbon, Articles 206 and 207 TFEU read in light and in combination with Article 21 and 3(5) TEU, provide the Commission and Council with a clear mandate for the integration of social interests into EU trade policies. In fact, in *Opinion 2/15*, the CJEU made clear that trade policy makers are under an obligation to integrate sustainable development and social protection into trade policy development and implementation. The constitutional set up has therefore changed fundamentally when compared to the pre-Lisbon configuration. This chapter has sought to examine whether such changes have been carried through to the current practice of trade policy. It has done so in two fields where conflicts amongst values may arise and hierarchical choices require resolution.

Previously, sustainable development and human rights could only be pursued by development and CFSP policies and as part of trade policies only when ancillary to trade. The new structures give social interests a fixed role in trade policy making on par with trade liberalisation. However, it remains unclear what the legal consequences for the trade policy makers are in cases of a conflict between economic and social interests. That is especially true in light of the CJEU's practice to grant a wide discretion to the policy maker in economic decision-making and foreign policies. The most recent EU trade policy has undertaken major steps towards increased integration in particular with the adoption of self-imposed guidelines on SIAs and the coherent inclusion of the Sustainable Development chapters in all trade agreements. Nevertheless, with regard to both instruments, SIAs and Sustainable Development chapters, the responsiveness towards and enforcement of social interests, especially in comparison to the enforcement economic commitments, remains weak. This enforcement bias may in practice lead to economic commitments prevailing over social interests.

The case of public services in EU trade agreements has followed a different path. Unlike sustainable development, the justification for their reflection in EU trade agreements rests on the interplay of several different Treaty provisions. These provisions confirm the role of general interest services as a shared value of the Union which was the case before the Lisbon Treaty (which introduced only minor changes of relevance). The expression of this role is reflected in the EU's trade agreements though three layers of exemption clauses. The above analysis reveals that each layer provides a high degree of protection for public services, but their scope is somewhat narrow. More importantly, what is demonstrated is that public services are not seen as a value to be promoted alongside trade liberalisation. Instead they are considered exceptions to which the EU's trade goals will occasionally give way. The wider societal concerns regarding the restriction of public services by future EU trade agreements suggests there is a need to reconsider the weight of expression given to such services.

The study of both these fields reveals that there appears to be no overarching concept of how to reconcile trade and social interests. This is despite the fact that EU external policies and especially trade is constitutionally linked to the fundamental values and general principles of the EU which include human rights, sustainable development, free and fair trade – and therefore 'social' values – as well as the principle of coherence. However, in both fields, the EU seems to employ a piecemeal approach that is greatly influenced by traditional responses stemming partly from WTO level, partly from international developments on sustainable developments and from its own previous competence fragmentations. Social interests are therefore treated as exceptions or mere political matters. In the absence of overarching concepts, the isolated instruments that are adopted to protect public services or to promote sustainable development are being pursued detached from each other. However, the EU possesses a strong constitutional basis that would allow and may require it to adopt holistic visions that integrate social interests into global economic regulation and to re-evaluate traditional approaches.

Notes

* This chapter is the product of a joint reflection. Section 4 has been written by Vivian Kube, while section 5 has been written by Luigi Pedreschi. Sections 1, 2, 3 and 6 have been written jointly.

1 Delia Ferri and Fulvio Cortese, 'Introduction', in this volume.

2 Stephen Weatherill, *Law and Values in the European Union* (OUP, 2016) 350.
3 Opinion 2/15, *EU-Singapore FTA*, EU:C:2017:376.
4 Piet Eeckhout, 'A Normative Basis for EU External Relations? Protecting Internal Values Beyond the Single Market' in Markus Krajewski (ed.), *Services of General Interest Beyond the Single Market* (Asser Press, 2015) 219, at 222.
5 Article 3(b) EEC Treaty.
6 Article 110(1) EEC Treaty.
7 Joris Larik, 'Global Governance through Trade: Constitutional Moorings' in Jan Wouters, Axel Marx and Dylan Geraets (eds.), *Global Governance Through Trade: EU Policies and Approaches* (Edward Elgar, 2015) 47.
8 David Kleimann, 'Taking Stock: EU Common Commercial Policy in the Lisbon Era' (2011) *CEPS Working Document No 34 8*; Markus Krajewski, 'The Reform of the Common Commercial Policy' in Andrea Biondi, Piet Eeckhout and Stefanie Ripley (eds.), *EU Law after Lisbon* (OUP, 2012).
9 Article 177(2) of the Treaty establishing the European Community, [2002] OJ C 325/33 (ex-TEC).
10 Article 11(1) of the Treaty on the European Union, [2002] OJ C 325/01.
11 Article 181(a)(1) EC Treaty (n 9).
12 EU Sustainable Development Strategy, first adopted in 2001, aimed at mainstreaming sustainable development across different policy fields, Communication from the European Commission, 'A Sustainable Europe for a Better World: A European Union Strategy for Sustainable Development', COM(2001)264 [not published in the Official Journal]; The Commission first stressed the need to mainstream human rights into all external policy fields in Communication from the European Commission, 'The European Union's Role in Promoting Human Rights and Democratisation in Third Countries', COM(2001)252.
13 Case C-45/86, *Tariff Preferences*, EU:C:1987:163, paras 17–18.
14 Lorand Bartels, 'The Trade and Development Policy of the European Union' in Marise Cremona (ed.), *Developments in EU External Relations Law* (OUP, 2008); Joris Larik, 'Much More Than Trade: The Common Commercial Policy in a Global Context' in Panos Koutrakos and Malcolm Evans (eds.), *Beyond the Established Legal Orders: Policy Interconnections between the EU and the Rest of the World* (Hart, 2011) 13; Nicolas Hachez *et al.*, 'FRAME: Report on the Integration of Human Rights in EU Development and Trade Policies' (2014) *Leuven Center for Global Governance Studies* – Work Package No. 9 – Deliverable No. 1.
15 GSP offers non-reciprocal preferential market access to developing countries (Regulation No 978/2012).
16 GSP + offers full removal of tariffs for 'vulnerable' countries which ratified and effectively implemented 27 core international conventions in the fields of human and labour right, the environment and good governance.
17 The EBA programme grants duty-free quota-free access to all products, except for arms and ammunitions.
18 For a critical assessment of all the integration of human rights instruments into these agreements, Hachez et al. (n 14), at 56.
19 Ibid., at 60–63.
20 Markus Krajewski, 'The Reform of the Common Commercial Policy' in Biondi, Eeckhout and Ripley (eds.), *EU Law after Lisbon* (n 8), at 294.
21 Angelos Dimopoulos, 'The Effects of the Lisbon Treaty on the Principles and Objectives of the Common Commercial Policy' (2010) *European Foreign Affairs Review* 153, at 160.
22 General Agreement on Trade in Services, paras 2–3; and, North American Free Trade Agreement, Article 102.
23 Piet Eeckhout, *EU External Relations Law* (OUP, 2011) 440.

24 Angelos Dimopoulos, *EU Foreign Investment Law* (OUP, 2011) 201. For a thorough overview; Marise Cremona, 'The External Dimension of the Internal Market' in Catherine Barnard and Joanne Scott (eds.), *The Law of the Single European Market: Unpacking the Premises* (Hart, 2002) 354.
25 On the other hand, foreign policy objectives are not unknown to nation state constitutions but they are rarely that explicit, Joris Larik, *Foreign Policy Objectives in European Constitutional Law* (OUP, 2016).
26 *EU-Singapore FTA* (n 3).
27 In 2006 and 2010, the EU Commission elaborated on its strategy to conclude a 'new generation' of trade agreements that will cover multiple areas of international economic regulation (for instance public procurement, competition policy and investment protection), Communication from the European Commission, 'Towards a Comprehensive European International Investment Policy', COM(2010)343.
28 *EU-Singapore FTA* (n 3), para 141.
29 Ibid., paras 146–147.
30 Ibid., para 146 with reference to Case C-201/15, *AGET Iraklis*, EU:C:2016:972, paras 61–104.
31 Opinion of AG Sharpston, *Opinion 2/15*, EU:C:2016:992, paras 491, 495 and 498 with reference to Opinion 1/78, EU:C:1979:224; Case 45/86, *Commission v Council*, EU:C:1987:163; Case C-62/88, *Greece v Council*, EU:C:1990:153; Case C-281/01, *Commission v Council*, EU:C:2002:761.
32 *EU-Singapore FTA* (n 3), para 165.
33 Ibid., para 154.
34 Marise Cremona, 'A Constitutional Basis for Effective External Action? An Assessment of the Provisions on EU External Action in the Constitutional Treaty' (2006) *EUI Working Paper Law* 29; Markus Krajewski, 'The Reform of the Common Commercial Policy' (n 8), at 295.
35 Case 112/80, *Firma Anton Dürbeck*, EU:C:1981:94, para 44; Case C-150/94, *Chinese toys*, EU:C:1998:547, para 67.
36 Dimopoulos, 'The Effects of the Lisbon Treaty on the Principles and Objectives of the Common Commercial Policy' (n 21), at 160–161.
37 *AGET Iraklis* (n 30), paras 61–104.
38 *EU-Singapore FTA* (n 3), para 146.
39 For a detailed discussion on the concept of fair trade under EU law, Marise Cremona and Gracia Marín Durán, 'Fair Trade in European Union: Regulatory and Institutional Aspects' in Brigitte Granville and Janet Dine (eds.), *The Processes and Practices of Fair Trade: Trust, Ethics and Governance* (Routledge, 2012) 151.
40 Vedder, 'Linkage of the Common Commercial Policy to the Objectives for the Union's External Action' (n 22), at 119.
41 Krajewski, 'The Reform of the Common Commercial Policy' (n 8), at 298.
42 Such as the UN Conference on Environment and Development in 1992, the Earth Summit, the Rio Declaration, the World Summit for Sustainable Development in Johannesburg in 2002 and the Doha Development Round that began in 2002; Marise Cremona, 'Economic and Social Rights in EU External Policy' in Francesco Bestagno (ed.), *I diritti economici, sociali e culturali: promozione e tutela nella comunità internazionale* (Vita e pensiero, 2009) 256.
43 Communication from the European Commission, 'The 2005 Review of the Sustainable Development Strategy: Initial Stocktaking and Future Orientations', COM(2005)37; Communication from the European Commission, 'The Review of the Sustainable Development Strategy: A Platform for Action', COM(2005)658; Communication from the European Commission, 'Trade for All, towards a More Responsible Trade and Investment Policy', COM(2015)0497.

44 The United Nations Development Group (UNDG) adopted the UN Statement of Common Understanding on Human Rights Based Approaches to Development Cooperation and Programming (the Common Understanding) in 2003, which serves as a reference point for all UN agencies and other international development bodies at <http://hrbaportal.org/the-human-rights-based-approach-to-development-cooperation-towards-a-common-understanding-among-un-agencies#sthash.H7zQsbcv.dpuf>.
45 Strategic Framework and Action Plan on Human Rights and Democracy of 25 June 2012 (2012 Action Plan), at 5.
46 Jan Orbie, 'Promoting Labour Standards through Trade: Normative Power or Regulatory State Europe?' in Richard Whitman (ed.), *Normative Power Europe Empirical and Theoretical Perspectives* (Palgrave Macmillan, 2011) at 165.
47 Communication from the European Commission, 'Trade, Growth and World Affairs: Trade Policy as a Core Component of the EU's 2020 Strategy', COM(2010)612, at 8.
48 Communication from the European Commission, 'Towards a Global Partnership for Sustainable Development', COM(2002)82, at 4.
49 Pascal Lamy, 'Sustainable Impact Assessment: Towards Sustainable Development' (Speech at the SIA Seminar Borschette Center Brussels, 6 February 2003).
50 Strategic Framework and Action Plan on Human Rights and Democracy of 25 June 2012 (2012 Action Plan), Point 1 and Point 11(a); Point 25 (b) and 28(a), Council Conclusion on the Action Plan on Human Rights and Democracy 2015–2019 (2015 Action Plan).
51 All documents and the toolbox can be found at <http://ec.europa.eu/info/strategy/better-regulation-why-and-how_en>.
52 European Commission – DG Trade, *Handbook for Sustainability Impact Assessment* (2016).
53 European Commission – DG Trade, 'Guidelines on the Analysis of Human Rights Impacts in Impact Assessments for Trade-Related Policy Initiatives' (2015).
54 European Commission – DG Trade, *Handbook for Sustainability Impact Assessment* (n 52).
55 Ibid., at 20.
56 European Commission – DG Trade, 'Guidelines on the Analysis of Human Rights Impacts in Impact Assessments for Trade-Related Policy Initiatives' (n 53), at 5.
57 Ibid., at 7.
58 Ibid.
59 European Commission, 'Tool #28: Fundamental Rights & Human Rights: European Commission' at <https://ec.europa.eu/info/files/better-regulation-toolbox-28_en>.
60 European Commission – DG Trade, 'Guidelines on the Analysis of Human Rights Impacts in Impact Assessments for Trade-Related Policy Initiatives' (n 53), at 12.
61 European Commission – DG Trade, 'Sustainability Impact Assessment (SIA) in Support of an Investment Protection Agreement between the European Union and the Republic of the Union of Myanmar, Final Report' (2016) at <www.eu-myanmarsia.com/data/info/201607080324172956pic.pdf> at 158.
62 Clive George and Colin Kirkpatrick, 'Have Sustainability Impact Assessments of Trade Agreements Delivered on Development Issues? A Reflexive Analysis of the Emergence and Main Contributions of Trade SIAs' in Paul Ekins and Trancrède Voituriez (eds.), *Trade, Globalization and Sustainability Impact Assessment* (Earthscan, 2009) 67, at 81.
63 *Técnicas Medioambientales Tecmed, S.A. v the United Mexican States, Award*, [2003] ICSID Case No ARB (AF)/00/2 [154]. In this case, the tribunal inferred from the objective in the preamble to intensify the economic cooperation, that the provision should be interpreted in favour of foreign investors.

64 *Grand River Enterprises Six Nations, Ltd, et al v United States of America*, UNCITRAL [1976], paras 69–71.
65 EU-Korea FTA, formally ratified in December 2015, L:2011:127:TOC.
66 CETA, Article 22.3.2(a)(b).
67 CETA, Article 23.3.1, FTA Singapore, Article 13.3.3, FTA Vietnam, Article 3.2 SD Chapter.
68 FTA Vietnam, Article 1.1 SD chapter; CETA, Article 23.3.2.
69 FTA Singapore, Article 13.1.1 SD chapter; CETA, Article 22.1.1.
70 CETA, Article 23.2.
71 *EU-Singapore FTA* (n 3).
72 FTA Colombia-Peru, Article 288.
73 CETA, Article 23.4, FTA Singapore, Article 13.12.
74 FTA Singapore, Article 13.16; *EU-Singapore FTA* (n 3), para 154, in which the Court stressed this exclusion when deciding on whether the CCP covers the SD chapter.
75 CETA, Article 23.8.5.
76 Axel Marx, Brecht Lein and Nicolas Bando, 'The Protection of Labour Rights in Trade Agreements' (2016) 4 *Journal of World Trade* 587, at 599.
77 United Nations Treaty Series, vol. 1155, signed in Vienna on 23 May 1969, at 331.
78 *EU-Singapore FTA* (n 3), para 161.
79 Narine Ghazaryan, 'A New Generation of Human Rights Clauses? The Case of Association Agreements in the Eastern Neighbourhood' (2015) *European Law Review* 391, at 405; Nicolas Hachez, '"Essential Elements" Clauses in EU Trade Agreements Making Trade Work in a Way That Helps Human Rights' (2015) *Cuadernos europeos de Deusto* 81, at 19.
80 Case T-292/09, *Mugraby*, EU:T:2011:418, paras 68 and 69.
81 Markus Krajewski, 'Investment Law and Public Services: Clashes of Interests or Peaceful Coexistence' (2012) *Investment Treaty News* at <www.iisd.org/itn/2012/07/19/investment-law-and-public-services-clashes-of-interests-or-peaceful-coexistence/>.
82 Wolf Sauter, *Public Services in EU Law* (CUP, 2015) 11.
83 Erik Andre Andersen and Birgit Lindsnaes, 'Public Goods: Concept, Definition and Method' in Erik Andre Anderson and Birgit Lindsnaes (eds.), *Towards New Global Strategies: Public Goods and Human Rights* (Martinus Nijhoff, 2007) 34–35.
84 Olga Batura, *Universal Service in WTO and EU Law: Liberalisation and Social Regulation in Telecommunications* (Asser Press, 2015) 1.
85 UN High Commissioner on Human Rights, *Human Rights, Trade and Investment* (E/CN.4/Sub.2/2003/9) available at <http://www.ohchr.org/EN/Issues/Globalization/Pages/ReportsHC.aspx>.
86 Elisenda Malaret Garcia, 'Public Service, Public Services, Public Functions, and Guarantees of the Rights of Citizens: Unchanging Needs in a Changed Context' in Mark Freedland and Silvanna Sciarra (eds.), *Public Services and Citizenship in European Law: Public and Labour Law Perspectives* (OUP, 1998) 81.
87 Hellmut Wollmann and Gérard Marcou, 'Introduction' in Hellmut Wollmann and Gérard Marcou (eds.), *The Provision of Public Services in Europe: Between State, Local Government and Market* (Edward Elgar, 2010) 3.
88 Juan Jorge Piernas López, 'Services of General Economic Interest and Social Considerations', in this volume; Silvia Pellizzari, 'Social Services, Service Providers and Non-Economic Activities in the Realm of the EU "Social Market Economy"', in this volume.
89 Caroline Wehlander, 'Introduction: The Constitutionalisation of the EU Concept of SGEI as a Story of Exit, Voice and Loyalty for Public Services in EU Law' in Caroline Wehlander, *Services of General Economic Interest as a Constitutional Concept of EU Law* (Asser Press, 2016) 3, at 14.

90 Pierre Bauby, 'Ambivalence of the European Strategy in External Relations on Trade Agreements' in Krajewski (ed.), *Services of General Interest Beyond the Single Market* (n 4), 233, at 240.
91 Ibid., para 146 with reference to *AGET Iraklis* (n 30), paras 61–104.
92 Piet Eeckhout, 'A Normative Basis for EU External Relations? Protecting Internal Values Beyond the Single Market' in Krajewski (ed.), *Services of General Interest Beyond the Single Market* (n 4), 219, at 231;
93 EU-Korea, Articles 7.4 and 7.10; EU-Columbia and Peru, Articles 111 and 118; EC-CARIFORUM, Articles 66 and 75; and, EU-Central America, Articles 163 and 169. Similar lists are found more recent EU trade agreements: CETA, Articles 8.2(2)(a) and 9.2; EU-Singapore, Articles 8.3 and 9.2; and, EU-Vietnam, Chapter II: Investment, Article 1 and Chapter III: Cross-Border Supply of Services, Article 1.
94 EU-Korea, Articles 7.4(3)(b) and 7.9(c); EU-Columbia and Peru, Article 108; EC-CARIFORUM, Article 75(2)(b); and, EU-Central America, Article 169(2)(b).
95 EU-Singapore, Article 8.1(2)(b); EU-Vietnam, General Provisions on Services; and, CETA, Article X-01(2)(a).
96 GATS, Article I:3(c).
97 EU-Korea, Articles 7.4(3)(c) and 7.9(c); EU-Columbia and Peru, Article 108; EC-CARIFORUM, Article 75(2)(c); and, EU-Central America, Article 169(2)(b). It is also identifiable in the newer agreements: EU-Singapore, Article 8.1(2)(b); EU-Vietnam, General Provisions on Services; and, CETA, Article X-01(2)(a).
98 CETA is based on a negative list approach which may be followed in the EU-Japan FTA or a hybrid as proposed in the EU-China bilateral investment treaty, European Commission, 'Services and Investment in EU Trade Deals: Using "Positive" and "Negative" Lists' (2016) at <http://trade.ec.europa.eu/doclib/docs/2016/april/tradoc_154427.pdf> at 5.
99 EU-Korea, Annex 7-A-2; EU-Columbia and Peru, Annex VII, Section B; EU-Ecuador, Annex VII, Section B; EC-CARIFORUM, Annex IV-A; EU-Central America, Annex X, Section A; Draft EU-Vietnam, Schedule of Commitments on Establishment; EU-Singapore, Annex 8-A-2; and, CETA, Annex II.
100 Found in: EU-Korea, Annex 7-A-2, Footnote 6; EU-Columbia and Peru, Annex VII, Section B, Footnote 2; EU-Ecuador, Annex VII, Section B, Footnote 201; EC-CARIFORUM, Annex IV-A, Footnote 2; EU-Central America, Annex X, Section A, Footnote 169; EU-Singapore, Annex 8-A-2, Footnote 6.
101 Draft EU-Vietnam, Schedule of Commitments on Establishment, Footnote 6. The same supplementary definition has been adopted in CETA, Annex II.
102 Krajewski (ed.), *Services of General Interest Beyond the Single Market* (n 4), at 25.
103 Austrian Federal Chamber of Labour, 'Services of General Interest in Bilateral Free Trade Agreements' (2007) *AK Position Paper* 4.
104 European Commission, 'Reflections Paper on Services of General Interest in Bilateral FTAs (Applicable to both Positive and Negative Lists)' (2011) 2.
105 EU-Columbia and Peru, Annex VII, Section B (Establishment), Footnote 4; and; EU-Ecuador, Annexes VII, Section B (Establishment), Footnote 246; EC-CARIFORUM, Annex IV-A (Establishment), Footnote 1; EU-Central America, Annex X, Section A (Establishment), Footnote 216; and, EU-Singapore, Annex8-A-2 (Establishment), Footnote 59.
106 Krajewski, 'Public Services Exemptions in EU Free Trade and Investments Agreements' in Krajewski (ed.), *Services of General Interest Beyond the Single Market* (n 4), at 264.
107 European Commission, 'Protecting Public Services in TTIP and Other EU Trade Agreements' (2015) at <http://trade.ec.europa.eu/doclib/docs/2015/july/tradoc_153614.pdf>.

108 Such exceptions can be identified in: EU-Korea, Article 7.50; EU-Columbia and Peru, Article 167; EC-CARIFORUM, Article 224; EU-Central America, Article 203; EU-Singapore, Article 8.62; EU-Vietnam, Chapter VII, General Exceptions, Paragraph 1; and, CETA, Article X.02(2).

109 Report of the Appellate Body, *European Communities: Measures Affecting Asbestos and Asbestos-Containing Products* (12 March 2001) WTO/DS135/AB/R, para 168.

110 Report of the Panel, *Thailand: Restrictions on Importation of an d Internal Taxes on Cigarettes* (7 November 1990) DS10/R–37S/200, para 73.

111 Report of the Appellate Body, *Korea: Various Measures on Beef* (11 December 2000) WT/DS161/AB/R and WT/DS169/AB/R, para 164.

112 *United States: Gambling*, 2005, para 306; *European Communities: Asbestos*, 2001, para 172.

113 Report of the Appellate Body, *United States: Import Prohibition of Certain Shrimp and Shrimp Products* (12 October 1998) WT/DS58/AB/R, para 156.

114 Ibid., para 168.

115 Markus Krajewski, 'Comment: *Quis custodiet necessitatem?* Adjudicating Necessity in Multilevel Systems and the Importance of Judicial Dialogue' in Marion Panizzon, Nicole Pohl and Pierre Suavé (eds.), *GATS and the Regulation of International Trade in Service* (CUP, 2008) 400.

16 The social dimension of EU investment law and policy

Sondra Faccio

1 Introduction

Foreign Direct Investment (FDI) can be defined as the transfer of funds or materials from one country to another country to be used in the conduct of an enterprise in that country in return for a direct or indirect participation in the earnings of the enterprise.[1] It reflects the objective of obtaining a lasting interest by a resident entity in one economy in an entity resident in an economy other than that of the investor. The lasting interest implies the existence of a long-term relationship between the foreign investor and the enterprise and a significant degree of influence on the management.[2]

FDIs are commonly undertaken by multinational enterprises (MNEs). FDIs have increasingly become part of the entrepreneurial and organizational strategy of firms, which find it advantageous to produce goods and services outside rather than inside their national borders and/or to create a base in foreign countries from where trade their goods and penetrate new markets.[3]

International investment agreements (IIAs) are international law instruments negotiated between States and, after the entry into force of the Treaty of Lisbon, between the European Union (EU) and third countries too,[4] with the aim of promoting and protecting MNEs' activities abroad. IIAs seek to restrain the behaviour of States by defining a standard to which they must conform in the treatment of foreign investors and investments.[5] IIAs' key provisions usually guarantee investments after their entry into a foreign country and impose to the host State to treat the investment fairly and equitably, to avoid discrimination between investments and/or investors on the basis of their nationality (the so-called national treatment and most favoured nation treatment), as well as to refrain from direct and indirect expropriation without compensation. IIAs also provide a mechanism for international dispute settlement: in case the State breaches the provisions of the IIA, the investor is entitled to resort to *ad hoc* arbitration against the State.[6] The right recognized to investors to have their dispute heard and decided by a neutral third party, rather than through State-led proceedings, is considered to be the most attractive aspect of IIAs and one of the main reasons for their success.

The main purpose of IIAs is to promote and protect FDIs. IIAs focus on the 'market', as they are traditionally meant to enhance international investment inflows into the States, the development of new enterprises and, eventually, States' economic growth, through the guarantee of some standards of treatment to foreign investors. However, a new generation of IIAs has started to address, albeit quite broadly and somewhat indirectly, social considerations, by including general clauses on the respect for human rights (arguably including social rights), environmental protection and labour standards.[7] This new generation of IIAs is grounded on the idea that States shall not lower their standards of protection of human rights, the environment and other social issues for attracting FDIs and that they shall retain the power to take actions to protect public interests, without incurring in any responsibility for IIAs' violations.

This chapter aims to analyse the EU investment policy, as shaped by the European Commission after the entry into force of the Lisbon Treaty, and EU IIAs and investment chapters of trade agreements, to discuss whether and to what extent they include social considerations and they embed the EU value of the social market economy. Socially oriented provisions within EU IIAs and investment chapters of trade agreements will be taken into consideration both from the point of view of their content and of their enforcement in investor-State disputes. The remainder of this chapter is divided into four sections. Section 2 briefly examines the EU competence on foreign direct investment, beyond the so-called common commercial policy (CCP); Section 3 analyses EU IIAs and investment chapters of EU trade agreements in details to verify whether and how they take into consideration social issues; Section 4 verifies how social provisions included in EU IIAs and in investment chapters of trade agreements can effectively be implemented in investor-State relations and, more generally, whether and to what extent investment arbitrators are dealing with social issues in settling investor-State disputes based on IIAs; Section 5 concludes with brief remarks on EU IIAs provisions on expropriation, arguing that the latter reflect current balance existing between the 'market' and the 'social' within the EU Common International Investment Policy.

2 The 'new' EU competence on investment agreements: beyond the CCP

2.1 The 'pre-Lisbon' era

Until the entry into force of the Lisbon Treaty, the EU had no express competence on FDIs and IIAs were negotiated and executed autonomously by Member States. Each State established its own investment policy and agenda, deciding State partners and purposes, autonomously. Upon the entry into force of the Lisbon Treaty, EU countries had negotiated almost 1.200 BITs with European and non-European countries.[8] Despite some variations,[9] these treaties were almost uniform in their structure and content,[10] usually including a few provisions on: the definition of the investment, the protection against unfair and unequitable treatment, the application of the principle of non-discrimination through the standards of the most favoured nation treatment and national treatment, the obligation to pay compensation upon the exercise of the State's right to expropriate and a neutral arbitration mechanism of investor-State disputes.[11] The purpose of IIAs was to 'create favourable conditions for greater investment',[12] to stimulate 'individual business initiative' and to 'increase prosperity',[13] to strength 'economic cooperation between the States'[14] or to stimulate the 'transfer of funds and technologies between the Countries',[15] with no reference to social issues and to the protection of social rights.

Trade agreements, by contrast, were considered to be part of the exclusive competence of the EU, as falling within the scope of its common commercial policy (CCP),[16] discussed by Kube and Pedreschi,[17] even before the adoption of the Lisbon Treaty and they were negotiated directly be the EU. EU trade agreements include custom unions, association agreements (AA), free trade agreements (FTA) and partnership and cooperation agreements. Customs unions aim to eliminate customs duties in bilateral trade and to establish a joint customs tariff for foreign importers; AAs and FTAs have the purpose of removing or reducing customs tariffs in bilateral trade; while partnership and cooperation agreements usually provide a general framework for bilateral economic relations, including a few provisions on investments, but do not affect custom tariffs. Since the early 1990s, EU trade agreements started to include express reference to human rights, democratic principles and sustainable development.[18] The EU-Russia Partnership and Cooperation Agreement of 1994 is exemplary in this respect as it provided that the treaty parties 'endeavor to cooperate on matters pertaining to the observance of the principles of democracy and human rights'.[19] Human rights are mentioned both in Article 2 as a general principle governing the parties' actions and in Article 6 as a subject of political dialogue between the contracting States.

2.2 The 'post-Lisbon' era

With the coming into force of the Lisbon Treaty, FDI has also been added into the list of exclusive external competence of the EU (Article 207 TFEU). This implied that EU Member States cannot continue concluding IIAs and that the Commission has taken over their competences, making the EU coming on stage as a new player in the international investment panorama. The EU Commission first outlined its approach to investment policy in its communication of July 2010, to then expand it with the European Commission Concept paper 'Investment in TTIP and beyond – the path for reform. Enhancing the right to regulate and moving from current and hoc arbitration towards an Investment Court' published on May 2015, the paper 'Trade for all – Towards a more responsible trade and investment policy' of October 2015, the 'Regulation establishing a framework for screening of foreign direct investments into the European Union' and the Communication 'Welcoming Foreign Direct Investment while Protecting Essential Interests' both of September 2017.[20] These documents establish what are the aims, principles and agenda at the bases of the EU (common) international investment policy and shape current EU's IIAs negotiations.

3 EU investment Treaties and social considerations

3.1 The commission strategy towards an EU common international investment policy

Kube and Pedreschi have highlighted how the CCP must be framed within the broader EU external relation policy. The general goals of EU external policy laid out in Article 21 TEU are of course relevant also when it comes to investment policy.[21] In line with Art. 21 and more generally with the EU objectives highlighted in Art. 3 TEU, the EU Commission's Communication of July 2010, that frames the EU international investment policy, clearly states that

> Investment agreements should be consistent with the other policies of the Union and its Member States, including policies on the *protection of the environment, decent work, health and safety at work, consumer protection, cultural diversity, development policy* and competition policy. Investment policy will continue to allow the Union, and the Member States to adopt and enforce measures necessary to pursue public policy objectives. A common investment policy should also be guided by the principles and objectives of the Union's external action more generally, including the promotion of the rule of law, human rights and sustainable development (Article 205 TFEU and Article 21 TEU).
>
> (emphasis added).[22]

Although the wording 'social market economy' is not mentioned expressly, it is clear that market and social goals go hand in hand as investment agreements shall be consistent with the EU policies on the protection of social rights, notably: 'decent work, health and safety at work, . . . development policy',[23] and – consequently – they shall preserve some leeway to States 'to adopt and enforce measures necessary to pursue public policy objectives'. This concept is reiterated in the Commission paper entitled 'Trade for all – Towards a more responsible trade and investment policy', released in 2015, where the Commission proposes a new trade and investment strategy, ensuring 'that economic growth goes hand in hand with *social* justice, respect for human rights, high labour and environmental standards, and health and safety protection (emphasis added)'.[24] According to the Commission, these principles shall apply to the EU trade and investment policy, and shall be implemented through concrete actions. In particular, the Commission envisages to implement 'modern provisions in bilateral agreements, putting stronger emphasis on the right of the State to regulate' and to transform 'the old investor-State dispute settlement into a public Investment Court System', with a clear code of conduct so as to avoid conflicts of interest and guarantee higher standards of independence and legal qualifications of judges.[25]

The Commission Concept paper 'Investment in TTIP and beyond – the path for reform. Enhancing the right to regulate and moving from current and hoc arbitration towards an Investment Court' (2015) also sets some important milestones of the EU common international investment policy. First of all, it establishes that EU IIAs shall guarantee the sovereign right of the States to regulate in the public interest and, secondly, it stresses the need that EU IIAs contain binding interpretations in order to limit the powers of arbitrators and to avoid that IIAs provisions are interpreted in a way which undermines the rights of States to achieve legitimate social objectives, such as 'public health, safety, environment, public morals and the promotion and protection of cultural diversity'.[26]

Finally, most recent documentation released by the Commission and concerning the EU investment policy recognizes that 'foreign direct investment has always been essential for the economic and *social* development of the European Union (emphasis added)'[27] and 'the need to maintain the necessary flexibility for Member States to screen foreign direct investments, taking into account their individual legitimate interests, different situations and national circumstances'.[28]

In substance, the Commission's guidelines on the EU common international investment policy establish that EU IIAs shall balance investment promotion and protection with social considerations. This equilibrium shall be achieved through the recognition to the State of the right of implementing regulatory measures in the public interest, on the one hand; and by limiting investment arbitrators' discretionary powers in the interpretation and application of IIAs provisions, on the other hand. In some treaties, notably the Comprehensive Economic and Trade Agreement (CETA) between the EU and Canada and the Transatlantic Trade and Investment Partnership (TTIP) between the EU and the United States, the Commission has gone even further by institutionalizing the settlement of investment disputes though the creation of an Investment Court System (ICS), to respond to the criticism expressed by some that *ad hoc* arbitration modelled after private dispute settlement is not the optimal mechanism for assessing the public interest regulation of States.[29]

3.2 *Preambular wording of EU IIAs and substantive provisions referring to social issues*

Further having discussed in a general fashion the EU current investment policy framework, this subsection analyses some EU trade agreements, with investment chapters and/or provisions, and investment agreements and highlight references to social issues contained in their texts. Some of the treaties discussed as follows are only drafts, currently under negotiation, others have been signed and ratified by States and are currently in force for the EU. Despite at different stages, these treaties give evidence that the EU international investment policy is increasingly sensitive to social issues and directed towards the inclusion in IIAs of provisions that preserve the States' power to take measures for their protection.

The first example is represented by the FTA between the EU and the Republic of Korea, signed on 6 October 2010 and entered into force on 13 December

2015. It does not provide for an *ad hoc* chapter on investment regulation, nonetheless it states that one of the aims of the FTA is 'to promote foreign direct investment without lowering or reducing environmental, labour or occupational health and safety standards in the application and enforcement of environmental and labour laws of the Parties'.[30] Article 13.3 also recognizes the right of the States to adopt or modify its laws and policies with the aim of safeguarding environmental and labour protection.[31] Article 13.7, paragraph 2, further states that '[a] Party shall not weaken or reduce the environmental or labour protections afforded in its laws to encourage trade or investment'.[32]

The AA between the EU and the European Atomic Energy Community and their Member States and Georgia signed on 27 June 2014 and entered into force on 1 July 2016 also recognizes that 'it is inappropriate to encourage trade or investment by lowering the levels of protection afforded in domestic environmental or labour law' and that the State shall not waive nor derogate from 'its environmental or labour law as an encouragement for trade or the establishment, the acquisition, the expansion or the retention of an investment of an investor in its territory' nor shall the State 'fail[s] to effectively enforce its environmental and labour law, as an encouragement for trade or investment'.[33]

In these agreements, the word 'social' does not appear, but reference is made to 'environmental and labor standards' that are material to the enjoyment of just and favourable conditions of work.[34] Other agreements, by contrast, contain express reference to the term 'social', among these the CETA, the EU-Singapore FTA, the draft investment chapters of the TTIP and the draft investment chapter of the EU-China FTA.

The preamble of the CETA between the EU and Canada, signed on 30 October 2016 and provisionally applied since 21 September 2017, recognizes 'the right of the Parties to regulate within their territories and the Parties' flexibility to achieve legitimate policy objectives, such as public health, safety, environment, public morals and the promotion and protection of cultural diversity'[35] and reaffirms the parties commitment 'to contribute to sustainable development in tis economic, *social* and environmental dimensions (emphasis added)'.[36]

In Article 8.9 (Investment and regulatory measure), the parties further establish 'their right to regulate within their territories to achieve legitimate policy objectives, such as the protection of public health, safety, the environment or public morals, *social* or consumer protection or the promotion and protection of cultural diversity (emphasis added)'.[37] This applies as general principle, carving out (at least in theory) on behalf of the States some room for manoeuvre to achieve domestic policy objectives, without incurring in any responsibility for the breach of CETA provisions. Annex 8-A, paragraph 3 of CETA goes a little further stating that 'except in the rare circumstance . . . non-discriminatory measures of a Party that are designed and applied to protect legitimate public welfare objectives, such as health, safety and the environment, *do not constitute* indirect expropriations (emphasis added)'.[38] It is interesting to notice that the latter provision, which refers to expropriation exclusively, is rather more precise, compared to Article 8.9, which only provides for a general 'right to regulate'; but, on the other hand, Annex 8-A does not include any reference to 'social' issues. The list, however, shall be intended as indicative, not exhaustive, and social considerations shall be implicitly included.[39]

The EU and Singapore completed negotiations for a comprehensive FTA on 17 October 2014. The agreement has not been ratified by the European Parliament yet, as in 2015 the EU Commission sought an opinion of the Court of Justice of the EU (CJEU) to clarify the EU competence to sign and ratify the FTA. The Court delivered its opinion in May 2017.[40] The latter, although it fed into the debate with the Council and the European Parliament on the best architecture for EU trade and investment agreements, has not affected the 'social dimension' of the treaty as it emerges from its text. In particular, in the Preamble of the FTA, the EU and Singapore state their determination to strength 'their economic, trade, and investment relations in accordance with the objective of sustainable development, in its economic, *social* and environmental dimensions (emphasis added)'[41] as well as their 'right to adopt and enforce measures necessary to pursue legitimate policy objectives such as *social*, environmental, security, public health and safety, promotion and protection of cultural diversity (emphasis added)'.[42] Chapter Nine of the EU-Singapore FTA, concerning 'Investment', also carves out some room for implementing domestic regulation aiming, among the others, at protecting human, animal or plant life or health, preserving exhaustible natural resources.[43]

Finally, there are a few international treaties that are not yet entered into force or are still under negotiation and whose texts or text proposals have been made public in the EU website, notably: the EU-Vietnam FTA, whose negotiations ended in 2016, the TTIP with the United States, whose last round of negotiation took place on October 2016, and the EU-China Comprehensive Agreement on Investment (CAI), whose last round of discussion took place on December 2017. These drafts-chapters reiterate the States' 'right to regulate within their territories to achieve legitimate policy objectives, such as the protection of public health, safety, environment or public morals, *social* or consumer protection or promotion and protection of cultural diversity (emphasis added)'.[44] The right to regulate of the States applies across all investment standards and, in particular, in relation to expropriation, excluding 'non-discriminatory measures designed and applied to protect legitimate public welfare objectives' from the scope of application of IIAs provisions.

From the above, it emerges that the strategy adopted by the EU Commission to guarantee the 'social' within IIAs mainly consists in preserving the States' policy powers to implement regulatory measures for social purposes (i.e. to safeguard environmental, labour standards, consumers protection); with the consequence that any measure adopted by the State with the view of achieving social purposes shall not be considered as a violation of IIAs standards or as a form of expropriation, even in the case they impact on investment, and shall not give rise to the State's responsibility under international law. These provisions, however, guarantee social instances only in theory as their practical application depends on arbitrators and on the interpretation they give to any relevant clause coming into play in investor-State dispute. As it will be discussed in the following paragraph, to overcome this problem, the EU Commission has introduced into IIAs some provisions to guide and limit arbitrators' discretionary powers in the interpretation of the treaties.

4 The interpretation and application of 'social provisions' in investor-State disputes and new rules adopted by EU IIAs to guide and limit arbitrators' discretion

4.1 *The interpretation and application of 'social provisions' in investor-State disputes*

Concerning the interpretation of IIAs, scholars and arbitrators have repeatedly highlighted the fact that IIAs clauses cannot be interpreted *in a vacuum*, but they need to be considered as a 'part' of the broader international law system to which States belong.[45] Under the general rules of treaty interpretation, as reflected in the 1969 Vienna Convention on the Law of Treaties (VCLT), interpretation must take into account together with the text and the context, including the preamble and annexes 'any relevant rules of international law applicable in the relations between the parties' (Article 31 (3) (c)).

Article 31 of the VCLT has often been applied in investor-State arbitration to consider human rights, and more broadly, social rights for the purpose of interpreting IIAs clauses.[46] For instance, in the case of *Suez, Sociedad General de Aguas de Barcelona S.A. and Vivendi Universal S.A. v. Argentina*, the tribunal expressly recognized that the host State 'is subject to both international obligations, i.e. human rights and [the investment] treaty obligation, and must respect both of them equally'.[47] In commenting the case, Tanzi observed that

> the Tribunal in its *ratio decidendi* took into account the human rights obligations relevant to the instant case in relation to the allegation of the breach of the obligation of fair and equitable treatment. . . . Indeed, the arbitrators appropriately referred to Article 31(1) of the Vienna Convention, according to which the provisions of a treaty must be interpreted 'in the light of its object and purpose'.[48]

The case of *Suez v. Argentina*, as many others involving Argentina, concerned a FDI in a concession for water distribution and waste water treatment services. In the Suez case, Argentina introduced new regulations in order to cope with the economic and political crisis and refused to revise upward tariffs and fees charged by public service companies, as the investors, and to renegotiate concession contracts. These measures impacted on the FDI and deprived investors of the necessary revenue to meet their financial obligations and to make required investments in the water distribution and waste treatment systems for which they were responsible. This situation led to the infringement of the Argentinian citizens' right to water and, eventually, led the State to terminate the concession agreement, in order to remedy the situation. All State's measures were perceived by the concerned investors as affecting the fair and equitable treatment they were expecting and led to the dispute before the ICSID arbitration tribunal. In its defence strategy, Argentina argued that 'it adopted the measures in order to safeguard the human right to water of the inhabitants of the country'.[49] Indeed, the human right to water is strictly related to the right to an adequate living standard, protected by Article 11 (1) of the Covenant on Economic, Social and Cultural Rights[50] and States must prevent private companies based on their territory from interfering in any way with the enjoyment of the right to water or from compromising equal, affordable and physical access to sufficient, safe and accessible water.[51] The Tribunal, nonetheless, concluded that Argentina's human rights obligations to assure its population the right to water do not trump its obligations under the BITs and that the existence of the right to water does not implicitly give Argentina the authority to take actions in disregard of its investment treaty obligations.

In the Case of *Suez v. Argentina*, the State made reference to its international obligations in relation to the protection and promotion of human and social rights to avoid responsibility for IIAs violations; in other cases, States used human and social rights obligations to ground their counterclaim against the proceeding investors. In the case *Urbaser S.A.and Consorcio de Aguas Bilbao Bizkaia, Bilbao Biskaia Ur Partzuergoa v. Argentina*, for instance, Argentina raised a counterclaim against the foreign investor (a water and sanitation service provider), arguing the latter alleged failure to provide necessary investments into the concession, leaving millions of people without water, thus violating its commitments and its obligations under international law based on the human right to water. In this case, the Tribunal recognized that '[t]he BIT has to be construed in harmony with other rules of international law of which it forms part, including those relating to human rights';[52] but it eventually dismissed Argentina's counterclaim, stating that the human right to water entails an obligation of compliance on the part of the State, not on part of any company providing the contractually required service.[53] The tribunal applied its discretionary powers and, taking into consideration 'serious concerns about the human rights implications' as well as the investors' 'failure to provide investments and to support expansion works assisting the needs of the population in the concession area', eventually dismissed the investors' claims on damages.[54]

Defence strategy of States based on human rights and social issues, so far, has not been successful in avoiding international responsibility for IIAs violation[55] and, only in a few cases, arbitrators dismissed investors' claims under IIAs arguing the prevailing powers of States to regulate in the public interest.[56] An example is represented by the set of decisions that brought to the elaboration of the so-called policy powers doctrine with reference to the interpretation of indirect expropriation.[57] Among these cases, the tribunal in *Saluka Investments B.V. v. Czech Republic*, recognized that

> the principle that a State does not commit an expropriation and is thus not liable to pay compensation to a dispossessed alien investor when it adopts

general regulations that are "commonly accepted as within the police power of States" forms part of customary international law today.[58]

However, the tribunal added that

> it has yet to draw a bright and easily distinguishable line between non-compensable regulations on the one hand and, on the other, measures that have the effect of depriving foreign investors of their investment and are thus unlawful and compensable in international law. It thus *inevitably falls to the adjudicator to determine whether particular conduct by a state 'crosses the line' that separates valid regulatory activity from expropriation.*
>
> (emphasis added).[59]

4.2 *EU IIAs clauses on the interpretation and application of investment provisions*

EU IIAs feature a series of clauses to guide, and sometimes limit, arbitrators' discretionary powers in the interpretation of IIAs, with the express aim of helping arbitrators in drawing 'the line' between lawful regulation and IIAs violation and of responding to the criticism expressed by some that current investor-State dispute settlement, modelled after commercial dispute settlement, is not the optimal mechanism for assessing the public interest regulation of States.[60]

CETA and the TTIP investment draft-chapter submit the resolution of investment disputes between investors and States to an ICS made up of a 'Tribunal' and of an 'Appeal Tribunal'. The Tribunal comprises fifteen members, appointed by an *ad hoc* committee (in the CETA is the Joint Committee), and hears each case in divisions consisting of three members. According to article 8.18 of CETA and article 9 of the TTIP investment draft-chapter, appointed members of the Tribunal shall

> possess the qualifications required in their respective countries for appointment to judicial office, or be jurists of recognized competence. They shall have demonstrated expertise in public international law. It is desirable that they have expertise in particular, in international investment law, in international trade law and the resolution of disputes arising under international investment or international trade agreements.[61]

By placing investor-State dispute resolution outside the traditional investment arbitration, the ICS, introduced by CETA and TTIP, has the aim of 'rebalancing' investor-State dispute settlement and avoiding outcome overly favourable to foreign investors to the detriment of States' public interests.[62] It, however, replaces one of the key features of investment arbitration, that is, the investors' autonomy to concur in the appointment of the arbitrators and the right to have the dispute heard and decided by a neutral third party, rather than through State-lead proceedings. This choice has given rise to some criticism and has been challenged by commentators on a number of grounds.[63]

As to interpretation, article 8.31 (Applicable law and interpretation) of CETA provides that '[w]hen rendering its decision, the Tribunal established under this Section shall apply this Agreement as interpreted in accordance with the Vienna Convention on the Law of Treaties, and other rules and principles of international law applicable between the Parties'.[64] Further, article 8.31 provides that

> [w]here serious concerns arise as regards matters of interpretation that may affect investment, the Committee on Services and Investment may . . . recommend to the CETA Joint Committee the adoption of interpretations of this Agreement. An interpretation adopted by the CETA Joint Committee shall be binding on a Tribunal established under this Section.[65]

Similar provisions are found in article 13 (Applicable law and rules of interpretation) of the TTIP investment draft-chapter.[66] Finally, Annex 8-A, paragraph 3 of CETA expressly states that expropriation provisions shall be interpreted in the sense that 'non-discriminatory measures of a Party that are designed and applied to protect legitimate public welfare objectives, such as health, safety and the environment, *do not constitute* indirect expropriations' (emphasis added).[67] Annex I of the TTIP investment draft-chapter features exactly the same provision with the inclusion, besides health, safety and the environment, of 'public morals, *social* or consumer protection or promotion and protection of cultural diversity' (emphasis added).[68]

This set of provisions safeguard social issues so far as the members of Tribunal are bound to interpret CETA (and TTIP) provisions in accordance with the VCLT and 'other rules and principles of international law applicable between the Parties' including, for instance, the Covenant on Economic, Social and Cultural Rights, to which both EU States and Canada are parties. Reference to the VCLT also allows arbitrators to take into account the Sustainable Development Chapter and the Labour Chapter of CETA (and TTIP) – which do not fall directly under the jurisdiction of the Tribunal – as forming part of the context of the treaty in accordance with article 31 (2) of the VCLT.[69] Moreover, in case of concerns, CETA gives to the Committee on Services and Investment – a forum set up by the Parties to consult on issues related to the application of the investment Chapter – the option to ask the Joint Committee – comprising representatives of the European Union and representatives of Canada – to adopt binding interpretation of the agreement. This safeguards the interests of the State-parties to the treaty against interpretations that distort the parties' intentions and unravel their bargain. Of course, the Committee on Service and Investment *may* refer to the Joint Committee to seek interpretation, as Article 8.31 provides for an option, not an obligation; however, it is safe to forecast that the Committee will be keen to revert to the Joint Committee for interpretation in any case the Tribunal departs from what the State-parties consider to be the meaning of the treaty and the content of their undertakings. Finally, Annex 8-A, paragraph 3 of CETA leaves no doubt that 'except in rare circumstances' certain social issues, such as health, safety and the environment, can be object of State's non-discriminatory regulation, without the risk for the State to incur in treaty violation for indirect expropriation. It will be interesting to see how arbitrators will interpret such 'rare circumstance' taking into account that the only guidance provided for by Annex 8-A is the excessive severity of the impact of the measure in light of its purpose. In this regard, Yotova has rightly observed that this formulation 'pitched a high threshold to be satisfied by the investor, requiring manifest excessiveness of the impact of the measure in light of its purpose, rather than the lower threshold proportionality analysis employed by some arbitral tribunals'.[70] This, *a priori*, leaves to the State more room for manoeuvre and, in any case, the Committee might intervene as a last resort to avoid overstretched interpretation, which might limit the 'social dimension' of the provision.

5 Conclusion

FDIs involve a long-term commitment by a foreign company to a business endeavour in a host State with (potentially) capital, knowledge and capacity flows that benefit the recipient economy.[71] However, FDIs may also have negative effects on the economy and social relations of the hosting community. For instance, the MNE may be a labour intensive enterprise which invests little in productivity and skills development and which sees labour more as a cost to be contained rather than a resource to be developed. In these cases, the MNE may create social and environmental distress and compromise the host State's prospects in terms of inclusive growth and sustainable development.[72] As a consequence, today, host States pay greater attention to the type of FDIs they attract and they tend to encourage only such MNEs that can make a particular contribution to the host economy, in line with its overall economic and social objectives. In other words, States increasingly seek to attract 'investment that makes a maximum contribution to economic, *social* and environmental development and takes place within mutually beneficial governance mechanisms while being commercially viable'.[73]

The EU has only recently acquired competence on FDI and its investment strategy perfectly reflects the above tendency, as it expressly attempts to strike a balance between economic growth and social justice.[74] The EU has a clear understanding that FDI is an important source of growth, jobs and innovation;[75] but it is also aware that the role played by IIAs cannot be limited to the development of the 'market', on the contrary they also should aim to safeguard the 'social'.

The EU value of the 'social market economy', therefore, has been embedded in those provisions of EU IIAs that aim to preserve States' powers to adopt measures in the public interest. In particular, the provisions on expropriation, included in EU IIAs, represent the perfect synthesis of the innate tension existing between the interest of the individual as an investor and the interest of the individual as part of the community and reflect the balance currently existing between the market and the social. Excluding from the scope of application of expropriation provisions such 'non-discriminatory measures designed and applied by the State to protect legitimate public welfare objectives', including social purposes, means subjecting the market to the claim of the social.

Notes

1 Stefan Riesenfeld, 'Foreign Investments' (1992) *Encyclopedia of Public International Law* 435.
2 Organisation for Economic Co-Operation and Development (OECD), 'Benchmark Definition of Foreign Direct Investment' (2008) at <www.oecd.org/daf/inv/investmentstatisticsandanalysis/40193734.pdf> at 48–49.
3 John Dunning and Sarianna Lundan, *Multinational Enterprises and the Global Economy* (Edward Elgar, 2008); Jeffrey Sachs, 'The Global Challenges Facing Emerging Markets' in Karl Sauvant, Wolfgang Maschek and Geraldine McAllister (eds.), *Foreign Direct Investments from Emerging Markets: The Challenges Ahead* (Palgrave Macmillan, 2010); Yair Aharoni, 'Reflections on Multinationals in a Globally Interdependent World Economy' in Sauvant, Maschek and McAllister (eds.), *Foreign Direct Investments from Emerging Markets: The Challenges Ahead* (n 3), at 42.
4 See below section 2.
5 Jeswald Salacuse, *The Law of Investment Treaties* (OUP, 2009) 9.
6 As to the difference between rules and standards, Federico Ortino, 'Refining the Content and Role of Investment "Rules" and "Standards": A New Approach to International Investment Treaty-Making' (2013) *ICSID Review* 152.
7 An extensive survey on IIAs reference to social issues, including labour, environmental and human rights, can be found in Kathryn Gordon, Joachim Pohl and Marie Bouchard, 'Investment Treaty Law, Sustainable Development and Responsible Business Conduct: A Fact Finding Survey' (2014) 1 *OECD Working Papers on International Development* at <http://dx.doi.org/10.1787/5jz0xvgx1zlt-en>; see among the others, Agreement among Japan-Republic of Korea-People's Republic of China for the Promotion, Facilitation and Protection of Investment, 13 May 2012, Protocol, 2 (c) at <www.mofa.go.jp/mofaj/press/release/24/5/pdfs/0513_01_02.pdf>; Agreement between Belgium-Luxembourg Economic Union-Colombia on the Reciprocal Promotion and Protection of Investments, 4 February 2009, Article IX (3) (c) at <http://fdfa.be/sites/default/files/atoms/files/822_Certificate%20in%20English.pdf>.
8 Communication from the European Commission, 'Towards a Comprehensive European International Investment Policy', COM(2010)343, at 4.
9 For example, the 2002 and 2008 Austrian Model BIT affirmed the commitment of the parties to promote internationally recognized labour standards, to create labour opportunities and improve living standards. The 2001 Finland Model BIT and the 2004 Netherlands Model BIT also include preambular wording referring to non-economic issues.
10 Communication from the European Commission, 'Towards a Comprehensive European International Investment Policy' (n 8), at 5–6; Rumiana Yotova, 'Balancing Economic Objectives and Social Considerations in the New EU Investment Agreements: Commitments versus Realities' in Frank Vandenbroucke, Catherine Barnard and Geert De Baere (eds.), *A European Social Union after the Crisis* (CUP, 2017) 271, at 282.
11 Agreement between Italy-Egypt for the Promotion and Protection of Investments, 2 March 1989 at <http://investmentpolicyhub.unctad.org/Download/TreatyFile/1081>; Agreement between United Kingdom-Republic of Argentina for the Promotion and Protection of Investments, 11 December 1990, Article 2 at <http://investmentpolicyhub.unctad.org/Download/TreatyFile/126>; Agreement between France-Argentina for the Encouragement and the Protection of Investments, 3 July 1991, Article 5 at <http://investmentpolicyhub.unctad.org/Download/TreatyFile/91>; Timothy Nelson, 'Going Dutch: The Many Virtues of the Netherlands Model BIT' (2012) *Dispute Resolution International* 6, at 161.

12 Agreement between United Kingdom-Argentina for the Promotion and Protection of Investments (n. 11).
13 Ibid.
14 Agreement between France-Argentina for the Encouragement and the Protection of Investments (n. 11).
15 Ibid.
16 Frederic van den Berghe, 'The EC's Common Commercial Policy Revisited: What Does Lisbon Add?' (2009) *Global Trade and Customs Journal* 275, at 279; Dorota Leczykiewicz, 'Common Commercial Policy: The Expanding Competence of the European Union in the Area of International Trade' (2005) *German Law Journal* 1673, at 1674; Opinion 1/75, EU:C:1975:145, at 1363–1364; Case C-22/70, *Commission v Council*, EU:C:1971:23, paras 17 and 22; Opinion 2/91, EU:C:1993:106, paras 9–11.
17 Vivian Kube and Luigi Pedreschi, 'The Social Dimension of Common Commercial Policy', in this volume.
18 Lorand Bartels, 'Human Rights and Sustainable Development Obligations in EU Free Trade Agreements' (2013) *Legal Issues of Economic Integration* 297.
19 Agreement between EC-Russian Federation on Partnership and Cooperation Establishing a Partnership, 24 June 1994 at <http://ec.europa.eu/world/agreements/downloadFile.do?fullText=yes&treatyTransId=643>.
20 European Parliament Resolution 2010/2203(INI) of 6 April 2011 on the future European International Investment Policy, [2012] OJ L296/34; European Council, 'Conclusions on a Comprehensive European International Investment Policy', 3041st Foreign Affairs Council Meeting of 25 October 2010, para 1 at <www.consilium.europa.eu/uedocs/cms_data/docs/pressdata/EN/foraff/117328.pdf>.
21 Article 207 TFEU establishes that '[t]he common commercial policy shall be based on uniform principles, particularly with regard to . . . foreign direct investment' and it 'shall be conducted in the context of the principles and objectives of the Union's external action'.
22 Communication from the European Commission, 'Towards a comprehensive European international investment policy' (n 8).
23 Article 151 TFEU refers to social rights as follows 'the promotion of employment, improved living and working conditions, . . . proper social protection, dialogue between management and labour, the development of human resources with a view to lasting high employment and the combating of exclusion'.
24 European Commission, 'Trade for All: Towards a More Responsible Trade and Investment Policy' (2015) at <http://trade.ec.europa.eu/doclib/docs/2015/october/tradoc_153846.pdf> at 22.
25 Ibid., at 21.
26 The European Commission Concept Paper, 'Investment in TTIP and Beyond: The Path for Reform: Enhancing the Right to Regulate and Moving from Current and Hoc Arbitration towards an Investment Court' (2015) at <http//trade.ec.europa.eu/doclib/docs/2015/may/tradoc_153408.PDF>.
27 European Commission, 'Proposal for a Regulation of the European Parliament and of the Council Establishing a Framework for Screening of Foreign Direct Investments into the European Union', COM(2017)487 at <https://ec.europa.eu/info/law/better-regulation/initiatives/com-2017-487_en>.
28 Communication from the European Commission, 'Welcoming Foreign Direct Investment While Protecting Essential Interests', COM(2017)494, at 9.
29 Rumiana Yotova, 'Balancing Economic Objectives and Social Considerations in the New EU Investment Agreements: Commitments versus Realities' (n 10), 271, at 295. As to the debate over investor-to-State dispute settlement (ISDS), Commission Staff Working Document, *Report Online Public Consultation on Investment Protection and Investor-to-State Dispute Settlement (ISDS) in the Transatlantic*

Trade and Investment Partnership Agreement (TTIP) (2015) SWD(2015)3 at <http://trade.ec.europa.eu/doclib/docs/2015/january/tradoc_153044.pdf> at 16.

30 FTA between EU-Republic of Korea, Article 1 at <http://eur-lex.europa.eu/legal-content/en/TXT/PDF/?uri=CELEX:22011A0514%2801%29&rid=1>.

31 Ibid., Article 13.3.

32 Ibid., Article 13.7.

33 Association Agreement between EU-European Atomic Energy Community and their Member States-Georgia, Article 235 at <http://eur-lex.europa.eu/legal-content/en/TXT/PDF/?uri=CELEX:22014A0830(02)>.

34 International Covenant on Economic, Social and Cultural Rights, Adopted and opened for signature, ratification and accession by General Assembly resolution 2200A (XXI) of 16 December 1966, entry into force 3 January 1976, Article 7 at <www.ohchr.org/EN/ProfessionalInterest/Pages/CESCR.aspx>.

35 CETA between EU – Canada, 'Preamble' at <http://trade.ec.europa.eu/doclib/docs/2014/september/tradoc_152806.pdf>.

36 Ibid.

37 Ibid., Article 8.9 'Investment and regulatory measures'.

38 Ibid., Article 8.12 and Annex 8-A.

39 Vid Prislan and Ruben Zandvliet, 'Mainstreaming Sustainable Development into International Investment Agreements: What Role for Labor Provisions?' in Stephan Schill, Christian Tams and Rainer Hofmann (eds.), *International Investment Law and Development: Bridging the Gap* (Edward Elgar, 2015) 390; Rumiana Yotova, 'Balancing Economic Objectives and Social Considerations in the New EU Investment Agreements: Commitments versus Realities' (n 10), 271, at 290.

40 Opinion No 2/15 of the Court 16 May 2017 at <http://eur-lex.europa.eu/legal-content/EN/TXT/HTML/?uri=CELEX:62015CV0002(01)&from=EN>.

41 FTA between EU-Singapore, authentic text as of May 2015, 'Preamble' at <http://trade.ec.europa.eu/doclib/docs/2013/september/tradoc_151729.pdf>.

42 Ibid.

43 Ibid., Articles 9.3 and 9.7.

44 FTA between EU-Vietnam, agreed text as of January 2016, Chapter 8 'Trade in Services, Investment and e-commerce', Article 13-bis at <http://trade.ec.europa.eu/doclib/docs/2016/february/tradoc_154210.pdf>; TTIP, Commission Draft Text, Chapter II, Article 2 at <http://trade.ec.europa.eu/doclib/press/index.cfm?id=1230>; European Parliament Resolution on the EU-China Negotiations for a BIT (2013/2674(RSP)), para 23 at <www.italaw.com/sites/default/files/archive/motion%20for%20a%20resolution.pdf>; European Commission Fact Sheet of 26 November 2013 at <http://trade.ec.europa.eu/doclib/docs/2013/november/tradoc_151916.pdf> at 7.

45 Case concerning Oil Platforms, (*Iran v United States of America*), Judgment, 6 November 2003, ICJ Reports 2003, para 41; Pierre-Marie Dupuy, 'Unification Rather Than Fragmentation of International Law? The Case of International Investment Law and Human Rights Law' in Pierre-Marie Dupuy, Francesco Francioni and Ernst-Ulrich Petersmann (eds.), *Human Rights in International Investment Law and Arbitration* (OUP, 2009) 45, at 58.

46 Tarcisio Gazzini and Yannick Radi, 'Foreign Investment with a Human Face, with Special Reference to Indigenous Peoples' Rights' in Rainer Hofmann and Christian Tams (eds.), *International Investment Law and Its Others* (NOMOS, 2012) at <http://papers.ssrn.com/sol3/papers.cfm?abstract_id=2030871> at 13–14.

47 *Suez v Argentina*, ICSID Case No ARB/03/19, para 262.

48 Attila Tanzi, 'On Balancing Foreign Investment Interests with Public Interests in Recent Arbitration Case Law in the Public Utilities Sector' (2012) *The Law and*

Practice of International Courts and Tribunals 47, at 58; *Suez v Argentina* (n 47), paras 215–218.

49 *Suez v Argentina* (n 47), para 252.

50 International Covenant on Economic, Social and Cultural Rights, GA Resolution 2200A (XXI) of 16 December 1966 at <www.ohchr.org/EN/ProfessionalInterest/Pages/CESCR.aspx>; UN Committee on Economic, Social and Cultural Rights, General Comment No 15: The Right to Water (Articles 11 and 12 of the Covenant), according to which 'the right to water clearly falls within the category of guarantees essential for securing an adequate standard of living'; *Suez v Argentina Republic* (n 47), para 256.

51 Pierre-Marie Dupuy, 'Unification Rather Than Fragmentation of International Law? The Case of International Investment Law and Human Rights Law' in Dupuy, Francioni and Petersmann (eds.), *Human Rights in International Investment Law and Arbitration* (n 45), at 54.

52 *Urbaser S.A. Consorcio de Aguas Bilbao Bizkaia, Bilbao Biskaia Ur Partzuergoa v The Argentine Republic*, ICSID Case No ARB/07/26, Award, 8 December 2016, para 1200; *Tulip Real Estate and Development Netherlands B.V. Republic of Turkey*, ICSID/ARB/11/28, Decision on Annulment of 30 December 2015, paras 86–92, where the *ad hoc* Committee refers to the 'principle of systemic integration', stating that resort to authorities stemming from the field of human rights is a 'legitimate method of treaty interpretation'.

53 *Urbaser S.A Consorcio de Aguas Bilbao Bizkaia, Bilbao Biskaia Ur Partzuergoa v The Argentine Republic* (n 52), paras 1205–1208.

54 Ibid., para 1233.

55 In two cases involving Argentina, arbitrators stated that the argument put forth by the respondent State, according to which the strict protection of the investor's property rights could potentially violate protected human rights, had not sufficiently been grounded to be considered in relation to the merits of these two cases; *Azurix Corp. v Argentina*, ICSID Case No ARB/01/12, Award, 14 July 2006, at para 254; *Siemens A.G. v Argentina*, ICSID Case No ARB/02/08, Award, 6 February 2007, para 75; Pierre-Marie Dupuy, 'Unification Rather Than Fragmentation of International Law? The Case of International Investment Law and Human Rights Law' in Dupuy, Francioni, and Petersmann (eds.), *Human Rights in International Investment Law and Arbitration* (n 45), at 56. In other cases, tribunals have reduced the amount of compensation awarded to the investor to take into account the human rights obligations of the host State towards its citizens; Attila Tanzi, 'Reducing the Gap between International Investment Law and Human Rights Law in International Investment Arbitration?' (2013) *Latin American Journal of International Trade Law* 299; *Compañía de Aguas del Aconquija S.A. and Vivendi Universal S.A. (formerly Compañía de Aguas del Aconquija, S.A. and Compagnie Générale des Eaux) v The Argentine Republic (I)*, ICSID Case No. ARB/97/3, Award, 20 August 2007, para 11.1.

56 Ian Brownlie, *Principles of Public International Law* (Clarendon Press, 1998) 532; Katia Yannaca-Small, *Indirect Expropriation and the Right to Regulate: How to Draw the Line?* (OUP, 2010) 445–477; Gorges Kaeckenbeeck, 'The Protection of Vested Rights in International Law' (1936) *British Yearbook of International Law* 16; Ministerial Statement on the Multilateral Agreement on Investment ('MAI'), 28 April 1998, para. 5; UNCTAD, Series on Issues in International Investment Agreements II, 'Expropriation', the U.N. New York and Geneva, 2012, xiii at <http://unctad.org/en/Docs/unctaddiaeia2011d7_en.pdf> at 80–86; *Charanne B.V. and Construction Investment S.a.r.l. v Spain*, Arbitration No 062/2012, Award, 21 January 2016, para 534.

57 *Saluka Investments B.V. v Czech Republic*, UNCITRAL, Partial Award, 17 March 2006, para 262; *Chemtura Corporation v Government of Canada*, UNCITRAL,

Award, 2 August 2010, para 266; *Methanex Corp. v United States of America*, UNCITRAL, Final Award on Jurisdiction and Merits, 3 August 2005, Part IV, D, para 9.

58 *Saluka Investments B.V. v Czech Republic* (n 57), para 262.

59 Ibid., paras 263–264.

60 Rumiana Yotova, 'Balancing Economic Objectives and Social Considerations in the New EU Investment Agreements: Commitments versus Realities' (n 10), 271, at 295. As to the debate over investor-State dispute settlement (ISDS), Commission Staff Working Document, *Report Online Public Consultation on Investment Protection and Investor-to-State Dispute Settlement (ISDS) in the Transatlantic Trade and Investment Partnership Agreement (TTIP)* (n 29), at 16.

61 CETA between EU-Canada, Article 8.27 at <http://trade.ec.europa.eu/doclib/docs/2014/september/tradoc_152806.pdf>.

62 Elisabeth Talbourdet, 'The EU's Investment Court System: A Possible Solution to Conflicts of Interest in Investment Arbitration', 10 April 2017 at <https://blogs.kcl.ac.uk/kslreuropeanlawblog/?p=1121#_ftnref11>.

63 Maria Deli and Maria Marceddu, 'Is the European Commission Issuing a Dismissal Letter to Arbitrators' (2015) *Kluwer Arbitration Blog* 4–5.

64 CETA between EU-Canada, Article 8.31 at <http://trade.ec.europa.eu/doclib/docs/2014/september/tradoc_152806.pdf>.

65 Ibid.

66 TTIP, Commission Draft Text, Chapter II, Article 13 at <http://trade.ec.europa.eu/doclib/press/index.cfm?id=1230>.

67 CETA between EU-Canada, Article 8.12 and Annex 8-A at <http://trade.ec.europa.eu/doclib/docs/2014/september/tradoc_152806.pdf>.

68 TTIP, Commission Draft Text, Chapter II, Annex I, para 3 at <http://trade.ec.europa.eu/doclib/press/index.cfm?id=1230>.

69 Rumiana Yotova, 'Balancing Economic Objectives and Social Considerations in the New EU Investment Agreements: Commitments versus Realities' (n 10), 271, at 291.

70 Ibid., 271, at 303.

71 Joseph Stiglitz, 'Regulating Multinational Corporations: Towards Principles of Cross-Border Legal Frameworks in a Globalized World Balancing Rights with Responsibilities' (2008) *American University International Law Review* 451, at 453.

72 *Técnicas Medioambientales Tecmed S.A. v the United Mexican States*, ICSID Case No ARB (AF)/00/2, Award, 29 May 2003.

73 Sauvant, 'The Regulatory Framework for Investment: Where Are We Headed?' (n 7), 407, at 410, 414; Karl Sauvant, 'The Times They Are a-Changin'-Again-in the Relationship between Governments and Multinational Enterprises: From Control, to Liberalisation to Rebalancing' (2012) *Columbia FDI Perspectives* at <www.vcc.columbia.edu/content/times-they-are-changin-again-relationships-between-governments-and-multinational-enterprises>.

74 European Commission, 'Trade for All: Towards a More Responsible Trade and Investment Policy' (n 24), at 22.

75 Communication from the European Commission, 'Towards a Comprehensive European International Investment Policy' (n 8); Communication from the European Commission, 'Welcoming Foreign Direct Investment While Protecting Essential Interests', COM(2017)0494, at 2; UNCTAD, Series on International Investment Policies for Development, 'The Role of International Investment Agreements in Attracting Foreign Direct Investment to Developing Countries' (2009) *The U.N. New York and Geneva* at <http://unctad.org/en/docs/diaeia20095_en.pdf> at 51–52.

Conclusion

Taking stock and looking ahead: the future of the 'social market economy' in the European Union

Delia Ferri and Fulvio Cortese

This book commenced by noting that the current 'melancholy' surrounding the future of the EU should not coincide with the abandonment of the foundational idea of a 'Social Europe'. The official proclamation of the European Pillar of Social Rights (EPSR), in November 2017, has brought new life to the long-standing debate on the relationship between the internal market and social rights, a theme on which much ink has been spilt so far. However, far less attention has been given to the constitutional framework that identifies, through the 'social market economy' clause, the merging of the social and economic dimensions within EU law.

Since the entry into force of the Lisbon Treaty, scholars have viewed Article 3(3) TEU with varying degrees of scepticism. In an article published in 2010, Semmelmann claimed that introducing the concept of the 'social market economy' within the EU legal framework amounted to a 'cosmetic and rhetorical step'.[1] More recently, Dale and El-Enany[2] affirmed that '[t]he social promise that Lisbon represented was . . . hollow'. Šmejkal and Šaroch[3] highlighted that in a practical sense, the 'social market economy' objective 'has not brought about any significant change of accents in favour of more social EU as it was expected when the Lisbon Treaty came into force'. They add that it 'does not imply any push towards "social Union" in the sense of specific EU measures that would harmonise social rights and benefits across the EU'. While the latter might be true, Garben[4] observes that reading this provision in combination with Article 9 TFEU and the TFEU's Social Title grant 'a significant measure of lawmaking and other competences to pursue' social objectives, 'resulting in a rich social acquis'.

The collection of contributions in this volume does not allow for clear-cut conclusions to be drawn on whether Article 3(3) TEU is becoming a constitutional parameter for EU action. Hence, in these short concluding remarks, it is not possible to claim that a collectively agreed outcome has been reached, nor is it possible to summarise the nuanced (and sometimes contrasting) views and conclusions that each of the authors has reached. Rather, we will try to put forward some thoughts stemming from the chapters, to identify common trends and highlight five particular strands that strike us as being conducive to further discussion.

First, there is a sense of uneasiness regarding the real meaning of the 'social market clause' emerging, in particular, from Part I. All of the contributions are premised, as O'Sullivan explicitly puts it, on the belief that the definition of what constitutes a 'social market economy' is dependent on the particular social, political, economic and even temporal context in which it is adopted and said to exist. Therefore, there is no shared notion of 'social market economy', but this depends on the constitutional nature of the EU legal order in which the Article 3(3) TEU is inserted. O'Sullivan, Dani, Civitarese Matteucci as well as Delledonne, to varying degrees and with different emphases, seem to evoke Asghiabor's notion of 'embedded liberalism' and, in Schiek's words, 'the gap between the EU's normative commitments to socioeconomic justice and the practical workings of its integration project' which has been causing 'a normative crisis with constitutional dimensions'.[5] Civitarese Matteucci, more pointedly, affirms that the actual living notion of the 'social market economy' in the EU context is disengaged from any specific concept of social rights, as conceived in European constitutional traditions. He questions whether Article 3(3) TEU even gives rise to the imperative to rebalance the EU's trajectory in favour of a more 'social Europe'.

Second, few authors point to the fact that the Union cannot take the necessary steps to apply a more dynamic and socially conscious interpretation of the 'social market economy' clause without an active restructuring of its competences, and without the CJEU re-orientating its own jurisprudence. O'Sullivan's arguments as well as Dani's discussion reinforce Semmelmann's affirmation that Article 3(3) TEU has been a cosmetic step. Nonetheless, none of them completely closes the door to further developments in the future. A conscious decision to reorientate EU law in light of this new provision remains possible. In this vein, Delledonne, while claiming that the idea of market citizenship has retained some of its early strength in the more recent case law of the CJEU such as *Dano*, *Alimanovic* and *Commission v United Kingdom*, suggests that those judgements, as controversial as they are, are not representative of a generalised trend in the case law of the Court. Delledonne states that the underlying and unresolved issue is the balance of powers between the EU and its Member States and that transnational solidarity must be strengthened in order to cement a lasting 'social' shift in the law relating to EU citizenship.

Third, all the contributors in Part II highlight that explicit references in legislation to the 'social market economy' and to Article 3(3) TEU are scant, if not completely absent. In most fields, legislation instead refers to the 'Europe 2020' strategy and its objectives, such as competitiveness and inclusive growth. Judicial decisions mentioning Article 3(3) TEU have also been rare. In fact, as Civitarese Matteucci already highlighted in Part I, there are two cases in which the CJEU refers explicitly to the 'social market economy'. One is *AGET Iraklis*, and the other is *Corsica Ferries France*. Against this background, a common trend in these chapters is that the influence of the 'social market economy clause' has, thus far, been modest, and in some cases imperceptible. The field of competition law, in which the 'social market economy' have most often been invoked, even prior to the entry into force of the Lisbon Treaty, is the one in which the influence of Article 3(3) TEU is perhaps most 'invisible'.

Fourth, the overall picture that emerges from Part II, with some exceptions (such as State aid law and policy, and foreign direct investment agreements), demonstrates that internal market goals still stand alone. Even when a limited number of social considerations are included, these are often secondary and subordinated to market goals. Consequently, and unsurprisingly, the practical challenges unveiled in Part II are linked to the contradictory constitutional nature of the EU, as illustrated in the first part of the book. For example, in relation to EU consumer law, Mak observes that this remains primarily concerned with the economic rights of EU citizens, despite containing certain openings for the pursuit of social rights and policies. In Mak's estimation, the recent Fitness Check carried out on the primary consumer law Directives appears to be a missed opportunity in this regard. Despite the incorporation of social concerns in energy law, Mete and Heffron affirm that a 'social' dimension to energy markets has yet to materialise. Paradoxical as it may seem, the fields that are, by their very essence, more socially oriented are those in which the social dimension is more contested, or thought to have been undermined by economic considerations. This emerges, to a different degree, in Doherty's contribution on labour law, in Bovis's chapter on public procurement, in Piernas Lopez's and Pellizzari's contributions on social services, and in Busatta and Hervey's contribution.

Finally, however, the latent nature of Article 3(3) TEU notwithstanding, some contributors to this volume have, in some instances, underlined that there is an emerging, yet still timid, 'social dimension'. In the field of State aid, Ferri and Piernas Lopez argue that the Commission has sought out, and potentially achieved, a more appropriate balance between the main objective of preserving competition in the internal market on the one hand, and social objectives on the other. In the field of external relations, Kube and Pedreschi highlight that, in *Opinion 2/15*, the CJEU has ultimately made clear that policy makers are under an obligation to integrate sustainable development and social protection into the implementation of trade policy. However, their evaluation remains somewhat cautious. Faccio arrives at a more optimistic conclusion in relation to foreign direct investment (FDI). She highlights that the EU has only recently acquired a competence on FDI and its investment strategy attempts to strike a balance between economic growth and social justice. According to Faccio, the 'social market economy' is embedded in those provisions of EU international investment agreements that aim to preserve States' powers to adopt measures in the public interest.

All in all, the extensive analysis carried by this book paints a picture of an EU legal order in which a more central role for social considerations has yet to be realised. Some authors express scepticism regarding the whole notion of 'social market economy'. According to Civitarese Matteucci, considering the historical legacy of the concept and the reasons for its insertion in the Treaty, the advancement of social rights at the EU level simply cannot be achieved under the ideal of a 'social market economy'. Others take the view that it remains, as yet, a paper tiger and has, thus far, failed to display its innovative potential in guiding the EU's economic policies. Many of the contributors to this book also highlight that the EU still bears the scars of the severe austerity measures that were adopted following the economic crisis. Nevertheless, the ideal and imperative of the 'social market economy', with its (still contradictory) juxtaposition of economic and social dimensions, is now embedded within the Union's conception of itself. It may provide a viable principle that is capable of breathing new life into EU policy in a moment of existential crisis, as well as in prompting the paradigm shift that O'Sullivan mentions. A 'soft paradigm shift', as Sganga puts it, has already happened in some distinct areas. Interestingly, and perhaps quite ironically, the realization of the EU 'social market economy' may not lie in the creation of laws, but in concerted political and social action.

Notes

1 Constanze Semmelmann, 'The European Union's Economic Constitution under the Lisbon Treaty: Soul-Searching among Lawyers Shifts the Focus to Procedure' (2010) *European Law Review* 516.
2 Gareth Dale and Nadine El-Enany, 'The Limits of Social Europe: EU Law and the Ordoliberal Agenda' (2013) *German Law Journal* 613, at 616.
3 Václav Šmejkal and Stanislav Šaroch, 'EU as a Highly Competitive Social Market Economy: Goal, Options, and Reality' (2014) *Review of Economic Perspectives* 393.
4 Sacha Garben, 'The Constitutional (Im)balance between "the Market" and "the Social" in the European Union' (2017) *European Constitutional Law Review* 23, at 24.
5 Dagmar Schiek, 'Towards More Resilience for a Social EU: The Constitutionally Conditioned Internal Market' (2017) *European Constitutional Law Review* 611, at 612.

Index